'It is clearly the most beautiful football book
that I have ever read.'
Giacomo Pellizzari, la Repubblica

'A thesis worthy of Scott Fitzgerald".'
Giuseppe Culicchia, La Stampa

'*The Match* by Piero Trellini is an exceptional undertaking.
(...) Books like this are no longer made. It's a super-novel. It
has a setting of absolute originality.'
Antonio D'Orrico, La Lettura – Corriere della Sera

'It is an ode to football, a poignant ode to the most
beautiful game in the world. (...) a sum of wonderful
stories, which keep you glued to the page…'
Walter Veltroni, La Gazzetta dello Sport

'I had never read, on a single game, anything so complete and
engaging. In its genre: a masterpiece.'
Darwin Pastorin – Huffington Post

'Have you read *The Match*? Beautiful. Trellini has turned the
carpet we all know upside down and shown the intricacies
that make it up. Spectacular coincidences, hidden roots,
historical premises.'
Luigi Garlando, SportWeek

THE MATCH

The Story of Italy v Brazil 1982

PIERO TRELLINI

First published by Pitch Publishing, 2023

Pitch Publishing
9 Donnington Park,
85 Birdham Road,
Chichester,
West Sussex,
PO20 7AJ
www.pitchpublishing.co.uk
info@pitchpublishing.co.uk

© 2023, Piero Trellini

This work has been translated with the contribution of the Center for the Book and Reading of the Italian Ministry of Culture

Every effort has been made to trace the copyright. Any oversight will be rectified in future editions at the earliest opportunity by the publisher.

All rights reserved. No part of this book may be reproduced, sold or utilised in any form or transmitted in any form or by any means, electronic or mechanical, including photocopying, recording or by any information storage and retrieval system, without prior permission in writing from the Publisher.

A CIP catalogue record is available for this book from the British Library.

ISBN 978 1 80150 424 9

Typesetting and origination by Pitch Publishing
Printed and bound in Great Britain by TJ Books, Padstow

Contents

Foreword 11

Prologue 17
The Man Who Came from Haifa 19
The Historical Memory of the Italians. 24
The Mundial 27

Prehistory 29
The Red Coast 31
The Land of Dreams 33
Brasil, Italia. 34
The Professor Who Missed the Titanic 37
The Man of the Mundial. 38
The Snake Smoked. 40
The Dasslers 43
The Count 47
Bernabéu's Right Hand. 49
The Revelation 51
La Dolce Vita. 52
Father and Son 54
Christmas 1956. 57
O Plano Paulo Machado de Carvalho 61
The Magnificent Seven 63
The Affront. 64
Hands in Pockets 67
The Terror 70
The Subversives. 74
The Timão 75
The War of the Sons 77
The Czarina 80
The Duellers 82
The Pact 85
The Gift 89
The New Rules of the Puppeteer. 91
Another 5 July 95
The Flood 96
The Best Deal of a Lifetime 99
From Total Football to Social Football. 101
The Chair Game 104
Real Vicenza 108
The Spark. 109
The Hidden Property .110
The Exchange 112
Hilton Hotel, 11pm. .113
The Silence 118
The Mason, Mason and Massera 119
Pablito 121

Marmelada Peruana 123
Suddenly the Last Mundial 124
The Scenario 126
The Package 127
The First Sponsor 129
The Fox and the Cat 130
Muddy 133
The Brazil of Telê Santana 134
Game of Four. 136
L'étranger. 140
The Mundialito. 142
One Kingdom is Not Enough 144
The Trial 147
The List. 149
Socratic Democracy 150
The Return 154
The Forbidden Place 156
A Ship in a Storm 160
The Call of Destiny 160

The Mundial 163
The Spain '82 Affair 165
All the Enemies of Saporta. 167
Rey's Madness 169
Ossie's Dream 171
The Boycott 175
The Two Masters. 177
The Blind Faith. 183
The Mystical Side of the No. 1. 183
A Dog Day Afternoon 185
O Canhão. 187
Telê's Binary Combinations 188
The Magic Square I 192
The Magic Square II 193
The Golden Cage. 194
The Great War 196
The Massacre Game 198
The Magic Square III 202
Meeting the King. 204
The Other Friulian 208
The Void 209
Deus é Brasileiro 211
The Stopover of Shame. 215
The Treatment 218
The Club of the Cuckoo Heads 220
Silence is Golden 221
The Group of Death 228
The Sarriá 234
The Eve. 236
The First Ballet. 238

The Revolt of the Excluded 242
The Brancazot Armada 245
The War of the Pens 246
The Grangiuàn 248
The Big Chill. 252
The Farewell Waltz. 258
The Flop 264
Achilles' Heel. 265
The Vecio's Plan 269
Serginho 272
War of the Worlds 276
The Tower Move 282
The Bluff 285
Hotel Majestic, Room 427 286
The Last Session 291
Quelli Che il Calcio 295
The Night. 301
Marathon–Sarriá 305
Against the Legend. 308
The Corsera Crew 312
The Artist 314
The Exercise 315
The Doubt 317
Lettera 32. 318
The Killer. 322
The Future, Now. 324

The Match. 327
Why 329
The Chairmen 331
Three Men and a Pipe 333
The Gentleman. 334
The Epic Poets 337
Italy, Make Us Dream 340
A Soul Split in Two. 343
The Game Is Not the Same for Everyone 344
The Last Words 346
The Italian 348
Fratelli d'Italia 350
In the Middle of the Pitch 352
Mr Tim's Certainties. 354
Zoff's Gloves 356

First Half 359
The Kick-Off. 361
The P Point. 362
The Fleeting Moment 363
O Galinho 366
O Doutor 368
The 12 Steps 370
The Clown 371

The Running Man 374
The Defence with a Moustache 377
The Right Choice 379
Lo Zio 380
The Last Fires 381

Half-Time 385
In the Grandstand 387
The Backup Plan 392

Second Half 397
The Second Act 399
The Last Souvenir 400
No Truce 403
The Scream of Judas 405
Tiziu's Moment 409
Three to Two 413
The Sorrows of Young Peres .415
The Last Quarter 419
A Caged Lion 420
The Envy of the Gods – Part One 422
The Envy of the Gods – Part Two 423
The Promise 425
The Blue Oak 427
Zoff's Oscar 429
The End 431

Conclusion 437
The Child of the Sarriá 439

Endings 441
José's Destiny 443
The Sarriá Tragedy 444
Towards Glory 448
The Black Jackets 454
The Scopone Plane 457
Jumping on the Bandwagon .460
The Fate of the 'Powers' 465
The Man Who Did Not Want America 472
Made in Italy 475
The Evolution of Football in Italy 477
Bearzot 478
After Bearzot 483
Santana 485
The Defeated Generation 487
The Search for Explanations .492
The Sad Destinies of the Champions 494
The End of the Sarriá and the Match of the Century 496

Author's Notes 499
The Air of the Mundial 501

To Dabò, Arturo and Olivia.

And to my family.

Like now, then. Always.

*In Barcelona we were in the most difficult group,
with Argentina and Brazil, the world champions
and the world's strongest national team. Nobody,
nobody at all thought we could have a chance.*

Mario Sconcerti

Foreword

It will be a party to remember which will be talked about when many years have passed and its main protagonists will then be just names linked to football mythology.

Mario Vargas Llosa
Un partido para la memoria, ABC, 7 July 1982

Football is a metaphor. It simplifies the concepts that shape our existence: justice, fatality, reason, instinct, compassion, cunning, gratitude, morality. Abstractions that find full expression in the moment of a game. A representation that can enter into myth, revealing the profound order that governs life, epicising themes that are rarely present in everyday experience: glory, courage, hostility.

For a young man in the early 1980s, attending a football match could prove to be a sentimental education, a process of change, a training course. And if this was done collectively it could become something important, an event capable of making and thus changing history. At that time we desperately needed heroes. The collective imagination was being renewed with new dreams capable, after years of darkness, of filling our expectations with hope. We were chasing a new epic, renewed utopias, sagas capable of involving the planet. It was the era of Star Wars, Rocky, Superman and Goldrake. In an Italy squeezed between an Italian Saturday and a bestial Sunday, in the light of the ball, people abandoned themselves with desperate euphoria because the rest of the week was pitch black. Inflation, intrigue, cabals, massacres and speculation. The country's colour was grey. But not yet pinstriped. Italians were still carrying around an idea of poverty and were experiencing times of waiting. And among the moments that punctuated the change that then took place, one cannot be forgotten.

On 5 July 1982, Enzo Bearzot's Italy beat Brazil, then became world champions six days later. It was a crucial moment in the redefinition of Italian identity. A moment that, as Giovanni Spadolini, Italy's then prime minister, had predicted when greeting the Azzurri before they left for Spain, would have had a far greater impact on our lives than any other political event.

It all happened on a summer afternoon, the longest, most dramatic and most illuminating of my entire life as a sports fan. I was 12 years old when I saw Italy vs Brazil. The perfect age to experience a match at the height of one's dreamy enthusiasm. A naive and uncontaminated impetus, able to open candidly the doors to the myth, to let it sediment inside you forever. I remember everything about those hours. My grandfather had left a month before the start of the Mundial (the World Cup), and I was with my family on the cool side of the house where we lived at the time, in front of the television. It was a Telefunken set with a two-button remote control. Due to a strange interference, if I sneezed it would change the channel and you had to go all the way around to go back to the channel. But on that summer afternoon I couldn't be cold. It was hot as hell and there was no air. In Rome, where I was, as well as in Barcelona, where the match was being played.

That Brazil side was unbeatable. And nobody was betting on Italy. But on that pitch, the team that seemed to have been born to conquer the world lost it, and the other team, which until then had not yet been aware of itself, managed to go down in history. The clearest memory I have of that afternoon is a bad feint by Júnior that made the ball go sideways. My father pointed out the naivety. And that image still remains for me the emblem of the match. A demigod who, in a daring gesture normal for him, spreads his legs to pass a ball. Failing.

But that match was much more than that, and this story tries to recount it, trying to overturn the commonplace (from the allegorical paradigm of attack against defence) or rehabilitate scapegoats (such as the wooden Serginho or the clumsy Waldir Peres, who played two of the most literary and fascinating roles in this match), overcoming the naive vision of the good guys defeating the villains. Because that Brazil was as beautiful as a god and as such had his Achilles' Heel. It was not a player. Its weakness was in the very condition of beauty. Fragility.

The match took place in a shabby stadium, a hot pit, now disappeared, called Sarriá, when the Cold War was in full swing, in the hottest summer of the century, during the most beautiful world championships ever (perfectly wedged between the two boycotts: that of the United States at the 1980 Moscow Olympics and that of the Soviet Union at the 1984 Los Angeles Olympics), of which it was the epicentre of beauty. It is so well calibrated that it has the same five-act structure as a film: triggering event (1-0), progressive complications (1-1 and 2-1), crisis (2-2), climax (3-2), resolution (the disallowed goal, the final parade, the epilogue). It is an ironclad script. An impeccable film. The way the match was going (Brazil just needed a draw, Italy had to win), the course of the result created an overwhelming alternation of moods. Ninety minutes of emotional beauty.

Two schools faced each other, the school of football as a spectacle and the school that was mistakenly associated with catenaccio, but which in reality represented strategy. Miltiades, winning at Marathon, freed the Greeks and the whole of the West from Persian domination. Giotto, by painting the Scrovegni Chapel, emancipated painting from the oppressive Byzantine rule, opening the way to modernity. Bearzot, by beating Brazil, not only prevented them from winning their fourth title but also bent the history of football at right angles. From that day on football lost in lightness but gained in commitment. The outcome of this match marked the death of Brazilian football and the rebirth of Italian football, which managed to shake off decades of 'catenaccio and counter-attack'.

Two schools, two continents, one ball, a thousand stories that all lead on to that field. Because a game is not just a game. It is

THE MATCH

a gateway that leads elsewhere. It is the point of contact between the two cones of an hourglass. It comes from a past and leads to a future. A unique and unrepeatable movement. A work of art. That would be enough. However, the game hides an impetuous tangle of underground stories. Interwoven threads, crossed destinies, fatal accidents (but also friendships, promises, oaths, fidelity, poisons, mortifications, rebellions, errors and rebirths) that crossed the lives of the men who were the protagonists, binding them together in a grip that now immortalises them for eternity.

At the centre of the story is a tale of gratitude and redemption: that of coach Enzo Bearzot and his blind faith in a player that everyone thought was finished – Paolo Rossi. Just as the 40-year-old goalkeeper Dino Zoff was considered finished, as well as old, when in the 90th minute he had the crucial ball in his hand that could change the fate of a nation. Around them a now vanished world of monumental celebrities sitting in the press boxes (on the one hand, the golden writers Gianni Brera, Oreste del Buono, Giovanni Arpino, Juca Kfouri and the three Marios: Soldati, Sconcerti, Vargas Llosa; on the other, the ravenous Italian reporters capable of massacring their national team as never before), in those of the authorities (João Havelange, Artemio Franchi, Primo Nebiolo), in the institutional seats (Sandro Pertini, Giovanni Spadolini, Juan Carlos, João Baptista de Oliveira Figueiredo), in those of power (Horst Dassler, Raimundo Saporta, Carlos Alberto Lacoste, Sepp Blatter) or even in those of the houses that matter (from Carmelo Bene to Umberto Eco via Vittorio Gassman).

In the background, the decline of the Brazilian dictatorship and the dawn of a new, ephemeral Italian boom. Behind them, unrepeatable childhoods: South American players afraid to leave their families for football, Italian players forced to earn a living (Zoff as a mechanic, Tardelli as a waiter, Gentile a worker, Conti a bricklayer, Causio a barber's boy). Common socio-genetic denominators of countries far and near, with an intertwined history (Brazil, discovered by a man from Florence, was to become the promised land of the

FOREWORD

Italians of the 20th century, until its stars, now improper daughters of Italian emigrants, returned to play in their country of origin). And precisely in their singers, the journalists, history still existed and weighed on the heads of the writers. They felt it was close. The Brazilian reporters still suffered from the cloak of the regime. For Italian reporters, the war was familiar: they had lived through it, their fathers had fought in it. And even in the most hurried lines, they managed to evoke leaders of every class (Pyrrhus, Hannibal, Augustus, Arminius, Napoleon, Leonidas, Carl von Clausewitz, Helmuth von Moltke, Emmanuel de Grouchy, Gebhard Leberecht von Blücher); historians of every age (from Tacitus to Machiavelli); battles of every place (from Thermopylae to the Piave, passing through Curtatone and Montanara). Men and battles now almost forgotten. Like the Brazilian soldiers who fought against Italy in the Second World War.

The match, despite the stakes, was a wonderful spectacle played in an incredibly fair and sporting manner. After that World Cup everything started to change. Football lost its last bit of innocence, spontaneity and naivety. And it was something else. I truly believe, like many, that Italians can be divided between those who 'lived' the Mundial and those who were born after it. Most of the people who like to talk about that match were my age when they saw it. Twelve years old. For many of them, football was born and died there. Nothing so beautiful has ever happened again. Because football itself has transformed along with us. But we are left with the indelible memory of that summer afternoon, of that piece of life that we lived in front of the TV sitting in the dining rooms of our homes, of that crazy happiness that unexpectedly attacked us all and that, making us feel for the first time, after what seemed like an eternity, brothers of Italy, came to convince us that, yes, we would make it to fulfil our dreams. That was Italy vs Brazil on 5 July 1982.

For a kaleidoscopic myriad of magnificent reasons, there were no more matches like that. The century we have left behind has now crystallised it as the most beautiful of the first 100 years of football.

THE MATCH

The way things have changed in the world and in football, it is not difficult to believe that it will probably remain the most beautiful of all time and that we will only have to look to the future with poignant nostalgia. Those 90 minutes were the sport, the football, the match, the stadium, the men, the stories of a precise moment, as they had never been before and as they would never be again.

I often think of that match. Of the endless vicissitudes of the men who took part in it, of the capricious tangles of chance that forever chained the characters in this plot to each other. But above all I think of my grandfather who was no longer there and my children who were not yet there. They were not there and they did not see. To them, my wife and my family I dedicate this story.

Prologue

My greatest passion is jazz, particularly Dixieland. That doesn't stop me getting goosebumps every time I listen to Stelutis Alpinis, but it's the voice of the blood: jazz...

Here, I would like a jazz team, great ensemble work, a lot of teamwork and suddenly the soloist comes out.

Enzo Bearzot

The Man Who Came from Haifa

Five o'clock in the evening, the time of the bullfights. A lone man stands in the middle of the field in Barcelona's Sarriá stadium. His name is Abraham Klein. He wears a watch on each wrist, one traditional and one digital. He cannot leave anything to chance, he certainly cannot afford to make a mistake. Not now, not today. This is his day. A few weeks ago he was devastated by the passing of one of his sons. Now he is about to referee his only match in the 12th edition of the World Cup being played in Spain: the last match of Group C: Italy vs Brazil. The semi-final is up for grabs. The winning squad will find themselves among the top four in the world.

It's a Monday. Klein has overcome all kinds of prejudices, difficulties and political manoeuvres to be here. But he is a survivor and is no longer afraid of anything. Maybe that is why he flaunts his forehead space by plastering his hair back, as was once the custom. Maybe it does not do justice to his 48 years, but it suits him just fine. Precision, rigour, clarity, honesty and courage are his values. And Klein belongs to a generation that entrusts looks with presenting them. He wears a long-sleeved cotton shirt, completely black except for the wide white collar and cuffs. At heart height is a pocket filled with all his pride. Printed on it is 'FIFA Referee' and wedged between those simple words, which make him an international referee for the game's highest body, are the two faces of the planet. On one is Italy, on the other Brazil. It is unbearably hot, 34 degrees in the shade; on the pitch it must be 40.

Klein came to Spain directly from Haifa, where he supervises the athletic activities of Israeli schools for the Health Institute. He trains every day. Ten kilometres of running, two hours of gymnastics, strict diet, heart rate checks. On the eve of the World

Cup in Mexico, he climbed the mountains of Galilee to get used to the altitude, and before the championships in Argentina he chose the climate of Cape Town. This time, fearing that his physical condition would not reach the levels of previous years, he hired a fitness trainer. Klein lost nine kilos in four weeks and trained his body to withstand a load of physical stress for 120 minutes so that he would also be ready for extra time, should it prove necessary. A nightmare for a man in his late forties. But he feels he has to do it; a referee is alone against 22 men. And he must always be in the right spot. Making a wrong decision would mean ruining a match. But he wants to dominate it, so he is constantly studying the videos. He tries to understand the tactics of the teams, get to know their players, see who among them has the tendency to intimidate their opponents. Or the referees. He avoids speaking on the pitch. His role is to manage the match without giving explanations. However, before each match he still tries to learn some basic expressions of the local language. He speaks perfect Hebrew, English, Hungarian and Romanian, but also German, Spanish, French and Italian, because he was taught Latin at school and European languages are all children of the same mother.

For more than a decade he has been taming the world's best players and now thinks he has learned everything about control. But the Spanish World Cup has just taught him a lesson he will never forget. A lesson punctuated by three crucial phone calls that will change the course of his life forever.

The first dated back to March. The list of referees who will take part in the Mundial is awaited but, with the qualification of Kuwait and Algeria, Arab TV stations have threatened to boycott the World Cup if an Israeli is allowed to direct a match. FIFA meets. The day of the verdict is set for Monday, 15 March, and on that morning Klein is shrouded in unusual anxiety. In 1970, Montezuma's revenge had prevented him from going ahead in the tournament; two years later the massacre of the Israeli Olympic team in Munich had not allowed him to take part in the 1974 World Cup in Germany; in the following

World Cup the Argentinian dictatorship denied him the final. Now what else could happen?

Spain's will be the World Cup of Zico, Platini, Rummenigge, Boniek, Maradona, and he does not want to miss it. He walks around the house impatiently, plays nervously with the phone, picks up the receiver to make sure there is a line. Until the phone finally rings. 'You are one of the 44,' says a voice on the other end. 'Abraham, you've made it, you're going to the World Cup!' His candidacy has been unanimously approved by the 59th meeting of the FIFA Referees' Committee. The solution adopted, suggested by Artemio Franchi, was the result of the usual diplomatic compromise: the television companies of the Persian Gulf States (Qatar, Bahrain, Oman, United Arab Emirates, Saudi Arabia and Kuwait itself) will be able to choose between not broadcasting the match or broadcasting it without showing his name in the overlay.

So Klein packs his suitcase two months later and leaves for Spain. Before his arrival, in London, three men shoot the Israeli ambassador Shlomo Argov in the head. It is 3 June. Using the attack as justification, three nights later Israel invades Lebanon. Exactly one week before the Mundial. That day the phone rings in Klein's hotel room. It is his wife: 'We are at war, Abraham!' Their son Amit is serving in the military and Klein's thoughts race to him: 'They cannot send a recruit into a firing zone.' Instead, he learns from that same phone call that Amit has already been sent to the front. Suddenly Klein's body is invaded by unfamiliar emotions. Fear prevents him from breathing. The fate of his son is in distant hands. And for the first time in his life, Klein finds he is not in control of the situation. All he can do is collapse on the bed and cry.

Three days later, when he learns that Amit is fighting in Damour's hottest spot, a few kilometres from Beirut, he asks for a meeting with Franchi. 'I can't do it,' Klein hisses. The UEFA and Referees' Committee president stares him in the eye: 'Are you sure?' 'Yes, one hundred per cent. I can't referee a match in this World Cup. My son is fighting in Lebanon and I haven't heard from him for days.

I don't even know if he is alive.' There is a special understanding between the two.

Like Klein, Franchi knows all the rules of football and the major languages of the world. In his youth he was also a referee. Now, as he is listening to Klein's story, he is the president of UEFA, the vice-president of FIFA, a member of the World Cup Organising Committee and, of course, chairman of the Referee's Committee. He is a fierce defender of football's interests but here and now he is only concerned for the Israeli referee. When Klein stops talking, Franchi abandons for a moment that tight, authoritative smile that has always given him the empathy to be accepted by everyone. He does not want to make a definitive choice. He has never done so. He has always left himself every possible room for manoeuvre. 'Compromise is always the most honest choice for a manager': his credo in ten essential words, as indispensable as the players of a team. He had whispered them a few months earlier to the Roman journalist of *Il Messaggero*, Lino Cascioli, who accused him of knowing the outcome of the World Cup draw in Spain in advance. Franchi understood Klein's dilemma and accepted his request not to have him referee, but invited him to stay in Spain: 'For now I'm only going to put you on the pitch as linesman.'

Almost two weeks pass, during which Klein does not receive a single piece of news from the front. He begins to fear that his son has passed away. It is the day of Italy vs Peru. It is 18 June, Amit's birthday. His son turns 20 at the front as Klein runs back and forth on the sidelines of the Balaídos, the stadium in Vigo. Klein tries to do his job, his eyes see Bruno Conti's amazing goal, Paolo Rossi's dull performance and the famous fall on the pitch of his colleague, the German referee Walter Eschweiler, but his mind is elsewhere. After the match he returns to the hotel and finds a telegram waiting for him on the reception desk. He hesitates. Then he grabs and opens it.

Shalom dear Dad,
Today, as you know, is my birthday. I am celebrating it here
in Lebanon; many of my friends have died and my heart
is broken, but we talk a lot about the World Cup and I am
looking forward to seeing you referee a game.
With love,
Amit

Klein cannot stop crying. He goes up to his room and hears the
phone ring. On the other end he thinks he can hear his son's voice.
He thinks it is a hallucination. How can Amit, who is in the middle
of a war, reach him in his hotel room? But it is him and Abraham is
seized by an uncontrollable emotion, the most powerful of his life.
His son has left the front line and begs him to referee. 'In less than a
week, I will be linesman again for Brazil–New Zealand.' But Amit
wants to see him on the field. 'I'll be there, son,' he promises him
through tears. So Klein, still stunned, rushes to Franchi: 'I'm ready,
give me a game.'

A few days later, on Saturday, 26 June, the Israeli referee is
assigned the third match of Group C between Brazil and the winner
of Italy vs Argentina. 'You'll do Argentina–Brazil, happy?' Franchi
tells him. It is a gift for him. Instead, he will find Italy and Brazil,
the teams of his destiny; before this match he has refereed them both
five times. In this World Cup he has already seen them both from
the sidelines. But this time he will conduct the orchestra.

Klein summons Zoff and Sócrates, the two captains, to the
midfield circle. He turns to the Brazilian and flips the coin. Heads
or tails, ball or goal. Sócrates loses the toss, and Zoff takes the field.
The sun is still high and the Azzurri goalkeeper chooses to field his
team on the right. When the sun goes down it will be the opponents
who will have it in their sights. Brazil kick off. The crowd is buzzing.
To comply with protocol, Klein has to wait until 5.15pm. He places
the ball on the ground, leaning over the midfield circle in perfect
alignment with the line that divides the field into two halves. He

is small in stature and lacks what is known as physical authority, but he still manages to impose his own law. In his erect posture, in his amplified gestures, in his theatrical glances, there is a solemn, authoritative, almost warlike mimicry.

The Brazilians look towards the grandstand. The centre of the pitch gathers only three figures: Zico, Serginho and Klein, who has his left arm raised and his eye fixed on the stopwatch. Galinho has the number ten wedged between his shoulder blades and his hands resting on his hips, as if he is about to start a walk. The clock is ticking as 44,000 gazes, 88,000 eyes stare at that strutting gentleman dressed in black. Klein understands that this is the moment, takes a breath and pushes all his authority into the whistle. Perhaps he already knows: it will be the last match of his life. It is his final.

The Historical Memory of the Italians

Italy start breathing the Mundial breeze 33 days before the match against Brazil. In the worst way: with slaps, spits and tears. For the national team it is the day of departure. In front of the Hotel Villa Pamphili in Rome, where the Italian team has gathered, the technical commissioner Enzo Bearzot, by now subjected to exhausting solicitations during which the criticism has largely exceeded the approval, is apostrophised 'bastard ape' by a fan – Anna Ceci, 22 years old, member of the Roman Club Boys Nerazzurri – furious with him for not having called up Evaristo Beccalossi, the Inter midfielder who is setting the crowds on fire. 'Criticism yes, insults no' is the credo carved into the conscience of the Friulian commissioner – Friuli is a north-eastern region of Italy. The *Vecio*, a dialect term meaning 'Old Man', as he has always been nicknamed, responds to the offence with a slap. It is a paternal, educational slap ('a father is also a father of other people's sons; I gave her a slap like I would have done with my own daughter'), holding back his hand just enough so that the lesson would not hurt her, but the gesture is consigned to history and goes around the world. The previous day, in the same context, the same

THE HISTORICAL MEMORY OF THE ITALIANS

scene, this time it was a Roma fan singing the praises of Roberto Pruzzo, who was also excluded from the squad, and spitting on the coach's arm. Bearzot, at that point, took off his official federal jacket and suddenly handed it to the invader: 'Here, this is the uniform, you be the technical commissioner!'

For the Italian press, the two episodes are yet another indication of an obvious state of nervousness. Shortly afterwards, at 4pm, on the Boeing 727 City of Sulmona AZ 8236 bound for Santiago de Compostela, Bearzot recalls his Argentinian past. 'We will suffer in the first phase with all three teams we meet, but we will rise in the second phase. In the long run, values always emerge and I am sure that my players will not betray me.' That's what the Old Man thinks, immensely confident, as he flies over Spain. The rest is Italian talk, while he doesn't talk at all. In this Enzo Bearzot is a different Italian.

In his country, the vicissitudes of football interest public opinion more than the enormous chasm that has opened up in the state budgets, the quarrels of the Pentapartite party, the painful aftermath of the armed struggle, the impressive sequence of Sicilian political murders or, again, the atrocious epilogues of the events of Banco Ambrosiano, one of Italy's best-known institutions at the time, which collapsed in 1982. It is a confused, immature and tumultuous Italy, but also tired, spartan and sleepy. The President of the Republic (Sandro Pertini), the secretary of the largest trade union confederation of workers (Luciano Lama), the figurehead of journalists (Gianni Brera), the coach of the national team and even the doctor of the Italian team (Leonardo Vecchiet) all smoke a pipe.

These are restless days. The previous Friday petrol broke through the 1,000 lire barrier, while the wind of crisis is blowing threateningly over the government, which, more than ever before, appears shaky. The desperate search for a solution to the problem of the escalator has created a worrying split between the parties and a chasm now seems to be dividing the Christian Democrat and Socialist ministers. It is the beginning of the most difficult week for Prime Minister Giovanni Spadolini, the first non-Democrat in the history of the Republic. He

THE MATCH

has just returned from his official visit to Spain, where he also had the opportunity to meet the Azzurri. He compared their destiny to his own. Saving Italy. The national team by reaching the semi-finals.

Spadolini averts the fourth consecutive early dissolution of the chambers. Solemn and good-natured, he loves history and is proud to be part of it. But he knows that history sometimes takes place in unexpected twists and turns. Apparently minor episodes that affect social life more than politics. When, on the eve of the Italian squad's departure for Spain on 1 June he welcomed the Azzurri to Palazzo Chigi, he suggested a bold and visionary hypothesis: 'If you win the World Cup, the historical memory of the Italians of 1982 will be much more closely linked to your names than to those of the Spadolini government.' He then said he was certain to meet them again in early July, on the occasion of the official visit to his Spanish counterpart.

And before leaving for Spain, he set to work, sounding out in three long talks the mood of the Republic's highest monetary authority, the governor of the Bank of Italy, Carlo Azeglio Ciampi, the most important private industrialist, Fiat chairman Gianni Agnelli, and one of the historic leaders of the Christian Democrats, Giulio Andreotti.

Work resumed in the morning, with a series of talks to be held by the president with Ciriaco De Mita, Bettino Craxi, Pietro Longo, Valerio Zanone and Oddo Biasini. This could be the last week of work for deputies and senators. If, at the end of the debate, the Spadolini government were to resign, the legislative activities would automatically be blocked and all the bills presented would lapse. The last word had not yet been spoken. While waiting for the fateful hour, the Chamber and Senate went ahead, ignoring the impending crisis. In the afternoon in Montecitorio, the case of the Christian Democrat councillor Ciro Cirillo, freed by the Red Brigade on payment of a ransom, would be discussed. It would certainly not be a fierce debate since the Chamber could even be deserted, due to the simultaneous Italy vs Brazil football game.

The Mundial

The same day, six years earlier. Joaquín Viola Sauret is sitting at his desk, reading his mail. The air is changing. Just 48 hours ago, Don Adolfo Suárez González became the first democratically appointed head of government since Franco. Viola was not chosen by the people. It was Rodolfo Martín Villa, the Gobernador Civil de la Provincia, who did it by appointing him mayor of Barcelona. He has been in that chair for ten months but it has been enough to qualify him as *el alcalde más impopular de Barcelona*, Barcelona's most unpopular mayor. He is 63 years old, his mouth perpetually half open and two bright eyes. He points them at an envelope that catches his eye. The sender is José Antonio Zalba, president of the commission in charge of preparing the World Cup in Spain. The letter contains a request for details of the works needed in order to be chosen as the venue for a World Cup match. Stadiums, car parks, roads, accommodation and services. At that precise moment, Viola takes his eyes off the paper and places them on the street map of the city he presides over: 'The World Cup will happen.' He knows that Barcelona, along with the capital, will be the main theatre. And he trembles at the thought of being part of the scene.

But his shining gaze has no foresight. The Presidente del Gobierno Suárez will remove him five months later and replace him with José María Socías Humbert, the last mayor to take office without the support of the ballot box, and Viola will never see the World Cup. Death suddenly appears to him as he is intent on reading another letter of directives. At stake is not the city of Barcelona but his own life. On the morning of 25 January 1978, four terrorists enter his house on the Paseo de Gracia, catch him in his pyjamas in his bedroom, wrap a bomb over his chest with adhesive tape and hand him a paper: 'Read carefully. If you do not pay within the terms, you will be blown up.' He would have followed those instructions; he has a rich wife and five children. But the device explodes before its time and his head flies through the air, taking all his dreams with it. The following year, Spain officially accepts the invitation. Yes, the World Cup will take place. Even without him. And it will be Barcelona that will host 'the game'.

The story of that challenge, however, begins much earlier.

Prehistory

No one would be shocked, or perhaps it is more accurate to say, will be scandalised by an elimination of the Azzurri.

Carlo Grandini, *Corriere della Sera.*

The Red Coast

Red is the colour of embers. That colour was the resin from the trees that covered the coast of the country. That is why they called it 'Brasil, ember' (*brasa*, in Portuguese). But Brasil (Brazil or Hy Brazil) was also a legendary place; geographers were certain that it existed beyond the visible ocean, to the point of writing it on their maps. In the past, Pliny the Elder had called it *Insulae Purpuraricae*, Purple Island. From the coasts of Italy he had spotted the purple colour of the sea, even though he could not see it, more than a thousand years in advance, before he died on the slopes of Vesuvius during the eruption of AD 79, wrapped in the purple fumes of the embers.

Italy and Brazil are linked by destiny, history and affection. The navigator who first sighted the Brazilian coast was an Italian, the Florentine Amerigo Vespucci, in 1499. He too was struck by the trees: 'They are so beautiful that it seems as if we are in paradise.' It was instead 'the fourth part of the globe', and he had just discovered it.

The Red Coast, even before Brazil became a world power in sugar production a century later during the era of Grand Duke Ferdinand I (1587–1609), began to attract the attention of Italian traders, especially from Tuscany, who were interested in the techniques of sowing, production and refining. One of them was the young Florentine Filippo Cavalcanti, descendant of the well-known poet Guido Cavalcanti and friend of Dante Alighieri, who, in 1560, decided to cross the Atlantic to observe the sugar plantations in Pernambuco at close quarters. Filippo left Florence, turning his back on a solid and promising future to move his destiny towards the unknown, to Brazil, where he married Catarina de Albuquerque, with whom he had 12 children. She could not have known that he, an Italian, was creating what would be considered by the Colegio Brasileiro de Genealogia – Brazilian Genealogy Committee – the largest Brazilian family descending from a single ancestor, larger than the Silva family. By the time the first riots against Pedro II broke out, the Cavalcanti family had spread throughout the country.

Those same vermilion shores that had attracted Filippo had been observed in 1835 by Giuseppe Garibaldi. He had embarked for Rio de Janeiro after learning that republican ideas were spreading in the southern province of Rio Grande do Sul, where people did not believe they could benefit from the imperial economic policy. When he landed in Brazil, a revolution was already underway, that of the *Farrapos* (ragamuffins) led by the *caudillo gaucho* Bento Goncalves, whose secretary was the Italian coalman Livio Zambeccari, who warmed the spirits of the Brazilian Giovine Italia. Garibaldi fought bravely, captured and emancipated the 'negro Antonio', the first freed slave of the entire Atlantic coast of Latin America (50 years before their total abolition in Brazil), was wounded and experienced imprisonment and torture. But he also met Ana Maria Ribeiro da Silva, whom he called Anita, the indomitable daughter of Paulist immigrants in southern Brazil who had revolted against the empire. Garibaldi was enraptured by her at first sight ('You must be mine'). She did not hesitate for a moment to follow him in the most risky of undertakings, becoming first his wife then the mother of his four children.

After dedicating 12 years of life and struggle to Brazil and Latin America, Garibaldi crossed the ocean again to reunite Italy: he spoke with Cavour, Mazzini and Vittorio Emanuele II, defended Rome, took part in the 1848 uprisings, the wars of independence and, like a *caudillo* at the head of his *gauchos*, in La Spedizione dei Mille – Expedition of the Thousand – in a headlong rush changed the history of Italy. He chose a purple-red shirt and a black handkerchief for the uniforms of his men, in memory of the lava from Vesuvius. He will remain forever linked to those two worlds of which he is and will be, par excellence, the hero.

The Land of Dreams

Italy and Brazil experienced their awakenings in the same years. Within the framework of an economy that was by now widely capitalist, newly united Italy began to be dominated by large-scale productive activities. But the impetuous industrial development of the late 19th century was inexorably relegating the rural world to the margins of modern life. In Brazil, Queen Isabel, daughter of the Neapolitan Teresa Cristina di Borbone, 'Mother of the Brazilians', was abolishing slavery for good (1888). This magnanimous gesture gave her the nickname *A Redentora* (The Redeemer) but cost her the throne, marking the end of the monarchy forever.

The newborn republic realised that it could count on an immense supply of land but did not have enough workers. It was at this point that the Society for the Promotion of Immigration, after an initial test with the Germans, who were not very inclined to interact with the locals, saw Italy as the ideal recruiting ground for the labour force it was seeking. Italians were perfect: white, Catholic, sociable, in need of employment and skilled in manual work. Thus, in 1894, the various Brazilian states began to promote the subsidised immigration of Italian families. Agencies promoting emigration began to appear everywhere in the Belpaese. More than 7,000 agents, often unscrupulous, travelled the country from head to foot, portraying Brazil as the country where dreams could come true. In the brochures, one can read 'Lands in Brazil for Italians' followed by 'Ships leaving every week from the port of Genoa. Come and build your dreams with your family. A country of opportunities. Tropical climate, plenty of food, mineral wealth. You can have your own castle in Brazil.'

Unwitting accomplices of the propaganda are also the stories of a chronicler of fantasy who, in those very years, makes Italians dream. In his pages, Emilio Salgari gives those red trees everything they need to live, from clothes to dishes, as well as juices, ointments, balms and terrible poisons. The Brazil he describes is a true paradise on Earth where man and nature live in perfect harmony. A happy country where you can ride a turtle or sail on a giant leaf. Like Pliny, he had never seen that land, he had never moved from Verona; at most he had moved to Turin, yet the novelist managed to describe in an astonishing way the Brazilian lands with all the exotic fauna, the impenetrability of the forests, the wild nature, the customs and habits of the Indios, contributing, together with the illustrator Alberto Della Valle, to introduce the young people of the time to the unknown world of the Amazonian lands and the tropics.

Enchanted by these suggestions, Natale Pastorin, a Veneto farmer who had run out of land in Italy, decided to take his wife, Policena, and son, Giovanni, to try the big leap by reinventing himself as a barber in South America. The Pastorins, who left a whole world of memories in Santa Maria di Sala full of yearning nostalgia, were only three units of the one million Italian souls who crossed the thin red line of the coast before landing in the ports of Santos and Rio de Janeiro between 1887 and 1902. The largest regional group of origin was Veneto, with 30 per cent of departures. The emigrants grouped together according to their regions of origin, rebuilding their rural communities in Brazil. Natale settled in Cascatinha, near São João Nepomuceno, in the state of Minas Gerais, where he divided his time between farming and barbering, while his wife found work in a textile factory. In the streets of the Italian neighbourhoods, the dialects of Verona, Lombardy, Trento, Emilia, Campania, Puglia and Calabria resound more than the Portuguese language. Italian are the names of the streets, the signs of the shops and the saints to whom they turn.

Brasil, Italia

A century before the Sarriá match, Brazil does not yet know what football is. In 1894, a 20-year-old Englishman from Southampton landed in São Paulo. Eleven years earlier, his father John, a Scottish engineer who had emigrated to Brazil where he had married Carlota

Alexandrina Fox Miller, a Brazilian of English descent, had sent him to England to study. His name was Charles William Miller and he arrived in Brazil with a bag in his hand. Inside were two leather balls, an air pump and a book on the rules of football.

The São Paulo Railway had just opened its doors and Charles found work in the accounting department. Not even a kilometre from his grandparents' house, at 24 Rua Monsenhor de Andrade, almost on the corner of Rua Rangel Pestana, in the Brás neighbourhood, where he was born on 24 November 1874, is the Várzea do Carmo. It is a field between the Gasômetro and Santa Rosa that the young people of the São Paulo Railway walk along every day on their way to work and that Charles considered perfect for a game of football, a sport he got to know at Banister Court School, in the old continent. So he starts tormenting his colleagues with stories and rules of a game, unknown to them, played by two teams kicking the ball from one side of a rectangle to the other. He formed a team with employees of the Estrada de Ferro São Paulo Railway, then another made up of members of the São Paulo Gas Company and the London Bank.

Once the training had been established, he organised the first regulation match: São Paulo Railway against Team do Gaz. On 14 April 1895, the players arrived at the field without kit, wearing their everyday clothes, chased away the grazing animals and played against each other. It was the first game of Brazilian football and it ended 4-2 to the railwaymen. When they left the field, the players, exhausted but enthusiastic, made a commitment to play a second match. It was the beginning. Born in a white environment and among the upper-middle classes, thanks to business trips it spread to all Brazilian states. Soon even the poorest strata of the population learned the rules and put them into practice wherever possible, with balls of rags.

When the Pastorins arrived in Brazil, one-third of the inhabitants of São Paulo were Italians. Their condition improved over the years. They formed a middle class that began to make the country great. The white slaves, the *carcamanos*, became entrepreneurs, architects, builders, journalists, writers and painters. The name of Antonio

Jannuzzi is linked to the entire building development of Rio, where there is no street where a building, a school or a house has not been built by his company; Pasquale Segreto, the 'manufacturer of merriment', the 'minister of entertainment', invented Rio's tropical belle époque, punctuated by bets, lotteries, gambling houses, *café chantantant*, cinemas and theatres; Francesco Matarazzo, who left Castellabate on 23 November 1881 at the age of 27, became a millionaire in São Paulo, Brazil, starting with a lard factory, then with his brothers founding a shipping company, fabric, liquor, majolica, matches, sugar, salt and soap factories; Giuseppe Martinelli built the first skyscraper in Latin America in São Paulo; Geremia Lunardelli became the largest coffee producer and trader in the world, so much so that he was nicknamed *Rei do Café*; and Giuseppe Guazzone and Pietro Morganti became the kings of wheat and sugar, respectively. Then there are the Italians who became, for better or worse, presidents of Brazil, Pascoal Ranieri Mazzilli (1961 and 1964), son of Montemurro parents, and Emilio Garrastazu Médici (1969–74), grandson of Palermo-born Raffaello. Not forgetting all those who were not personally successful, such as the newsagents in Rio de Janeiro, almost all of Calabrian origin (to the extent that the newsagent in Brazil is now an emblem of Italianness), or those farmers who, taking advantage of Italian experience, produced the best wines in South America.

And if Charles Miller was the founding father, in the years following his pioneering work it was the immigrants from Italy who spread the game through the foundation of clubs throughout the country. In 1913 and 1914, Pro Vercelli and Torino, two of the most representative Italian teams of the time, came to Brazil for a tour. Football was a sport on the rise and the Italian colony was the most numerous. So Luigi Cervo, Vincenzo Ragognetti, Ezequiel Simone and Luigi Emanuele Marzo, four employees of Industrie Riunite Matarazzo in São Paulo, came up with the idea of creating an Italian team. On 14 August 1914 an advertisement appeared in the *Fanfulla*, the newspaper of the Italians in Brazil, looking for footballers interested in the project. Forty-six people responded and on 26 August the Sociedade Esportiva Palestra Italia was born, with a tricolour uniform and the Savoia shield on its chest. These players paved the way for the country's most popular sport, without knowing that, one day, on the football pitch, Brazil would play its destiny with Italy.

The Professor Who Missed the Titanic

Among the Europeans shuttling back and forth between the old and new continents was Professor Faustin Havelange. He had been teaching mining engineering at the University of San Marcos in Lima for ten years and had to make long journeys from Belgium to fulfil his duties. Too much travelling had exhausted him so he was eager to change his life. He was about to embark on his last trip to Peru. On his return home, he married Juliette Ludivine Calmeau, the daughter of an industrialist from Liège, and with her he sought a new life in Brazil.

He chose a special ticket for his farewell: the inaugural ticket for the *Titanic*, the liner that would leave Southampton at 12 noon on 10 April 1912 under the orders of Captain Edward John Smith, also on his last voyage. The destination was New York, from where Havelange would take another ship to Lima. But on the morning of his departure he narrowly missed the train to Liège and, consequently, the boat to cross the Channel in time to reach the English port, thus saving his life. And in some ways also saving that of his son, Jean-Marie Faustin Goedefroid 'João' de Havelange, who was born four years later.

João was lucky enough to be born into the world and took full advantage of the unique opportunity of an earthly existence, facilitated by wealth. His father had started trading in arms for the Société Française des Munitions, but he also represented United States Steel, a company that was rapidly growing thanks to the immense deposit found at Chuquicamata in Brazil and the profitable acquisitions made by J.P. Morgan during the banking panic of 1907. The young Havelange studied at the French *lycée* (secondary school), graduated in law and followed football. He played as a midfielder for Fluminense and in 1931 became a champion in Rio with the academy team. But his father, who at the age of 18 had founded the Standard Liège football team with other students from the College of Saint-Servais, thought that the best sport for him was swimming.

Under his father's guidance, João trained continuously: 6,000 metres in the morning and the same in the evening, every day, including holidays, even on Sundays when the only pool open in the whole of Rio was at the YMCA. He had only one obsession: to become number one. So much perseverance bore fruit and suddenly he started winning at 400, 800, 1,000 metres. He became the champion of Rio, the champion of São Paulo, then of Brazil. Finally, he became the fastest man in South America.

In 1933 his father suffered a cerebral haemorrhage. A few hours before the final farewell, Faustin made his son a promise: 'You must continue to be the best, João. Swear to me that you will make every effort to represent your country at the Berlin Olympics.' The man who had avoided the wreck of the *Titanic* died in his bed, leaving his son with the burden of a word to keep. João qualified for the Olympic Games and, in 1936, after 21 days at sea, he reached the port of Bremerhaven a week before his race. There was no swimming pool on board and he did not have time to recover his form, but he was dazzled by the magnificence of the organisation orchestrated by Hitler. And by the hero of those Games: Jesse Owens.

The Man of the Mundial

At the time when Adolf Hitler took over the supreme command of the German armed forces, Raimundo Saporta was a child, spending his days at 145 Malesherbes Boulevard. It was here that the foundations of the Lycée Carnot – Carnot High School – were laid, where Raimundo studied with his brother Marc. The German invasion of France changed, among millions of destinies, the course of his own little story, imposing on him a secret that he would have to keep for the rest of his life. That is why Don Raimundo Saporta Namias would never be able to write his memoirs, to speak publicly about his childhood or to remember his origins in interviews. He had to lie. It was said that his father is Spanish and his mother French, but also that his parents are Moroccan and Armenian, respectively. Or that she is Swiss. Or that both are Romanian. The only certainty is her mystery. A secret that shrouds her family. Constantly protected by dry statements. Always his, always cutting. 'I was born in Paris to a Spanish father and a French mother.' Full stop.

Perhaps this is also why he always avoided any kind of prominence. With the World Cup, however, the spotlight was inevitably on him. On 9 October 1978, at the suggestion of Culture Minister Pio Cabanillas Gallas, and thanks to a decree signed by Juan Carlos of Bourbon, Saporta was crowned president of the Real Comité Organizador de la Copa Mundial de Fútbol. A bachelor and very attached to his mother, he would become the noble father of the organisation. 'The man of the Mundial.'

In all Spanish documentation, Raimundo was born on 16 December 1926 in Paris. The same information is given on his consular visa for Brazil in 1961. But only he and his mother knew the truth in 1982. His father Jaime Saporta Magriso was a banker born in Thessaloniki (then part of the Ottoman Empire, now in Greece) on 27 September 1887, his mother Simona Nahmias was born in Constantinople (also in the Ottoman Empire, now Istanbul, Turkey) on 8 February 1902. Both were Sephardic Jews, direct descendants of Jews expelled from Spain in 1492. Following the 1929 crisis, the family moved to Paris.

Ten years later, the Spanish consul, Bernardo Rolland de Miota, advised Saporta's family not to name eastern cities as their birthplace, as their Sephardic origins could be guessed. Jaime and Simona had never set foot in Spain, yet they were Spanish by virtue of a

1924 decree signed by General Miguel Primo de Rivera granting nationality to those who could prove their Jewish origins. In fact, Raimundo's parents appear in the files of the Spanish consulate in the capital. Raimundo's file, however, has disappeared. It does not exist in any register. There is no trace in the civil register of Paris (État Civil de la Ville de Paris).

Who was he then? To find out, it is necessary to follow his destiny backwards. By tracing his entire life against the current, we do not find any answers until his high school days in Paris. Report cards from other eras still lie quietly undisturbed in the school archives, and in the folder containing those from the 1938–39 school year is the report card of 13-year-old *Raymond* Saporta. He was born not in Paris but in Constantinople. His father had succeeded in having him omitted and his birthplace left blank in the file for the 1940–41 school year. A mysterious, compassionate and secret arrangement must have allowed him to fill it in with the 'Paris' that would appear from then on in all his Spanish documentation. This is how the war began to change the life of the creator of the Mundial.

The Snake Smoked

'It's easier for a cobra to smoke than for Brazil to go to war.' When the Second World War broke out, it was President Getúlio Vargas who hastened to calm things down: 'The country will remain neutral.' A proposal consistent with the policy of not aligning itself with any of the great powers in order to try to enjoy their advantages. By early 1942, however, the government had begun to support the United States by granting it the island of Fernando de Noronha and Brazil's north-eastern coastline to supply American military bases. The stance was paid for by the torpedoing of 36 Brazilian merchant ships by German submarines.

Shocked by the civilian deaths, public opinion demanded that Brazil recognise the state of belligerence against the Axis countries. On 31 August 1942, Brazil declared war on Germany and Italy. Thus

THE SNAKE SMOKED

a cobra fumou (the snake smoked). But it was only after almost two years, on 2 July 1944, that a first contingent left for Italy under the command of General João Batista Mascarenhas de Morais. Some 25,000 Brazilians, united in the Força Expedicionária Brasileira, known by the acronym FEB, driven by the motto 'The cobra is smoking', landed on the peninsula in five stages. They reached the ports of Naples and Livorno and crossed the whole country in the direction of the Apuan Alps. In Italy, the FEB was attached to the IV Corps of the 5th Army of Generals Willis Crittenberger and Mark Clark, both deeply convinced of the futility of sending unprepared troops to face a war they did not know.

From the very first days, the shortcomings in the FEB's training became apparent and all kinds of accidents occurred throughout the war. The drivers of the expeditionary corps lacked driving experience and 24 Brazilians died as a result of trivial road accidents far from the front line. To these were added seven from gunshot accidents, four from drowning, three from murder and one from suicide. The first Brazilian victim died at night, killed by the blast of a machine gun clumsily manoeuvred by a comrade. His name was Antenor Chirlanda, born in São Paulo; he belonged to 9th company of the II/6th and was nicknamed Mussolini because of his resemblance to the Italian dictator.

In the 200 or so days that followed, the FEB carried out almost 3,000 offensive sorties in the battles of Monte Castello, Montese, Fornovo and Castelnuovo, hitting over 4,000 targets. There were 460 Brazilians killed, almost 3,000 wounded, 35 taken prisoner and 15 missing. Monuments are dedicated to them in the provinces of Bologna, Pisa, Modena and Parma (in the place where German infantrymen and Italian Bersaglieri, defeated in the Sacca di Fornovo, surrendered).

Many football players were involved on the other side of the fence. Anti-fascist Vittorio Staccione, a midfielder for Torino, was rounded up and sent to Mauthausen, one of the worst extermination camps, where he died. The Milan player, Ferdinando Valletti, on the other hand, was saved by agreeing to participate in the prisoner tournament. Armando Frigo, a midfielder for Spezia, was captured and shot by the Nazis after the armistice. Napoli midfielder Aldo Fabbro died with his mother and grandmother under the bombing. The same fate befell the Juventus player Pietro Tabor. Casale captain Luigi Barbesino died in flight during a reconnaissance mission. Bologna full-back Dino Fiorini enrolled in the Republican Guard and lost his life in an ambush. Partisan Antonio Turconi, goalkeeper at Pro Patria, was killed by the Nazi–Fascists when he was not yet 24 years old. The last to fall was Cecilio Pisano, a centre-forward who arrived in Genoa from Uruguay and became Italian thanks to his emigrant ancestors. He was thrown out of a window at the end of the war. Two-time world champion Eraldo Monzeglio, who died seven months before the start of the Mundial, avoided being shot at Salò by the patriots because of his footballing merits (among those who should have put him up against the wall, many were enthusiastic about the Azzurri's triumphs in which he had played a leading role), while his technical commissioner, Vittorio Pozzo, did his best to help Jewish families and to help allied prisoners escape to Switzerland. Despite this, he would always be labelled a fascist.

At the end of the war, the government of Rio de Janeiro, which had initially confiscated all the property of German, Italian and Japanese citizens, overcame all resentment and returned the seized property to its rightful owners. With this gesture it closed all the wounds opened by the war.

Brazil, which was nevertheless one of the victors in the conflict, paid dearly for its participation. Excluded from the war reparations negotiations, it had to repay in full the loan that the United States had granted to Vargas in 1942. The last instalment of the $361m that had arrived in South America was paid on 1 July 1954. Four days later, Brazil was eliminated from the World Cup in Switzerland in the quarter-finals, defeated 4-2 by a legendary team, Puskás's Hungary. The final pitted the Hungarians against a Germany still reeling from the war. It all seemed to have been written. But another Adolf had secretly added a chapter that would be revealed just moments before the opening whistle.

The Dasslers

Everyone called him Adi. He spoke little, thought a lot and loved to run. In the hidden interlocking of his worlds, he noticed a gap. There were no shoes suitable for sports. So he had a simple, revolutionary idea: specific shoes for different disciplines. Athletes needed the right shoes to win. They just did not know it. Adolf Dassler went to meet them. His brother Rudolf then took care of closing the deal. They did not get along but they complemented each other. They sent their shoes to players, coaches and managers of sports clubs in the region. Adi left the book of possibilities open; he constantly modified his creations, tested his products himself and agreed on improvements with the athletes.

Since 1924, with the Gebrüder Dassler Schuhfabrik (Dassler Brothers Shoe Factory), the two sons of shoemaker Christoph von Wilhelm Dassler had started producing football boots in their mother Pauline's laundry in Herzogenaurach, a small town in Bavaria. Then 1936 proved to be a magical year. Adi had become the father of little Horst, and Jesse Owens had triumphed at Hitler's Games with Dassler shoes on his feet.

Owens' shoes were made specially for him. Adi had thought of every single aspect. He made the upper from tanned calfskin and covered it with cowhide. In the forefoot area he decided not to add any metal plates and, to increase flexibility, he inserted a chrome crust sole instead. To save weight he then created small eyelets and thin laces. Underneath was the darkest and most decisive work. To widen the tread, he angled the six nails outwards and graduated the length of the tips by hand, according to Owens' specifications, from 15 to 17mm. He named the model after the coach of the German national athletics team, Josef Waitzer.

Adolf Hitler saw the 1936 Berlin Olympics as a great opportunity to flaunt the theory of Aryan supremacy. Adi saw the same opportunity in that 23-year-old American boy, christened James Cleveland but known to all by the similarity of his initials: Jesse.

'I want Owens,' Adi told his brother.

'He is black, we cannot support him. We only support German athletes.'

'But he is the best.'

'You would blow the deal with the National Socialists.'

'I don't care, he will be the Olympic champion.'

Adi Dassler had boldly offered Owens his athletes' shoes through Waitzer. It was a risk for him, but he did it. And that gesture started the story.

When word spread that the fastest man on Earth had won Olympic gold with the German shoemakers' shoes, the fortunes of the Dassler factory changed. Shortly afterwards, however, the war changed the destiny of the two brothers. Rudolf was called up for military service, Adi was relieved of his duties, as an indispensable worker. On 28 October 1943, Albert Speer, the minister of armaments, issued a directive to stop production at the Dassler shoe factory immediately. Machines and personnel were redirected to the war effort.

When the war ended, the Americans were tasked with blowing up the factory. The Dasslers, looked upon with suspicion both by the Nazis for helping a black American defeat their athletes and by the Americans for making weapons used against them, tried desperately to prove that they were just shoe manufacturers. They failed. Everything seemed finished until Adi's wife Käthe picked up a photograph and pronounced a name. The needle in the balance was still Owens. The American officers believed the Dasslers and allowed the factory to remain standing, but in return they took their house and a batch of shoes for the army. It was the last order.

The world conflict had only suspended the family's conflict. Adi and Rudolf drowned in a swamp of suspicion. The latter was convinced that he had been imprisoned by the Americans because of a complaint by his brother. The former feared that Rudi had threatened his wife. And that, worse, he was Horst's real father. When the 'denazification' policy put them under separate surveillance, both were sure they had been betrayed. The acquittal changed nothing and the break-up was inevitable.

The Gebrüder Dassler Schuhfabrik was officially closed in April 1948 and the two brothers divided up the company and employees, with 73 labourers choosing Adi and 49 administrative workers following Rudolf. From then on the Dassler brothers no longer spoke to each other. The Aurach river divided their lives. Adi opened a factory to the north, near the railway station, Rudolf on the opposite side in Würzburger Strasse. The Dassler name could no longer exist, so Rudolf took the first syllable of his name and added it to the first of his surname. 'Ruda'. But the sound seemed wrong to him, so he changed the two consonants and in 1948 renamed the company Puma (Puma Schuhfabrik Rudolf Dassler). On 16 June of the same year, his brother Adi had the same idea and registered the trademark Addas (Adolf Dassler Spezialsportschuhfabrik Addas). But there was already a name 'Adda' used by a company that manufactured children's shoes, so on 18 August of the following year he added an 'i' in pen to the trademark registration form to create Ad(i)das.

The dispute between the brothers not only involved their employees but affected the whole of Herzogenaurach. Since at least one member of each family was employed by one of the two companies, hardly anyone could escape the effect of the fratricidal quarrel. And the town split into two factions. The Puma and Adidas families became Guelphs and Ghibellines. They had their own bakeries, their own butchers, their own separate pubs. When someone walked through the door, the eyes of the people present always went to their shoes. Herzogenaurach became 'the town of downcast eyes'.

To avoid disputes, Adi did not want to use the side seams used by the old Dassler Schuhfabrik, so he used three parallel straps, which gave the shoe and foot more stability. The innovation made his shoes very recognisable and the three white stripes became the company's trademark.

A few years later the shoes with the three stripes were on the feet of the German national team in the Bern stadium in the 1954 World Cup Final. Italy and Brazil were extras at that World Cup. The former lost a group stage play-off, the latter reached the quarter-final but went no further. The invincible army was Puskás's Hungary, who had not lost in over four years. It was Hungary that sent Brazil home, beating them 4-2, then humiliating the defending champions Uruguay in the semi-finals by the same scoreline. And it was also Hungary that, during the group stage, beat Germany 8-3, and now met them again in the match that must definitively sanction their glory. For the Germans, having reached the final was already an extraordinary achievement; the best they could hope for was to avoid another humiliating defeat. They clung to one hope. Rain. Only water could neutralise the Hungarians' skills. On the morning of 4 July 1954, the sky in Bern was blue. But as the players left for the stadium, an incredible downpour hit the city. For the Germans it was music.

Before the start of the World Cup, Dassler revealed to coach Sepp Herberger that he had just invented removable studs, which could be screwed or unscrewed depending on the condition of the pitch. In the changing room Sepp turned to him: 'Adi, screw them on.' The Hungarians slipped, Germany played. Six minutes from the end, Rahn's goal put an end to the supremacy of the unbeatable Hungarian team, 3-2. The winning of the Jules Rimet Trophy ended the years of misery suffered by the Germans after the war. Suddenly Germany was somebody again and Adi became the hero of the 'Miracle of Bern'.

In the same year, at the European Athletics Championships in Bern, 'Heinz' Ludwig Fütterer won the 100 and 200 metres in Rudolf's Puma shoes. The two brothers made history. But Adi's son Horst would soon change it forever.

The Count

During the war, the Jules Rimet Trophy, won by Italy in 1938, was kept in Rome, a stone's throw from St Peter's Basilica, in the home of the president of the Italian Football Federation located in Piazza Adriana. Ottorino Barassi kept it hidden from the eyes of the Nazis, who wanted to requisition it for gold smelting. But it was the calibre of Barassi as a manager that proved most valuable. After managing the organisation of the 1934 World Cup, he was appointed by FIFA to help the Brazilian managers with the 1950 edition. And it was he, an Italian, who made sure the event ran smoothly by ensuring that the Maracanã stadium was ready in time for the tournament. He was about to be appointed as a member of the FIFA Executive Committee and with that title he would contribute to the foundation of UEFA. In the meantime, he drafted the reform, the so-called 'Lodo Barassi', which was intended to set up the plans for the promotion and relegation of football divisions, reduced the number of players and limited the recruitment of foreign players in Italy.

Il Conte – The Count – had just got his hands on the draft of that statute. In Italy everyone called him that. The title was enough to understand who he was. He was the most influential shadow in Italian football. Alberto Rognoni from Calisese di Cesena, the son of a land-owning magistrate, founded the Cesena Football Association on 21 April 1940, when he was only 22 years old, a gesture that, among others, created an intertwined thread with the history of the national team. At one end was Azeglio Vicini, who was born in Cesena in 1933 and who, as well as leading the national under-23 and under-21 teams, in 1982 was Enzo Bearzot's deputy. At the opposite end of the table was an unknown coach, Arrigo Sacchi, who led the team to win the last Academy championship in 1981/82.

While Vicini played for Il Conte (he was one of the first to wear the Cesena jersey and it was he who scored the 12 goals that got them promoted), Il Conte played for football. When, in 1951, the reform of the championships had to be passed, Rognoni spent a whole night rewriting the statute. He was in a Florentine hotel with 18 senior managers, headed by Barassi himself. At dawn, Rognoni headed for the lobby and crossed the corridor, along which the rooms of the powerful men faced each other. Each of them had left their shoes to be polished in front of the door. Thirty-six. Il Conte took two pairs at a time, opened the window and, with seraphic calm, threw them into the River Arno. When it was time for the meeting, the delegates, overwhelmed by this unusual destiny, first furious, then bewildered, then surrendering, appeared in slippers and short socks to listen to what Barassi, reading Rognoni's notes, had to say. This is how football was reborn in Italy.

The 'Capanno sul porto' in Cesenatico, Il Conte's headquarters, became the Mecca of football and Rognoni the grand inquisitor. He was the creator of the Control Commission, the Investigation Office of the Football Association, the body responsible for unmasking offences. He did everything, he never delegated, he was always on the front line. He even hid in the boot of a car to find the culprit of a crime that led to Udinese's relegation to Serie B in 1955, and showed up disguised as a monk at the home of the main corruptor of football at the time, Gegio Gaggiotti, a farmer from Brescia.

The last blow was the Scaramella scandal, the offence that led to Catania's relegation from the league in 1955, the disbarment of the Roman referee Ugo Scaramella, the abandonment of the profession of his corruptor, *La Gazzetta dello Sport* correspondent Giulio Sterlini, and his replacement by a young Catanese named Candido Cannavò, who was to become assistant manager during the Mundial.

Until Il Conte bought the *Guerin Sportivo* it was the oldest sports magazine in the world. From its columns, the intelligentsia, not just the sporting intelligentsia, of much of the 20th century would shine through: from Indro Montanelli to Gianni Brera, from Luciano Bianciardi to Camilla Cederna, from Pierpaolo Pasolini to Rino Tommasi, from Oreste del Buono to Gianni Mura. A unique editorial experiment. A laboratory of revolutionary journalistic ideas that even Pope Paul VI liked: 'Il *Guerin Sportivo* is like Juvenal, who *castigat ridendo mores* [corrects customs by laughing at them].'

Between 1953 and 1973, Il Conte, as editor-factotum and absolute master, was in total control. He dictated precise rules to his staff. First, each article must begin well and end better, because a brilliant beginning invites the reader to continue and the ending must leave him or her satisfied. Second, never write that a match was bad. Third, always go to the press box, listen to what the journalists say and write the exact opposite. The recipe worked. Despite the newspaper wars, Il Conte's weekly magazine resisted fashions, crises and mood swings.

Once, Rognoni fired the entire Milanese editorial staff, crossed the station square, and hired four porters to invite them to *Guerino*, as *Guerin Sportivo* was affectionately called, to write about football: 'Want to bet that they are more capable than you?' After the unfortunate people had been staring at him for an hour, he smiled, sent them away with a generous tip and, as if nothing had happened, called his collaborators back to his office in Piazza Duca d'Aosta 8b.

It was here, in 1961, that the young Italo Cucci set foot for the first time, but he had to wait 12 years and the transfer of ownership from Il Conte to (Luciano) Conti before becoming head of the crew. One day Dino Zoff said to him, 'It would be nice to see the photos and drawings of the goals every week.' This pleased him and the suggestion brought the weekly magazine to its highest-ever circulation. A 'working director', like Il Conte, Cucci would write, headline, lay out, photocopy, cut and print for the newspaper. And he would go into the field. That is why, on 5 July, he was sitting in the stands at the Sarriá.

Bernabéu's Right Hand

Spain. The beginning of a new life. Raimundo began to savour it in 1941 when the Saporta family moved to Madrid, away from the German soldiers. While the Holocaust was taking away the rest of his family and almost the entire Sephardic community of Thessaloniki, it was time for Jaime, Simona, Raimundo and Marc to embark on a journey full of hope. The illusion, however, lasted only for a moment. A few days after their arrival, a tram ran over and killed Jaime Saporta. Doña Simona was left a widow with two children in a country she did not know, fresh from a civil war and governed by a dictator who sympathised with the Nazis from whom they had fled to survive.

Raimundo owed his mother his life twice over. She was the one who gave it to him and she was the one who saved it. Doña Simona was cultured and intelligent. In Madrid, she knew that she had to reinvent herself quickly, so she took the form of the French widow of a Spanish banker. Her perfect command of the French language and a surname that few would have traced back to a Jewish lineage did the rest. She enrolled Raimundo in a French school. There he was encouraged to take up sport. Aware of his lack of athletic ability, he devoted himself to organising the basketball team and became a school delegate at the age of 16. This position put him in constant contact with the top management of the Spanish Basketball Federation, in particular with its president, Jesús Querejeta. At the age of 19 he became a member of the federation, two years later was appointed treasurer and the following year he was elected vice-president. His management skills, a brain predisposed to numbers and his fluency in languages made him a key figure. But he could not live on sport alone; after high school, the early death of his father precluded the possibility of university and forced him to find a job.

He started out in a domestic appliance shop on the Gran Via, until he managed to get a job at the Banco Exterior de España, where he remained for the rest of his life. The federation grew and, in 1952, Santiago Bernabéu, president of Real Madrid, contacted him about a basketball tournament. Saporta was young but already knew his way around and Bernabéu didn't let him get away.

Raimundo joined Real Madrid as an accountant in 1953, a year later he became treasurer, a decade later Bernabéu's right hand: vice-president. His favourite position was that of a worker in the shadows, an obscure worker who was, nevertheless, the organising genius of the team: he lured Alfredo Di Stéfano (whom Gianni Brera would describe as superior to Pelé) to Barcelona, and put him alongside such greats as Raymond Kopa, Ferenc Puskás, José Santamaría, Francisco Gento and Pachín. One of the strongest formations ever.

The Revelation

During the Second World War, Abraham Klein's parents' entire family was deported to Auschwitz. In 1938 his father Vilmos, who worked as a tailor, fled to Palestine to save his life. His mother Sarah left him in Timișoara, Romania, on a train to the Netherlands. Little Abraham arrived in Apeldoorn after three weeks, exhausted and hungry.

After the war, he returned to Israel and ended up on a kibbutz. He did not find his father in Haifa until 1948. Abraham was old enough to wear long trousers but Vilmos was ill so his mother sent him to Mr Jonas. The man was closing his shop. 'I have to run to referee a game, come with me. We'll take care of the trousers later.' Abraham followed him.

During the match the tailor was injured. The man turned to him and handed him the whistle: 'It's simple, if there's a foul, blow the whistle.' Attitude is a predisposition of the soul. Often it can be innate, sometimes we do not know we have it, sometimes we discover it late. It manifested itself in Klein that afternoon. He knew the rules, his father had been a player at MTK Budapest, one of Hungary's top teams, and he himself played as a striker. He did not have his parent's skills. He could, however, read the game. Picking up that whistle started his future. Jonas noticed it too: 'If you work hard you can become a real referee.'

Abraham was now 19 years old. He moved to Tel Aviv, where he graduated in medical sciences and, during his military service, had his first experiences in the Military Games. It was there that he learned the importance of discipline, psychology and physical fitness, the three pillars of his training.

La Dolce Vita

At the end of the Great War, Giovanni Pastorin, no longer a child, returned to Verona to become a railwayman. By the time the republic and the constitution had come into being in Italy, his son Elio, together with his wife Leda had turned their backs on the destiny of their country to trust, like their grandfather, in the exotic dream of Brasiliano. In the new land, a few days after the 1954 World Cup Final, the conservative military forces revolted against Vargas and the statesman committed suicide. His heavy inheritance was received by a doctor, Kubitschek de Oliveira, the governor of the state of Minas Gerais. He was elected president of Brazil in 1955 and succeeded in giving a new impetus to the country's activities. He built the new capital, Brasilia, developed industries and financed public works. Brazil finally breathed an atmosphere of rebirth.

Rio and Rome lived their *dolce vita* almost simultaneously. Musicians, intellectuals and artists gathered along the beach of Ipanema and the pavements of Via Veneto. The world seemed to live only there. There was no other life. Brazilian life moved to a minimal but complex rhythm called bossa nova. João Gilberto and Tom Jobim had just invented it. They were later joined by Antonio Pecci Filho, known as Toquinho, of Italian origin.

At the beginning of September 1955, Livraria Martins Editora published *O pensamento vivo de Darwin* – the translated version of *The Living Thoughts of Darwin* – by Julian Huxley. Leda Pastorin found it in her hands a few days before giving birth and began to read it avidly. When her son was born on 18 September, she had no doubts about his name. It would be Darwin.

At the same time, at the Maracanã in Rio de Janeiro, the first match of the newly established tournament, the Bernardo O'Higgins Cup, was played between Brazil and Chile. The star of the Seleção was Júlio Botelho, aka Julinho. The world had become aware of this Brazilian with a Clark Gable moustache and an air of composure the year before, during the World Cup in Switzerland. He had also been noticed by the Italian coach that preceded Bearzot on the bench of the national team, Fulvio Bernardini. Fiorentina, in fact, had just bought him, as an international player, for $5,500. The discovery of a grandfather from Lucca, a certain Bottelli, in the family tree of the Brazilian champion, was providential for his registration.

However, the Confederação Brasileira de Desportos only picked players from domestic leagues for the national team. Brazil could not therefore use their best right-winger from the Italian club, although they decided not to follow the practice. Brazilian football was living a particular moment in history. The memory of the *Maracanazo*, the home defeat at the 1950 World Cup, was still in the collective memory. The responsibility for that defeat, ascribed to goalkeeper Barbosa and left-back Bigode, both black players, had given rise to racist issues and a need to approach football in a rigorous manner, conditions that did not sit well with the characteristics of the country's greatest winger: Manuel Francisco Dos Santos, known as Garrincha.

Brilliant but unpredictable, undisciplined and individualistic, Garrincha was looked upon with scepticism, not least because of his excessive pursuit of dribbling. Julinho himself, however, refused to be called up: 'It hurts me to take away the place of someone who has earned it by playing in his homeland,' he said. There were less famous and less well-paid team-mates who simply wanted this opportunity. It was a generous gesture that changed the history of football. In his place, Brazil agreed to field the 'angel with crooked legs', who otherwise would not have had the chance to explode on to the scene.

So the day of Darwin's birth coincided with Garrincha's accidental debut for the green-and-yellow national team. He would become the greatest of all time in his role. A few months later Julinho provided Fiorentina with the Scudetto and the following year the final of the European Cup. It was played at the Santiago Bernabéu in Madrid and the opponents were the formidable Real Madrid of Kopa, Gento, Muñoz and Di Stéfano. The team orchestrated by Saporta. The Viola went down in the final part of the match when Di Stéfano punished them with a penalty conceded for a foul committed outside the area and Gento added a second goal six minutes later. The Continental dream thus ended. Back in Brazil, Julinho understood that he would never win a World Cup. His role was now occupied by the man to whom he had given way. With Garrincha (and Pelé) on the field, the Seleção never lost again.

But the echo of the Italian boom was stronger. Three years later, the 1958 World Cup arrived in Brazil. The Pastorins had decided to leave forever the land that had bewitched three generations of their family to return to the Belpaese. It was the centenary of the unification of Italy. Turin was the new Mecca. Darwin thus found himself growing up in Via Madama Cristina, in the city of the Mole Antonelliana and Fiat, supporting Juventus and becoming a journalist for the city's sports daily *Tuttosport*, for which he would be sent to Spain during the 1982 World Cup.

Father and Son

The roots of all the events that follow rest on the conflict between a father and son. A psychological drama with a 19th-century flavour will in fact be the first motionless engine of the events that will contribute to creating the physiognomy of Italy in 1982. A private grudge that will change history, the government, Sandro Pertini's choices and the minds of Italians, combining to accompany the explosion of the Italian catenaccio, the rise of Luigi Carraro to CONI (the Italian National Olympic Committee) and Federico Sordillo to the FIGC (the Italian Football Federation), to create the technical DNA of Enzo Bearzot and the unreliable possibility of a Spadolini government. As well as involving, for better or worse, other slices of the Spanish Mundial: the choice of a director, the ownership of the biggest sports newspaper, the flight of a bigwig, the advent of the Azzurri's lucky charm, the bitterness of some reporters and even the expedition of a 70-year-old man to Hispanic soil.

Angelo Rizzoli, the old man, had always had a ruthless attitude towards his son Andrea. The *cumenda* – a term from the Milanese

FATHER AND SON

dialect meaning boss – had grown up in an orphanage, experienced the anguish of poverty and had built himself up. He had launched newspapers such as *Annabella*, *Oggi* and *L'Europeo*', had printed the *Treccani* encyclopaedia, published all the literary classics, and produced memorable films and won all the highest awards in cinema (the Oscar and Silver Ribbon for *8½*, the Golden Globe for *Giulietta degli spiriti*, the Palme d'Or for *La dolce vita*, the Golden Lion for *Deserto rosso* and *L'anno scorso a Marienbad*). The cultural history of Italy revolved around him. Without him, the imagery of Italian cinema would have been different. Yet he proudly flaunted his ignorance and detested the rich. Especially those who had had it easy. And his sons were also included in this category.

Andrea, the eldest, was publicly humiliated on every occasion. At public dinners, the *cumenda* would show the bottle to his guests: 'This high mountain is me.' Then, grabbing a bicchiere (glass): 'And this little mountain is Andrea.' Despite this, his son, who joined the company when he was still a child, tried all his life to rise to the occasion. When he was very young, he convinced Vittorio Metz and Giovanni Mosca to leave the *Marc'Aurelio* in Rome and come to Milan to found *Bertoldo*. And it was also he who gave life to Guareschi's *Candido*, successes that never prevented his father from humiliating him mercilessly in public, in front of the company's top management: 'Tas ti, bamba,' (Shut up, stupid). Andrea did not look like his father and, to create his own diversity, for better or worse, he tried in every way to distance himself from him. He contrasted his father's jovial certainty with an insecurity. Optimism versus suspicion. Worldliness versus reserve. Even in his clothes: Panama versus grisaille. And yet Andrea wallowed in wealth. He played golf, gambled in casinos, owned the largest yacht in the Mediterranean, the *Sereno* (a 50-metre boat jokingly dubbed 'the yacht of toilets' because of the large number of bathrooms on board), a private plane and a villa at Cap Ferrat (acquired by the actor Curd Jürgens, who died in 1982 on the day of Italy vs Peru and Brazil vs Scotland).

Andrea found the opportunity for his own glory in 1954, when his father was busy producing the saga of *Don Camillo*. The technical director of AC Milan, Tony Busini, was looking for someone willing to sign seven-figure cheques without a second thought. Andrea, at 40 years old, was forced to ask his father for permission. 'Do as you like, but don't ruin me.' Having obtained his consent, Andrea threw himself into his new venture, organising the company as if it were one of the family businesses. If his father had made the history of publishing and cinema, Andrea managed to make the history of football. He was the president of Gipo Viani, Nereo Rocco, Cesare Maldini, José Altafini, Angelo Sormani and Gianni Rivera. He helped his team win four league titles and a European Cup, the first for an Italian team. A victory that came from afar, from the football of the *poareti* – the poor, in Venetian dialect – and that marked the triumph of the catenaccio. That Milan team also dug the deepest furrow in Italian football and the course that ran through it would flow into the blood of future coach Enzo Bearzot. But it was not enough to overcome his father, possessed by an obsession that was about to take shape in those very years. A newspaper.

Angelo had always missed his empire. He had presented himself in Monte Carlo before Giuseppina Fossati Bellani Crespi, wife of Aldo, owner of the *Corriere della Sera*. The idea was ambitious: to put together the Rizzoli periodicals and the daily newspaper of Via Solferino to create a cartel on advertising sales. But she did not think he was up to it and threw him out: 'Put your heart at rest, dear Rizzoli, you will never have the *Corriere* with us.'

Humiliation gave him new energy. Over the years, he tried to get his hands on *Il Giorno*, *La Notte*, *Il Tempo* and *Il Messaggero*. In vain. So he got the idea into his head of creating his own daily newspaper. He went to Indro Montanelli: 'Come and be the editor of my newspaper, it will be called *Buondì*, so when you say goodbye to the newsagent you will automatically buy it.' Then common sense led him to *Oggi*, which would be, as the slogan said, 'The newspaper of tomorrow'. The crowning achievement of an entire life. His own.

And he began to invest a fortune in it. For this reason, in 1963, immediately after Andrea's triumph in the European Cup, Angelo

Rizzoli withdrew the toy from his son, ordering the divestiture of the family from Milan. He bought the presses, organised the editorial staff, hired two editors (Gianni Granzotto and Gaetano Afeltra, who left the *Corriere* for the job) and had ten edition zero issues printed. In the meantime, he kept accounts. He did it his way, on the white back of a Turmac cigarette box, and he only needed three columns: credits, debits and liquidity. After three years of work, it was this that made him realise that tomorrow's newspaper would ruin him. And he had the courage to throw away the 11 billion lire he had spent so as not to squander any more. He had the biggest empire in publishing but he understood its limits, beyond which the empire itself would crumble.

The withdrawal from Milan proved to be pointless but Andrea had left his mark. In the following two decades, leading up to the 1982 World Cup, the nine years of his son's presidency would always be remembered as the golden age of the Rossoneri's history.

Christmas 1956

It was the autumn of 1956. A year of existential turmoil. Bearzot and Santana, the future coaches of Italy and Brazil, were two young men playing football in the shirts of Inter and Fluminense. Both of them were forced to chase down those destined for the title. The Brazilian title was now in the hands of Vasco da Gama, while the Italian flag was destined for the AC Milan team produced by Andrea Rizzoli, directed by Gipo Viani and played by Cesare Maldini. The national teams had met a few months earlier in Milan and the Azzurri had beaten, 3-0, the same Brazil that would become world champions two years later. Bearzot was not on the pitch. The Azzurri jersey that he wore for the first time on 27 November 1955 would remain his only one.

In Brazil, Juscelino Kubitschek initiated a period of strong industrialisation, which culminated in the construction of the new capital, Brasilia. It was also a year of firsts for Italy. Cortina d'Ampezzo hosted the Winter Olympics; Anna Magnani won an

Oscar as best actress for the film *La rosa tatuata*; *Il Giorno*, the daily newspaper owned by Enrico Mattei's ENI, was born; and the first stone of the highway Autostrada del Sole was laid. Every Saturday night, Italian television kept half the country glued to its screens, thanks to Mike Bongiorno and his *Lascia o raddoppia* (Leave it or double it); on the big screen, on the other hand, the year was marked by four Totò films, all directed by Camillo Mastrocinque (from *La banda degli onesti* to *Totò Peppino e... la malafemmina)*. For the world, it was the year of stellar marriages: Grace Kelly and Rainier of Monaco were matched by Marilyn Monroe and Arthur Miller. But it was also a year of excellent divorces, such as the artistic one of Dean Martin and Jerry Lewis after a decade. Or of illustrious deaths, such as those of Jackson Pollock, Alfonso de Bourbon, brother of the future King Juan Carlos and, above all, Jules Rimet, the inventor of the World Cup. One birth, however, was to prove crucial for Italy and Brazil. The autumn of 1956, in fact, was the first of a child who had just come into the world: Paolo Rossi.

At the same time, on the other side of the planet, the destinies of Havelange, Rimet's future heir and undisputed ruler of the 1982 World Cup, and Horst Dassler, the man who would give him power, crossed paths. The two threads were knotted under the same sky, that of Melbourne, when, during the Australian summer, the Olympic Games were held for the first time in the southern hemisphere. Sport was thirsty for universality and wanted to go beyond Western borders. But the Suez crisis and the Soviet occupation of Hungary threatened to overshadow the event. Fooled by fate, Hungarian and Soviet water polo players found themselves pitted against each other in the same pool during the famous 'bloodbath'. The Neapolitan swimmer, Carlo Pedersoli, who one day would become Bud Spencer, also moved in the same Olympic water.

And water was even about to enter Horst Dassler's head. He was only 20 years old, he did not yet know that he would be founding a sportswear brand for swimming and that in 1982 he would change football forever. For the time being, he was keeping his feet on the ground. After all, it was the shoes he had to think about. His mother, Käthe Dassler, nicknamed Catherine the Great, placed the fate of the company in her hands. Horst was the only one in the family who spoke English. His job was to promote Adidas during the first Olympic Games to be televised. It was not an easy task for him. He had to contend with his uncle's Puma and the Japanese Kihachiro Onitsuka's Tiger. But above all he had to contend with IOC president Avery Brundage, who strenuously defended Pierre de Coubertin's amateur ethics.

These were the first Games held under Brundage's presidency and he was unable to adapt those principles to modern times. He did not accept the idea that the Olympics should come to terms with the market. He did not understand that it was precisely from the market that he could draw the means to organise his own life and development. 'Sport,' he declaimed, 'is a pastime, an entertainment, a moment of recreation, the opposite of work.' Deluding himself that he could block the nascent avenues of professionalism by edict, he forbade athletes from accepting compensation or free products: athletes must buy their own equipment or have it assigned to them by their respective Olympic federations. But Horst found a loophole. IOC regulations allowed athletes to gradually obtain the 'technical equipment' they needed for their sport. And for Adidas, there was no more technical equipment than their shoes. 'Function First' was the company's slogan. And the loophole became a highway.

Before leaving, Horst popped into the factory and emptied it. On the eve of the Games, however, the Australian port authorities withheld all his goods. Young Dassler managed to free them, thanks to the North American athletes, who wrote letters of indignation. At the same time he arranged for Puma's delivery to be held at customs until the end of the Games. As soon as he arrived at the Olympic village he went to dinner with the heads of delegations, drank with the coaches, strolled with the managers. But above all, he went in and out of the athletes' rooms. He offered them all shoes – his own brand. The athletes appreciated the gesture and started walking, running, jumping and competing, unwittingly sponsored by Adidas. The symbol of the three stripes started its world tour from there. Horst was young but he had already understood everything, well in advance: 'Having friends means doing business.' To increase demand, he filled a sports shop with stacks of his boxes. They became known as 'Melbourne spikes'. Entire teams rushed to pick them up for free. For them, Christmas had already arrived.

The strategy proved to be a success. The athletes with the three stripes on their feet brought home 72 medals. In the 400-metre relay, the three best runners wore Adidas shoes. Among those were the winner Bobby Joe Morrow, the last great white sprinter from the United States, who was also Olympic champion in the 100 and 200 metres. The Texan athlete's time of 20.6 seconds over the latter distance equalled the world record and set the Olympic record, beating Jesse Owens' time after 20 years. From father to son, the US Olympic laurels of Owens and Morrow remained united in the name of Adidas. On 10 December, *Life* chose the champion for its cover as he crossed the finishing line. His shoes caressed the red band on the cover. Adidas improperly became the Olympic brand and synonymous with victory.

While Dassler had been sent to Melbourne by his mother, Havelange was invited by the Brazilian Olympic Committee as head of the delegation. He had returned to Brazil from Berlin without a medal around his neck, with clear memories and uncertain prospects. His father's business had passed into other hands. He had started working in the administrative department of Siderúrgica Belgo Mineira. Ten dollars a week to manage the affairs of employees and customers. After four years, the most anonymous and alienating of his life, he knocked on the boss's door: 'I quit. I will never work for anyone else in my life.' He made an exception for the next two years, where he became a lawyer for a bus company. He managed to return to the Olympic Games once more, in 1952 with the national water polo team.

This time Havelange was not competing; this was his first political step. And he desperately needed to bring home a medal to make his country proud. Dassler, too, was looking for visibility, podium athletes who were destined to bring prestige to his company. Brazil was not considered a winning nation, so the two crossed paths but without exchanging a word. They would have to wait almost 20 years to do so. Horst actually knew that of the 47 athletes on the Brazilian team only one was destined for glory – the triple jump Olympic gold medallist Adhemar Ferreira da Silva. Horst wasted no time on Havelange and presented Da Silva with his revolutionary shoe designed to take the pressure off the body at the tip of the foot. Perfect for a jumper. The competition was fierce but, for the Brazilian, it would still be gold. The only Olympic medal for Havelange's delegation. Thanks to Horst.

O Plano Paulo Machado de Carvalho

Havelange, like Saporta, was seduced by sports politics. And, like the Spaniard, he moved up the ladder: he became head of the Paulist Swimming Federation, president of the Metropolitan Swimming Federation in Rio and a member of the Brazilian Olympic Committee. Until, in 1958, he was crowned president of the Confederação Brasileira de Desportos, the number-one sports federation, including football, in his country. He was just 41 years old. It was the year of the World Cup and Brazil had never won one. To cure the team's ills, he applied the same organisational principles he used for Viação Cometa, the transport company he had become owner of. The company needed a large number of specialists to solve a wide range of problems, from mechanical to administrative. For every aspect there was a diagnosis and a remedy.

Players do not just need a coach but specialists. Havelange got a new coach, Vicente Feola; a team doctor, Hilton Gosling; a psychologist, João Carvalhães; even a dentist, Mário Trigo (because in a World Cup you have to foresee and prevent everything). All from São Paulo. Many of the professional players came from the *favelas*, from areas of great deprivation, and in a short time they had to acclimatise to a totally different context, accepting rules and discipline. 'They have to abandon their natural violence,' Havelange told Carvalhães. In the 'Battle of Bern' (the quarter-final against Hungary in the 1954 World Cup), two Brazilian players had been sent off. On the 1956 tour there had been aggression against Austria in Vienna. Havelange wanted to put an end to such indiscipline and took it upon himself to create a project to present the image of a modern country to the world.

To build the winning mentality, psychology would play a vital role in the process. Dr Carvalhães carried out aptitude tests on the entire team. The results suggested to him that Pelé and Garrincha could not be fielded. Seventeen-year-old Pelé was found to be 'clearly childish' and 'too irresponsible to play in a team', while Garrincha, who scored the lowest in the test (38 out of 123, less than what is required to drive a bus in São Paulo), was deemed unfit to withstand the pressure of a World Cup. Technical director Vicente Feola mediated between the president and the psychologist: 'Doctor, you may be right, but you don't know anything about football.' Between 1958 and 1966, Pelé and Garrincha would play together in Brazil 40 times: 36 victories, four draws, no losses.

The person most responsible for the feat, however, was not on the pitch. His name was Paulo Machado de Carvalho, known in his homeland as 'Marechal da Vitória', and he was the head of the delegation. Embarrassed by the players' attitudes, Havelange relied totally on Machado. 'I need a team that will make people forget the defeat of 1950, a winning team, a champion team. You do whatever you have to. You have carte blanche.' And that was put in writing. But Machado, a person already influential in the politics of football in São Paulo, with the collaboration of some journalists drew up a written plan, 'O Plano Paulo Machado de Carvalho', to 'civilise' the players who would represent Brazil in the World Cup.

The operation worked. For the first time in the history of the tournament the Brazilian national team was prepared in a professional and organised way. Carvalho took care of the group's logistics, passed on information to the athletes, studied Sweden (a country unknown to the players) and took precautions against the temperature. The plan turned out to be perfect. Brazil twice became world champions, in 1958 and 1962.

The Magnificent Seven

The purple Italian-Brazilian blood colours much of football history. Brazil becoming world champions for the first time in 1958 was thanks to at least seven 'Italians'. The Seleção was led by Vicente Italo Feola, the son of a craftsman and a peasant woman from Castellabate, in Cilento. Captain of that team was Hideraldo Bellini, son of an emigrant from Comacchio, who would be world champion again in 1962. When they handed him the cup, the local photographers, obstructed by the height of their Swedish colleagues, shouted at him to hold it higher. He heard them and raised it to the sky. His team-mates were Mário Jorge Lobo Zagallo, born in Brazil but of Italian descent, who also won the next World Cup and, as coach, the 1970 World Cup, together with left-winger Roberto Rivellino, also known as 'Rivelino', born in São Paulo to a Molise family, and defender José de Anchieta Fontana.

In that same team Feola, surprisingly, played two youngsters, aged 17 and 19. The first was called Pelé. The other José. The father of the latter, Gioacchino, who harvested pumpkins, had forced his son to divide his time between school and work until he got a diploma in mechanics. Piece of paper in hand, José João Altafini found himself at Palmeiras, where they kept a photo of the great Torino in a beautiful setting. His team-mates found him identical to Mazzola, so they christened him that but with only one 'z'. And 'Mazola' was the name with which he would go down in history (having become a naturalised Italian, he played the following World Cup in the Azzurri shirt, later returning to play in the Italian championship as Zoff's team-mate).

The 1958 World Cup did not see the presence of Italy, ousted during qualifying after losing 2-1 to Northern Ireland on 15 January 1958. The only Italian goal was scored by Dino da Costa, born in Rio de Janeiro, son of an Italian trolley bus driver, who entered the youth team of Botafogo at the age of 14 and then became a naturalised Italian, after having formed a formidable attacking trio with Garrincha and Luís Vinício.

Before Dino da Costa, Amphilóquio Marques Guarisi, also known by his Italianised name Anfilogino Guarisi, known in Brazil as 'Filó', played for Corinthians and the Seleção in the mid-1920s before joining Lazio (called Brasilazio in those years due to the massive presence of Italian-Brazilian players: 14) and becoming world champion with the Italian national team in 1934.

The opposite fate befell José Oscar Bernardi, a defender for Santana's Brazil against the Azzurri in 1982. His family came from Lucia, in the province of Rovigo. That is why, as a boy, they called him 'the Italian'. Surely, if he had not become a footballer, he would have worked in Monte Sião, the small town in the state of Minas Gerais that survives thanks to the textile sector (no needles though, just crochet, that is the tradition). His mother was one of the pioneers. His father Dino was part of a family of shoemakers who left Italy to settle in Brazil. For Oscar, it was the example of how to live. Nobody in the family had ever known wealth, they had always worked. This taught him a lot. Humility, above all else. Traditionalists (six children) and religious (attending mass every Sunday, processions on every occasion, pilgrimages to Aparecida every year), the Bernardi family were the first people of Italian origin to move to the area.

Angelo Benedicto Sormani had the same origins: paternal grandparents from Garfagnana and maternal from Rovigo. Nicknamed 'the White Pelé', team-mate of the original O Rey at Santos, he ended his brilliant career at Lanerossi Vicenza, who bought an unknown youngster with an all-too-common name: Paolo Rossi.

The Affront

Felice Riva took Andrea Rizzoli's place at AC Milan. Platinum bob, scarves and silk shirts. Not to mention the Lacoste. The same ones that RAI correspondent Beppe Viola wore at the Spanish Mundial. But he was the first to show them off outside a tennis court. They called him 'the blondie' and he had just found himself holding the keys to an empire. Like Andrea Rizzoli, he was the son of a self-made man. Four years earlier, when he died suddenly, that parent left him orphaned (his mother had died of cancer in 1955) but tremendously rich. From his father Giulio, he inherited the family business, Cotonificio Vallesusa, the textile group that produced the famous Popeline Capri shirts, one of the symbols of the Italian economic boom, a colossus with 30 factories and 15,000 employees.

Milan were on top of the world and Riva, who was studying to be a tycoon, wanted the club. In taking it, he claimed to belong to the golden world that fate had given him, but distractions, missteps and wrong investments quickly ruined him. In 1965, Felicino's companies drowned in an abyss of 46 billion lire. Vanished. It was bankruptcy, the closure of all the factories, with 8,000 workers and employees losing their jobs overnight. The director of the Rivarolo Canavese plant committed suicide to avoid signing another 1,480 dismissal letters. The strikes of his employees were followed by the unrest of his players, who refused to train due to non-payment of bonuses. The bankruptcy at first was hidden with falsified balance sheets but later Riva was sentenced to four years' imprisonment. He had been arrested at the exit of a cinema but luck did not desert him; he remained in the cell only for a few days because the warrant had a formal defect. He realised that nobody had seized his Italian passport, so he fled to Nice, then to Paris, then to Athens and finally he settled in Beirut.

On 27 October of the previous year, during the extraordinary shareholders' meeting called in the theatre of the Cassa di Risparmio in Via delle Erbe, the newly appointed president had asked his young lawyer, Federico Sordillo, to join the secretariat of the Milan board of directors and a football-loving manager, Luigi Carraro, to be his deputy. The vacant post was temporarily filled by Sordillo, who played the role of commissioner for a couple of years until Luigi Carraro decided to sit at the highest chair on 20 April 1966.

THE MATCH

The World Cup in England was just over two months away. A couple of weeks later Havelange showed up in Milan. He wanted to talk to Carraro. Brazil were the reigning world champions thanks to their victory in Chile, where Pelé was injured, immediately leaving his place to Amarildo, who ended up at AC Milan the following year. Havelange wanted the player to be left free to allow him to train and thus participate in the World Cup. Luigi didn't speak the language and his son Franco was in charge of dealing with the president of the Brazilian federation. The Carraros were totally willing, in exchange only asking that Amarildo sign a contract for the following season. But the amount proposed did not satisfy the player and the negotiation was prolonged. The days passed and, in that time, punctuated by lunches and dinners out, a friendship was born between the Carraros and Havelange.

In England, Havelange was certain that Brazil would win its third World Cup, the one that would remain at home for good. And he wanted to make sure that Machado did not overshadow his triumph. The credit for this feat must be linked to his name alone. So he got rid of him. The team was the same one that had won twice: there would be no problems. But the players, compared to 1958, had aged eight years and were eliminated in the first round. For Havelange it was an affront. The president of FIFA was an Englishman. In the three matches against Bulgaria, Hungary and Portugal, the Seleção were refereed by a West German and two Englishmen. For him this meant only one thing: 'The plan was to take Brazil out.' After the elimination, according to him, England and West Germany would settle the tournament to meet in the final. And the epilogue promptly saw the two teams fighting for the title, which went to the hosts.

In October, Havelange returned to Milan to thank the Carraro family. He complained about how Brazil had been treated at the World Cup and announced to Luigi: 'One day I will be president of FIFA.'

Carraro could not know how things were going to turn out because a few months later, on 7 July 1967, as a result of the palpitations for his team, he died of a heart attack while the shareholders' meeting was in progress. His place was dramatically taken by his son Franco. Three years later, in 1970, Angelone Rizzoli, also 27 years old, found himself on his father's throne. It was the year of the World Cup in Mexico. Havelange waited another four years to win that third coveted title that the English had snatched from him. But destiny had a surprise in store for him: he found England in his group.

Hands in Pockets

He had his hands in his pockets that day, Abraham Klein. He was 36 years old and about to referee his first World Cup match.

'Come on, take the envelope,' a Hungarian colleague had urged him a few days earlier. He held it between his fingers, thoughtful. 'I can't,' he replied, 'I'm nervous.' Then he made up his mind:

Match number 15

Guadalajara, 7 June 1970

England vs Brazil

The reigning champions against the likely heirs, the cradle of football against the land of football. And underneath, written in black marker, his name: Abraham Klein.

The young Israeli referee must have impressed FIFA observers two years earlier at the Mexico Olympics. They had studied him since his debut. His springboard was in Rome. Italy were on the pitch against Poland in the World Cup qualifiers. His first big match. Klein was 31 years old. Until then he had refereed in Israel in front of 20,000 people but now he was about to referee in front of almost 70,000 spectators. He did not want to be found unprepared, so on the morning of 24 October 1965, a week before the match, he boarded an Alitalia flight, paid out of his own pocket, flew to the Stadio Olimpico, bought a ticket and went to see Roma vs Napoli. Nobody knew who he was and Klein learned a lot, above all from the crowd that shouted and cried as he had never seen one do.

THE MATCH

When he returned home late in the evening, he wrote to a friend in Poland asking for information about the national team and convinced the editorial staff of *Gazzetta dello Sport* to send him dozens of clippings: he knew that in Italy the sports newspapers knew more about the players than their families. He thus discovered that Gianni Rivera was the star that the defenders tried to knock out throughout the game. As a football lover, Klein always wanted to see the game flow. He was an advocate of the advantage rule, his favourite rule of the game. He therefore decided that in those cases he would let the match play out as much as possible. When he returned to Rome he felt that his preparation could not have been more thorough. He was calm, decisive and confident. Italy won 6-1. Three of the Italians' goals came from playing the advantage. The FIFA observers took note.

The year before the World Cup, in the summer of 1969, while the world was waiting to turn its eyes to the moon and its ears to Woodstock, Bayern Hof and Hapoel Nahariya faced each other. It was the first time a football pitch had hosted a German and an Israeli team since the war. The most suitable referee had to be chosen. The issue was political. The Germans wanted the best Israel had to offer. Abraham Klein was already the best but the federation knew the history of the Klein family. A man who had had to wear the yellow star as a child and had lost his family in the Holocaust could not referee such a match. 'Are you up for it, Klein?'

He hesitated for a moment, then gave a sharp 'yes'. He added: 'I am a referee, not a judge.' That 12 July was the best day of his sporting life. For once he left his fears at home. He treated the men on the pitch as players, all equally, without victim or executioner.

But now no one, not even he, could understand why he had been appointed. *FIFA is taking a big risk*, he thinks. On one side Pelé, on the other Bobby Moore, two legends. But also Jairzinho, Bobby Charlton, Rivelino, Geoff Hurst, Carlos Alberto and Gordon Banks. The most important match of the World Cup so far, the final before the final. Some say sending him there was like sending a boy scout to Vietnam. But the unknown Klein had faith in his abilities and that same faith was also placed in him by Sir Stanley Rous, the president of FIFA, and Ken Aston, the president of the Referees' Commission, former match director in the infamous 1962 Chile vs Italy match, the Battle of Santiago, the man who, enlightened by the sight of a traffic light had just introduced the use of the yellow card for cautions and the red card for sendings-off.

Klein had already refereed four international matches but none was remotely comparable to the one he had been called upon to officiate now. A $20 reimbursement would pay for his expenses but he would have gone there for free. And now he was faced with a footballing masterpiece.

That is why his hands trembled like a violin string and Klein put them in his pocket. He did not want the players to see them. Then he led the teams out and decided to be strong. After all, he had given his soul to be there and he deserved it. He had already been in Guadalajara for a fortnight and had ignored all possible temptations in order to concentrate solely on his preparation. He had not left his hotel for a single day. In his head there had only been the match. He knew he could not miss it.

He came out of the dressing room, went to meet the captains, took his hands out of his pockets and greeted them with a firm grip. The players looked at him, wondering who that man in the middle of the field was. They knew nothing about Klein, but he knew everything about them. That was his advantage. So he looked first one way, then the other, and whistled for the start of the match. He controlled it calmly, running with confident grace from one end of the pitch to the other. And he soon realised, looking into their eyes, that the players were respecting him. When Pelé fell in the box after a clash with Alan Mullery, Klein was not seduced by the world's greatest player. He simply shook his head no to him to continue playing. He would later describe this as the best decision of his life.

In the 90th minute Klein blew his whistle with all the breath he had left in his body to end the match. But he quickly realised that none of the players had heard him. He had witnessed an incredibly hard-fought match, he had witnessed what was to be called 'the save of the century' (Banks from Pelé), he had directed a battle that, he imagined, would go down in football history, regardless of whether it was the reigning world champions or those who would become world champions. So, for once, the first and last time, he decided to give in to instinct, letting the match continue for a few more moments. The only heartfelt choice of his career.

The Terror

In 1962, under the presidency of João Goulart, known as 'Jango', the American Chamber of Commerce and the First National Citybank created the IPES, a research centre financed by 300 US corporations, designed to penetrate all sectors of Brazilian society in order to seek consensus among ordinary people and at the same time promote their own interests. To succeed, the centre had co-opted radio, television and newspaper editors to spread manipulated news about bad governance, crime and the cost of living. With the help of John Fitzgerald Kennedy, the IPES succeeded in creating a new climate – which would also arrive in Italy, inspiring Licio Gelli's Piano di Rinascita Democratica (Plan of Democratic Rebirth) and the Loggia P2 – and in preparing the field for the imminent military coup that took place two years later, from the night of 31 March. Just when Goulart was launching the social reforms that would change his country's fortunes.

All of Brazil's future ills came from there. It was from that moment that the best part of an entire generation was killed and thrown into mass graves. The disintegration of the country began in front of the eyes of millions of innocent people. Leandro was a five-year-old boy, Luizinho was six, Éder a year older. Cerezo was about to turn nine, Júnior, Oscar and Sócrates were ten, Serginho, Zico, Falcão and Paulo Isidoro were 11, Waldir Peres 13. Generals Castelo Branco (1964–67) and Da Costa e Silva (1967–69) twisted the Constitution to their liking, governing through the enactment of

THE TERROR

special laws, AI (Institutional Acts), created ad hoc to legitimise the extra-constitutional actions of the military regime. These succeeded in shutting down Congress, ousting politicians, infiltrating false professors into universities, imposing lusory bipartisanship, turning strikes into crimes, establishing censorship and starting the practice of torture. In March 1968, the killing of the student Edson Luís in Rio exploded the student movement. But the fire of youth conquests in Brazil was nipped in the bud. Sérgio Paranhos Fleury became commander of the police Death Squadron, his men, Brazilian torturers, trained in the 'torture manual' published by the CIA. Faced with the scandalous number of suspected suicides among political prisoners, the students were forced to turn off their anger. With the infamous AI-5 (13 December 1968) the civil rights of Brazilians were effectively cancelled and arrests carried out without a judicial warrant.

All newspapers were occupied by the regime's auditors. Daily newspapers such as *O Globo* or television stations such as Rede Globo lied to the people by constantly manipulating well-known news and polls. Others tried to let readers know that the well-known newspapers were under censorship. They inserted messages to be interpreted, cryptic allusions. Even weather bulletins reported that 'the air is unbreathable' or that Rio, on the eve of a sultry summer, would be swept by strong winds. Writers, musicians and even the authors of telenovelas found the AI-5 was arousing a desire to seek ways of deflecting a censorship that also affected the ways in which people's intimate spheres were depicted (gone were love triangles, unmarried couples, homosexuals and naked body parts).

During the military dictatorship of the third general, Emilio Garrastazu Médici, the period of greatest terror of the entire regime, everything was militarised, from the Brazilian Sports Confederation to the technical commission of the Seleção. The 1970 World Cup became a real propaganda machine. The Seleção's fitness trainers, Admildo Chirol and Carlos Parreira (who would make his coaching debut in Spain in 1982 on the Kuwait bench), came from the army's physical education school; Jerônimo Bastos, head of the delegation, was a brigadier general; Cláudio Coutinho, the fitness trainer, was an artillery captain. Sócrates and Júnior were 16, Zico and Falcão 17, Cerezo only 15, Éder just 13. The boys of Telê Santana were just teenagers. Pelé and the other players of the Seleção, on the other hand, were considered gods. They could speak, they would be heard. But they preferred to remain silent.

But the one who would not shut up was actually coaching the Seleção. His name was João Saldanha, a journalist who smoked four packs of Continental a day, drove around in a Volkswagen and handled a short-barrelled 32-calibre gun with little hesitation. He was given the job directly by Havelange, president of the Brazilian Football Federation. Saldanha had lived a thousand lives up to that moment: born in Rio Grande do Sul, the scene of the exploits of Garibaldi (there was never any certainty about his hometown), a weapons smuggler as a child, a student leader in his twenties, a notary's apprentice in his thirties. But also a footballer. He was a member of the Brazilian Communist Party, took part in the Long March with Mao, landed in Normandy with Montgomery and attended all the World Cups. Havelange knew his history but he also knew he was the right man to resurrect Brazil after the collapse of 1966.

On the day of the press conference to present the new technical commissioner, Saldanha left the editorial office of *Ultima Hora* as if nothing had happened and headed for the federation. When Havelange pointed him out in the crowd as the man who would lead Brazil to Mexico, his colleagues were stunned. Saldanha got up, sat down at the middle of the table, put his hand in his pocket, pulled out a piece of paper and grabbed the microphone: 'Dear colleagues, I know that in the past the other selectors who preceded me started with a list of 40 or more names that only a couple of months before the World Cup would be reduced to the final 22 to be communicated to FIFA. I also know that the World Cup is now almost two years away, but I am still officially telling you who the 11 starters and their reserves will be.' The journalists were increasingly incredulous. This had never been seen before. 'My team will be made up of 11

THE TERROR

men who are prepared to do anything. For glory or for the grave.'
Saldanha asked the government for a decree to humanise Brazilian
football: fewer matches and more spectacle. He chose Brazil's best
players and entrusted them with a simple recipe: 'No one owns an
area of the pitch, there are no fixed positions. Four men on the same
line are only good for military parades.'

Within just a few months Saldanha's Brazil had won all their
qualification matches for the World Cup (22 goals in six matches,
only two conceded), restoring the joy lost after the fiasco at the
English World Cup to an afflicted people. A poll revealed that 68 per
cent of the population of São Paulo and 78 per cent of the population
of Rio supported him. Never in the history of Brazilian football had
a selector enjoyed such popularity. The dramatist Nelson Rodrigues
called him 'João sem medio' (João without fear): 'A warrior more
fiery than the dragon of Saint George, capable of leading Brazil
to *tricampeão* [third World Cup] in the midst of the thicket of
gangsters that is a World Cup.'

However, Saldanha's communist sympathies became intolerable.
He spoke openly about torture and political prisoners. The military
did not like his interviews with *Le Monde*, so it surrounded him with
spies. When the minister of education, Jarbas Passarinho, learned
that Saldanha was a follower of Stalin and Mao, he sent his order to
army captain Cláudio Coutinho (who would be Brazil's selector at
the 1978 World Cup in Argentina): 'Tell President Médici that the
Brazilian national team is in the hands of a man who totally disagrees
with the ideas of the military revolution: a Bolshevik subversive.'

But what cost Saldanha dearly were three television interviews.
When asked in Hamburg what he thought of the genocide of the
natives in the Amazon, he replied: 'In 469 years of Brazilian history,
we have killed fewer people than you Germans have in ten minutes.'
In London, as a guest of the BBC, he smiled when asked about
the alleged dishonesty of South Americans: 'If the English are so
honest, what is Scotland Yard's reputation for?' He was not afraid of
authority either. When General Emilio Garrastazu Médici, whom he

considered 'the greatest murderer in Brazilian history', asked him to let Dario play in the national team, Saldanha replied directly in front of a Porto Alegre television station: 'Let's make a pact, Mr President: I won't tell you who to select for your government and you won't tell me who to put in the team.'

Médici called Havelange: 'You have to take him out. Immediately!' Havelange obeyed. On Tuesday, 17 March 1970, three months before the World Cup, Saldanha seraphically accepted the verdict: 'It is very easy to understand why they threw me out. It is more difficult to explain why they hired me.' The next day, Zagallo, his former player, was called up in his place. The first thing he did was to summon Dario. He took him to Mexico, where he didn't play a single minute. The most beautiful Brazil ever won its third Jules Rimet Trophy against Italy and handed it over to Médici. The team was the same as that indicated by Saldanha in his first press conference as coach. The '11 men willing to do anything' jotted down on that piece of paper two years earlier.

The Subversives

With the 1970 victory, the kind of militarised organisation tested by the Seleção also spread to the country's clubs. Athletes were required to comb their hair, shave their beards, accept total confinement in training camps and train according to army physical education rules.

Afonso Garcia Reis, known as Afonsinho, a 23-year-old medical student and a Botafogo midfielder, was a promising Brazilian footballer and the only one protesting about the players' working conditions. He understood that he was on a borderline. His visibility protected him from repression. He decided to fight the regime by using the football stage. In 1970 he grew a beard and his hair. He was classified as a *comunista de carteirinha* (card-carrying communist). His coach, Mário Zagallo, ordered him to shave. The national team closed its doors to him but he didn't give up. They punished him by preventing him from training and playing. Santos wanted him to play for them but Botafogo would not give him up. They wanted to make him disappear by keeping him away from the limelight.

Afonsinho raised his head and, encouraged by his railwayman father, went to the Supreme Court of Sporting Justice with his two lawyers, Rui Piva and Raphael de Almeida Magalhães, to ask for his release. To choose his own future. In Brazil no one had ever been the master of deciding where to play but he won his case. He was the first to succeed. He went on to play for Santos, Flamengo, Atlético Mineiro and Fluminense, continuing to fight for the rights of the weakest.

He was followed a few years later by José Reinaldo de Lima, Atlético Mineiro's striker and top scorer in the 1977 and 1978 championships. Called 'Rei' by his fans, he was a king who cheered brazenly with a clenched fist. A revolutionary gesture that was too much for the Brazil of the military. Before the World Cup in Argentina he was brought before the president of Brazil, General Ernesto Geisel: 'Boy, leave politics to us, you just think about football.' Terrified, he agreed, but he did not keep his word. On 3 June 1978 in Mar del Plata, after the goal against Sweden, he raised his fist. After the second match, during an interview he called for the return of democracy. He never played another minute. His place was taken for the rest of the Mundial by Roberto Dinamite.

Training camps became barracks. The apparent formal order contrasted with the precarious working conditions of the players and a football scenario totally spoilt by the presence of politicians and generals in the teams' places of command. In this context, in 1971 the Brazilian championship was born with 20 clubs divided into two groups. The team that achieved the most points in the first round was Corinthians.

The Timão

Sport Club Corinthians Paulista, the Timão, is the team of São Paulo's working class. It was the first team in Brazil to accept players of working-class origin and the second, after Rio's Bangu, to accept black athletes. It was founded in 1910 by a group of workers and labourers, mainly of Portuguese, Italian and Spanish origin, with the aim of creating a football team for the lower strata of São Paulo society, in opposition to the existing elite clubs. Here, seven decades later, Sócrates Brasileiro Sampaio de Souza Vieira de Oliveira, known simply as Sócrates, met, for the first time, other like-minded people: players, coaches and fans. Here he started to talk about democracy, about a different way of living the professional reality of football.

The football organisation in Brazil was feudal and oppressive, especially for the players, on whom it imposed a way of working, thinking, dressing and living. Inside Corinthians, Sócrates found the space to talk not only about a footballer's duties but also about rights. Because only knowledge can make you free. This was what his father, Raimundo, had taught him. Freedom is knowledge, and Sócrates found this knowledge in books, opening one after another. Classic texts. He became so passionate about the point that he named his first three children after books. Sócrates, Sófocles and Sóstenes. Culture was a daily conquest for him, the discovery of a reservoir from which he could draw in order to emancipate himself from his condition.

In 1964, the year of the coup, the day the army seized power, young Sócrates saw his father forced to set fire to the books the regime considered subversive. For the parent it is an unbearable but necessary pain. For the son it was the beginning of a desire that became a necessity: to fight for freedom. Sócrates was ten years old and that gesture remained engraved in his mind. He felt like a child of a dictatorship. His heroes were Machiavelli, Che Guevara, Hobbes and John Lennon. And, of course, Plato. His father had chosen his name after reading Plato's *The Republic*.

Seven years later, when he started attending the Faculty of Medicine at the University of São Paulo in Ribeirão Preto, Sócrates had already started his football career with Botafogo but refused to sign a professional contract. He would do so three years later, with one condition: to continue his studies. The club had no choice but to accept.

When Sócrates became 'O Doutor' (the Doctor), he divided his time between the hospital and the football pitch. Times were hard, as football was not a land of privilege but of deprivation of freedom. The players earned little, the referees were corrupt, the pitches were in poor condition, the payments were always late. Nobody talked about rights. The ownership of the most important clubs was in the hands of powerful men linked to the military hierarchies, who managed the *futebol brasileiro* with authoritarian methods. The so-called *concentração*, the pretence of Brazilian clubs to keep players under observation like troops in an army, dominated, hindering every possible form of freedom, even of thought. 'The ultimate aim of *concentração*,' said Sócrates, 'is to humiliate people.'

The War of the Sons

Adi Dassler disagreed with his son's methods and way of life. A fervent Catholic and dedicated to duty, he could only disapprove of Horst's marriage to Monika Schäfer, a Protestant circus performer. The only thing he managed to convey to him was his visceral hatred for his brother's family. The fathers' war was carried on by the sons and Horst had to deal with his cousin Armin, Rudi's heir.

The 1966 World Cup Final at Wembley was Horst's masterpiece: the two finalists, England and West Germany, wore his three stripes. After warming up, England goalkeeper Gordon Banks and defender Ray Wilson left the pitch with Adidas boots on their feet. A surprise awaited them in the changing room. A few moments later they were back on the pitch in Pumas. For that run, both would have earned 10,000 francs.

In 1968, Lee Evans won the selection trials for the Olympic Games by breaking the 400m world record of 44.1 seconds, but the record was not recognised because his spiked shoes were deemed not to comply with the regulations. They were Pumas and had more than the regulation six spikes. The first person to appeal to the athletics federation was neither an athlete nor a manager but the entrepreneur

Dassler: the studs must count as nails. At the 1968 Olympic Games in Mexico City, Evans won the gold medal with a new world record of 43.86 seconds, then at the same Games repeated the gold medal and the record when running the final leg of the 4×400m relay. The four athletes appeared at the prize-giving ceremony wearing black berets and waving a closed fist as a sign of solidarity with the Black Panther movement. Exactly as Tommie Smith and John Carlos had done earlier at the 200m awards ceremony. As they raised their fists to the sky, they wore only black socks on their feet. The spectators were impressed, America was divided. But one small detail brought the scene back to earth. Each of them had arrived at the podium with a Puma shoe on his shoulder. They then remembered to leave it in full view on the platform. A protest, but with a sponsor.

At the same Games, high jumper Richard Douglas 'Dick' Fosbury climbed over the bar, tipping his body backwards for the first time and falling on his back. He won the gold medal, revolutionised his discipline and set a new Olympic record with a height of 2.24 metres. In the event that made history, he wore two different-coloured shoes. But they were Adidas.

Two years later, Puma agreed to pay Pelé $120,000 to wear their boots at the 1970 World Cup (Armin Dassler asked him to lace them up before the whistle blew, so that they would be shown on television), and at the next World Cup Horst managed to put his Adidas boots on Franz Beckenbauer's West Germany. And by the 1970 World Cup he had also provided the official match ball.

When Horst developed the first leather tennis shoe, he named it after Robert Haillet, the best French player, but then, to expand into the American market, he turned to Stan Smith, who had just become number one in the world, with Haillet shoes on his feet. In the years that followed, Stan Smith shoes became more famous than the tennis player. But that was not enough for Horst: times were changing and the recent past was showing him the way.

In the 1960s, Mark McCormack, a lawyer from Cleveland, Ohio, founded IMG, International Management Group. His first client was golf legend Arnold Palmer. The pairing marked the advent of television in golf and the subsequent golden age of the sport. Ski manufacturer Franz Kneissl was also conquering the international Nordic sports market through his sponsorships. Photos of the winners with their skis clutched to their chests for his Austrian company were worth their weight in sales. On the eve of the 1972 Winter Olympics in Sapporo, the International Olympic Committee (IOC) disqualified the world champion Karl Schranz because of a breach of the law on amateurism due to his contract with Kneissl. At the Munich Olympics in the same year, the script was almost identical. Horst asked swimming champion Mark Spitz to hold his shoes on the podium during the anthem. IOC president Avery Brundage was furious and opened an investigation, and Spitz retired from swimming. It was then that Dassler decided to focus on water. In response to Speedo, he founded Arena, a brand of competition swimwear that adhered to the body like a second skin. Finally freed from the constraints of Olympic amateurism, Spitz signed a contract with Horst. Three years later, at the World Swimming Championships in Colombia, two-thirds of the swimmers were wearing Arena suits.

When the IOC threatened to ban all athletes who advertised sports equipment or clothing from competitions, Dassler took action and called a summit with Europe's biggest sports manufacturers: 'It's no longer enough to pay the athletes, we have to buy the federations. In other words, officially sponsor the national teams.' If Kneissl had to deal with the International Ski Federation, Dassler had to play his game with FIFA, whose president was Sir Stanley Rous, who was also firmly attached to the idea of sport as an amateur activity. Amateurs in sport, for Horst, were just that in appearance. Most athletes were in fact professionals. To be active at a high level, they had to work full time, which is why they needed to be sponsored. The proponents of amateurism knew this well, since they had allies in Eastern European countries where 'state amateurism' reigned. Dassler, in order not to see the efforts of the industries (which paid the athletes) thwarted by the decisions of gentlemen who wanted to reduce sport to an elitist activity, destined only for a small circle of rich people, openly railed against the hypocrisy of fake amateurism. The IOC president, the aforementioned 19th-century American-born Brundage, ended up in his sights, but he left office that same year and died shortly afterwards.

The Czarina

When Angelo Rizzoli died, his three sons inherited the leadership, a 100 billion lire fortune, no liabilities and only one warning at the end of his will: 'Do not get into debt with the banks, always love each other and remain united among yourselves.' None of these wishes would be respected.

At that time the *Corriere della Sera* was in the hands of the Crespi family and was directed by Giovanni Spadolini. The young, wealthy and nonconformist Giulia Maria Crespi, known as 'the Czarina' for the decisive style of her management, called him to create a more democratic and open newspaper. However, he was too closely linked to power to distance himself from the traditional parties, refused to warn bourgeois public opinion about the danger of a reactionary backlash and remained insensitive to the new turmoil of the 1968 rebellion. When on 16 December 1969, a few days after the massacre of Piazza Fontana, he crucified Giuseppe Pinelli on the front page in order to side with the police, Crespi understood that her *Corriere* had become the headquarters of the ministries and its director unfit to deal with the present.

Born rich, with an important father, into a family that had made its fortune in yarns and silk, Crespi realised they were living in a period of profound change and decided to take a left turn. In order to launch the new line, the company even dismissed its director and replaced him with Piero Ottone. This had never happened since the Crespi family had become owners of the newspaper. He shouted: 'You are ruining me as a public figure.'

But that exit was his good fortune. The following day Spadolini was approached by Ugo La Malfa to join the Italian Republican

THE CZARINA

Party. Two months later, on 8 May 1972, he was elected and became a senator. The *Corriere*, on the other hand, was sinking. Money for salaries began to run out. To try to raise it, Giulia Maria Crespi sold two-thirds of the shares to Angelo Moratti and Gianni Agnelli. She tried everything. She involved the *Washington Post* and, above all, Carlo Caracciolo, Gianni Agnelli's brother-in-law (who married his sister Marella) and editor of *L'Espresso*. He spoke to her about the possibility of a holding company to unite the *Corriere*, *L'Espresso* and *La Stampa*. But nothing came of it. It was Agnelli who extinguished the last hope. In agreement with Moratti, he turned his back on her, there was no more money in the till, the banks demanded the repayment of debts, the paper for printing was finished. Crespi began to realise that perhaps she no longer had any cards to play. Montanelli, whom Spadolini had turned against her, branded her a 'Guatemalan despot' at the end of a long disagreement that would never be reconciled. She had just ordered Ottone to fire him. She did not know it, but it was his last act. Andrea Rizzoli sniffed the air and made an offer. She didn't have the courage to cut a nearly century-long cord. She still hoped for a miracle. A sign. It came but was not what she had hoped for.

She felt a pain in her shoulder and rushed to see a doctor. She had breast cancer. The news put an end to her uncertainty. She had to be admitted to hospital and did not know if and when she would be released. Her first thought was about her children. And her first fear concerned the inheritance of the *Corriere*. A weight too great for them. The liabilities of the group's publications amounted to 7 billion lire. So she offered Rizzoli his 33 per cent of the newspaper that had belonged to his family for almost 90 years. It cost 21 billion lire. But it could cost 100 billion. What Andrea Rizzoli had in front of him was not a business deal but a suicide. And although he was a prudent person, endowed with common sense and entrepreneurial skills, his family background prevented him from assessing the situation clearly. The woman handing him the newspaper was Giulia Maria Crespi, daughter of the Giuseppina, who slammed the door in her father's

81

face. And all his common sense was devoured by the resentment he had accumulated over the years towards his parent.

She, Giulia Maria, knew that father. One evening in 1960 her friend Franca Santi Invernizzi suggested going to Angelo Rizzoli's house to see a film. She was the wife of producer Lionello Santi: 'We'll only be a few people, it's only a preview.' She refused but her friend insisted: 'Come! It seems to be something special, Fellini worked on it.' Giulia Maria Crespi thus entered the Rizzoli home for the first time. That evening, her parents were among the first eyes in the world to see *La dolce vita*.

The Duellers

'I want to spread the Adidas brand all over the world.' When he heard these words, the Italian executive smilingly replied, 'I want to do the same with the Italy brand.'

It was during the 1966 World Cup in England that the paths of Dassler and Franchi crossed. They were very different but found common paths that made them friends. During the 1962 World Cup in Chile, the Italian team had suffered an intolerable injustice. The Battle of Santiago, in which Italy found itself playing with nine against eleven Chilean 'boxers', had only one person responsible, the referee Aston, and only one cause, the Italian federation counted for nothing. Franchi was the leader of the expedition and was beginning to take his first steps in UEFA. He did not live off football alone. On the contrary, it was his work that guaranteed him the well-being that sport, to which he dedicated himself out of passion, could not provide.

In 1954 he and other partners founded Angiolo Bruzzi Spa, a company for the marketing of oil and its derivatives. Italy's economic recovery required a great need for raw materials and fuels and the choice proved to be a winner. The company imposed itself on the market, became a partner for citizens, businesses and public administrations, and established a preferential link with ENI, founded by Enrico Mattei, inspired by a modern economic and political vision.

The same vision that Franchi pursued in his company and also in football. The understanding turned into a true partnership, so much so that AGIP became a partner in Bruzzi Spa. The decisive factor that convinced the company was Franchi's presence.

Even in football his sense of proportion, persuasive diplomacy, sharp irony and ability to smooth out the edges already make Franchi a point of reference. Italy had not won anything since before the war and he was looking for a way to bring them back, to give them the respect they deserved. As a true Sienese and therefore a true connoisseur of the Palio, he knew that having the best horse was not enough to win. A strategy was needed. He realised that Dassler could become a formidable ally and with him he began a propaganda campaign to make football known in Africa and the East. Dassler gave away jerseys and boots, conquering virgin markets, and Franchi began to strengthen the image of the Italian national team. But also his own. The following year he became president of the Italian Football Federation. With him in that role Italy won the 1968 European Championship and came close to the World Cup in 1970. With merit, but also thanks to favourable circumstances. Circumstances that always exist and that few know how to orchestrate. He did not want to take credit for himself, he kept out of the limelight. He regretted that second place in the World Cup, but he didn't lament it: Italy had finally re-entered the circle of the teams that counted.

In 1973 he became president of UEFA and in 1974 vice-president of FIFA. When he took over as head of the European football federation, he made it clear that UEFA could do without FIFA – because football in Europe was more solid and organised – but FIFA could not do the same with UEFA. Franchi's aim was to get the best players into the Olympics and to bring the game of football to the whole world. It was a strict programme that not only displaced FIFA but also the IOC. The Olympics had always been for 'amateurs'. Franchi wanted to remove this inconsistent and unfair rule. Of course, he did not get the support of the Eastern European countries, but he did get Dassler's support.

In the meantime, the oil crisis disrupted the economy in Italy and the Western world. The sudden and unexpected interruption in the supply of oil from the OPEC nations also caused an energy blackout in Italy. Artemio Franchi was not surprised. He knew his way around the world scene and knew some very influential people, even beyond the world of football and soccer. He made good use of his friendship with Mohammad Reza Pahlevi, the last Shah of Persia, who ruled Iran until the Islamic revolution of 1979. The sovereign, thanks to Franchi's solicitations, took steps to have a ship loaded with black gold arrive in Italy. It was to be the only one en route from the Middle East to dock on the Italian coast. If, in those difficult days of austerity, some assembly lines were able to function or some cars were able to travel, it was thanks to him alone.

Shortly afterwards he was granted a privileged insight into the structures and organisation of the energy sector in immense China: a country that was in many ways unknown and isolated within the walls of its power. After the death of Mao Tse Tung, his successor Deng Xiaoping began a process of reform. For a long time the giant of the East boycotted all sporting events where Taiwan was recognised, but now the Chinese authorities wanted to steer the nation towards a future as an emerging great power, including in sport. So they identified Franchi as the international manager with whom to start a dialogue for their return to the world of sport. Artemio was invited to Beijing, passing through doors considered almost insuperable. In a short time, the red flag with the yellow stars would resume flying on the flagpoles of the Olympic world, together with the five rings.

But the astral conjuncture took place in 1974. For different purposes (respect, business and power) three men found themselves pursuing an identical goal. Franchi had just taken office as president of UEFA, Dassler now controlled most of the federations that he showered with gold in exchange for visibility. At the dawn of the German World Cup in June, in a room of the Steigenberger hotel in Frankfurt, the duellists Stanley Rous and João Havelange, the latter fresh from three world titles under his regency, were vying for the FIFA sceptre. Whoever won would be the third man: the future king of football.

The Pact

In order to succeed, Havelange embarked on a gruelling and expensive tour that took him around the world to spread his beliefs. During the presidential campaign he visited 86 countries in ten weeks, promised to increase the number of World Cup places for countries outside Europe and America, as well as to help build stadiums and offer technical, educational and health support. To be more convincing, he was accompanied by the most dazzling star of his national team (as well as the world it represented): Pelé. But he left behind a $6 million hole in the coffers of the Brazilian sports federation. Havelange had become friends with local bosses, an accomplice of South American dictators and was compromised in everything. Not even Horst Dassler could get to see him. Havelange seemed to be the darling of the military councils of Brazil and Bolivia, involved in arms sales, implicated in illegal gambling in his country. However, it was not such activities that bothered Dassler. Havelange had just rejected his deal to equip Brazil in the World Cup. He already had a Brazilian company for that; therefore Horst's support could only go to the Englishman Rous.

In the last week of the campaign, Havelange landed in Mexico and six Central American countries. He then headed to London, hired a Mystère-Falcon and flew to Strasbourg to watch the friendly match between Brazil and Racing Strasbourg ahead of the 1974 World Cup. After the match, he left the Stade de la Meinau, returned to the airport where the Mystère was waiting for him, and flew back to London. He drank a coffee, took a bath, closed his hotel room, disconnected the phone and slept for 24 uninterrupted hours. The next day he got on a plane and flew to Frankfurt for the election. In the German city a correspondent of *The Times* identified a deployment of West African diplomats around the Steigenberger hotel. High-ranking personalities with a high French education. Diplomats probably, certainly disconnected from the world of sport. Their presence was bad news for Rous. However, the Englishman believed in his chances. He had been FIFA secretary since 1934 and president since 1961. Doing the maths, even with the African and South American countries, Havelange was down by about 20 votes. Europe and Concacaf (Central America, Canada, the Caribbean and the United States) were for the Englishman.

Shortly before the vote, Dassler was warned by Blagoja Vidinić, the former Yugoslav goalkeeper, gold medallist in Rome in 1960, now coach of Zaire fresh from winning the African Cup of Nations: 'Friend, you are riding the wrong horse.' Havelange had African, Asian and Latin American support, so he had victory in his hands. If Dassler wanted to spread his gospel in the 'unexplored' world, Havelange was the man, so he had better be on his side. Not only that but the Brazilian was much more like Dassler than he thought. Rous's FIFA was still not a business. It moved without billion-dollar sponsorships, it was little televised and its executives did not even have a $10 dollar daily allowance. Havelange, a man of great power who knew how to hide his mysteries, wanted to turn it into a multinational: professional football, free marketing, television rights and major international tournaments. He had convinced the federations with gifts. Just like Horst did.

When he met him in private the evening before the vote, Dassler was clear: 'You have to help me, if you do we'll both get rich.' The plan was this: Havelange had the consent of the Third World to whom he had promised participation in the World Cup. In order to satisfy his voters, he had to increase the number of participants in the final phase to create permanent seats for Asian, African and South American countries. But to do this he needed money. If Dassler guaranteed it, he would have free rein in international affairs and FIFA would be his home. The two looked each other in the eye. They were inflamed by common ambitions. African, Asian, Latin American and Eastern European countries were the passport to power.

Dassler knew that their reduced purchasing power would not lead to an expansion of his economic activities. Politically, however, they carried considerable weight because together they represented the majority of votes. To hold them was to hold the gold. Horst Dassler made sure that the Brazilian would keep his promises. In the contract with FIFA for the advertising exploitation, he inserted a clause: if the number of teams remained at 16, he would pay 18 million marks, but if they increased to 24, the figure would double to 36 million marks, a sum that no organisation could ever refuse. But the hosts must also be encouraged (more teams meant more facilities). So, for the use of the brand and mascot, Horst promised them 30 million marks (instead of 15 million) if the tournament was expanded.

The secret of victory is in friends. Havelange's father had always recommended this to him. Shortly after his father's death during the Berlin Games, the young Havelange met a friend who would later become director of Lufthansa in Brazil. When he was offered a promotion in Australia he thought about leaving the company. It was Havelange who convinced him to accept the promotion by extolling the virtues of the Australian continent. Shortly before the election Havelange travelled to Sydney and visited his friend. 'To thank you for the advice you have given me,' the man told him, 'I will send you six men to Frankfurt.'

To win in the first ballot the candidates had to get two-thirds of the votes: 79. Whoever won on the first ballot was almost certain to shake up the delegates and thus make it to the second ballot. The first round ended 62 to 56. Havelange was up by six votes. The friend from Lufthansa had kept his promise and found the six delegates. It was not enough but the cards were on the table. In the second round of voting, only the majority counted and 30 minutes later the Russian vice-president announced the end of an era. The votes was 68 to 52. Havelange was the new king of football, all due to those six friendly votes in the first round.

After the election, the delegates offered Rous the honorary presidency. Havelange then persuaded him to accept a pension of 6,000 Swiss francs per month. Rous declined the offer: 'It's not fair to be paid like that for a job you're not doing.' Havelange tried again and said they could call the World Cup the Stanley Rous Cup. Rous declined again. It was not his style. Money and the desire for fame belonged more to the winner. The eyes of the generals were on Havelange. They wanted back the millions from the Brazilian federation that had vanished into thin air. But now, accusing the head of the most popular sport on the planet, a Brazilian, of corruption would bring shame on an entire country. His network involved too many people. The investigation could become a boomerang. He was now untouchable.

On 11 June 1974, thanks to the support of the Third World federations, Havelange became the first non-European FIFA president. Dassler did not forget Vidinić and remained forever grateful to him. A few days later, however, the Yugoslavian coach's boys went down in history as the worst team at the German World Cup, made immortal by the dramatic 'reverse punishment' in the match against Brazil. The Zaire players sported yellow-green kit with a roaring leopard on their abdomen. On the shoulders, the three stripes. Friend Horst's signature.

To raise money for FIFA's ambitious goals, Horst had to look beyond his sportswear business. His future and that of football would depend less and less on box office receipts and more and more on television. Whereas in the past a photo was enough to generate an advertising revenue, now the widespread use of cameras could multiply it indefinitely. Similarly, whereas before his work focused on an individual athlete, then on a team, then on a federation, now, with the advent of television, it was the sporting event itself that could be bought and sold. And an event like the World Cup could attract capital from outside the industry. Horst multiplied the business potential: TV reached everywhere in the world and sponsors from all sectors now came from it.

The Gift

Faced with the possibility of buying the *Corriere della Sera* and thus succeeding in the enterprise failed by his father, Andrea Rizzoli could not resist. If he conquered the newspaper and most of the rest of the market, his editorial group would surpass the one created by his parent and his figure would finally overshadow that of Angelo Rizzoli. Blind revenge against his past drove him to go beyond the Herculean columns of common sense, thus deluding himself that the future would be his. But there was another story that flowed impetuously and could save a doomed destiny.

Indro Montanelli left the *Corriere* on 18 October 1973 due to incompatibility with the ownership. Three times Giulia Crespi had blocked his appointment as editor, preferring first Alfio Russo, then Giovanni Spadolini, and then Piero Ottone. Some of his statements of clear dissent appeared in the *Mondo* and called for the creation of a newspaper that would wage war on the one he worked for. Crespi, who once loved but could no longer stand him, could not believe it and sacked him.

Eight months later, in the middle of the 1974 World Cup, his 'brand-new newspaper' appeared on the news-stands, put together with 28 journalists from the *Corriere* who had followed him. Among them were Alfio Caruso and Carlo Grandini, to whom he had entrusted the sports section. Shortly before, however, Montanelli had gone to see the Rizzolis.

'I offer you the *Giornale Nuovo*.'

'Thank you but we are not interested,' Andrea replied.

'You've been courting me for three years to edit one of your newspapers, and now that I've got it all ready to go, you say no?'

'We are going to buy the *Corriere*.'

'Are you kidding? This is a huge mistake!'

Angelo, who was sitting between them, was stunned. He didn't know either.

'I give you my newspaper. You be the editors, I run it.'

THE MATCH

'I'm sorry, but you're too late. I've already concluded with Angelo Moratti and I'm on speaking terms with Crespi and Agnelli for their shares. We will be the publishers of the *Corriere*.'

'Do as you like, but remember, as soon as you set foot in that company you will lose everything. Everything!'

Montanelli left the office, thinking, *Poor Angelo, you will end up paying for everyone's mistakes.* He would see him again in prison.

In order to get the *Corriere*, however, negotiations with the Christian Democracy Party were necessary. The secretary was Amintore Fanfani, who gave his approval on one condition: 'Within 24 hours you have to get rid of the director Piero Ottone who made us lose the referendum on divorce.' Andrea agreed and invited Ottone to lunch at his house in Via Gesù to fire him. But when they reached the coffee, he renewed his contract for another three years. Ottone had gained sales of 40,000 copies compared to Giovanni Spadolini's management. And for Andrea Rizzoli only that counted in the end. But he paid dearly for this gesture. Fanfani swore revenge on him. He spread the word that the Rizzolis were unreliable, dangerous and subversive. In order to strangle them, he blocked the administered price of newspapers and ordered the big banks, all state-owned at the time, to close credit to the family.

The Rizzolis tried to make amends but Andrea's shyness prevented him from facing the situation head-on. So he sent his son to Rome. Fanfani received Angelone on the terrace of his attic in Via Platone, sitting on a rocking sofa. His feet did not touch the ground and his wife Maria Pia was forced to push him. The scene increased young Rizzoli's embarrassment as he was showered with insults: 'Liars! Irresponsible! Incapable! Idlers!' He did not let Angelone utter a single word. He concluded by admonishing him with his finger: 'Don't come asking us for anything more. We Christian Democrats no longer exist for you Rizzoli.' And so it would be.

To pay for the *Corriere*, the Rizzolis had to sell the hotels that Angelo had built in Ischia. Angelone's father referred Angelone to an INPDAP (National Welfare and Assistance Institute for Civil

Officers) official with connections in the real estate market. His name was Umberto Ortolani. In his office in Via Condotti in Rome, Angelone found Licio Gelli and Roberto Calvi waiting for him. Lined up at their side were Alberto Ferrari, general manager of the Banca Nazionale del Lavoro; Giovanni Cresti, superintendent of Monte dei Paschi di Siena; and Gaetano Stammati, president of the Banca Commerciale Italiana, who would shortly become finance minister in Moro's fifth government and treasury minister in Andreotti's fourth.

During the negotiations, Angelone, who only had a degree from Pavia and a specialisation from Columbia in New York behind him, noticed the deference of all those present towards Gelli. He later met him at the Quirinale, Palazzo Chigi, the Christian Democrat headquarters in Piazza del Gesù, Carlo Donat Cattin's office, and Giacomo Mancini's house. Wherever he went, he was there.

Angelo told his father that the group was willing to finance them by keeping the family at the top. Andrea stepped aside and left the field free for his son. But reality would be infinitely greater than that ambitious young man. During the hot months of the takeover of the *Corriere*, Ottone also turned to Caracciolo and Scalfari to find an alternative solution to prevent such a risky operation for the country's democratic balance. The two involved Pirelli. But nobody was ready to take on such a burden and every attempt failed. On the day of the Rizzoli takeover, Ottone himself broke the news to Caracciolo and Scalfari. That evening, the idea of founding their own newspaper was born in both their heads.

The New Rules of the Puppeteer

Having helped to elect Havelange, Dassler turned to Patrick Nally, a specialist consultant who in 1970 founded the West Nally Group, a public relations agency specialising in sports event management, with BBC sports journalist Peter West. In a pioneering way, the company, located at 12 Berkeley Square, London, began to redefine the business of sport by inventing sponsorship packages and acquiring the rights to the world's biggest sporting tournaments on behalf of sports federations. Horst invited Nally to Landersheim, Adidas's French headquarters. He told him about how sport was changing and the commercial wars behind the World Cup and the Olympics. Nally was stunned. Horst noticed this and invited him to dinner a stone's throw away. Next to the factory was the Michelin-starred restaurant, Auberge du Kochersheim, a kingdom of French nouvelle cuisine. The Auberge was Horst's second office: 'I want to talk to you about how I see the future,' he told Nally. That same evening, the two men began to construct the plan that would change the world of sport.

'Havelange promised African countries access to the World Cup,' said Horst.

'By when?' asked Nally.

'1982.'

'And how is he going to do that?'

'With my help.'

'And how are you going to do that?'

'With your help.'

'You should get them to rewrite the FIFA rules first.'

'No problem with that.'

'Not to mention that the federation needs to modernise its commercial structure.'

'We are its commercial structure.'

'We should first do a run-in.'

'Yes, just to see if the game can work.'

'Something like a world youth championship. Does that exist?'

'Not yet.'

'Then let's start with this.'

'That would be perfect. A global event but without being too conspicuous.'

'Let's do it directly in Africa.'

'A big sponsor would be needed.'

'How about Coca-Cola?'

'That would be great.'

'If we can convince them we are on the right track.'

'If we have Coca-Cola everyone else will follow.'

American managers were unfamiliar with football; they only knew that it was a sport that was conquering new countries, including their own: the 47,000 youth players in 1965 had grown to almost 600,000 by 1975. Nally showed the Coca-Cola executives the numbers. The largest crowd in the world? A football match. Brazil versus Uruguay, in Rio de Janeiro in 1950: nearly 200,000 spectators. The largest television audience for a sporting event ever? Again, a football match. The World Cup Final between West Germany and the Netherlands in Munich in 1974: 400 million viewers. The sport with the most participants in the world? Football: 18 million professional players, 42 million semi-professionals and amateurs, not counting the millions of young people who played without being registered. That was the picture.

But despite its worldwide popularity, football was still competitively dominated by the same nations from Europe and South America. The youth tournament conceived by Dassler, Nally and Havelange was therefore structured in such a way that teams from Africa and Asia would be placed alongside the other finalists. The FIFA World Youth Tournament would be open to 16 youth teams (two African, two North and Central American, three South American, two Asian, six European plus the host country) and would provide a showcase for future World Cup stars. It would give footballers the opportunity to compete at a high level, in front of large crowds, with television coverage. And of course it would give Coca-Cola a very strong identification with football. The Coca-Cola Company would be the only one to have the rights to advertise around the stadiums for the final and semi-finals, it would be the only soft drink sold in the stadiums and its name would be linked to the trophy that the winning team would win: the Coca-Cola Cup. There was also room in the agreement for Horst Dassler. In a competition like this, the presence of a sports manufacturer was essential. Adidas would supply prizes (Adidas Golden Ball and Adidas Golden Boot), kits and equipment.

'It is in the interest of all parties involved,' concluded Nally, 'that the Coca-Cola Cup can become the most important championship after the World Cup.'

The negotiation lasted 18 months. The two proved convincing. The company was far-sighted and the deal was done. Coca-Cola invested $8 million to become the first exclusive sponsor in the history of sport and the first brand partner of FIFA. Soon after, Dassler and Nally convinced Havelange that, to fulfil his campaign promise and expand the federation's global development programme, FIFA's rules and regulations needed to be reformed. The work in progress again passed through the hands of Nally and Dassler and again involved the Atlanta-based company. Coca-Cola and FIFA were not interested in an isolated event.

For both players there was a strong desire for 'evangelisation'. This was a process that would require perseverance and a long time. And the only way to be legitimised was to create a development programme. The FIFA/Coca-Cola World Football Development Programme, patented by West Nally, was initiated by four 'pools' (two English-speaking, one French-speaking and one Spanish-speaking), recruited directly by FIFA, consisting of experts in administration, coaching, refereeing and sports medicine. Between 1976 and 1979, the teams intended to visit some 100 football-developing countries (particularly in Africa, Asia and Oceania). They would spend between six and twelve days in each country, involving local schools and associations, during which they would hold seminars, conferences, tours, practical demonstrations, competitions (involving Coca-Cola bottle tops), certificates and prizes. The participants would use the knowledge they had acquired and spread it virtuously, thus accelerating the rate of development of local football.

The young players of the mysterious Cameroon, who would qualify for the World Cup in Spain, where they had Italy in their group in June 1982, were involved in the programme in May 1977. The equally unknown New Zealand, who would face Brazil in June 1982, was visited by FIFA emissaries in January 1977.

The brochure addressed to the area heads of the World Football Development Programme warned them that the task would not be a walk in the park but 'an ongoing affair'. And 'it will require years of hard work to bring maximum benefit to both parties' – FIFA and Coca-Cola. Dassler had found a way to make Havelange's promise come true: with money from the American soft drinks company, FIFA would be able to develop the developing nations that voted for it. Football changed from there. But in this ripple effect everyone was happy to be part of the game. In the countries to be colonised, football was so important that the governments themselves had an interest in promoting it. A winning team illusorily exhibits the power of a state. If it helped those countries in their football development, then Coca-Cola would find itself building relationships with governments all over the world and attracting influence and respect.

In the meantime, Nally planned the FIFA World Youth Championship, which would be held in Tunisia in 1977. The billboards around the pitches would advertise just one drink, that of a country far away from Africa and from football. This was the general rehearsal. The real test was scheduled for the following year: the World Cup in Argentina.

Another 5 July

The Italian hero of that World Cup was little more than a boy when he first sighted the shores of Brazil. He had been called up for a tour of the footballing country by Carlo Parola, the man who has been etched into footballing iconography thanks to a spectacular reverse kick he invented in the year of the *Maracanazo*.

Paolo Rossi was born with the myth of Brazil. At the age of 12, his father took him on a Lambretta to see Fiorentina's friendly match against Santos. He didn't take his eyes off Pelé for the whole 90 minutes. Two years later he saw him while at home in the 1970 World Cup Final. From then on, Brazil invaded his imagination, even when he kicked his first ball with Sporting Santa Lucia, the team of young players set up by the doctor from his village, Dr Paiar. He played with his brother Rossano, was the youngest of them all but already knew his way around. He was a fast and instinctive right-winger. The chalk line became his reference and in the limited space of the pitch he unleashed his creativity like a painter with his canvas. The following year he was at Cattolica Virtus, coached by Enrico Orioli, with few resources, had a lot of passion and humanity. He played 153 matches and scored 119 goals. He wore the Juventus shirt. He seemed to have arrived but instead it was the beginning of an ordeal.

On his debut in the Primavera team, during the derby against Torino, he broke his right external meniscus. He lost a year, morale and conviction. He returned and broke his wrist. He recovered and finally made his first-team debut. Dino Zoff was in goal. Paolo was only 17 years old and it seemed like a dream. Instead, again against Torino, the meniscus problem recurred but this time on the left. Once again he managed to recover. It was at this point, in the summer of 1975, that Parola called him up for a tour. Paolo found himself sharing a room with a 38-year-old native of Italy at the end of his career, who at his age had been world champion with Brazil: José Altafini. The competition against Flamengo bore his name: Taça José João Altafini 'Mazolla', and it would take place on 5 July. In the evening, José told Paolo stories of green lands, crystal waters and magic feet. Paolo Rossi listened, bewitched.

The Flood

On Friday, 25 July 1975, at 4.30pm, Carlo Caracciolo and Eugenio Scalfari got into an olive-green Alfa Romeo Giulia rented in Milan and, under a river of water, drove along the A4 motorway until they were ready to take the exit for Sommacampagna, south-west of Verona. After 5 kilometres, they turned right on to a dirt road on Provinciale 54. The journey came to a halt in front of a large wrought-iron gate surmounted in the middle by the letter 'M'. It was raining. The world seemed suspended. Even football had stopped. When it

THE FLOOD

resumed after the summer, the national team would find Bearzot on the bench for the first time. Caracciolo and Scalfari cared little or nothing. On the contrary, they were planning to make a newspaper without sport. And they were there for that.

They would never have made it to that closed railing if a few months earlier they had not been among the guests at an art exhibition organised by Andrea Rizzoli on the terrace of Milan's Hotel Palace. The occasion was the relaunch of the *Mondo*. Present were the best names of the *Corriere*, from Biagi to Ronchey, passing through Siciliano. Invitees were everyone: Spadolini, Rusconi, Mondadori, Visentini, Ottone, politicians, journalists, editors and competitors. In the midst of them Andrea Rizzoli was finally ruminating on his revenge.

When he saw Scalfari, Rizzoli approached him: 'It's going to be a great weekly and no expense will be spared.' It was a war against the weekly news magazines *L'Espresso* and *Panorama*.

'You have tonight opened a game of which you do not measure the consequences. Are you going to bring war into our house? Well, we will bring it to yours. If you want to undermine the supremacy of *L'Espresso*, we will attack the *Corriere*,' replied Scalfari.

Rizzoli laughed without understanding and clapped a hand on his shoulder: 'Bravo, always fighting.' Scalfari also laughed to soften the tone, but on that evening any residual doubt was overcome.

A week later the business plan was ready: 20 pages, 65 journalists, 150,000 copies. Break-even in three years. However, the money was missing. Five billion. The project was stuffed in a drawer. Shortly afterwards, however, *L'Espresso* reduced its format, paper costs fell by 20 per cent and sales increased by 20,000 copies. Profits became substantial but not enough. A publisher was needed. A big publisher. They began to weave a web of relationships. They went through it all. The last thread, the thickest one, had accompanied them through that summer storm.

At the gate of the villa, two men with large umbrellas wrapped in yellow tarpaulins were waiting for them. The dim light of the torches guided them along a muddy avenue to a canopy. Scalfari and Caracciolo stood at the foot of a flight of steps. On the last step there was an outstretched hand waiting for them. It was that of Giorgio Mondadori: 'Welcome.'

The entire Mondadori staff was in the house. After the pleasantries, the company sat down to eat. It was late, the diners were tired and they pretended to talk about something else: the Juventus championship; Lazio, who lost it when Maestrelli was diagnosed with liver cancer; the Apollo–Soyuz space mission, the first collaboration between the programmes of the US and USSR superpowers; the new Mondadori headquarters inaugurated the previous year and designed by Oscar Niemeyer, the architect who created the city of Brasilia for Kubitschek. And the film produced by Andrea Rizzoli, *Amici miei*. Its director was Mario Monicelli. His father Tomaso was the first author published by Arnoldo Mondadori.

Born, like Angelo Rizzoli, in 1889, to an illiterate peddler, from that book published in 1912 he came to contend for the supremacy of Italian publishing. The following year Arnoldo married Tomaso's sister, Andreina, an event that made Giorgio Mondadori and Mario Monicelli cousins. This was the talk card. The topic for which they were all there was postponed until tomorrow.

The next morning the rain subsided and at breakfast Mondadori got to the point. 'What should it be called?' asked the host.

'*La Repubblica*,' replied Scalfari, 'like the Portuguese newspaper, the one from the Carnation Revolution.'

'Mhh, *La Repubblica* ...' The conquest of the *Corriere* by Rizzoli still stung at Mondadori.

'It can be done.'

Thus the draft of the articles of association was prepared. Under the heading 'planned exit' Caracciolo wrote '14 January 1976'.

In the evening the sky opened up. The full moon illuminated Verona. The group dressed in suits and ties and ran to the Arena to see Aida. Alberto Mondadori joined them. He was dressed in a tailcoat and wore a tuba hat. The pact was sealed at night at the Tre

Corone restaurant, in Piazza Bra, with four bottles of champagne. It was a perfect evening and Scalfari had caught it in time.

A few months later, as soon as Alberto Mondadori had realised his dream, his sisters put him in the minority by combining their shares. Designated by his father Arnoldo as his successor, he suddenly found himself robbed of the sceptre. In 1976 he sold his shares and never set foot in Segrate again. Exactly one month after the publication of the newspaper, on 14 February, Alberto died of a heart attack. On the seventh toast of that magical evening, exhausted, he suddenly collapsed on the table and fell into a deep sleep. When he woke up, *La Repubblica* was already a reality.

The Best Deal of a Lifetime

In the space of a few days, Horst Dassler, through the SMPI (Société Monégasque de Promotion Internationale, registered in Monte Carlo, 55 per cent his and 45 per cent West Nally's), signed a $2.2 million contract with the Argentinians for the use of the World Cup brand. With FIFA, he signed an $8.3 million agreement for the sponsorship and distribution of advertising and television rights to the World Cup (to be repackaged and resold to companies around the world). The total to be paid out was $10.5 million, a sum that Dassler did not have but that Coca-Cola guaranteed him by becoming the main sponsor of the World Cup, leaving him, in exchange for management, 30 per cent of the profits.

It was the world's largest corporate sponsorship programme. The agreement, signed in 1976, marked a turning point in the evolution of the sports business. Until then companies wishing to advertise paid stadium owners to rent space to display their brands. FIFA received nothing. Dassler and Nally patented a new logic. The valuable asset was football and FIFA owned it; therefore, FIFA should control advertising in stadiums. Once the principle had been established, the rules needed to be organised, and these were translated into packages of rights. Dassler and Nally positioned themselves under

FIFA to buy wholesale and resell retail. For Nally it was 'the best deal' of his life.

However, Dassler's dealing never stopped. He managed to acquire the Le Coq Sportif brand at a time when the French company was suffering from Asian competition in the textile market and rising raw material prices due to the 1973 oil crisis. For his family, he bought 49 per cent of the company. In fact, through a friend, he also controlled the remaining 51 per cent. The friend, André Guelfi, nicknamed Dédé la Sardina, was a shady businessman who, before becoming a racing driver, made his fortune fishing for sardines. Horst decided to give the brand an international dimension, a worldwide network of distributors and agents. Thanks to this operation, Guelfi also managed to get his hands on FIFA's advertising business.

But to manage Coca-Cola's money, you needed the right man. The Atlanta-based company's marketing executives insisted on a representative who could protect their interests at FIFA. Someone who knew the sport, could negotiate and spoke several languages. Dassler met him on one of his regular business appointments as public relations director for the Longines watch brand. He was struck by the dialectic of the man, a Swiss who was involved in organising the 1972 Munich Olympics on behalf of his company. His name was Joseph Blatter. He was Horst's age, 40, and had many past lives. He had been an amateur footballer, director of public relations for the Office du Tourisme Valaisan, general secretary of Swiss Ice Hockey, and sports journalist and manager of the Neuchâtel Xamax football club. The two liked each other and felt like kindred spirits.

Horst brought Blatter to Adidas in Landersheim to train him and to teach him everything he knew. Blatter had the right profile: he was multilingual, had a business background and had worked in sport all his life. The employees saw the Swiss man repeating Horst's instructions exactly, like a puppet, but the young Blatter was ambitious and quickly learned every nuance of the company's machinery. When he considered him ready, Horst sent Blatter to FIFA, initially salaried by himself, as technical director to manage the new international development programmes that the organisation was putting in place with the money obtained from Coca-Cola.

Meanwhile, Horst's father, Adi, was increasingly uncomfortable. He was shocked to find out that at the 1974 World Cup the West German team had asked for money to wear his products. He had not resolved his relationship problems with Horst and wrote long, bitter letters repudiating his son's actions. He spent most of his final years in the workshop, doing what he knew how to do, shoes, increasingly uninterested in the commercial aspects of his company. He had no idea how many Adidas factories there were in the world and, frankly, he did not care. He died shortly after the conclusion of the World Cup in Argentina and was buried in the Herzogenaurach cemetery, far from the grave of his brother Rudi, who had died four years earlier. At that time the Adidas company, which employed over 3,000 people in Germany alone, was redistributed in equal parts to Horst, his four sisters and their mother Käthe. However, many of Horst's businesses were not shared with the rest of the family and remained off the Landersheim company books. The sports marketing empire, which he had built up over the past decade, thus remained hidden from even the closest of people.

From Total Football to Social Football

Not everyone liked him: his shyness was mistaken for arrogance, his silent work for conceit. By following his uncompromising path Enzo Bearzot had made many enemies, but he had won the trust of a group of young people. They were the same ones with whom he now wanted to try to go down in history. He was the 'Old Man', not only because of his age but because his face was marked by fatigue, hardened before its time, his hair was thin, his forehead wrinkled. A life in football and few friends among journalists, yet he gave them everything they were entitled to, in great detail. His availability was always absolute with everyone. At the helm of the national under-23 team he met a young generation of reporters who would go on to have a career with him: Giuseppe Pistilli, Bruno Bernardi, Piero Dardanello and Franco Mentana, who stuck to him like a postage stamp. His first great ally was Giovanni Arpino at *La Stampa*. It was he who gave him the label of 'Old Man'.

When Valcareggi ended his role as Italy's coach in the summer of 1974, Rivera, Mazzola and Riva were at the end of their journey. The national team had to be rebuilt and Artemio Franchi thought of Fulvio Bernardini, the only one who had the courage to risk a revolution. The president asked the new coach to choose his most direct collaborator from Bearzot and Vicini, who were already working as technicians for the Italian federation. Bernardini summoned them to Rome to his house on the Balduina and asked his wife to entertain them in the living room. He then received the two technicians separately, spoke with them and dismissed them.

'I prefer Vicini,' his wife whispered.

'You're right,' replied Bernardini, 'he's open and sunny. Bearzot is a closed and shady Friulian, but he knows about football.' And he chose the latter.

After six matches and only one victory, Bernardini was flanked by his deputy. Bearzot would be the coach of the top Italian representative team, so the summer of 1975 gave him a place on the bench of the national team. Azeglio Vicini was entrusted with the under-23 squad. Franco Mentana of *La Gazzetta* was the first person the Old Man talked to about his idea: a team where men counted more than feet, with a young framework, to which older players could also have access, who knew how to create play and assist their less-experienced team-mates. He had to invent a squad from Bernardini's ashes, keep those who were still good and discover new recruits. After an initial draw with Finland, Bearzot immediately encountered the top players in European football, Poland and the Netherlands, who had just become the third and second world football powers, respectively, and against whom Italy drew and won.

Thanks to Bearzot, Italy began to emerge from the tunnel. The coach applied psychology to football, defended all the players, mentioned a family of 22 children and believed in human relationships and team spirit. After a handful of matches he started to outline his principles, to talk about eclecticism, to want players who could do everything. The coach no longer believed in football locked in defence and only willing to go forward on the counterattack. For him, the 'Italian game' was dead. He wanted to overcome the too rigid specialisation of tasks that characterised Italian football and was oriented towards a more accurate athletic preparation, a more careful coverage of space, which was only possible if everyone ran, a greater participation of the attackers in the defence and vice versa. It was a new way of conceiving football but the press was distracted by names and manners, so no one noticed that the national team, by renouncing catenaccio, had reached a tactical turning point.

The year was 1976. A crazy year of births and rebirths. Eugenio Scalfari's daily newspaper *La Repubblica*, Steve Jobs' Apple computer, Jorge Rafael Videla's military dictatorship in Argentina, among many others, all saw the light of day. *Rocky* came out, *Star Wars* was filmed, Niki Lauda resurfaced from his terrible accident in Germany, Felice Gimondi won the Giro d'Italia, Björn Borg won the Wimbledon tournament, but Adriano Panatta won everything else: Rome, Paris and even the Davis Cup in Chile. Enzo Bearzot had only been Italy's coach for a handful of months.

However, it was not a good period for the country. The lira was devalued by 12 per cent, the Moro IV and V governments fell one after the other to make way for the third Andreotti government, which obtained a 'no confidence' vote from the Chamber of Deputies with the abstention of the Italian Communist Party, socialists, social democrats, republicans and liberals. Bearzot, however, had his mind elsewhere. In autumn, the qualifying matches for the World Cup in Argentina would begin and the coach was searching for his gamestyle. The vanguard was the Netherlands with its total football. But the football of the tulips was perhaps too free for the characteristics of Italy. And Bearzot had the lucidity to understand this immediately, choosing the Polish team as a reference model, still modern but less uninhibited. The debut was discouraging: two defeats, against England and Brazil, in the American Bicentennial tournament. Bearzot was ready to resign but before communicating his decision he gathered the players in the dressing room on the eve of the friendly match against Romania at San Siro.

'Guys, in my opinion this is the right path, it is worth insisting on. Be careful, though: if you follow me, I will risk more, but you will also pay a price.'

The players didn't think twice about it and they all declared themselves in favour of the new tactical method, without reservation: 'We are with you, let's go ahead, coach.'

On the day of the match, the bench was greeted by a barrage of vicious insults and the players on the pitch were booed. San Siro was hostile. The reason can be guessed, as the stadium was linked to Rivera and Mazzola, still players but excluded from the national team by Bernardini. Bearzot, who had taken over the reins, avoided calling them up so as not to offend the man whose deputy he was. The coach was disheartened but did not give up; he had the trust of his players and Italy carried on. They won 4-2, but perhaps the result was of little importance. The date was historic for another reason: for the first time the national team abandoned the Italian style of play. Bearzot's team was born on 4 June 1976.

The Chair Game

The *Guerin Sportivo* did not perceive the change. It rejected the team, the plans and above all the coach. The weekly magazine was one of Bearzot's fiercest enemies. In those days it attacked him mercilessly. 'The national team is there, the coach is missing.' The new game expressed by Bearzot 'was all based on the frenetic dynamism of the midfielders who in reality ended up being of little help to the forwards and of no support to the defence, a sector in which another disastrous flaw of our bench players was realised'. This is why Italo Cucci was calling for 'a new coach, more intelligent, modern, prepared and confident'. But the director's resentment had sentimental origins. It was a story of fathers. Lost and found.

Cucci's father left him when he was still a boy and secretly taking his first steps in journalism, careful not to let his father's eyes fall on the first crime articles in the newspaper *Il Resto del Carlino*. He would have liked to show them to him with pride, in fact. By now he had understood that this would be his job. He was then rejected by the editor Giovanni Spadolini and forced to choose the path of sports journalism. But in the course of his previous activity as a judicial reporter, he had happened to write in *Stadio* about Bologna, involved in the 'Doping Case'. It was on that occasion that the young Italo Cucci met Fulvio Bernardini.

Cucci was fascinated: Bernardini was generous, intelligent, had class, football knowledge and a rare ability to treat the game of football with culture and humanity. As a player he had been a goalkeeper, midfielder and striker. He had played exceptionally well for Pozzo's national team but had been sensationally excluded from the squads that took part in the victorious 1934 and 1938 World Cups, as the coach had deemed him unsuitable for the technical project: 'You see, Bernardini, you are currently playing in a superior manner; perfectly from the point of view of individual performance. The others cannot reach your conception of the game and end up being in awe. I should ask you to play less well. Sacrifice you or sacrifice everyone else? How would you adjust in my place?'

Bernardini was one of the few sportsmen with a university degree at the time (he was called 'the Doctor') and began to work seriously as a journalist in the aftermath of the Azzurri's success in Paris, later writing for *Corriere dello Sport*, *Il Resto del Carlino*, *La Gazzetta dello Sport* and *Il Messaggero* (for which he would cover the World Cup in Spain). As a coach he managed to win the Scudetto for the first time in the post-war period for two non-Turin and non-Milan teams: Fiorentina and Bologna, as well as the Coppa Italia in 1958 for Lazio, the first official trophy in the history of I Biancoceleste.

THE MATCH

After the 1974 World Cup collapse, Cucci thought Bernardini was the right man for the national team, so he asked him to do an article indicating how he would rebuild it. 'I'll do the article for you,' the coach replied, 'but it's not enough; I want more, I want to say things, propose solutions, make a programme of renewal and then carry it out myself, not give it to the federation.' The Palazzo does not want him. They consider him 'inconvenient', 'old' (he was in his seventies), if not 'senile'. But when Cucci called Franchi, the 'Grand Duke of Tuscany' immediately replied: 'I've already thought about it, he's the right man, we'll just have to get someone to accept him ...'

At his debut on the Azzurri bench, on 28 September 1974, in Zagreb, a friendly match against Yugoslavia, Bernardini caught a cold and had a stomach ache. It was a start that made the suspects gloat. Bernardini went on his way, however, choosing the most complicated route: the summonses. In just three call-ups he brought together over 50 players. He brought together the whole of Italian football, a confused army that should be part of two hypothetical national teams: the senior and the youth team, the one followed by Bearzot. The Old Man knew the merits and faults of those faces and pointed out that such work could prove counterproductive. Bernardini continued but, despite their differences, found in Bearzot the friend and ally he was looking for. When it became clear to him that his brief interlude with the Azzurri was destined to end, he let loose in front of Cucci, with tears in his eyes: 'Now they can say and do anything to me, but I had the national team, I worked on it with enthusiasm, it was the aim of my life, I launched many good young players who love me. When they decide to take it away from me, I will give it back to them without any fuss.' That day, in Bogliasco, his hand clutched his wife's. 'And when that happens,' he told her, looking at her with a knowing smile, 'it won't be a drama. We'll still love each other, won't we, Ines?'

Shortly afterwards he began to foreshadow the end: 'Soon Bearzot will be able to walk on his own. And he will do very well.' Cucci could not believe it and in the *Guerino* he attacked the Old Man in a merciless way. 'Fuffo' Bernardini was the father he had lost.

106

He could not tolerate such an injustice. But it was the Doctor himself who reassured him: 'You may be right in many cases, but not in this one. Bearzot is loyal, he's the right man.'

Meanwhile, the game of musical chairs continued. The successes of Milan landed Carraro at the FIGC as president of the technical sector. Sordillo followed in his footsteps, first occupying the Rossoneri's chair, then entering the federal council of the national team. Carraro then moved on to the football league and, when Franchi's mandate expired, he took his place in the FIGC, while Sordillo went to occupy his old chair in the technical sector.

A few months later, Fulvio Bernardini, the coach of the national team, went to Carraro and told him: 'I've finished my job, I'm quitting.' Carraro hesitated but Bernardini insisted: 'Listen to me, let me go, put Bearzot in. You'll see, with him the national team would do very well.' On the evening of 8 June 1977 in Helsinki, at the end of the World Cup qualification match between Italy and Finland, there was a banquet based on raw fish organised at the hotel of the Italian national team. Among the journalists was Elio Domeniconi, correspondent of the *Guerino*, who was assigned to follow Bearzot. However, he was unexpectedly approached by Carraro, who begged him to join him in his suite. 'Domeniconi, I need a big favour. You have the right connections in Genoa. You should beg your friends at Sampdoria to take Bernardini back.' Back in Genoa, Domeniconi phoned the vice-president Roberto Montefiori. He immediately interrupted him: 'Carraro has already phoned me too. Calm him down, we'll get Fulvio back as sports director.' And the national team became Bearzot's alone.

But Cucci could not digest the sacking of Bernardini by the federation. When the bench was handed over to the Friuli coach, he wrote a fiery editorial: 'I'm ashamed to be Italian.' And again in the *Guerino* he exclaimed that if Bearzot was a real man he should show gratitude to his predecessor. From that moment on, Bearzot refused to speak to Cucci and his newspaper. Yet, without wanting to, the *Guerino*, through its correspondent, had done Bearzot a favour. For years there was no dialogue until one day Cucci sent Bearzot the young Darwin Pastorin. He had high hopes, kind manners, Brazilian serenity and great admiration for the Vecio. The coach opened up and Pastorin returned to the editorial office, excited: 'Bearzot is a wonderful person!' But there was still a cold war with the rest of the newspaper.

Real Vicenza

In three years he had more injuries than matches and he now knew he was at the last stop of the journey. The decisive one. The young Paolo Rossi still knew nothing of what awaited him, he only knew his past.

With a Scudetto, not his own, sewn on his chest, he was loaned to Como, to cut his teeth, he was told. He did not get the chance. He struggled to settle in, played only six matches and became depressed on the bench. He was sent back before the end of the season. Juventus were not expecting him, so when Giuseppe 'Giussi' Farina showed up with 100 million lire to take him to Vicenza, president Boniperti was happy to sell him. All Rossi had to do now was hope. Football was his life but he had to start thinking about the possibility of not making it. If the opportunity did not arrive, he would be forced to build his own future. He would have to finish his studies, find a job in a bank and become one of the many who had tried to chase a dream. He would still have the enthusiasm of his twenties, a single meniscus, a car, a blue A112 Autobianchi with folding seats, a slim physique and a clean-cut, good-guy face. Perfect ingredients to become a Mr Rossi.

It was with these thoughts in mind that the aspiring champion Paolo Rossi entered the gates of the Menti Stadium in Vicenza on the morning of the first day of August 1976. Lanerossi had just left behind a dreadful season during which they risked being relegated to Serie C. They had no dreams of glory, sold the few who were worth anything and only bought experienced players on the wane or unknown youngsters at bargain prices. Like Rossi. There were a few onlookers in the stands, mostly pensioners. 'And this is the new striker?', 'With that physique, how can he get into the area?', 'Good thing he'll be a reserve.' The starter was Alessandro Vitali, a centre-forward who had exploded a few years earlier and had also played in Serie A with Fiorentina and Cagliari. Paolo Rossi was actually a right-winger who was promised 50,000 lire for every appearance. *Who knows if I'll ever see them*, he thought. *Here the risk is that I'll be watching the championship from the bench.*

But fate knocked on his door. Vitali, during the negotiations for his signing, quarrelled with Farina and absconded at night from the Rovereto training camp, thus ending his career. He ended his life by crashing into a plane tree on the outskirts of Bologna on 26 August 1977, dying instantly at the age of 32. Rossi, who in the meantime had earned the trust of coach Giovan Battista Fabbri, known as 'Gibì', found himself a starter. President Farina, a couple of months earlier, had not been too subtle when introducing him to the team: 'Gibì, I think this Rossi is a dud, he even has a broken meniscus ...' Fabbri, seeing Rossi's pace, decided to try him as a centre-forward in the second half of the season. His knees found new connections, he began to blossom with forgotten strengths and from that moment on he never stopped scoring.

It was the dawn of an unforgettable season. That of 'Real' Vicenza. Rossi was fast, reactive and got on well with his team-mates: Cerilli, rejected by Inter; Salvi, who was given the boot by Sampdoria; Carrera, who couldn't find a place at Reggiana and Filippi, known as 'Calimero' because of his short stature, rejected by Bologna. Each of them had something to prove. Fabbri, who had also had Bearzot among his players, was inventing total football before it even existed, without even going to study in the Netherlands.

The Spark

Ten years before Joaquín Viola Sauret opened the envelope containing the requirements to be chosen as the venue for the Mundial, the congress in London decided on the potential venues for the 1974 and

1982 World Cups. The 1978 one, destined for an overseas country, would be in Argentina. The two European venues that were defeated at the 1966 World Cup, Spain and West Germany, were to vie with each other. The candidates, in order to bring home the result, agreed: the Spaniards withdrew from the race for the nearest World Cup and the Germans from the one furthest away. In 1966 nobody could have imagined what would happen in the meantime. Argentina and Spain, oppressed at different times and in different ways by dictatorial regimes, went into their World Cups in completely different moods. FIFA's decisions, after the 1976 coup d'état, gave the Argentina of the generals an immense propaganda opportunity. Spain, which would confirm its acceptance on 31 August 1979, when Don Adolfo Suárez González completed the dissolution of the Franco regime, was given the opportunity to demonstrate that its military past had been buried forever.

At the same time, the Real Federación Española de Fútbol set up a commission to prepare for the World Cup. Its planning was part of the post-Francoist democratic transition.

The Hidden Property

'True power resides in the hands of the holders of the mass media.' Behind this certainty lay Licio Gelli's P2 masonic lodge. And the only way to put it into action was to bring Italy's largest daily newspaper into subservience to its dark designs.

To complete his takeover of the *Corriere*, Gelli was assisted by his right-hand man, Umberto Ortolani, the banker Roberto Calvi, the businessman Eugenio Cefis and the coffers of the IOR, the Istituto per le Opere di Religione. All he needed was a publisher interested in buying it. The sacrificial victims were the Rizzolis. Financed by Eugenio Cefis, a well-known Italian entrepreneur, in 1974 the new publishers were persuaded to buy. Until then, the shares of Editoriale Corriere della Sera were divided between three families: the Crespis, the Morattis and the Agnellis. It was

THE HIDDEN PROPERTY

therefore sufficient to acquire two of the three shareholdings to become the new owners. But Andrea Rizzoli was not satisfied with a controlling stake and took over 100 per cent of the publishing company. However, he soon realised that the operation was much more expensive than he had expected. He was forced to look for more funds from the banks, unaware that many of them were chaired or directed by P2 members and that the decision to grant him new money was therefore conditioned by Gelli's opinion.

In July 1977, forced to recapitalise the company, Rizzoli found the 20 billion lire he needed. At the time it was not clear where the money came from. The first hypotheses point to the two strongholds of the international Right: Bavaria and Texas. The better trail, however, leads to Milan. With some reasonable deduction, there are those who think of the president of Banco Ambrosiano, Roberto Calvi, 'the banker of God', and the financier, Umberto Ortolani, both very close to the Catholic world and to the Christian Democrats. No one, however, identified the weavers of the plot that was enveloping the publishing group.

As a pledge, Rizzoli gave Calvi 80 per cent of the shares, to be redeemed after three years at a higher value. In practice, he handed over the company, allowing the penetration of hidden ownership in all the publishing and financial ganglia of the group. The indebtedness increased and the presence of Banco Ambrosiano as a creditor depository of the pledged shares was a sign of the invisible change in ownership. With the Rizzoli family increasingly weak in financial terms, Calvi became the real boss.

Under the covert rule of Calvi–Gelli–Ortolani–Cefis, the control room was repopulated. Bruno Tassan Din, who joined Rizzoli in 1973 as an employee, became managing director and owner of part of the company. Umberto Ortolani, a lawyer and Gelli's right-hand man, joined the board of directors. Franco Di Bella, after a carbonara dinner with businessman Silvio Berlusconi, became the new editor of the *Corriere* in place of Piero Ottone. Gelli thus achieved his first objective: to put his men in key positions at Rizzoli.

The Exchange

Shortly before the Mundial, the Comité pour le boycott de l'-organisation par l'Argentine de la Coupe du Monde, an association formed by French and Argentine left-wingers behind the periodical *L'Epique* (which in turn has a following of intellectuals and artists of the calibre of Jean-Paul Sartre, Roland Barthes and Ives Montand), succeeded in raising the awareness of the main associations in defence of human rights, including Amnesty International. At first, Sweden, the Netherlands and France, the countries most involved in the battle against the horrors of the Argentinian genocides, seemed to want to join the boycott of the 1978 World Cup, but in reality their respective national teams never considered staying at home.

If the teams wanted the World Cup, they would try to change the country in which it was to be held. The military coup had made it necessary to hold the 11th edition of the championships in a country that was not dominated by a dictatorial regime. Human rights associations suggested that FIFA president Havelange should think about an alternative venue. They were thinking of asking Spain, which was due to host the World Cup in 1982, for the heroic feat of a four-year advance. Or Brazil, to respect the continental alternation. Bureaucratic quibbles were sifted through until a small, big event brought history back on track.

In 1975, two young Brazilians were arrested by the Argentinian army's 'working groups'. Their names were Paulo Antônio de Paranaguá and María Regina Pilla. Paulo's father, a member of the Paulist high society, moved heaven and earth to get his son back home: the union of Brazilian bankers, the American democrat Ted Kennedy, Cardinal Eugenio Sales, the Brazilian general Danilo Venturini and the UNESCO ambassador Paulo Carneiro. Nothing happened. When the ball passed to Antonio Leite, Paulo's maternal grandfather, he needed only two degrees of separation to reach his goal: he begged football's highest representative, Brazilian João Havelange, to raise the issue with the highest representative of the country that would host the World Cup, General Jorge Rafael Videla. The exchange of words between them changed the fate of the kidnapped youths and puts things in place.

'All right, we'll get them out,' promised the dictator, 'but in return we need FIFA to confirm Argentina as the venue for the World Cup.'

'General, you have my word,' counter-promised Havelange.

Paulo was transferred to Paris and welcomed by Robert Mitterrand, friend of the Paranaguá family and brother of François. Spain only had to think about 1982. The last World Cup of the 1970s would be an Argentinian affair.

Hilton Hotel, 11pm

In view of the Argentinian Mundial, Pier Cesare 'Pierce' Baretti went with Cucci to Budapest to see Hungary vs Czechoslovakia. Bearzot was also there. Hungary could be one of Italy's opponents at the World Cup. It was a spring night in 1977, the night before the match. The three of them met in the lobby of the Hilton Hotel. When Cucci saw Bearzot he stiffened, closing himself in silence. Baretti knew them both and, after an initial moment of embarrassment, brought them closer: 'You still don't understand each other, why don't you try it tonight?'

It was 11 o'clock. Cucci and Bearzot began to talk. They confronted each other, explained themselves, understood each other. They finished at five in the morning. During those hours they discussed everything: their common roots, the classical high school, the Jesuits, politics and, of course, football. Bearzot did not talk to him about methods or footballers but of men. Cucci was dazzled. He suddenly understood Bearzot's moral qualities even more than his technical ones. And he found in him an extraordinary innovator. That night Cucci sided with Bearzot. His fiercest enemy thus became his most ardent defender. It was the beginning of a friendship. It was one of the few friendships the coach formed with journalists. But it would not be the only one.

THE MATCH

A few months later the coach was in Buenos Aires for the World Cup draw. Cucci stayed in Bologna and sent Elio Domeniconi along with photojournalist Guido Zucchi: 'I recommend you stick to Bearzot, he's a friend of ours.' At Linate airport in Milan, Domeniconi met his colleague Giampaolo Ormezzano.

'Where do you sleep?' asked Domeniconi.

'At the Grand Hotel. You?'

'At the Lancaster.'

'I almost came there.'

'Bravo, Bearzot is there too.'

A few years earlier Ormezzano, a lifelong Granata – Torino fan – was convinced that after Valentino Mazzola there would no longer be a captain worthy of wearing the Torino armband, or indeed 'from Torino' as Italy's captain. And instead Enzo Bearzot arrived. When he heard his name, the director of *Tuttosport* had no doubts: 'I'm coming there.'

The two correspondents of *Guerino* were more than happy to have Ormezzano on their team because he spoke all the languages of the world. And thanks to him, in fact, they immediately managed to find the coach of the Argentinian national team, César Luis Menotti, at the Bagni San Giorgio in Mar del Plata. Ormezzano had also written a book about Omar Sívori and had become a friend of his, so in the afternoon he got him on the phone:

'I'm here in Baires, would you like us to visit you? I'll bring the Vecio too.'

'Bearzot? Of course! Then I'll invite you out to dinner. Enzo has never seen me on the pitch, so he can finally do it.' And Sívori burst into laughter.

Ormezzano reported back to the coach. Bearzot laughed and accepted.

Sívori was out of football and spent his time with his wife María Elena Casas and his three children, Néstor, Miriam and Humberto, on a huge estate in San Nicolás de los Arroyos, overlooking the Paraná river. When he saw it, Ormezzano mumbled: 'Boniperti got it all wrong.'

'Why?' asked Sívori.

'He continues to live in a block of flats in Corso Agnelli.'

'Don't worry, he'll get his own villa on the hill too.'

But in the meantime he christened his home 'La Juventus'. The dinner was organised on the fly at Boca, in the restaurant of an Italian native, Los Años Locos (The Crazy Years). Néstor Rossi, another Argentine champion, also joined in. The evening proceeded cheerfully and sports memories emerged with each course. But when the conversation turned to the subject of generals, Sívori changed tone. Four years earlier, he had been dismissed from leading the Albiceleste because of his lack of sympathy for Juan Domingo Perón, who had just returned to Argentina. He had not kicked a ball since that day.

'It's bullshit what you write in Italy about military repression.'

'Omar, just today an Italian journalist working here told me about the cars without number plates of Videla's police,' says Ormezzano.

'I live here and know better than you. I have never seen anything like this. There is no dictatorship in Argentina.'

It was the southern hemisphere winter and it was hot. To calm everyone down, the owner of the restaurant suggested an Italian ice cream at a place not far away: 'Leave your jackets here, no one will steal them. Argentina is a safe country.'

Everyone followed the invitation and reached the ice cream parlour. They parked and after a few seconds a car came screeching in. It was a Ford Falcon and it had no number plate. Afer some violent braking, some figures got out, each with a machine gun aimed at the group.

'Documents!'

Only Ormezzano had them with him; the others had left them in their jackets at the restaurant.

Sívori, El Cabezón, the angel with the dirty face, the landlord, the national hero, also found himself without papers. Feeling cheated in the eyes of the others, he nervously shouted to the policemen: 'I am Sívori!' believing that was enough. But those guys in uniform had never seen him play. They did not know who Omar Henrique Sívori was. To them, he was just a stranger without papers. They decided to arrest him but he managed to escape the police's grasp. He had always been restless and quarrelsome and had spent his career picking fights. In his 12 years in Italy he had served 33 days of suspension.

'I was a great footballer, I also played for our Argentina team. Even a short time ago I was the technical commissioner of your national team, it's impossible that you don't know me! This is Néstor Rossi, idol of your fathers.' But in Argentina the great Sívori, the 1957 continental champion, the 1961 Ballon d'Or, was now an ordinary man.

Bearzot whispered to Ormezzano, 'You, who are more familiar with him than I am, try to calm him down. His nerves are shattered. If he explodes he'll get us all killed.' In the meantime, the policemen were speaking among themselves in tones that were not at all reassuring. Ormezzano understood Spanish and was afraid. He had heard about the night killings of Videla's secret police. They all had their hands resting on the bonnet of their car, under a lamppost, the policemen right behind them, the barrels of their machine guns touching their backs.

'Why did you park here?'

Sívori became more and more furious: 'Because there was room.'

'Do you take us for fools? Tell us the real reason!' Another car arrived, also without number plates.

When one of the police pointed the torch at the Italian coach, Sívori shouted: 'This is Bearzot!'

Ormezzano was about to say, 'He was the captain of Torino!' but his voice was muffled by that of the Argentine: 'He leads Italy at football, he's here for the draw, his picture is in all the papers today.'

One of the policemen whispered to his colleagues, 'He's the coach of the Italian national team.'

Bearzot at that time had won the sympathy of the Argentines thanks to Miguel María Muñoz, the prince of local commentators, who had invited him several times to be on the radio. Ormezzano took advantage of the unexpected moment of suspension and, in two words, in Castilian, he explained who they were, where they came from and where they were going. An internal consultation followed in a low voice. Then the order: 'Get out of here. Now!'

The group started to leave, but Omar wanted an explanation and started to flail about. It was at this point that Bearzot went towards him. At that moment it was as if he saw him enter the area, his mouth wide open in search of oxygen, his arms spread like wings, his legs unable to stay still. This time Bearzot knew how to mark the opponent of a lifetime. He picked him up and dragged him away, throwing him into the car, which then went off into the night. Once calmed down, Sívori begged Ormezzano not to say anything. The next day there was the World Cup draw. Bearzot was hesitant but agreed. Such news could be dangerous and inappropriate.

At dawn, Ormezzano met the Italian colleague who had warned him about Argentina, Giangiacomo Foà, correspondent of the *Corriere della Sera*, who told him, 'That's the street of the villas where the generals in power live. And you have parked under the house of Galtieri, the number two in the Videla government. Yours could have been a car bomb. It's only by chance that they didn't kill you by shooting you at a distance. They could have taken you out right away and thrown you in the river.' Ormezzano agreed not to write about it, but he would always regret it.

The following morning, 14 January 1978, the draw for the group stage was made live on television in Buenos Aires, in the presence of the FIFA president, Brazilian João Havelange, the general secretary, Swiss Helmut Käser, and the vice-president, German Hermann Neuberger. A three-year-old boy, Ricardo Teixeira Havelange, pulled the cylinders containing the tickets with the names of the participating teams from the urn. The grandson of the FIFA president.

On the eve of the draw, there had been no lack of insinuations that the system was not fair. Previous draws involving children were evoked, which, in a very simple way, had probably been altered to favour the home team. Franco Mentana was the only journalist who knew in advance what the fate of Argentina's group would be, where Bearzot's Italy also ended up. A week before the draw he sent the scoop to the *Gazzetta dello Sport* but the editorial staff did not take it into consideration. When he returned to Italy, he realised that his pieces had never been published, a wrong that left him astonished and bitter. He could not have known that the *Gazzetta* had ended up under a hidden ownership linked to the Argentinian powers.

The Silence

When, on the eve of the Argentinian World Cup, Andrea Rizzoli left the reins of the group to his son Angelo (known as 'Angelone'), the P2 pushed Rizzoli to also acquire *La Gazzetta dello Sport*. The control of newspapers gave the P2 an enormous capacity for manoeuvre: it could condition the conduct of politicians, whose adherence to the P2 area had been rewarded with compliant articles and interviews that guaranteed visibility in public opinion. At the same time, it could control journalists. Giovanni Russo was censored, Giangiacomo Foà was transferred (from Buenos Aires to Rio de Janeiro), Enzo Biagi was warned. Di Bella invited him to go to Argentina in Foà's place on the occasion of the World Cup but urged him not to offend the sensibilities of the generals. 'You know, Enzo, it's not for anything else, but they might favour Rizzoli in the purchase of some newspapers in the country.' Biagi refused to leave.

Gelli punctually put the publisher in touch with Admiral Emilio Eduardo Massera. 'Licio is a great friend of mine and I cannot refuse him anything.' This was the beginning of the Milanese publishing group's fortunes in Argentina. Rizzoli first acquired at a very good price the plants of Editorial Abril, the largest Argentinian publishing house expropriated from the Italian Civita brothers; then, thanks to the interventions of Gelli and Ortolani who managed to get it an 'extraordinary' authorisation from the Argentinian authorities, it opened Editorial Crea. In exchange, Gelli bought the silence of the *Corriere* with regard to the human rights violations carried out by the military. The Milanese newspaper limited itself to providing a 'reassuring portrait' of the country, hiding the drama of the desaparecidos (the missing), the tortures of the dictatorship, the disastrous economic situation and the protests over Massera's visit to Italy in the autumn of 1977.

The Mason, Mason and Massera

On the eve of the World Cup, the Federazione Nazionale della Stampa Italiana (National Federation of the Italian Press) appealed to Italian journalists in Argentina not to limit themselves to reporting only sports news but to use the occasion to testify to human rights violations by the military junta.

The unconditional support of the World Football Federation could not, however, completely shield Videla from the dangers of objective and independent international information. In order to improve Argentina's image abroad, the military junta turned to the world's largest public relations agency: Burson-Marsteller of New York. The agency drew up a report (costing $1.1 million) emblematically entitled 'What is true for products is also true for countries'. One could therefore sell the product 'Argentinian dictatorship' like any other commodity to be launched on the market. The essence of the report was condensed into one recommendation: it was necessary to 'influence those who influence public opinion' – journalists – by showing them the image of an orderly and peaceful society very different from the one painted by 'subversive propaganda'. In fact, a crowded programme of entertainment was planned for the reporters: an abundant supply of propaganda material, tourist trips, lunches with Argentinian businessmen, shows at the Colón Theatre in Buenos Aires, evenings in fashionable nightclubs and even 'personal encounters with Argentinian youth' in order to offer a 'sample of the variety of entertainment existing in the country' and the 'normality of daily life'.

THE MATCH

The appeal of the Federazione Nazionale della Stampa Italiana was taken up by the two correspondents in Buenos Aires of *La Repubblica*, Franco Recanatesi and Saverio Tutino. The *Corriere della Sera*, on the other hand, in view of the World Cup, unexpectedly provided a 'reassuring' image of Argentina.

On 10 December 1977, as the Italian national team had just qualified for the World Cup, the *Corriere della Sera* published on its front page an article by Leonardo Vergani entitled 'L'industria del gol dà lavoro e speranza all'Argentina' (The goalscoring industry gives work and hope to Argentina), aimed at conveying a festive and cheerful image of the country, without mentioning the repression that produced thousands of innocent victims among the Argentinian people: 'The military government that governs Argentina is making an enormous effort to ensure that everything works properly during the World Cup: stadiums, roads, telephones. There will be no security problems ... The World Cup will leave a more modern Argentina, because astronomical sums are being spent on infrastructure ... In spite of the police regime, the cities are cheerful, people stay up late at night, record shops are open at night and songs come out that we used to sing thirty years ago, Claudio Villa tunes.'

Vergani's article became the subject of criticism by *Il Manifesto*, which, the following day, asked: 'Why, then, does Di Bella's newspaper so brazenly cover the propaganda of the Argentine military junta?' *Il Manifesto* could not yet know what lay behind the 'good-natured' attitude of the *Corriere*. But the article from Via Solferino that aroused the most reaction was undoubtedly the one signed on 29 May 1978 by Paolo Bugialli, the correspondent in Argentina for the World Cup: 'Let the footballers play their World Cups, let hundreds of millions of people all over the world enjoy them, let the Argentinians express without further qualms the satisfaction of having organised them, and well, and paying out of their own pockets. Perhaps it is time to stop this nonsense. But, we repeat, it can't be that they are all policemen and fascists who stop you in the street and ask you to tell the truth. Which is this: the whole country is striving for everything to work, for visitors to find friendship, the whole country feels under scrutiny and faces it with trepidation. Videla passes, Argentina remains.'

The substantial silence on Argentina during the years of repression by the main Italian press could only be explained by the manoeuvres of the P2. Gelli, in fact, carried out parallel diplomacy between Italy and Argentina, weaving ever closer links between the political and economic apparatuses of the two countries, and exercising his occult power over the mass media. The ties between Gelli and the South American country dated back to the immediate post-war period, when he, a fascist fighter in the Spanish Civil War and a former republican, fled to Perón's Argentina, which welcomed Italian fascists and German Nazis. He became part of Perón's entourage and became especially close to López Rega, enrolling him in the P2 Lodge. After the death of Perón and the coup, Gelli, notwithstanding his previous ties with the Peronist right, was able to remain in his post thanks to the protection of General Suárez Mason and Admiral Massera, both members of the P2 Lodge. Thanks to his friendship with Suárez Mason, president of the Argentine State Oil Corporation, he was able to strengthen his role as an international broker of oil contracts.

Pablito

At the end of 1977, Bearzot included the name Paolo Rossi in his list of those called up. The test was a friendly match in Liège against Belgium. It ended 1-0 to Italy, with a goal from Antognoni. When he was about to leave the Stade de Sclessin, the Vicenza striker looked at the coach. He said nothing but held out his hand. From the way he shook it, Rossi understood that his chance was gone. A month later, Bearzot played the same team against Spain at the Bernabéu in Madrid. Italy lost 2-1 but Rossi stood out. Even Lazlo Kubala, the selector of the Red Furies, praised the new arrival: 'Me gustó muchissimo Rossi,' (I really liked Rossi). The press was full of praise for him and, on the plane that was bringing the Italian journalists home from Madrid, his nickname was coined.

Giorgio Lago, head of the sports services of the *Gazzettino*, was sitting next to Piero Dardanello, of *Tuttosport*, when Sandro Ciotti, who was carrying out some interviews for an RAI radio programme, approached. 'Italy has found its centre-forward for the World Cup, from now on we can call him Pablito,' said Lago, likening him to the little gaucho symbol of the upcoming World Cup in Argentina. Ciotti smiled, Dardanello wrote it down. The next day Paolo Rossi was Pablito to everyone, a perfect name to accompany him in the future World Cups that he might play, all in Latin countries.

On 9 May 1978, in Rome, at the same time that a red Renault 4 was parked by the Red Brigade in Via Caetani with the body of ex-Italian prime minister Aldo Moro locked in the boot, Enzo Bearzot delivered to the Italian Football Federation the list of the 22 players who would play in the World Cup in Argentina. The same day a telegram arrived at Vicenza football club: 'We confirm that your player Rossi has been called up and we kindly ask him to be at Villa Pamphili in Rome by 18.30 on Friday 12 with his game clothes, valid passport and vaccinations.' It was the official invitation.

However, the news was overshadowed by that of the assassination of Moro, politican of the Christian Democrat. His kidnapping, which took place on 16 March, had also overshadowed the worst tragedy of modern prisons, which occurred almost simultaneously at Villa Devoto, the largest prison in the Argentinian capital, where political prisoners were held. By setting fire to mattresses, the guards had triggered a fire that caused the death of 150 prisoners. The press close to the military regime did not fail to 'recommend' to the Italian government an 'Argentinian solution' in the fight against terrorism. Videla himself tried, through the Moro kidnapping affair, to obtain international solidarity in the Argentinian government's war against terrorism and subversion: 'We Argentines feel we share in the anguish experienced today by other peoples, who are also victims of terrorism. As a consequence of these harsh circumstances we will perhaps find at this time the understanding that we did not have when subversion chose us as the preferred target of its criminal projects.'

At the end of the national championship, Rossi, with 24 strikes, was the king of goals. Vicenza, in second place, surrendered in the final sprint only to Juventus, who at this point would have gladly bought back the co-ownership of Rossi. Farina, however, did not give up. The fate of the best player in the Italian championship was decided in a sealed envelope. The war of the envelopes was won by Vicenza. Some say that Juventus had to restrain themselves because of Fiat's difficult moment, with workers laid off. There were cries of scandal, Carraro resigned from the league, the Vicenza president was immediately accused of immoral squandering, the sum offered was more than the Paul Getty Museum in Malibu had spent to buy a Van Gogh, a Renoir, a Cézanne and a Matisse. Farina defended himself: 'Sport is like art and Paolo is the Mona Lisa of our football. A work of art worth over five billion lire.' Never before had a player been valued at such a figure. But at the same time, with a contradiction in perfect Italian style, that Mona Lisa was invoked by the people for the World Cup. Deployed as a surprise starter in place of an unresponsive Graziani, who had, however, had the merit of getting the national team to Argentina with his goals, Rossi accompanied Italy to the top. The world noticed him.

Marmelada Peruana

A few months before the World Cup, Argentina captain Jorge Omar Carrascosa left the national team without explaining why. No journalist from the Argentinian press tried to delve into the reasons that may have prompted the leading man of the home team to turn his back on fame, money and a chance at immense glory that was just around the corner. His armband was inherited by Daniel Passarella. In the first round of the Mundial, Argentina was in the same group as Bearzot's Italy. Rossi shone, both national teams defeated France and Hungary, the other two teams in the group, and qualified for the second phase.

THE MATCH

The format next saw two groups of four teams, with direct access to the final for the group winners. The hosts had Brazil, Poland and Peru in Group B. In Group A were Italy, the Netherlands, West Germany and Austria.

After the first two matches, the qualification of Group B was a two-way fight between Brazil and Argentina. Both had one win and had drawn with each other. The last match for each remained. In the event of a win for both, goal difference would count. In Group A the last matches had been arranged for the same time (1.45pm). Initially, the matches in Group B were also to be played at the same time (4.45pm), but it had since been decided that 7.15pm would be reserved for the hosts. Brazil tried to ask for the two matches to be played at the same time but to no avail. Argentina would play knowing the result of the Cariocas. A couple of hours before the Argentina match, Brazil beat Poland 3-1. At this point, the goal difference read plus five for Brazil, against plus two for the Albiceleste, who therefore needed to beat Peru by four goals to reach the final. The task would be desperate if it were not for the fact that defending the goal of Peru, who had nothing left to play for in the World Cup, was Ramón Quiroga, an Argentine born in Rosario, incredibly the same city where the match was being played, who had taken Peruvian citizenship just a few months earlier. The Argentinians scored six times. That result would go down in history as the *Marmelada peruana*, Peruvian marmalade.

Four days later, Argentina became world champions after beating the Netherlands. The referee was the Italian Sergio Gonella, for Ruud Krol, the captain of the Dutch, 'the best Argentine defender'. The day before, the match between the teams finishing second in the groups was held: Italy, Brazil and Klein.

Suddenly the Last Mundial

Estadio Monumental, Buenos Aires on the afternoon of 24 June 1978. Italy vs Brazil. The great disappointed met. One against the other, in the 'final' they did not deserve: Brazil without having lost a match, Italy having played the best football. And in the middle of it all, Klein, who should have been in the final between Argentina and the Netherlands. The hosts, in the person of Rear Admiral Carlos Alberto Lacoste, known as 'El Gordo', managed to get FIFA (i.e. João Havelange) to replace Klein in the name of possible political connections between the Netherlands and Israel. The real reason, in fact, lay in Klein's inflexible managing of the only match lost by Argentina: the one against Bearzot's Azzurri – the most difficult match of Klein's career.

Both teams had already qualified for the second phase, so it seemed like a formality, although in reality the loser would leave Buenos Aires, the favoured venue for both teams. The intimidating weight of the military junta had so far managed to crush every single refereeing decision, even the most innocent, because this World Cup had to have only one winner: the hosts. And that match was no exception. Victory was not an option but an obligation. Argentina did not want to play elsewhere and, to avoid that, the referees had already helped them against Hungary, with two red cards, and against France, with a penalty. For someone like Klein, the crowd, the generals and the pressure did not scare him. In the first half, under a storm of 70,000 whistles, he had the cheek to deny the hosts a penalty. But on his return after the break, to avoid feeling the weight of such disapproval, he decided to delay his exit and, instead of leading the teams out, he let the Argentina players go ahead of him. With the organisers he pretended not to understand the language. Instead he whispered to the linesmen, 'We're not moving until I see Kempes's head.' The moment the Argentinian shirts came out, the crowd went crazy. Klein's return to the pitch was lost in this hero worship. In the 67th minute the Azzurri scored the winning goal with a masterpiece of action orchestrated by Giancarlo Antognoni and Paolo Rossi, and magnificently finished by Roberto Bettega. They had told Klein to be careful: 'The crowd can kill you!' At that moment he thought, *If I'm right, no one will ever blame me.*

When the whistle blew for the end of the match, the teams lined up to shake Klein's hand. He was now a certainty for the final. Instead, it was his impartiality that would seal the fate separating the righteous from the maligned, giving him a direct pass to the consolation match rather than the final act. And on the pitch of the Monumental in Buenos Aires, on that afternoon of 24 June 1978, Klein could already see six-elevenths of the Spanish Italy (Zoff, Cabrini, Gentile, Scirea, Antognoni and Rossi) and a couple of stars of Santana's Brazil (Oscar and Toninho Cerezo), as well as meeting the faces of Tardelli, Graziani, Zico and Waldir Peres, then extras sitting on their respective benches, later protagonists of the 1982 World Cup. Italy scored through Causio and hit the post four times, but Brazil needed only two shots from distance to take third place in the final of the disappointed.

The Scenario

After the World Cup, in July 1978, the Rizzoli group's general management had a book prepared for internal circulation. It was called *Scenario 1979–1981* and aimed to predict the evolution of Italian society. All the journalists in the group had to comply with these directives. It was a way of telling them how they should run their newspapers. This was a blatant violation of the contract for the category, which provided for complete autonomy of the editorial staff with respect to the administration.

It was in this climate that Carlo Grandini returned to the *Corriere* on 3 September 1979 as sports editor-in-chief and special correspondent; three years later he would follow Italy's journey to the World Cup in Spain. When the Rizzolis had joined the *Corriere*, he had left at Indro Montanelli's invitation to found the sports editorial office of the *Giornale*. One day, while in the editorial office, he was informed of his father's death. Before leaving, he decided to finish the piece he was writing. When he went up to Montanelli's to deal with the last editorial matters, the editor looked at him in amazement.

'But good god, what are you still doing here with your father who just died?'

'I'm leaving soon, I prefer to finish my work first.'

Montanelli laid a hand on his shoulder. 'Now go to Ferrara, to your father's grave. And when you come back, know that you have another one here.'

But Grandini also parted ways with that second father, making way for Alfio Caruso.

The Package

After the World Cup in Argentina, Horst and Nally started working on the World Cup in Spain. The two partners had a double mission. On the one hand, they had to get FIFA to grant them the marketing rights to the World Cup. On the other, they had to find the 36 million Swiss francs that the host country claimed from FIFA.

Havelange's promises forced the extension of World Cup participation to 24 teams but this made the costs of the competition even more prohibitive. Dassler met with Nally in the Congress building in Madrid. He invited him into the bathroom and turned on the water tap. 'The first thing is already settled. For a million dollars we have the contract in our pocket.' Now there remained the 36 million deal for Spain. He would find it by focusing on the rights of the television market. However, advertisements had a new enemy: the remote control. During breaks, viewers could change channel and revenues would drop. But Dassler had a solution: 'We have a sports event that is broadcast worldwide. We show the advertisements directly in the programmes.' In other words, they would be shown during the matches. This was a new idea and needed to be sorted out. By writing the rules, their relationship with the federation became total.

West Nally was awarded the rights to all FIFA and UEFA competitions, including the UEFA European Championship. The Spanish World Cup (the rights to which they bought for 25 billion lire) represented the maturity of their company. They created a four-year package called InterSoccer4 that guaranteed an exclusive sponsor for each commercial category (a new idea – Coca-Cola, for example, became the 'official' drink of the 1982 World Cup), advertising exposure, tickets and VIP access. The model proved to be an immediate success and quickly became the new standard by which sponsorship rights for international sporting events were managed.

Dassler and Nally became the exclusive group that changed the methodologies of sports management, the founding fathers of sports marketing. With them, football was beginning to structure itself, the price of television rights was experiencing a sharp rise for the first time and money was beginning to flow. In a short time every commercial aspect of the big events came under Horst's control through a chain of companies that influenced the destiny of football. With one of them, Rofa Sport Management, he had the right to appoint exclusive sponsors for the World Cup, set the match times, allocate places for the service staff and those for the photographers, and had obtained a guarantee from FIFA that the advertising hoardings he managed would never be covered, even partially or temporarily.

Horst pulled the strings of world football and became the *drahtzieher*, the puppetmaster. His proposal for static advertising in the stadiums and television rights for the Mundial arrived on a table at the Real Comité Organizador on 13 March 1979. Seated around it were Raimundo Saporta, who led the Spanish delegation gathered at FIFA headquarters in Zürich, Manuel Benito, Pablo Porta, Augustín Domínguez and the president of the FIFA Organising Committee, Hermann Neuberger. One month earlier FIFA had already accepted, for 36 million Swiss francs, West Nally's contract, which also included the television rights for the United States and Canada. Three months later (on 20 May 1979) Havelange, for the sum of 30 million Deutsche marks, offered the same company the rights for the commercial exploitation of the World Cup products (mascots, symbols, posters, etc.). For the management of the deal, Saporta proposed a mixed company between West Nally and the Real Comité Organizador.

The First Sponsor

Unfinished fairy tales do not get second chances. At the end of the 1978/79 Italian championship, Paolo Rossi's Real Vicenza were relegated (the player having exploded at the World Cup in Argentina in the meantime, scoring three goals). However, the year brought another surprise: Franco D'Attoma's 'Perugia of miracles'. They completed the Serie A tournament undefeated, finishing second, three points behind AC Milan. The red-and-white president felt he was one step away from glory, so he wanted to bring the Vicenza bomber to Perugia. However, he needed to find a way to lower the salary and to find the money. Players could only change clubs if they were bought outright but D'Attoma invented a new formula – the loan. He made a simple speech to Vicenza's president, Farina: 'With the team in Serie B, a player of this calibre will be devalued. Isn't it better to park him at Perugia for a year?' He proposed 700 million lire. Vicenza, remaining the owner of the player, could take him back at the end of the season. The agreement was there. Having lowered the price, they now needed the money.

Perugia's coffers could not afford such an investment. D'Attoma, together with the managing director, Spartaco Ghini, and the lawyer, Gabriele Brustenghi, asked the Perugia pasta company Ponte for 400 million lire to sponsor the team. But the FIGC objected; the company's logo could not appear on the athletes' shirts as the regulations only allowed the name of the technical sponsor. D'Attoma was not discouraged. He realised that the rules contained in the federal papers lent themselves to double interpretation and resorted to an admirable stratagem to get around them. His wife was the Perugian noblewoman, Leyla Servadio, who, together with her brother Leonardo, set up the Ellesse clothing company in 1959. It was child's play for D'Attoma to set up a knitwear factory with the same name as the pasta factory. Within 48 hours Ponte Sportswear had been born, formally as a simple technical supplier of the jerseys but, in fact, as the first real jersey sponsor of Italian football. At the end of the summer of 1979 Marino Mignini of the Ponte pasta factory and Perugia president Franco D'Attoma presented the new sponsored kit of the red-and-white club for the 1979/80 season.

On 26 August 1979, on the occasion of the Coppa Italia match against Roma, Perugia sported a jersey with a sponsor for the first time in an Italian championship. The operation succeeded in financing the signing of Paolo Rossi. Curiously enough, the same player, already bound by a previous personal advertising agreement in the same agri-food sector (with Polenghi Lombardo), was the only red-and-white player who could not display a sponsor on his shirt. The federation, however, did not tolerate the ploy and fined the Umbrian club. But D'Attoma did not give up and had the name of the pasta factory written on the grass of the stadium and on the nets in two shades of white. No one had ever thought of that. He continued to be fined but the road was now marked out.

The situation was no longer containable. The federation understood that it must adapt. The modern era of football was about to begin. Paradise for Rossi seemed near. A team that was as young and ambitious as he was, aiming to win the championship. Too bad that it all went wrong. Perugia lost their captain Franco Vannini and Rossi scored few goals. The worst, however, was yet to come.

The Fox and the Cat

While Havelange, Horst and Saporta were discussing the fate of the Mundial around fiery tables, a Roman greengrocer was making a decision that, within the space of a few months, would prove crucial for Italian football and for the centre-forward of his national team. He was 30 years old and owned a wholesale shop in Via di Porta Fabbrica 18, a stone's throw from St Peter's. Together with his brother, he sold vegetables to the Vatican cardinals. The business was healthy, his bank account immaculate and his turnover high. His days were tiring; the fruit boxes had swelled his biceps, but also dampened his enthusiasm. His only diversions were betting on horses at the Tor di

Valle racecourse. And football. He devoted all his free time to it. He would rush to training sessions, follow the footballers everywhere, had his photo taken with them and covered the walls of the shop with hundreds of souvenir photos (in one of these, taken during a friendly match in Rome and displayed prominently, he proudly stands next to Pelé).

Not only that, he invited them to his stall, filled their boots with fruit and offered a thousand services. In return he asked only for a small dream: to be recognised, to stand out from everyone else. A hug when they got off the bus, a greeting when he passed them on the street, a privileged entrance to join them in their hangouts. But also access to their changing rooms, their cars, their hotel rooms. He insinuated himself into their lives, capturing their habits, vices and secrets. He also got hold of their words, to distribute them, together with his fruit, the next day at the market. Deluding himself that he too was part of the golden world of football – Massimo Cruciani, the footballers' friend. The first player he met was Franco Cordova, a customer in his shop, who not only made him the supplier of the Leonardo da Vinci hotel, owned by his father-in-law, Alvaro Marchini, but also introduced him to other footballers, such as Giordano, Manfredonia, Wilson, D'Amico, Garlaschelli and Cacciatori, plus the staff of Lazio.

Club president Umberto Lenzini was convinced that the seafood risotto and grilled sea bream eaten at La Lampara restaurant in Via dell'Oca would bring the team good luck, so every Thursday they had a reserved table. The owner's name was Alvaro Trinca, a former fishmonger, known for his ability to make frozen sea bream and swordfish look fresh. He owned stocks and flats, lived on the French Riviera, dressed eccentrically and always wore a pair of smoky white-rimmed glasses. Appearance was everything to him. Because of this, he was considered a person of respect, even by bookmakers. He was one of the few people who could bet up to 100 million lire 'by finger', meaning by voice, without paying a penny, or even by telephone. He had been doing this for three years, since he was approached several times in one week by a group of illegal gamblers. His friends knew that he was a friend of the footballers, that champions such as Giordano and Manfredonia invited him to their wedding. He, on the other hand, knew that around football there was billions of lire swirling around linked to illegal betting. So he was not surprised when he was invited to bet on a football match.

For the first three years he staked little. However, he began to learn the secrets of that world. The bookmakers controlled the game mainly from Genoa, Milan and Turin, the largest number of bets were placed on international cups rather than on the Italian championship and the strongest bets were diverted and 'dumped' across the border, in Switzerland, Austria and England, because that's where the operational centres were.

Trinca and Cruciani became friends. The general markets were their gym. Football was their passion. Since 1977 Cruciani had also been his supplier, so Trinca involved him in betting. They did not always win but their relationship with the bookmakers was excellent and the appointment to collect the winnings or pay the losses was respected by all: the Thursday after the Sunday of the match.

One day in October 1979 the two went to Fiumicino airport to greet the Lazio players leaving for a friendly against Palermo. At the ticket office Wilson approached Cruciani. 'This match counts for nothing, the result is shared. We're agreed to draw. You can bet on it.' And he handed him a phone number, which belonged to a Palermo player, Guido Magherini. When he received the call, the player was not at all surprised. He said, 'It's better to bet a lot of money on the draw because the result is guaranteed.' He then dismissed him with an indication: 'This is a friendly, but we can also play on other Serie A and B matches.' Trinca proposed to Cruciani that they pool their knowledge. 'You convince the players to fix the result of the match in advance, I'll take care of the betting.' Then, looking his friend in the eye, he said, 'Massimo, this time we'll make real money!'

In December, the arrangement took off. Cruciani, the public relations officer, began making quick trips throughout Italy to involve the players. Where he did not appear in person, his telephone book, overflowing with numbers of private homes, training camps and beach houses, facilitated his task. Trinca waited for tips and then moved according to agreement. Fabrizio Esposti, a garbage collector for the municipality of Rome, Cruciani's trusted man, who was also responsible for the budget in the newly founded company, helped him out. The budget was made up of just two items: expenditure (cheques to players) and income (winnings). All the conditions were in place for their idea to become the business of the century: maximum profit with minimum risk. But the betting business had the trajectory of a boomerang and what followed became the winter of their failure.

The cat and the fox immediately started losing. In order to make up for it, they set up martingales, combined bets that link several matches where the winnings of the first count as the stake for the next. But it took nothing to blow their bet, such as a player's change of heart or an unexpected goal. The swansong came on Sunday, 13 January 1980. It was the day of their redemption. Trinca and Cruciani set up a martingale over four matches, three of which were fixed: Lazio's win over Avellino, Juventus's draw against Bologna (agreed, according to them, by the two chairmen, Boniperti and Fabretti), and Genoa's draw against Palermo. In the fourth match, Pescara vs Inter, the only clean one, they bet on the victory of the Nerazzurri. They bet 177 million lire, in addition to the bets in the names of other players. If all went well, the stake was 1.35 billion lire. For them, that meant they could pay off all their debts with the bookmakers. The draws were respected, and so was Inter's victory, but Lazio drew with Avellino, which blew the whole martingale. The debt with the bookmakers thus reached 950 million lire.

Muddy

On 27 December 1979 Rossi was due to play in a friendly match organised by UNICEF, Borussia vs Rest of the World. When at the last moment the match was moved to the next day, a Friday, the centre-forward thought about the championship: on Sunday there was Avellino. So he chose not to go. It was a decision that would change his life. Instead of Germany, Paolo was with the Perugia team in a training camp in Vietri sul Mare on the Amalfi coast. It was raining outside. After dinner he was playing bingo with the team in the hotel lobby when Mauro Della Martira approached him: 'Two friends want to meet you.' Rossi could not say no and got up from the table. This apparently innocuous choice created one of the most dramatic crossroads of his career.

Facing him were Massimo Cruciani and Cesare Bartolucci, a porter at the general markets in Rome.

'Paolo, what are you doing on Sunday?' Cruciani asked him.

'Let's win, or at least try to.'

'What if you draw? Maybe even score two goals?'

Rossi did not like the direction the discussion had taken, and he cut it short: 'Sorry, they're waiting for me over there, Mauro you do it.'

Two days later, on a rain-soaked pitch, the player's unknowing destiny unfolded: he scored after 30 seconds. Avellino equalised, then took the lead. But Rossi scored again to equalise. That innocent brace remained muddy.

A few months later, the Lega Nazionale Professionisti (National Professional League) authorised Perugia to take to the pitch with the advertising brand on the shirt. The sponsor made its debut in Serie A with all the trappings of officialdom. It was 23 March 1980, a day that would change the destiny of football. For much more serious reasons.

The Brazil of Telê Santana

The Brazil of 1982 was born from a combination of factors. On 15 March 1979, João Baptista de Oliveira Figueiredo came to power, the fifth general in a row since the 1964 coup. He inherited the baton from Ernesto Geisel, a president overwhelmed by insurmountable economic problems: foreign debt generated by the Médici government, an international oil crisis and high inflation. Geisel, however, had

THE BRAZIL OF TELÊ SANTANA

begun to espouse an unusual democratic opening that was continued by his successor. Figueiredo abolished censorship, allowed the return of exiled politicians and reintroduced multi-party rule. He also freed football from power interests.

The first step was the dismemberment of the historic Brazilian Sports Confederation controlled by Admiral Heleno de Barros Nunes. Created to overcome the contrasts between the Federação Brasileira de Futebol and the Federação Brasileira de Sports, the Confederação Brasileira de Desportos throughout the 1970s had progressively expanded the league for political purposes: from the initial 20 clubs in 1971, it had gone up to 42 in 1975, 74 in 1978, and 94 in 1979. The multiplication of Brazilian clubs was a consequence of a government policy based on the propaganda use of football. When the Confederação de Desportos was dissolved into the newly formed Confederação Brasileira de Futebol (CBF), the Brazilian Football Federation, Giulite Coutinho was chosen as its president and decided to appoint a popular coach, admired by the fans and respected by the press, to lead the Seleção.

In order to make his choice, he was waiting for the results of the poll being carried out by the Paulist newspaper *O Estado de S. Paulo*, with 218 sports journalists from Brazil, to decree the best coach in the country – 197 voted for the same man: Telê Santana, thanks to the excellent year of his club Palmeiras. On 18 January 1980, Giulite Coutinho officially announced him. The coach, however, was reluctant. His decision did not depend on the 750,000 cruzeiros per month he would receive as he had a company of metallurgical products that brought him 900,000 cruzeiros every month, he was the director of a real estate agency and also a testimonial in the advertisements of Banco Bradesco. He accepted the job when his only condition was set down in black and white: no more ties with club teams. 'Independence will allow me to impose my style without making concessions.'

There were eight principles on which to base this independence: 1) having a permanent coach and fitness trainer; 2) total autonomy in

135

summoning and dispensing with players; 3) organising the calendar, so as to reconcile the interests of the CBF and the federations; 4) personally observing the players who stood out in each state, to give everyone an opportunity; 5) travel around Brazil to maintain direct contact with the players at the training grounds; 6) seeking greater proximity with Brazilian coaches who formed a marginal and uninformed class; 7) demanding time to coach the national team, even if it was only for one match; 8) periodically following the evolution of football in other countries, especially in Europe.

In the history of Brazil, Telê Santana was the first technical commissioner exclusively employed by the federation and at the service of the Seleção. Until then, the coaches who had preceded him, when they came to manage the national team, did not leave the club team they were with, thus provoking inevitable conflicts linked to preferences and envy; and they also remained sensitive to external influences, which generally led them to summon a dozen players from Rio, another dozen from São Paulo and only a couple from Minas Gerais and Rio Grande do Sul, states where football was not as strong, at least politically. These practices had been followed until his predecessor, army captain Cláudio Coutinho, a coach always willing to comply with superior orders, was called upon in 1970 as the national team's fitness trainer before being promoted to technical commissioner. As a coach he imposed his enlightened imprint, moving away from the talent of individual stars and relying on the cohesion of the players. The team did not dazzle, but in Argentina in 1978 they did not lose a match. It was he, however, who would lose his life a few months before the Spanish Mundial, drowning in the waters that caress the beach of Ipanema.

Game of Four

1980 was the year of the European Championships in Italy. Bearzot's national team, fresh from the excellent World Cup in Argentina two years earlier, dreamed of the continental title. In attack they could count on a phenomenal duo formed by Rossi and Giordano, respectively top scorers in Italy in 1978 and 1979. The country dreamed but, for some, football was taking away their sleep. Alvaro Trinca, four months before the start of Euro '80, urgently summoned his brother-in-law Nando Esposti, husband of his sister Laura. 'Let's meet at Massimo's right away, I have to talk to you.'

When they met at Cruciani's, Trinca said, I'm ruined. I bet a billion on the matches and lost it all.' He railed against the players who had not respected the pacts, both on the field, by changing the results, and off it, by not paying the money lost from the bets.

'I'll take you to a lawyer who defends the underworld,' his brother-in-law reassured him. 'He's a good one, he'll tell you what to do.'

Two days later, on 12 February 1980, Trinca and Cruciani were in front of the criminal lawyer Goffredo Giorgi. It was a particular day. A few hours earlier, at the Sapienza University, an armed commando of the Red Brigade assassinated Professor Vittorio Bachelet. Panic spread through the university city. The entire university was under siege by armoured vehicles, and thousands of students were barred entry. Giorgi welcomed his two new clients in a state of shock. It was cold in Rome and the lawyer was wearing a waistcoat and wool jacket over his striped shirt. Trinca and Cruciani cared little about the weather or the umpteenth murdered person. This was now routine. Bachelet was the 11th victim of terrorism since the beginning of the year. Sitting in front of the criminal lawyer, they recounted the whole affair in excited tones and asked to recover only one thing: the money they had lost.

Giorgi was an authority in the legal field but knew little about footballing affairs, so he called on a colleague, Marcello Lorenzani, a Roma partner. The four quickly made their moves. Three days later, Giorgi deposited in a notary's office the evidence given to him by his clients, who had been swindled by 27 footballers (22 of them from Serie A) by not having respected the agreements, and gave an interview to *Il Messaggero*. Cruciani's home phone started to ring repeatedly.

THE MATCH

A week later came the second move. At Lorenzani's suggestion, Giorgi picked up the phone and called the *Corriere dello Sport*, asking them to pass on to him details of who was dealing with the case. His response came from Paolo Biagi, who had been asked by his editor Giorgio Tosatti to investigate the matter. 'If you come to us you will hear everything directly from those concerned.'

The meeting was scheduled for a couple of hours later. Tosatti made only one recommendation to his envoy: 'Listen to everything and say nothing. Then we will talk about it together.' In the meantime, three young men from the Nuclei Armati Rivoluzionari (Armed Revolutionary Nuclei) used an excuse to break into a house on the fourth floor of via Monte Bianco 114, in the Roman quarter of Monte Sacro. Valerio Verbano, who was returning from school, lived there. When he arrived he was shot in the back before the eyes of his parents, a ministerial official who was a member of the Italian Communist Party and a nurse.

In the Lorenzani studio, meanwhile, Biagi listened to Trinca and Cruciani's astonishing revelations. 'The matter is serious. I can't make such an important decision. You have to talk to Tosatti.' So the group went to Piazza Indipendenza and was received by the director of the *Corriere dello Sport*. Tosatti had in his hands the scoop of a lifetime, the one that could change the course of football history. But caution overwhelmed him. The deal was too big and the two men did not convince him. He and his newspaper could risk a libel trial. 'Gentlemen, we are not going to do anything for the moment, but I suggest that you inform the ordinary judiciary and the sports judiciary.'

At 8.30 the next morning Biagi rushed to see his friend Franchi. He could not conceal from him such a big affair that concerned him so closely. The FIGC president, on learning the facts and the names involved, had a jolt. 'I thank you, my friend. I will tell Judge De Biase right away.' But the head of the investigation office, having read the first news of the scandal in the newspapers, had already contacted Giorgi, who replied dryly, 'We are not interested in sports justice. Only the ordinary courts can get his clients' money.' But then he had second thoughts: 'I would only be willing to talk to the president of the Italian Football Federation.'

While De Biase rushed to Franchi, Giorgi ran to Lorenzani. The appointment was set for that same evening in the Via Allegri headquarters at 7.30pm, 13 hours after the meeting with Biagi – Giorgi and Lorenzani on one side, Franchi and De Biase on the other. Defence against attack. In the car parked in front were Trinca and Cruciani.

The first request came from the lawyers: 'Down here are the interested parties. Why don't we let them up?'

Franchi distanced himself. 'No, forget it.'

Giorgi then went on the assault. 'The players have caused our clients to lose a billion, we have evidence galore. What can the Football Association do to help them?'

Franchi smelt the scent of blackmail. The next step would be the judiciary. If the scandal broke, it could become a bombshell for Italy, both the championship and the imminent European Championship. But the president did not bend. 'The Football Association can do nothing.'

Giorgi tried again, suggesting that Franchi could intervene on the presidents of the teams concerned. Franchi hesitated for a moment. 'I can't contact all of them. I will only hear one, he will hear the others. For the time being, just forget it.'

The lawyers took to the streets with a promise that smacked of victory: 'Don't worry, it will all work out.' But Franchi may have misjudged the situation. He called Umberto Lenzini, in the midst of a financial crisis. The Lazio president nipped the initiative in the bud. Manin Carabba, De Biase's right-hand man, also tried. He went to Lorenzani's office with a list of names: 'Let's blow seven heads off at the end of their careers and we'll close the scandal.' But the deal was not done. After a week of silence, the lawyers convinced their clients to present the complaint to the Public Prosecutor's Office. 'You will see that, as soon as it is public, the people concerned will rush to bring us the money. Then you can also withdraw.'

So, on the morning of Saturday, 1 March, Cruciani and Trinca arrived at the Roman court in a black Renault. They quickly climbed the steps with four sheets of paper in their hands. Full of names. Among them were those of Paolo Rossi and Bruno Giordano, players who would make noise and be useful to them. At 1.10pm the lawyer Giorgi presented the bettors' complaint to the Rome Public Prosecutor's Office. Later that afternoon, Cruciani and Trinca returned to the editorial office of the *Corriere dello Sport* and gave Biagi a copy of the papers. Tosatti, however, for prudence, decided not to publish the document. The next day, there were two derbies, Milan vs Inter and Lazio vs Roma. The bombshell must wait.

It exploded on Monday, 3 March. The names of the 27 denounced footballers came out. Four days later the first to end up in handcuffs was Alvaro Trinca, flushed out by the financial police in his house in Via degli Ammiragli 82, in Rome. Five days later Massimo Cruciani gave himself up at the Court of Rome. In front of the magistrates, the two main accusers confirmed names and facts, providing evidence and clues. Judge Ciro Monsurrò nicknamed Cruciani 'the watch', because of the wealth of detail with which he enriched the plot of his story. And the mystery had its twist.

L'étranger

It was 4.45pm on 23 March 1980. The sanctity of the stadium had been desecrated. Police cars entered the athletics track at the Stadio Olimpico in Rome. At the end of the match two officers arrested Della Martira and Zecchini of Perugia for conspiracy to commit aggravated and continued fraud. The two were in tears and begged not to be handcuffed. The officers also handed Rossi a notice from the judicial police inviting him to appear before the magistrates. Pablito remained motionless with the paper in his hand while he observed his companions disappearing into the Alfa 2000 of the Finance Police. Destination: the Roman prison of Regina Coeli, like two criminals.

At the same time, in other Italian stadiums, Bruno Giordano, Ricky Albertosi, Giorgio Morini, Pino Wilson, Massimo Cacciatori, Lionello Manfredonia, Stefano Pellegrini, Guido Magherini, Sergio Girardi and AC Milan president Felice Colombo were arrested. Gianfranco Casarsa, Rossi's team-mate, and Claudio Merlo turned themselves in during the night. The president of Lazio, Umberto Lenzini, collapsed on hearing of the arrests.

When Rossi's name was mentioned, the country was split in two: is he guilty or innocent? The journalist Giorgio Lago asked him face to face: 'Paolo, tell me the truth.' The player's reply was just as direct: 'Believe me Giorgio, I am innocent, I have nothing to do with this story.'

On Wednesday, 14 May 1980 in Milan, in the offices of the football league, the sports trial for clandestine betting began. It began with the AC Milan vs Lazio and Avellino vs Perugia matches. In court, Rossi was calm: 'It was the classic draw accepted by two teams who didn't want to get hurt.' He said he knew nothing about the betting. But the sporting judiciary did not believe his version. His fate was in the hands of a greengrocer. His word against the other's. Not one piece of evidence, one photo, one sheet of paper, one cheque that could incriminate him. Rossi went through the trial as if it was something unreal, as if someone else was in his place. He hardly reacted to the accusations. He impersonated Meursault, the Camusian étranger. Everything was so absurd that he thought, *They can never ban me for such an irrelevant episode.*

The disciplinary commission of the FIGC needed only four days to issue its sentence, which arrived on a Sunday at 10am: AC Milan relegated to Serie B, Avellino and Perugia penalised five points. To Paolo Rossi the judges inflicted a ban of three years. It seemed incredible to him. but he understood that it was all true when he returned home and saw the faces of his parents. Fabio Dean, the tall, burly lawyer who defended him together with Brustenghi, called him: 'Paolo, it was a marked sentence, they wanted to set an example. But we are going ahead, there is the appeal.'

Two months later, in the glass building on the small Via Allegri, Rossi's career was decided. At 9am on Friday, 18 July, the player appeared before the president of the Federal Appeal Commission, the Neapolitan magistrate Alfonso Vigorita. After consulting the defence brief, structured in five points spread over seven pages contesting Cruciani's version of events, and asking for a full acquittal, the judge raised his head and stared at him: 'Pablito, I hold you in high esteem as a footballer. I will tell you that you made me live moments of happiness at the World Cup in Argentina. But we are discussing other matters here. Do you have anything to add?'

Hearing himself called Pablito gave Paolo hope. 'I am innocent, I repeat this to you, certain that I will be believed.' Just 24 hours later, in room 312 of the Hotel Leonardo da Vinci, he learned the verdict. The court was split. Two judges for acquittal, three for guilt. The ban was reduced to two years. Bruno Giordano's was increased to three years. Football had lost its innocence. Bearzot his spearheads. The shadow of the 'totonero' obscured the Italian championship and the imminent European Championship. Franchi felt responsible, seeing in the events the first sign of a moral degradation destined to spread. He resigned. He did not want to express a judgement and he whispered only a few words to the FIGC general secretary Dario Borgogno: 'I will never be federal president again, even if they re-elect me. What happened is also my fault.' Franchi attended the Federal Council without strength and with one last brilliant speech convinced his friends to elect Sordillo. The lawyer received 4,077 votes out of 4,337 voters.

The Mundialito

With the Geisel-Nunes-Coutinho era over, the new president and the new Brazilian technical commissioner drew up a plan together to make 1980 a running-in year to gradually tackle the Copa de Oro de Campeones Mundiales, better known as the Mundialito, the elimination rounds for the World Cup and the eagerly awaited

THE MUNDIALITO

Mundial in Spain. The new coach only had a handful of matches before the event, which, in the intentions of the military junta in power in Uruguay after the 1973 coup d'état, was to relaunch the image of the Latin American country and its coup government on the international stage, thus breaking its political isolation. It included the national teams of Argentina, Brazil, West Germany, Italy (despite the public denunciation of the Uruguayan dictatorship signed by 41 Serie A players) and the Netherlands (in place of England, who did not want to participate in a propaganda tournament invented by a coup d'état).

The Mundialito became a television event destined for record ratings, the stage where Santana's team could show all its spectacle. A Panamanian company stole the TV rights from Eurovision and within 24 hours sold them to Canale 5 for the staggering sum of $900,000. For the newly established private Italian broadcaster, this was a big deal. To broadcast in Europe, however, it needed a satellite, managed by Telespazio, owned by RAI. The impasse was only resolved after feverish negotiations with state television, which granted Canale 5 the satellite in exchange for live broadcasts of Italy's matches. But for Silvio Berlusconi, the Mundialito was in any case the first major sporting event broadcast by his network. The matches, broadcast live in Lombardy and deferred in other Italian regions, reached record viewing figures for a private TV station. Eight million Italian viewers got to know the wonders of Telê Santana's Brazil. They first drew with Argentina, in a match that seemed to be decisive, and then beat West Germany. The final was the one that was hoped for: Uruguay against Brazil. The Celeste was a young team, Brazil a collection of soloists: Cerezo, Éder, Sócrates, Oscar, Júnior and Batista were already certainties, while Zico unfortunately stayed in Rio with an injury. Brazil had the match in hand but the Uruguayans responded on the counter-attack. It ended as it should have, with the hosts winning 2-1. But it was Brazil that penetrated the TV screens.

Shortly afterwards, Brazil arrived in Europe for a tour of friendlies with potential World Cup opponents. It began with England, in the temple of Wembley, where Zico gave Brazil their first-ever victory on English soil. Three days later it was France's turn: at the Parc des Princes, where the Seleção won 3-1. Four days later it was the turn of West Germany, the reigning European champions: the music remained the same, with Santana's team winning 2-1. A triumph. Back home, it was Spain, the future World Cup hosts, 1-0. The whole of Europe bowed to Brazil. And Italy? Not in the plans. It was a small and unresolved team, discredited by the betting scandal.

One Kingdom is Not Enough

If Havelange was the king of football, Dassler was its emperor. One kingdom was not enough for him. He wanted the whole sport. Football was just one of the federations of the IOC. His goal *was* the IOC. His showcase was the Olympics, so, to achieve his aims, he cultivated relationships with all those involved on a global level and trained his staff to do the same. He had public relations managers in all countries where Adidas was present. He constantly monitored local sports policies, looked for new opportunities, big contracts or simply new friends. He had an encyclopaedic archive of all kinds of information on athletes, coaches, managers and officials. For each name he opened a file. Tastes, dishes, vices, weaknesses and shoe size. He noted everything.

But he was also spied on. The Stasi followed his steps and those of his men. The best source was the unofficial collaborator Karl-Heinz Wehr, alias 'Gaviota'. For 20 years, the East Berlin executive informed the Stasi in detail about the intrigues of Dassler's 'lobbyist' group, to which he had been admitted. Dassler knew this and he became a victim of the paranoia he himself had generated. He also placed microphones in the two hotels owned by Adidas: the Auberge in Landersheim and the Sporthotel in Herzogenaurach. He travelled through Eastern Europe only if he had a telephone intercept detector with which he searched for hidden microphones in hotel rooms before unpacking. Dassler also taught his trusted people to use the detector.

He organised training courses for agents, during which he advised his men to keep false documents in leather briefcases in order to confuse policemen, secret services or thieves.

A few years earlier, in 1972 in Munich, an employee of his, Christian Jannette, head of protocol of the German Olympic Games, met his counterpart and IOC Executive Board member Juan Antonio Samaranch Torelló. Two years later, Samaranch told him, 'I would like to meet Mr Adidas.' The ambassador relayed the message. Dassler knew the end of the story and arranged a meeting. Samaranch made the ritual pilgrimage to Landersheim, where he played tennis with Horst. He was affable, courteous, helpful. For Dassler, he was the ideal candidate for the IOC summit.

The Spaniard had a lot in common with Havelange. Both sportsmen, favoured by wealthy families as youngsters and military dictatorships as adults. Known 'for how good he is at keeping quiet', Samaranch, a year after joining the IOC, was appointed National Delegate for Physical Education and Sport by Francisco Franco in 1967, with whom he forged a strong professional bond and friendship. He remained in office until 1971, then between 1973 and 1977 he was president of the Barcelona Provincial Council. After Franco's death, the people dismissed him. 'Samaranch, go away!' the furious people shouted at him in front of his office. He escaped through a side door protected by security guards and went as ambassador to Moscow, where the 1980 Olympic Games were being celebrated. There he received Jannette, Dassler's assistant, 72 times in five years. Thanks to Horst, Samaranch was elected president of the IOC in 1980. Gratitude in business can be rare and the new king of sport reciprocated by granting the Adidas boss the management of Olympic marketing for more than a decade.

In 1980 in Moscow, when Juan Antonio Samaranch, a Catalan from Barcelona, professor of economics, former ambassador to the USSR became president of the IOC, sport was not a universal religion, recognised and worshipped everywhere, but a small faith in difficulty. Fractured by the boycott, full of divisions, its coffers strained. Samaranch changed everything: style, manners, costs. His predecessor, Lord Killanin, an Irishman from Eton and Cambridge colleges, a former boxer, a knight, a former journalist, a volunteer in the Normandy landings, only went to Lausanne a few times a year because he claimed that the price of hotels was 'exorbitant'. Samaranch increased the number of members of the Olympic Committee, signed billion-dollar contracts, democratised the system, widened the pyramid of command, promoted local Olympic committees, managed television rights and opened up to multinationals. The IOC became the UN of sport. And Samaranch its *deus ex machina*. A year after his coronation, on 29 September 1981, at the Baden-Baden congress, he finally opened the way for professional athletes to participate in the Olympics: 'The IOC cannot run the risk of the best athletes participating in world championships organised by international federations and finding the door to the Games closed.'

To make his web more effective, Dassler, who could already count on the head of football and that of Olympic sports, wanted his own man in the most important federation – athletics. The International Amateur Athletic Federation (IAAF) was currently deciding whether to confirm its president. Horst had a contract with the IAAF until 1983. Since 1976, the head of the IAAF had been an esteemed Dutchman, Adriaan Paulen, known for his independent attitude and therefore considered unlikely to protect the interests of the German federation. His re-election was a foregone conclusion. For Horst, however, the right man was the Italian Primo Nebiolo, for whom he would use all his influence and ability to steer decisions in order to get what he wanted. So, in 1981, Nebiolo was elected president of the IAAF and Dassler was awarded marketing contracts for another 20 years.

Ambiguous but revolutionary, megalomaniac but concrete, storyteller but modern, Nebiolo changed sport. In 1982 the organisation began paying athletes for their appearances in competitions and openly accepted sponsorships. He is accused of having turned an entire world upside down, of having introduced merchants into a sacred temple, of having transformed a pure discipline into a circus. It is true, but with him, athletics was leaving the suburban fields to make its triumphant entry into the big world. He also created an Olympic Solidarity Commission, with the aim of managing the proceeds of television rights by redirecting them to athletes from poorer nations, to ensure their presence at the Games. It was a system that worked and was therefore also used by his friend Samaranch in the IOC. Nebiolo hammered the newspapers with information about the extraordinariness of the events and the reports finally moved from short articles to big titles. The discipline he represented was becoming a modern spectacle, with no downtime, marked by exploits. A sport that highlighted the efforts of its people.

The Trial

The verdict for Rossi was a ban until 29 April 1982. Two very long years. It seemed impossible to him that they could have convicted him for a few words exchanged while he was playing bingo. And if those goals scored at Avellino had been the result of a fixed match, why had none of the opposing defenders been prosecuted? Two words, two goals, two years. Flimsy evidence, imaginary clues leading to a concrete sentence and a real conviction. Rossi in one fell swoop lost his credibility, his career and the European Championship in Italy. But the World Cup in Spain was also compromised as it was very unlikely that he would be able to arrive in an acceptable physical condition at the appointment with the national team a few weeks after his return. With the start of the new championship, in fact, a long period of inactivity began for him. He returned to Vicenza, the owners of his contract, and trained with the team that had sadly sunk to Serie B. A few exercises with his former team-mates, the midweek match with the reserves, but then on Sunday at home or in the stands.

At the criminal trial, Rossi's future was in the hands of Cesare Bartolucci, the porter at the general market, Cruciani's friend and an eyewitness to the meetings between the greengrocer and the players. After Cruciani and Trinca's discordant versions, it was Bartolucci's turn to give his account on the morning of 13 November, and his words could prove decisive for the former Perugia centre-forward, on whose head there were infamous but at the same time contradictory accusations. If Bartolucci confirmed Cruciani's version, there was no escape for Rossi. If not, Rossi would face a certain acquittal, because the 'castle' would fall.

'What I said in Milan,' Bartolucci declared, 'no longer counts. I was irritated by the heavy provocations of Rossi's lawyers, who almost insulted me. Here, in court, I will tell the whole truth, as I did in the preliminary investigation. It is true that I introduced Cruciani to Della Martira and accompanied him to Vietri sul Mare, but I never heard that Rossi should have taken money and he never said he would have scored two goals. Cruciani then never spoke of a match in my presence.'

Rossi, wrapped in a brown leather jacket, listened attentively to the interrogation. These were the worst moments of his trial. At the end of the deposition, he let out a long sigh that relieved months of tension. 'Bartolucci said some true things. I am pleased that he has acknowledged that he told some lies. The truth is coming out.' And then: 'Excuse me, I'll stop here, I don't want to disrespect the judges, and then every sentence of mine can be misinterpreted. It would also be incautious and offensive to come out of court and display triumphalism.' But Paolo started to believe in the acquittal. After more than six months of trial and ten hours in the council chamber, the sentence came. The judges of the fifth section of the criminal court of Rome acquitted Rossi and the other players on trial because of lack of factual evidence. The centre-forward rejoiced: 'I had always said I was innocent and now you have to believe me. I'll soon be back playing, I'll even train at Christmas. The nightmare is over.'

In reality, for the sporting justice system, the non-punishment sanctioned by the judiciary did not mean innocence. There was still a year and a half of the ban to be served.

Even for Giordano that was a mocking victory: 'My conscience is clear, my bitterness enormous. I didn't take any money and I didn't do anything wrong, but Paolo Rossi and I are the most important players in Italy and it was convenient to mention our names. Unfortunately, the judges decided to believe those who accused us, even in the absence of evidence. So even I now find myself standing still or only playing amateur matches with friends. It's a very high price to pay because the federal disqualification has prevented me from playing a European Championship at home and above all it will prevent me from taking part in the 1982 World Cup.'

Boniperti followed the Pablito affair closely. He had never digested Farina's 'disrespect' and when he returned to the office in March 1981 he found the Veneto president much more willing, ready to sell the player to make up the deficit of his club. Juventus paid Farina's fee with interest and Pablito returned to wear the Bianconeri shirt. The new signing did not hesitate and immediately attacked the sporting justice: 'I want to think that Juventus thinks I'm innocent, but if it happened again, I wouldn't appear before the sporting judges. The trial was a joke. It's terrible to be judged by people like that, to be accused of crimes that were never committed, to be condemned without the slightest proof. And who will erase this stain now?'

The List

The list of members of the P2 Lodge was found on 17 March 1981 during the search of Licio Gelli's villa in Castiglion Fibocchi, not far from Arezzo, as part of the investigation into the alleged kidnapping of Michele Sindona. The Presidency of the Council of Ministers decided to make it public two months later, on 20 May 1981. One year before the Mundial.

The list of the 963 members appeared in all the newspapers, also in the *Corriere*, but in a grey and illegible page with the names in succession without the headings. Among the affiliates were 44 parliamentarians, two ministers, a party secretary, 41 generals (including Carabinieri, Guardia di Finanza, Army and Air Force) and eight admirals, in addition to magistrates and public officials, journalists and entrepreneurs. The institutional figures included politicians who held or had held strategic positions, while the high finance sector was almost fully represented.

Naturally, journalism was also affected by the scandal. The list included all the top managers of Rizzoli and its satellites: Angelo Rizzoli (president of Rizzoli-Corriere della Sera), Bruno Tassan Din (general director of Rizzoli Editore), Franco Di Bella (director of *Corriere della Sera*), Paolo Mosca (director of *Domenica del Corriere*), Roberto Ciuni (director of the newspapers *Il Mattino*, *Il Giornale di Sicilia* and *La Nazione*), Maurizio Costanzo (director of *'Occhio*), Stefano de Andreis (founder of the press agency Il Velino), Massimo Donelli (director of *Epoca*), Giampiero Orsello (vice-president of RAI), Giampaolo Cresci (vice-director general of RAI and director of *Tempo*), Giuseppe Pieri (vice-director of RAI), Luigi Nebiolo (director of TG1), Mario Tedeschi (director of *Borghese* and senator for two terms of the Italian Social Movement), Carmine (Mino) Pecorelli (murdered in 1979) and Roberto Gervaso. The repercussions on Rizzoli-Corriere della Sera were enormous. The top management was arrested (Angelone Rizzoli was held criminally responsible, as were Calvi and Tassan Din), *L'Occhio*, the *Corriere d'Informazione*, the weekly supplements, the television network were closed down and *Il Piccolo*, *L'Alto Adige* and *Il Lavoro* were sold. The storm involved every sector of the country. Starting with the institutional one.

Socratic Democracy

A year after the Mundial in Spain, internal electoral rules forced Vicente Matheus, who had been president of Corinthians for a decade, not to stand again. In order to remain at the top, he proposed a puppet in his place, the timid Waldemar Pires, convinced that he could continue to exercise power in the role of vice-president. Once Pires had been elected, Matheus remained the de facto boss. He

SOCRATIC DEMOCRACY

did not introduce him to the players, he did not let him have the presidency room, he did not allow him to take decisions for the team.

Corinthians were in disarray. Sócrates' performances were fluctuating, coach Brandão had left the scene and the team, which found itself coached by fitness trainer Julinho, was playing one of the worst championships in its history. In order to shift the blame for relegation on to Pires, Matheus ran away to Europe. It was a false step. The team did not disintegrate during his absence. On the contrary, it regenerated. Pires took it in hand and rebuilt it in record time. The majority of the players earned below their needs and he promised salary increases.

The number of purchases, disposals, renewals and loans reached the ears of Matheus, who returned to the command post, but found it occupied. Surprising everyone, the timid and submissive Pires decided to stay in his seat: 'You have to have courage and break with the past.' Matheus laughed but, when he realised he had lost control of his puppet, the hilarity turned to anger: 'Beware Waldemar. I created you, I will destroy you.'

Pires remained calm: 'The country is changing, there is no more room for personal management.'

It was the same thought that Sócrates had in his head. He tried to convey it to his companions: 'What do we want to change? What do we want to decide on?'

The first topic was the retreat. Then came the training times. The salary. And then everything else. It almost seemed like a game, but it was happening. Pires became aware of his role. Without even realising it, he created the first spark of a revolution. Instead of directing, he allowed people to participate. Everyone. The first thing he did was to appoint a sociologist as sports director. His name was Adilson Monteiro Alves and he had no football experience. He offered only one guarantee: 'I promise you new ideas, ideas of change.'

When Alves introduced himself to the boys in the gymnasium at Parque São Jorge, he warned that it would be a ten-minute chat. 'I just want to tell you one thing: I don't understand much about football and I don't know how to do it yet. But I know for sure that this is not the way to do it. And I think you will have to tell me where to start, because only you know what needs to be changed. That's why I came here today to tell you that I'm here to listen.'

Sócrates could not believe his ears. They were the words he had been waiting to hear all his life. The quick presentation turned into an assembly. Alves and the players remained in the room for six hours. Without knowing it, Alves had built the foundations of a project that would be revolutionary.

The first to take the floor was Sócrates himself. 'We players should no longer be excluded from the club's decisions.' Alves looked at him and agreed. 'We have thousands of fans out there crushed by 15 years of dictatorship, let's make our voices heard.'

'How?' whispered someone.

'Voting,' intervened Sócrates, as if he had always had that word in his mouth. Six letters that weighed like lead. In Brazil no one had the right to vote. 'We are the ones who go on the field, we are the ones who lose or we win, we make money for the club. We have to talk. We must vote. We implement what hasn't happened in our country for almost 20 years. We decide in a direct way.'

Sócrates demanded that everyone should be involved in the moves of society, from first to last: 'The time for silence is over.' Thus began a small revolution. Every proposal, whether it came from the players, the technicians or the club managers, was discussed by everyone. In the end, a vote was taken and the majority decided. The coach set the number of training hours but it was Sócrates, together with the other players, who proposed the time and location. Same with the match prizes. The coach was not the only one who set them and, another revolution, they were divided equally between all players, both starters and reserves. Sócrates, together with his team-mate Casagrande, known as Casão, started an incredible self-management of the club. Alongside them were Wladimir, Zenon, Biro-Biro, Juninho, Alfinete and all the others.

SOCRATIC DEMOCRACY

In Brazil, there was a footballers' union that had the task of protecting its members, but for the 'heel of God' what his members lacked was the consciousness of being workers like everyone else. For him, running after a ball was like being a worker in a factory: 'We are paid to produce a good game and we work every day for our physical preparation. There is only one difference. The player is also an artist. For him, football is a spectacle.' But he turned his nose up at the performances of the retired Pelé, who, like Buffalo Bill, put on a show in American social circles. Sócrates detested those who lived off their image and swore that he would never be able to play the puppet.

In the Brazil of dictatorship, the Corinthians team was transformed into a small democratic republic. Thanks to one of those rare coincidences in history, people with different heads but pointing in the same direction suddenly gathered in the same place. Not everything happens by chance. The architects of this change were enlightened people. Alves, in order to carry out his project, armour-plated the players: only technicians and doctors were allowed to enter the dressing room. No interference from journalists or *cartolas*, top hats: the managers. Even the executive car park was removed. Alves knew he was risking it but it was only the beginning.

Pires called the coach Mário Travaglini to the Parque São Jorge. The new coach found good but discouraged players. The first decision was drastic: 'Only those who believe in it remain.' He also proposed that the team should choose who started. And the group decided. Travaglini warned: 'Every cut is dramatic, but there will be no black list. The players will be treated as human beings and the club will take care of their redistribution to other teams.' The squad was halved and Travaglini brought forward 18 men to whom he conveyed confidence: 'You go out there and do your part. If you make mistakes, don't worry. I trust you.' Plus a new concept: the 'Carousel'. Travaglini invented a rhombus that must rotate without stopping, like a pinwheel, in midfield. But the most important lesson he passed on to the players was another: 'Freedom is an illusion if it is not accompanied by responsibility. Otherwise it is anarchy. And voting becomes the tool to demonstrate this difference.'

In interviews, players started talking about equality, participation, freedom. A handful of them pulled out, limiting themselves to doing their duty only on the field. This too was a sign of democracy. But morale rose and they started to play and to win. A footballer could sink in his qualities or blossom. The new internal democracy allowed the players to explode, losing their innermost fears of the self. Alves's boys united and started to become strong. Each one complemented the other and there was the joy of playing football; 25 matches without a defeat. However, it was not enough to reverse the bad start to the season. The placement in the Paulista state championship compromised the access to the Serie A of the following Campeonato Brasileiro, popularly known as Brasileirão. Thus, at the end of 1981, Corinthians were facing relegation. But nobody was discouraged, Sócrates most of all. He turned down a million-dollar contract with Barcelona at the beginning of 1982. It was a strong signal.

Travaglini started experimenting with the youth team. The start of the championship was good and four wins in a row allowed Corinthians to return to Serie A. With Magrão, Casão, Biro-Biro and Zenon, Corinthians had the best attacking core ever seen. An era of victories began. But Sócrates spoke more about democracy than his goals. Journalists wondered whether it made sense to give the players the right to vote. He swept away any doubts: 'It has always worked, ever since Athens, in ancient Greece.' And if someone whose name is Sócrates says so, you have to believe him.

The Return

It was the afternoon of 12 November 1981, Thursday, the eve of Italy vs Greece, the second-last qualification match for Spain. The Azzurri were training on the pitch of the old Combi in Turin. Bearzot followed them with unusual detachment. His attention turned increasingly to the adjacent pitch, where Juventus were playing with the Primavera team. Once the session was over, the coach pretended to leave but, once he was sure that the reporters had left, he returned. He had a valid reason. Paolo Rossi was on the pitch.

Bearzot had not seen him for a long time. He had put on weight. He had been out for over a year and a half, with six months' ban left to serve. At the end of the match, Bearzot walked up to him. They were both embarrassed. The Old Man put his hands on Paolo's hips: 'They look like those of a Norman broodmare.' Rossi sketched a smile. He understood that the coach was waiting for him. 'From today I have a good reason to bring them down,' Rossi replied.

Bearzot was convinced of Rossi's innocence but his role imposed on him the respect for a sentence and a 'federal' detachment. During the winter, even before addressing the issue in technical terms, he questioned the moral problem. The World Cup is the ultimate competition for a professional and Rossi, once he had paid his debt, would be in good standing. Once the ban was over, he would take him to Spain.

When the player returned to life he was a different man. Pale and withdrawn. The months of absence lay heavy: two lost years that he could not erase. Recently married, he turned a quarter of a century old in September. He no longer felt like a boy but needed to live his life. He continued to do charity work. A counsellor for a foundation, he appeared on Mike Bongiorno's TV quiz show *Encore*, donating his winnings to children with heart disease in Vicenza. He was disappointed by the people and the journalists and did not expect such nastiness. 'Paolo is very sensitive and generous,' explained his wife Simonetta to Antonio Corbo. 'He gave a lot, he didn't say no to anyone, neglecting his loved ones. He expected more affection, perhaps.' That is why he closed himself off. But he wanted above all the Azzurri jersey. 'Because the ball,' said the player, 'is a love, and because only the national team can help me.'

On 2 May 1982, exactly one month before Italy's departure for the Mundial, in Udine, Rossi took the pitch for the first time. Brera in *La Repubblica* welcomed him like a son: 'Paolo did not return pure because he was never contaminated, he remained a victim of human respect.' After 49 minutes he scored. Pablito was back. A few days later, the call-up for Spain arrived. Despite only making three appearances in the league, Rossi was called up for the national team. Pruzzo stayed at home and Bearzot called up Selvaggi, Cagliari's centre-forward, in his place.

'Coach, if I wanted to come to the World Cup, I would even bring my suitcases,' said Selvaggi.

'No need, just leave your boots at home.'

The idea was clear: protect Rossi. The technical commissioner knew well that Paolo's condition was precarious. He needed to play to regain his form but with the top scorer breathing down his neck it would not be possible. So, instead, he wanted to keep him on the pitch to the bitter end. The harsh criticism was not long in coming but this was the only way to protect Rossi, taking all the responsibility. Bearzot knew that there are no more matches available. Rossi could only regain his form during the Mundial. An enormous risk that no coach would normally take.

The Forbidden Place

In an effort to help indebted Brazilian teams and players who had been out of work for months, the National Sports Council ratified a measure liberalising team shirts for advertising purposes. While other clubs were coming to terms with the potential new revenue that would come in, Adilson Monteiro Alves was going in the opposite direction. The fans must be involved in this revolution. They had the right to know that in Corinthians the vote of a warehouse manager was as valuable as that of the president. So, to fill that space on the jersey, he was not looking for a company but for a man. This man was a Corinthian, 30 years old, with a bizarre name and descending from Italians from Liguria. His name was Washington Olivetto.

As a young man on his way to college in his 1969 Volkswagen Karmann Ghia, Olivetto got a puncture in front of an advertising agency. Instead of asking for help, he asked for a job, with a slogan: 'I'm here because of a flat tyre. But this is a great opportunity for you. Because a tyre doesn't get a flat twice on the same road.' The strategy worked and it was the beginning of a brilliant career, which now brought him in front of the sporting director of the team of his heart: 'I want you to help us with your findings. A lot of things are changing and with your ideas we can get them to the people.'

Olivetto accepted. He did not want any money and had only one condition: 'Nobody should benefit from this handshake, only Corinthians and its people.' Then he started to involve his network: TV presenters, singers, radio presenters, women, fans, opponents of the regime. The new revolutionary decision-making processes within the club become a topic of discussion. Corinthians ceased to be a marginal team and became a headliner, a brand, the fashion club. To talk about this new form of decision-making, the team was invited to the TUCA, the theatre of the Pontifícia Universidade Católica de São Paulo, which used to be the heart of the country's democratic opposition. Participants included Alves, Sócrates, Wladimir and Washington Olivetto. The moderator was Juca Kfouri, the young director of *Placar* sports magazine – curly hair, informal T-shirt, smiling face, a past difficult to forget.

Under the Médici government, José Carlos Kfouri was arrested in São Paulo on 7 September 1971. He was 20 years old. The car of one of his friends, Eduardo Ralston, had been found full of leaflets considered subversive. Together with Ralston and another friend, Fabio Iunesco, Kfouri and his wife Susanna were also picked up. They were handed over to the dreaded DOI-CODI (Department of Information Operations – Center for Internal Defense Operations) in via Tutoia, from which they nearly failed to come out alive. The branch of hell. The military undressed Eduardo and hung him from the torture pole. Kfouri was in the room next door. His friend's desperate cries filled his ears. When a soldier threatened his wife,

THE MATCH

Kfouri smacked his hand on the table: 'Sir, this is my wife, I demand that you treat her with respect.' He could say no more. A fist knocked him out. It was only the beginning but he was saved.

He was now 32 years old and already an established journalist. To better recount the incredible story of Corinthians, Kfouri resorted to an analogy, stealing a phrase from Millôr Fernandes: 'Falling into a Corinthian democracy.' Washington Olivetto shook himself. He grabbed the last two words, pulled his notebook out of his pocket and hurriedly scribbled them on to the paper. If he was to sell the country on their change, he needed not a slogan but a battle cry. And in that moment he thought he had found it. Corinthian Democracy was the label they needed to push the product. And democracy was starting to be talked about everywhere.

Sócrates became the catalyst of the new verb. In the spring of 1982, he wrapped his hair in a bandana and recounted the most singular, courageous and fascinating experiment in the history of world football. At first, part of the press followed him, then the crowd. His 200th goal was worth the victory in the first leg of the Brasileirão quarter-final. At the end of the match, journalists surrounded him. 'The government doesn't want free speech and we do. It doesn't want the citizens to decide directly and we do. Write it down.' The reporters knew that Sócrates tore the sports pages out of his comrades' newspapers. 'In this country everyone understands about football but no one understands about politics. If we keep talking only about football people will continue to neglect everything else. Ignorance is oppression. And football is a means to maintain it. Only with more information can we break this cycle.' It seemed like suicide but, incredibly, Mário Travaglini's Timão won the Brasileirão semi-final, while the club's budget, wisely managed by the players, reached an unexpected surplus.

With only a few days to go before the World Cup, the question of players' rights had become a national issue. Even Zico went to meet Wladimir to establish a common strategy. Brazil had the impression that it was one step away from regaining the right to vote for the President of the Republic. In the streets the first yearnings for freedom had begun to be felt and one had the impression of walking in a forbidden place. The Corinthian Democracy was no longer just football. It had become a wonderful and healthy interference, on a social and behavioural level. The first slap in the face of a Brazil inebriated by too many years of dictatorship. The other teams may be winning more but they were not doing anything for the country. Creating a team with money was easy but there were some things money could not do.

The conservative right-wing press was attacking them by all means, using every pretext. Even false ones. Until one morning the umpteenth poisoned article about the new form of management broke something. The Corinthians answering machine was flooded with messages of solidarity. Students, fans, even journalists. They wanted to give an answer to those who were trying to boycott the Corinthian Democracy. They even called opposing footballers, telling them they had also introduced the vote. And they thanked them. It was a delicate moment, the beginning of a crystal dream that nothing was able to shatter.

Monteiro Alves stood up for his boys: 'The players are not children, they know what decisions to take.' But he saw with his own eyes what pressure they were under. And he understood that they needed support. It was May 1982 and Brazil were between two championships, the national and the state. The Mundial was just around the corner. Alves telephoned the pop star of Brazilian psychotherapy, a columnist for the *Fohla de S. Paulo*, Flávio Gikovate: 'Nobody uses psychology in football, we would like to. The boys are going through a difficult time, they need support. And we need someone who has our ideas.' Gikovate was flattered but stalled, reserving his response until after the World Cup in Spain, although not before offering some advice: 'You have to make sure that the World Cup does not relegate you to second place.' Alves smiled: 'If Sócrates plays the way he does, the effect will be the opposite. A whole revolution is now weighing on his role.'

A Ship in a Storm

Overwhelmed by a double collapse caused by the P2 scandal and the economic disarray, and now reduced to a pile of rubble, the *Corriere della Sera* was facing its first dramatic year of reconstruction. The scandal created an earthquake that also involved Italian politics. The resignation of Prime Minister Forlani led Pertini to take a crucial decision. To deal with the crisis, he entrusted the job to Spadolini, the first non-Democrat to lead a government in the history of the Republic. Also at Pertini's instigation, Alberto Cavallari was called to direct the *Corriere*. To convince him, he went so far as to encourage him like a father: 'Only you can remove the mud and prevent failure. If you don't accept you are a coward.' So, a year before the Mundial, Cavallari took command of a piece of Italian democracy. To rebuild it.

While his correspondents were in Barcelona to cover Italy vs Brazil, he was waging his desperate battle, with the hostility of everyone: competitors interested in causing the *Corriere* to die in order to divide up its copies; parties eager to subject him to their power; creditors focused only on suffocating it. With an editorial staff torn apart by endless infighting, two owners in prison, a third found hanged under a bridge, collaborators fleeing, ink and paper running out, the new editor began to steer his ship out of the storm.

Until then, he had had an overwhelming career as a special correspondent (culminating in the first interview with a pope, Paul VI). His memory was full of history, his eyes saturated with events, his drawers full of reportage. But perhaps he was creating his masterpiece right now.

The Call of Destiny

The 'moral issue', which Pertini, Spadolini and Cavallari considered to be the main Italian problem, was mocked as a senile urge. And yet it was precisely in the name of this issue that Cavallari left his Paris residence to enter Via Solferino. He faced the task with determination but in total solitude. He already knew it would be so. But the *Corriere* had been his newspaper during the good years, so he could not refuse the commitment in the darker ones. However, he did not arrive until after the newspaper lost one of its key players. Nine days before Cavallari's appointment, Enzo Biagi, declaring that he was not willing to work in a newspaper controlled by Freemasonry, had left *La Repubblica*. So, in view of the World Cup, the new editor decided to acquire a name of the same weight, send it to Spain and make it say what was on its mind. Without brakes, limits or rules.

The *Corriere* crew at Sarriá was joined by an exceptional companion: writer Mario Soldati, one of the few intellectuals willing to believe in the impossible. After a legendary career divided between novels, films, reportage and television programmes, he made his debut as a special correspondent at the age of 76. Cavallari came to him with his proposal after adding up three considerations: Soldati loves football; Soldati has never seen Spain; Soldati always pursues the unknown. Incredible as it was, this man who had lived a thousand lives and in a thousand places had never set foot on Iberian soil. And to think that at the age of 28 he had touched it.

In 1934, being in Lourdes for a report to be published in the *Gazzetta Padana*, Soldati proposed a series of Spanish correspondence to *Lavoro* in Genoa. It seemed to be agreed but a telegram from the director Nello Quilici reached him: 'We only recognise your French per diem. We cannot pay you for the articles.' Finding himself short of money, Soldati could not cross the Pyrenees and renounced Spain. He tried a second time. For the love of a blonde girl. She was waiting for him in Zaragoza but there was Franco and the civil war. Soldati could not reach her and lost her. The regret haunted him all his life. The 'invitation of destiny' arrived almost half a century later. The writer from Piedmont, followed by the artist Antonio De Rosa, thus joined the patrol of Milanese chroniclers. Soldati set off on his adventure with shrewd enthusiasm, the eternal cigar in his mouth and a fragment of Heraclitus as a talisman: 'He who does not expect the unexpected will not discover the truth.' For him, immersing himself in this 'cosmopolitan shambles' was an 'irresistible, explosive return to youth'.

The Mundial

The Brancazot army grew up in the image and likeness of its bony leader whose shady, uninspired, monotonous game, stuck in outdated tactics, materialises characters that are not ours and do not belong to us because they belong to Bearzot, who for just ten kilometres was not born on the other side, in Yugoslavia.

Gianni Melidoni, *Il Messaggero*

The Spain '82 Affair

There is only one man whose job it is to turn the party into a business. That's Saporta. They say that where he puts his hand, money gushes out. And that he has managed to sell the air of the Bernabéu stadium, an advertising space above the catwalk. He offered it for 700 million pesetas, first to Coca-Cola, who refused, then to Pepsi. When he was turned down for the second time, he went back to Coca-Cola: 'If you give us half, we won't give it to the competitor.' Gone. Same stratagem with Pepsi. Result: the 700 million arrived anyway, but by selling nothing. Not to mention that the space was then bought by another company. Faced with the first doubts about the numbers of the World Cup, he flaunted confidence: 'All the expenses have already been covered; from now on, every income will be an asset for the Spanish treasury.'

When he was entrusted with the organisation of the World Cup he accepted only on two conditions: appointment by royal decree, so as to avoid government interference, and no remuneration. The Real Comité Organizador de la Copa Mundial de Fútbol is a gigantic bandwagon that holds the eight faces of España 82: laws, finance, transport, security, relations, calendar, facilities and communication. Both the relevant ministries and the main private companies, such as Iberia, Aviaco, Telefónica, Renfe and RTVE, collaborate with the Real Comité. Officially, Saporta is not a politician but he has always been on the side of power, yesterday with the Francoists and today with the moderates. Yet, for the tax authorities he is a simple banker. When Gianfranco Civolani, correspondent of the *Guerin Sportivo*, went to Madrid to investigate, Saporta looked at him with horror: 'You are wrong, I work for the Mundial free of charge because I am a man of sport and because the king has entrusted me with this task.' He invited the sceptics to visit him in Doctor Fleming Street, number 34, the headquarters of the Banco Exterior de España: 'Ask for Raimundo Saporta, I am one of the six compartmental directors of the Banco.'

But while he holds 'the most billionaire World Cup in history', Spain continues to flounder in the ocean of its economic frustrations. With three million unemployed, 26 per cent inflation and a foreign debt of $30 billion, it is going through the worst political crisis in its history. Saporta cannot hide it: 'It's not the best time to set up a World Cup. It would have been better to organise it ten years ago or in ten years' time, with autarky or democracy already established.' Transition is not the ideal time, and Saporta is studying how to cope with the large amount of money needed to organise a sporting event of this magnitude without having it financed by public money. No waste for the state. Not at this time.

However, the country faces a large amount of work, some of which cannot be postponed, in order to meet the minimum conditions required by FIFA. Among the work is overcoming the obsolete telecommunications system and renovating the stadiums according to the new standards. The Sarriá stadium in Barcelona alone requires over 200 million pesetas. Too much money for such a poor country. The press controversy soon begins to affect Saporta's actions, but inside his head he has already drawn the four lines to be followed to finance the World Cup: tickets, television rights, advertising and merchandising.

Ticket sales revolve around Mundiespaña, a private company made up of four travel agencies (Wagon Lits, Ecuador, Meliá and Marsans) and four hotel chains (Entursa, Hotasa, Hursa and Meliá). It is said that 39 million Swiss francs have come from the consortium of multinational television companies for TV, radio and video rights. Another 36 million have come from West Nally for advertising in stadiums and US television rights, to which a further 30 million German marks have been added for the exploitation of World Cup products, from the mascot to posters (he has entrusted the Maeght

Gallery in Paris with the creation of 14 posters corresponding to the cities hosting the World Cup; the Barcelona poster was designed by Antonio Tapis: it is worth 750,000 pesetas with the signature, just 15,000 without). The licences for the exploitation of products branded with the mascot or symbol of the World Cup should yield at least 120 million pesetas and go through IberMundial 82, a company authorised by FIFA and owned by West Nally and Real Federación Española. The shirts with the Mundial symbols are produced by Mundi-Fútbol, another company that was born around the event. In addition to this income, the Real Comité adds extraordinary lotteries, special football pools, minting of coins and four editions of stamps.

It seems that nothing can stop the Spain '82 affair.

All the Enemies of Saporta

For decades, every day, with impeccable punctuality, he enters his office at the Banco Exterior de España half an hour after eight o'clock. Once his workday is over, he has to wait until two o'clock in the morning to reach his beloved mother at home. First he has to synchronise his obligations with the needs of Real Madrid, the urgencies of the basketball federation and the tasks of the Mundial (occupations for which he never wanted to receive a penny).

When he returns home exhausted, Saporta finds an answering machine jammed with messages that he cannot answer. The telephone is his greatest enemy. He receives hundreds of calls every day. And, of course, he cannot cope with them all. The backlog is piling up in an eternal chase that he is playing on many fronts: in addition to the organisation of the Mundial, he is also organising the basketball world championships to be held in Spain, which will start on 5 July 1986 (and which will require him to deal with the difficulties of building new facilities, the endless logistical problems and, above all, a series of publicity issues that are already causing him great concern). Commitments that overlap with everyday ones, not to mention conflicts and emergencies. Everywhere he turns he finds enemies:

in the ministries, in all the sporting bodies, in the public companies, in the entire Spanish federation and even among politicians (he has fought publicly with both Ambassador Raimundo Pérez-Hernández and Treasury Minister Jaime Julián García Añoveros).

From the beginning, the Real Comité has had to clash with the administrations and parties linked to the Mundial cities. And the pressure from the latter has always been very high. But Saporta wanted a committee in the hands of the sportsmen and he made his fears public: 'If the committee does not return to its initial principles, independence and sport, I will not continue.' So, since the future of the World Cup is in great danger, it is the government that saves him: 'Continue your work, Saporta, you are the best person to do it.'

He goes ahead, but whatever decision he takes he inevitably comes up against a brick wall, that of the Spanish federation itself. Saporta and Porta, the two most influential executives of the World Cup, have found themselves the protagonists of a power struggle to the death in order to have control of crucial decisions. Porta systematically rejected any of Saporta's proposals: funding for new projects, renovation of stadiums, rental of venues, choice of strategic collaborators.

The organisation of the Mundial continues to hang in the balance. Havelange decides to mediate in the conflict using a mutual friend: Juan Antonio Samaranch. A dinner is arranged for early December 1981. The World Cup is just six months away. However, Samaranch is unable to get on a plane, so at the Zalcain restaurant in Madrid, Porta, Saporta, his deputy Anselmo López and Havelange sit around the table. In an atmosphere of high tension, the umpteenth act of a stale crisis unfolds before the astonished eyes of the FIFA president. Havelange emerges distraught from a dinner that should have been used to mediate, unravel, resolve, but has instead made things worse. 'If I had known beforehand that Porta and Saporta could not be seen, I would never have dreamed of granting Spain the organisation of the World Cup.' The time for irrevocable decisions now seems near.

Rey's Madness

Less than two months before the Mundial, Saporta, the man who built the whole toy, is in pieces. His work has been impeccable but the enormous pressure of the committee and the exhausting infighting have cost him the loss of his health, the onset of a breakdown and the beginning of a depression. The first to realise this are his friends. They do everything they can to cover for him but, as his disorders worsen, protecting him becomes impossible. His irreproachable behaviour is beginning to dissolve.

Perhaps it is also the fault of the stars. Saporta is capable of concentration, tenacity and realism. He is an efficient and pragmatic man, endowed with logical and synthetic skills. These qualities enable him to see problems and solve them quickly, without getting lost in superfluous or irrelevant questions. However, his sense of duty distances him from the real purpose of his life. He would have liked to achieve independence and freedom and finds himself imprisoned in an existential frustration that he did not want. And it is this enigmatic destination that has been influenced by the luminous messages compiled in the darkness of his sky.

According to the astrologers Héctor and Karin Silveira, the Sagittarian Raimundo Saporta established his first connection with the universe in the hour of Capricorn. But his 'birth star', the dreaded Saturn, impressed order and control on him. It was Saturn who revealed himself as his true 'cosmic father', imposing on him the personality to lose himself in adventurous yet dispersive outbursts, strictly adhering to responsibility, commitment and adherence to all his commitments.

No privileges for him, only obligations. Restrictions and blocks that inhibit his enthusiastic and ardent Sagittarian soul. The submergence of hidden passions, hidden behind his well-known capacity for tolerance, generate in him incredible tensions accompanied by constant states of worry. Effects that he managed to alleviate until the Mundial, thanks to the daily ingestion of magnesium and *complejo vitamínico B*, but which have now emerged in sudden bursts of nerves.

His health has not been good since December, but Saporta had held out until the World Cup draw. In spring, taking advantage of his regular stays in Switzerland, he and his inseparable mother underwent a new check-up. The newspapers say he is under medical treatment, forced to take all sorts of medicines, pills that help him relax but cause him an unavoidable drowsiness at all public events, such as when he was in Baden-Baden for the Olympic Congress, special guest of his dear friend Juan Antonio Samaranch. Or drugs that cause him to behave in very unusual ways during institutional visits.

In February, he disrupted protocol during the visit of US Secretary of State Alexander Haig. At the start of the plenary session of the Conference on Security and Cooperation in Madrid, the American politician was approached by an overweight man who grabbed his hand and confusedly repeated words such as 'football' and 'Kissinger'. The gentleman in question was none other than the president of the World Cup Organising Committee, who, after skipping a police check and an invitation from a hostess to leave the plenary stage, had interrupted Haig to take a photograph, attempting to invite his predecessor Henry Kissinger to visit the Mundial. From that moment on, Saporta began to occupy the front pages of newspapers with strong and impatient statements. The most famous of these went around the world: 'I depend on the King of Spain, and him alone!' A phrase that created embarrassment and irritation. Some say he has gone mad but he finds the strength to reply: 'They may lock me up, but I hope to resist until the end of the World Cup.' He failed.

When Manuel Benito, his leading man and secretary of the Real Comité, resigned, the 'Pact of Puerta de Hierro', named after the area where the meeting was held, stripped Saporta of all power, transforming him into a decorative figure (with the formal satisfaction of coordinating Cultural-82) and Benito into the architect of the Mundial's success. After five gruelling years at the helm of the Real Comité, Saporta relinquishes his hand just two months before the inauguration. A mockery that came to fruition on the day Havelange returned to Spain to find everything in order but nothing in place.

Indifferent to the changes within the Real Comité and the humiliation suffered by Saporta, Havelange storms into his office and slams a packet of four hundred tickets on to the table. They are for Brazil's opening match: 'You can take them back. These are not the ones I asked for!' In the room is a map of Seville's Ramón Sánchez Pizjuán stadium. Havelange points his finger at the authorities' stand: 'This is where I want my seats.'

Saporta looks at him in amazement. 'I can't have them, I'm not in charge of them.'

The king of football at that point explodes. 'I can't give these seats to my friends, so listen to me carefully, Raimundo. I can do without eating, sleeping and going to the bathroom for three days, so I won't move from here until you find me four hundred seats for the authority tribune.'

Saporta observes him as he sits serenely on the chair and points to the phone. 'Why don't you call?' says Havelange.

The Spaniard, now at the limit of his strength, hesitates. 'I don't work for you.'

Havelange dryly replies, 'You call.'

Saporta mechanically picks up the phone, makes a phone call, frets, wanders around the office, calls again and again and again, until an employee walks in with tickets for the grandstand. Havelange takes them, says thank you and leaves. Politicians, judges, publishers and presidents have their place in the grandstand.

Ossie's Dream

Brazil and Italy have reached the second phase of the Spanish tournament. If this outcome could be taken for granted for the

Brazilians, favourites for the trophy, the same could not be said for Italy, for whom a quick and less than glorious return home is expected. The team is still searching for the game physiognomy that four years earlier, in Baires, had made it shine and that now seemed irretrievably lost. Results and the group tables have pitted them against each other. But first the draw and then the war tried to play with their destiny.

The two teams found themselves swallowed up in a World Cup with a completely new look: the African confederation, together with the Asian confederation, after having pressed FIFA for more weight on the world football field, obtained an increase in the number of their representatives. Europe demanded a quid pro quo in return, and its teams were thus increased to 14, in addition to the six from America, the two from Asia and Oceania and the other two from Africa. The finalists, having risen from 16 to 24, were divided into six groups of four, a choice that greatly complicated the work of the Spanish organisation, which made the first group the top seeds, the second the Eastern European countries, the third the remaining European and South American teams and the last the 'also rans'.

In the draw, which took place in Madrid on 16 January 1982, Italy were placed in Group 1, Germany in Group 2, Argentina in Group 3, England in Group 4, Spain in Group 5 and Brazil in Group 6. The arrangement favoured the Spanish hosts, who should avoid meeting the Brazilians until the final, and would play their last match of the first phase having the opportunity to work out the best odds for progression. The top two in each group would advance to the second phase (in the event of a tie, the best goal difference would apply). The second phase consisted of four Italian-style groups of three teams each. In particular, the runners-up of the groups that included Italy and Argentina would have to face the winner of Brazil's group, almost certainly Brazil.

In the group draw, however, the first European drawn from the third tier, Belgium, ended up with Italy, and the second, Scotland, with Argentina. Bearing in mind that Chile and Peru could only go where there was a European (each group could not contain more than one South American), FIFA general secretary Joseph Blatter, on his debut in a planetary competition, blatantly blocked the procedures, making them start all over again. So Belgium ended up in Group 3 with Argentina, Peru took their place with Italy, and Scotland moved to Group 6 with Brazil. If even only one of these teams had remained where they were, the story would have been different and the fate of Italy and Brazil would probably not have been sealed on 5 July.

The complexity of such an organisation is reflected in the 36 matches of the first round, played from 13 to 25 June on 12 peripheral pitches (with the exception of the opening match at Camp Nou in Barcelona), followed by those of the second round held only in Barcelona and Madrid.

But there is one event that threatens to change the course of the Mundial. The bloody escalation of the conflict between Great Britain and Argentina in the remote Falkland Islands. England, Scotland and Northern Ireland, in fact, could drop out of the draw, revolutionising the World Cup. Initially, the British government is calling on British sports authorities to prepare an international boycott plan against athletes from Argentinian teams. Sports Minister Neil McFarlane calls for the immediate expulsion of Argentina from the Mundial but both FIFA and the Spanish organisers find the proposal unacceptable. For FIFA, a World Cup without the defending champions would be unthinkable: 'We are concerned with football here, not politics,' Havelange says sharply.

In the freezing desert of the Malvinas, among the ranks of the 'best youth' of Argentina sent to the front by General Galtieri, the destinies of the football players also move. Like that of Private Omar De Felippe, a Huracán defender who, at the age of 20, wounded and lost, while the English Gurkhas also shoot at blades of grass, the very ones he would like to step on with a ball between his feet, finds himself desperately stealing bread from the dead. Some 649

Argentines will not see the World Cup, among them José Leónidas Ardiles, 28, captain of the 6th Air Brigade, shot down by the British on 2 May in the South Atlantic aboard his Mirage M5 Dagger. He is a first cousin of Osvaldo, an immovable starter for Menotti's Argentina, divided between the country where he grew up and the one where he now lives.

When, a month earlier, 'Ossie' touched the ball for the first time in the FA Cup semi-final at Villa Park, he had been drowned out by the booing of the Leicester City fans, not because he was the Tottenham midfielder but because he was Argentine and therefore an enemy. Leopoldo Galtieri, a few hours earlier, had started a war between the two countries. For the British it was an attack on national sovereignty, even though most of them did not even know they owned the Falklands. Osvaldo, on the other hand, had spent the night of 2 to 3 April on the phone with his family in Argentina. At dawn, together with Ricky Villa, Tottenham's other Argentine, he informed the coach, Keith Burkinshaw, that their two nations were at war: 'It is one of the worst moments of my life, it is terrible for me to see the two countries I love against each other.'

On that day, while his family was under escort, Ardiles chose to take to the pitch. When the Leicester supporters chanted 'England, England', his own fans, the Tottenham fans who had come to love him, responded with a chorus of 'Argentina, Argentina', displaying a magnificent banner: 'You can keep the Malvinas if you leave us Ossie'. Football had slapped the war in the face. They dedicated a song, 'Ossie's Dream', to him, a player capable of dragging them to the triumph at Wembley in the FA Cup the previous year. But the war metaphors of that hymn now sound stridentstrident, describing as they do how the 'boys from Keithy's army' will be 'marching off to war'. 'Soldiers', 'General Burkinshaw', 'enemy' and 'battle' add to the war metaphors in the third verse of the song before concluding that 'the kings' will be 'marching home' in triumph.

José's death shattered Ossie's dream. Like many of his generation, he had always considered war to be a distant event but now it has entered his home. His subsequent departure to Buenos Aires to join the Argentina national team was interpreted as a political gesture and when, on the eve of the World Cup in Spain, he and his team-mates were dragged into the 'Malvinas are Argentinian' commercial, he realised that it would be impossible to return to play in England.

The Boycott

Spain is not eager to do the British a favour, as Britain does not intend to surrender Gibraltar, long claimed by the Madrid government. At the United Nations, the Spanish delegate abstains from voting on Resolution 502, which defines Argentina as an aggressor state. Therefore, the Anglo-Saxon authorities change direction: 'If they don't withdraw, it will be the British teams that won't participate in the World Cup,' Scottish Sports Minister Alex Fletcher informs the press. 'It is not good for English football to have to stay at home because of the faults of others, but we are experiencing extraordinary circumstances.'

'At certain times sport takes a back seat,' he is echoed by English federation president Bert Millichip. 'We will do what our government tells us to do.' He is followed by his main employee, the English team coach Ron Greenwood: 'It will be painful for our boys, but football is not everything in life, there are more important values and we must be willing to make sacrifices to defend them.' Also the Scottish Footballers' Association, through the mouth of its secretary Harry Lawrie: 'We are in favour of the withdrawal of our team from all matches with countries that agree with Argentina in the Falklands conflict.' The Irish national team cancels the friendly match against Argentina. The captain of the English national team Kevin Keegan: 'We cannot expect our boys to go and get killed in the Falklands and in a few days face Argentina in a football match.' And finally Jimmy Greaves, the most prolific striker in the history of the English First

Division, proposes the organisation of a tournament between the Home Nations only in order to donate the proceeds to the families of the soldiers involved in the Falklands.

The situation throws FIFA, the Football Association and the Foreign Office into chaos. Prime Minister Margaret Thatcher will decide whether or not to leave England, Scotland and Northern Ireland at home. It would be an earthquake, although there have been plenty of precedents: in 1938 Austria, after the German invasion, decided to renounce the World Cup in France, and in 1974 the Soviet Union refused to meet Chile in Santiago.

The possible boycott by the British teams is noted by the coach of the Brazilian national team Telê Santana: 'A bad thing for the Mundial, but very good for us.' His team would lose Scotland in their group, to be replaced by Sweden: 'We will then have a weaker opponent and we will not risk facing England, one of the favourites.' On the other hand, Enzo Bearzot, coach of the Italian national team, is worried: 'The more people die, the more the World Cup will suffer. Apart from the question of the British teams, with the war going on, this would be a competition without enthusiasm, burdened by a heavy atmosphere. I would advise all the national teams to play the same: it could be the World Cup itself that brings them closer together.'

In the meantime, the work of Artemio Franchi, president of UEFA and chairman of the refereeing commission, has also been affected by the ongoing war. In order to organise the referee designations, additional precautions are needed. The Englishman Clive White, for example, could not referee Argentina vs Belgium.

From the political and logistical point of view, it is a 'terrible' Mundial: 104 match directors have to move within a Spain that suffers from communication problems. But the Italian manager does not show concern: 'Everything will return to normal.' If not, the first to suffer would be Great Britain itself. In order to curb boycotts, there are mechanisms in place to impose drastic sporting and economic sanctions. Moreover, a boycotting country would be excluded from the next tournament. For England, who had failed to qualify for the 1974 and 1978 World Cups, it would mean missing out on four World Cups in a row.

It was Margaret Thatcher who unravelled the matter in front of the House of Commons: 'A good performance by the British teams in Spain will be an excellent incentive for the military in the Falklands.' The boycott issue then fades into the background. From his throne in Madrid, Raimundo Saporta has been quiet the whole time. The idea of boycotts never crossed his mind. 'You will see,' he said, 'there will be no surprises. It will be a wonderful Mundial.'

You have to believe him. For the first time, a World Cup is hosting all five continents and all six confederations. For Spain it is a debut in society. Perched beyond the Pyrenees, for decades it danced alone, but since the death of the Caudillo de España Francisco Franco, the country has discovered its Western vocation. Just 35 days ago it joined NATO and this championship seems to have come on purpose to tell the world that the nation is now a democracy. In the inaugural match in Barcelona, the head of the government, Don Leopoldo Calvo-Sotelo y Bustelo, who a year earlier had been holed up under the benches of parliament amid the crack of machine guns from 200 rebels of the Guardia Civil, stood proudly on the stage of the authorities, while Antonio Tejero, the coup colonel who, gun in hand, had held him hostage, is locked up in prison, in Alcalá de Henares, sentenced to 30 years.

One country, one month. All in 30 incredible days, during which, for once, it is space that marks time.

The Two Masters

The pipe and the cigarette butt. Jazz and samba. The school and the street. Two parallel tracks, two distant worlds, two lines destined never to meet. Yet a common destiny has brought them face to face for the first time, showing that in the end they are not so different.

Bearzot is an 'old man' of only 55, who has spent his life on the football pitch, listens to Dixieland records and smokes a pipe. He is tall, angular and spirited, with a long face, a boxer's nose, nervous hands and a sulky smile. He was born in Aiello del Friuli, a closed, reserved, shy people, used to defending themselves but always wrapped in the flash of a rematch. His village was on the route of the American planes that went to bomb Germany. Germans, partisans, Cossacks – everyone passed through her land. Those of 1926 were called up, many were sent to Germany and never returned. If the war had lasted a few more months, they would have pulled Bearzot in too, as he was born in 1927. And Bearzot felt he had been lucky. 'Those who are not Friulian cannot understand certain things: in a frontier land you have to redo things from night to morning. That's why the Friulian is diffident, I would say counter-attacker.' This is why the Vecio has found his trusted men in the Friulians: the captain, Dino Zoff, the team doctor and his fitness advisor, Leonardo Vecchiet. And Fulvio Collovati, the key player in his plan to defeat Brazil, is Friulian.

Telê Santana da Silva, too, is O Mestre, the maestro, for his people. But he is not a thinker like Bearzot. He has the worn, tanned skin of men who have lived in the open air in all sorts of weather, and a wonderful hawk-like profile that is beginning to sag under his chin. He spends his time on the bench chewing his gum, as if he hates it. In contrast to Cláudio Coutinho, his predecessor and perfect polyglot, he boasts that he can only speak Mineiro, the dialect of the state of Minas Gerais (and Mineira is his left wing: Luizinho and Éder). That's where he comes from. Born in the small town of Itabirito (in the ancient Tupi language it means 'stone that scratches red'), in 1931, four years after Bearzot, the third of ten children of 'Seu' Zico, a foreman in a steel company, and 'Doña' Corina Silva, a housewife. His first childhood passion was football, as a goalkeeper. At the age of eight, a village party after a rally complicated his plans for the future. A firecracker landed on his left hand, causing him to lose the use of two fingers. Necessity pushed him forward, so much so that, despite his tiny build, he found himself a starting forward for Itabirense's young players and later for the América Recreativo of São João del Rei, of which his father had been the president.

THE TWO MASTERS

In 1938, Santana and Bearzot watched their first World Cup as children. They both listened on the radio to the match between their two nations that would see one team through to the final in Paris, won 2-1 by the Azzurri. On the night of 19 June, Bearzot, together with the whole town, was in the square in Gradisca to hear Carosio's voice over the loudspeakers. The 4-2 victory in the final against Hungary, which decreed Pozzo's Italy as world champions for the second consecutive time, included two goals by Gino Colaussi, known as 'Ginùt', who was from Gradisca. That was the day Bearzot decided: 'I'm going to be a footballer,' without knowing where he might end up but knowing that his parents preferred him to become a doctor, a pharmacist or at least a banker, like his father Egidio, director of the Cassa Rurale di Cervignano and San Vito al Torre.

But destiny knocked on Bearzot's door when a scout of Pro Gorizia saw him playing first in the team of the classical high school at the student tournament and then in Aiello, in a real championship. They asked him to come to Verona on loan for a match and that was the start of his career. He was a teenager who loved music and smoking. Every now and then he stole a Tre Stelle from his father and smoked it in instalments. He rode around on a Lambretta and listened to 'Ma l'amore no e Polvere di stelle'. He already knew how to play the piano, having learned it from his father, who was the church organist on Sundays. Locked up in a Salesian boarding school, he was struck by Horace and Socrates. He had passion for humanistic culture. He excelled in his studies, was disciplined and the rector reassured his parents that he would become a doctor.

At the age of 12, however, Telê, who by then lived alone with his aunt and uncle after his father went to work in a textile factory 120 kilometres (75 miles) from home, was employed by the Cooperativa de Alimentos Esperança, in Queiroz Júnior, an occupation that he changed shortly afterwards to become an assistant in a shoe shop. At that time he had two addictions: smoking cigarettes (of which he would later be one of the fiercest critics, not allowing anyone to smoke near him) and chewing the roots of the field grass (which he would later replace with chewing gum).

Young Enzo could also distract himself during breaks by playing football in the courtyard. The Salesians instilled in him principles of life. One of them entered his veins: to succeed, you have to know how to fight. The spirit of sacrifice seeped into him. The boarding school became his workshop, from which he emerged a man. But he only brought out his combativeness on the pitch. The Pro Gorizia team realised this and he found himself a footballer without even realising it. His family disapproved, the faculty of medicine moved away. Football was about to enter his life for good.

At 18 years old the two future coaches had the life of their dreams. The young Telê saw Rio de Janeiro for the first time, auditioned for the Fluminense youth selection, scored five goals and was signed as a centre-forward for the following season. Inter played a friendly in Gorizia, where Bearzot played the match of his life and was hooked. The father gave in to his son's destiny. The doors of Milan opened to Bearzot. However, he resisted the temptations of the big city and was an example of education. He did not go out, he was not a star. He loved to be alone. One morning in September 1948, on the number 3 tram passing through Corso Italia, he met a girl, Luisa, the love of a lifetime. Santana was the same age as him when, in 1951 in Rio he met Dona Ivonete, whom he married two years later.

Two tragedies touched Bearzot and Santana closely. In 1949 the Superga tragedy and in 1950 that of the Maracanã shattered, in different ways, the dreams of their generation. The following year Santana had already earned a starting place in the first team, employed as an advanced right-winger. He was not a refined player but rather a hound, a tireless scorer from midfield and a relentless opportunist in the penalty area. This was inspired by his speciality of scoring goals for which Brazilian journalists in the early 1950s coined the expression *ladrão de bola*. He put the ball into the net like a machine gun, and in his 11-year career at Fluminense he scored 162 goals.

THE TWO MASTERS

Bearzot was also at home in midfield. He was a solid and stubborn midfielder, the classic 'seven-lunger' who ran for others without ever making the headlines and stuck like a shadow to the ankles of the opposing forward to stifle his flair and space. He had two children, Cinzia and Glauco (Santana followed him, becoming father to Sandra and Renê), and conquered the peak of football: Turin. He played 442 matches, starting against Silvio Piola and finishing against Sandro Mazzola, passing through Sívori, Charles and Schiaffino. He had the history of football on his shoulders. He nostalgically remembers the days of the Filadelfia. There were no hot showers, but everything else warmed the heart. 'We trained on the bowling greens, we were poor, but we were also Toro.' He earned an unfortunate presence in the national team in Hungary. He had to mark the immense Ferenc Puskás. He didn't let him touch the ball. Ten minutes from the end a cross came in from the right, the temple of both hit the ball with a glancing blow. The trajectory became mocking and thus displaced the Italian goalkeeper.

For Santana, the greatest opportunity to play in a World Cup came in 1954. The coach of the national team was Zezé Moreira, the man who had launched him as a professional when he led Fluminense. He was in a good period and in his team he was the starting right-winger in a system created by Moreira himself, to which he adapted perfectly. This time he had hopes of being called up but Zezé preferred to bring in Julinho and the Paulista Maurinho, who could also play on the left. Santana stayed at home to cheer on his clubmates, Pinheiro, Castilho and Veludo. He could have made up for it in later years had he not come up against some real football legends – Vavá, Garrincha and Pelé blocked his way. In 1962 he found himself at the end of his career and realised he had no hope. He would always see the World Cup from afar.

But the public loved him and, according to Brazilian custom, gave him more than one nickname, mostly related to his physical appearance. His 57kg (9 stone), distributed over 171cm (5ft 7in), triggered the fans' imagination and affectionate irony. *Magro* (skinny),

THE MATCH

Banquete de cachorro (puppy's meal), *Fiapo* (weak) and *Tarzan das Laranjeiras* (Fluminense's Tarzan) were just a few of the names given to Telê Santana. The *Jornal dos Sports*, owned by the journalist and publisher Mário Filho, after whom the Maracanã stadium was named in 1966, a month after his death, launched a competition with a prize of 5,000 cruzeiros to rename the skinny Fluminense goalscorer. The winning name was *Fio de Esperança*, a nickname inspired by a 1954 American film, *Prisoners of Heaven*, starring John Wayne, which in Brazil was translated as 'Thread of Hope'.

Bearzot, on the other hand, was given the label 'il Vecio', because at 38 years of age he was still on the pitch. During his last season, 1963/64, a long series of injuries enabled him to play only two matches. It was then that Nereo Rocco, the Granata's head coach, formally invited him to play a part: 'Hey, you brute, when are you going to give me a hand?' Bearzot, as a captain who was not a player, made himself available to the Parón as long as he was in charge of Torino. In three seasons he learned 'the culture of the group', for Rocco – and later for himself – the first of the founding values of a team. For these credentials, the president of FIGC, Franchi, appointed him to a provincial club, Prato. Bearzot helped the team save their lives and he passed the test. Franchi then brought him on to the staff of the national set-up, entrusting him with the responsibility of the under-23 team and collaboration with the senior national team.

Santana hung up his boots a year after Bearzot, when, having passed the age of 30, he realised that his chances were no longer the same. He opened an ice cream parlour in Vila da Penha, where he lived. His most popular flavour was cheese, a creation of his uncle Eurico, with whom he lived during his childhood. But he didn't pull the plug on football, agreeing to take part in charity matches for ADEG (the Sports Association of the State of Guanabara), alongside veteran stars such as Barbosa, Nilton Santos and Zizinho. And it was there, when everything seemed to be over, that he discovered he had a vocation: to be a coach. Now he finally had the chance to take part in his first World Cup.

The Blind Faith

Bearzot and Santana have a lot in common. They want a clean game, without tricks. They are radically against violence. They believe in men, even before the players. And they choose them for their moral qualities. Neither of them have an easy life on the eve of the Mundial. Bettega, the lighthouse of the Italian attack, is injured, Paolo Rossi has only just returned to play after two years of inactivity, Antognoni has taken a hard blow to the head, Tardelli is drained and Conti has a damaged knee. If Bettega is not there, it will only be because the player himself says no. Bearzot counts firmly and stubbornly on his boys. For years he has always played the same players, against everything and everyone. He knew that the national team was precarious by its very nature: 'Changes only added to the precariousness.'

Santana, on the other hand, finds no peace. In the 17 matches of the previous year he used 35 players without managing to resolve his dilemmas. And just a few months before the Mundial he still has four key roles unclear: goalkeeper, right-back, left-wing and centre-forward. After trying out six goalkeepers he finally chooses one.

The Mystical Side of the No. 1

Peres smiles. Deep down he already knows. It is a gift he is convinced he has always possessed. Divinatory, prophetic, premonitory. It's his mystical side. It has not always been so but it has happened in most matches. Even before he played he was certain of the result of the match and with him in goal Brazil has never lost. Several times the Brazilian press criticised him for this tendency to smile while playing. Some think it is a defence mechanism: laughing to avoid crying. For him, the smile is a certainty. He has understood that certain signals can be a gift, a warning or perhaps even divine protection.

A few years earlier, on the eve of the Brazilian championship final between Atlético Mineiro and São Paulo, he dreamed of being

THE MATCH

in a cave and trying three times to get a handkerchief. The match ended on penalties. Peres did not save one but the title still went to his team, São Paulo, thanks to the three shots from the penalty spot missed by their opponents.

On the eve of the call-up to the World Cup in Spain, he dreamed of standing on top of a very tall building, looking down and feeling dizzy. It was confirmation that he would be called up; it had already happened in 1974 and 1978, the previous World Cups for which he had been called up.

In 1980, three goalkeepers were experimented with in the Seleção. Raul, Carlos and João Leite. Waldir Peres did not even think about joining the group. For him, the game is long over. After his São Paulo team lost the title, he indulged in a month of rest by spending the December holidays at his home in Guaruja. From there he would watch the Mundialito on television.

And indeed, on 4 January 1981 he was comfortably watching Brazil vs Argentina on his sofa when, in the 20th minute of the second half, Carlos dislocated his elbow. Leite entered the fray and the staff began to tremble. 'Telê,' the assistants intimated, 'call Waldir! Call him now!' The following day, after a whole month off, Waldir returned to his flat in São Paulo to start the Paulista pre-season. When he opened the door, the phone was already ringing. It was Roberto Silva from Radio Bandeirantes: 'Waldir, Carlos is out. You have been summoned, you are going to Uruguay!'

'Man, I don't know anything about that!'

An hour later, São Paulo Futebol Clube called him: he had to be at the airport at 7pm. He was completely out of shape but it was the invitation to the land of wonders. A magical door to the World Cup. The same evening he took the plane to Montevideo thinking that maybe he would have the chance to play alongside the likes of Zico and Sócrates. As soon as he arrived he was taken to the Brazil rally. When the treasurer entered, he put $1,000 in his hand. 'What is it?' he asked.

'It's the match prize for the draw with Argentina.'

184

'Even though I watched it from the sofa?'

'You became one of us while you were sitting there.'

He thus became part of the golden generation. But he earned the credit on the pitch, during the European tour against European champions West Germany on 19 May 1981 in the Neckarstadion in Stuttgart. Fischer opened the scoring for the Germans but Toninho Cerezo and Júnior put Brazil 2-1 ahead. Then the whistle blew for a penalty for West Germany. Breitner was taking it and he had never missed one before. Breitner and Peres faced each other, the stadium silent, preparing to explode at the equaliser. Breitner started, stopped, looked at Peres, carried on and shot weakly to his right. Peres dived and caught the ball. Almost a miracle. But the penalty has to be retaken as Peres moved before the kick was taken. Breitner then changes everything: he shoots hard and to the opposite side of the goal. Peres blocks. Again. Two out of two. This time it was a real miracle.

The next day, the whole of Brazil was with Peres. He was voted man of the match and earned the front page of the *Jornal da Tarde*. That was the match in which he became the Seleção's starter. The day Brazil accepted him. Until then, his name only aroused controversy. And the country had other good goalkeepers.

Peres plays again against the Germans on 21 March 1982, on the eve of the World Cup, at the Maracanã, under the gaze of 150,000 people. He makes some great saves, one of them memorable, flying to deflect a high shot with the fingertips of his right hand. The image of that unique moment is then used for the advertising campaign of the Topper ball, the Seleção's sponsor, with the slogan 'A bola que o Waldir Peres convocou' – The ball Waldir Peres deflected. The two matches against West Germany have brought him to a World Cup: the 1982 one, finally as a starter.

A Dog Day Afternoon

The position of right-back remained vacant until the last day. Edevaldo de Freitas, the revelation of the Mundialito, thought he had the starting role in his pocket. He has contended with Getúlio Costa de Oliveira and Perivaldo Lúcio Dantas, but after 17 matches Santana removes him ahead of the Spanish expedition, replacing him with young José Leandro de Souza Ferreira.

On the left wing, however, Santana's doubts are tangled around three players: Zé Sérgio, Éder and Mario Sérgio. José Sérgio Presti, known as Zé Sérgio, young, fast and with great dribbling ability, named in 1980 as the best player of Brazil, seemed predestined for glory, but his career has been devastated by injuries. After breaking his right arm against Mexico, he was out of action for two months; he recovered but, on his return, against Noroeste, he was fouled and broke his arm again. Just a few days before the call-up, a third injury puts him out of the World Cup for good. So the coach's torments focus on his 'godson' Éder, whose undeniable technical merits would guarantee him a place if his countless disciplinary problems were not added to them.

Santana therefore turns to Mário Sérgio Pontes de Paiva, an extremely skilful and intelligent player. On the pitch he looks like an old man: balding and stocky, with a thick beard. He looks at the horizon, never at the ball. It is not an occasional trick but the way he plays. In Brazil, it has earned him the nickname 'cross-eyed'. In reality he has excellent vision of the game. He is a talent and the World Cup could be his showcase. After four years at Vitória, a small team that few care about, he joined Fluminense. It was the big leap but he could not handle the pressure and started drinking. To make matters worse he has a sharp tongue and explosive temperament. At the age of 29, Mário Sérgio has still achieved nothing in life and finds himself relegated to a remote corner of the Argentinian league. It was then that Falcão, the Internacional star, recommended the forgotten man to his club. Mário Sérgio grabbed the opportunity with both hands and, at the age of 31, finally made his debut for the Brazilian national team.

The 1982 World Cup is approaching, Santana's line-up is overloaded with equally talented, less elderly and more reliable creative midfielders. Mário Sérgio, however, in 1980 and 1981, wins selection for the *Bola de Prata* as the best player in his role. His visa for Spain. But his nature re-emerges as he travels the last stretch of road that separates him from the Mundial. On the afternoon of a dog day, in a moment of euphoria, he pulls out a gun and shoots out the window of the bus at a group of fans who are daring to challenge him. The gimmick works, the crowd disperses, but it kills his career. Palmarès, talents and matches are no longer enough: Mário Sérgio stays at home. Santana goes with his heart and chooses Éder.

O Canhão

Éder Aleixo de Assis. A name like a gun cocked and discharged. He is almost getting the shot of a lifetime: to enter the mythology of his football. To become a demigod of the torcida (Brazilian ultras). With a face that has nothing to fear, because they have already done everything imaginable to him.

There is no preparation behind his talent. It just comes to him. It is an instinctive thing that he has always done since he kicked barefoot in his native town of Vespasiano. He would have stayed there if Telê Santana had not brought him out of anonymity, giving him, at once, a shirt in the Grêmio team, the entrance into the professional world and economic independence. But Éder was a restless boy, hanging out with gangs of thugs, smoking 30 cigarettes a day and sinking into alcohol at night. The impetuousness of his twenties also swallowed up his gratitude. In return for Santana's favour, he disputed his mentor's tactical methods, failed to show up for training sessions and even defecated in his shoes. In the first derby, when all eyes were on him, he punched Batista in the face.

Telê Santana tried to help him, but Éder would not listen to reason and kept getting into trouble again and again. One one occasion it was nearly fatal. It was a night in May 1978, just a few days before the World Cup in Argentina. In a discotheque in Porto Alegre he started to pursue a woman who was already accompanied. He was shot twice. He was hit in the right arm and missed the World Cup. He was left with a scar as a warning but it was not enough for him. When he recovered, he seduced and then abandoned the daughter of the president of the club for which he played.

Santana did not abandon him; he gradually convinced him to break with bad company, to follow the training sessions, to stop smoking. He almost succeeded, but in 1980 it seemed that their paths would separate: while the young left-footer was sold to Atlético Mineiro, Santana became selector of the Brazilian national team. However, the coach left the door ajar, first as a reserve for Zé Sérgio, then Mário Sérgio. Éder then won the starting spot just before leaving for Spain. His play has ignited passion and imagination in his fans. He has the right foot of an infant but an unforgiving left foot. And that left foot is enough to make him proud, especially after he scored two goals at Zico's Flamengo from 40 yards out. That is why he has been nicknamed 'Exocet', 'Dinamite', 'Torpedo' and 'Bomba de Vespasiano'. But for everyone he is now 'O Canhão', the Cannon.

Telê's Binary Combinations

The problem that most distresses the Brazilian coach is the choice of centre-forward: eight players in two years, it was a cross to bear for him. Match after match, Telê Santana has to decipher his team's binary code by playing his own abstract battle, a football mastermind. When Sócrates, Serginho, Nunes and Zé Sérgio run on to the pitch, Telê doesn't see yellow and blue kit, only players in the right or wrong place. He may have great champions but he does not have a solid formation. Unlike Bearzot, he has not yet managed to create a family. The Seleção is not for him what the Azzurri is for the Vecio: his boys, always the same, trusted and confirmed in good times and bad. If Bearzot has made an iron pact with his players, Santana is undecided, doubtful and a slave to the latest sensations. And the question of the spearhead afflicts him above all else.

TELÊ'S BINARY COMBINATIONS

The summer of 1980 was the mirror of his fatigue, a rough sea in which, each time, the last impression drowned any previous certainty. On 8 June, in the first real match against a national team – Mexico – he lined up Serginho as a starter. The centre-forward scored and helped Brazil win 2-0, but Zé Sérgio also scored. A week later Telê experimented, kept Zé Sérgio, removed Serginho and inserted Nunes. The experiment didn't work, Brazil lost against the USSR 2-1, but it was Nunes who scored. Ten days later, against Chile, he alternated Nunes and Serginho, the scorers in the last two matches. They won 2-1. 'It's done,' he thought. A few days later, on 29 June against Poland, he confirmed Serginho and Zé Sérgio as starters for the first time together on the pitch. Brazil drew 1-1, played badly and were challenged. The following month, on 27 August, he removed Serginho and left Zé Sérgio: Brazil beat Uruguay 1-0, but the match was won by a new defender, Getúlio, who Telê naturally confirmed as a starter the next time around. At the end of the summer, on 25 September, with Zé Sérgio up front, Telê's Brazil beat Paraguay 2-1. After Sócrates had left the field, his replacement, Reinaldo, scored, adding to Zé Sérgio's goal. Thirty days later, again against Paraguay, Zé Sérgio was still unassailable and Sócrates was only destined to play one half (a choice that brought Serginho back), and the result was a winner: 6-0 with Zé Sérgio scoring a brace, but Sócrates also scored. So in the last friendly match of the year, on 21 December, Sócrates returned to play as centre-forward (before being replaced by Serginho again). Brazil beat Switzerland 2-0, with goals from Sócrates and Zé Sérgio.

The attack remains at the centre of Santana's thoughts: Baltasar, Cesar, Roberto and even the league's top scorer Nunes burn themselves out. Careca is perhaps too young, while Reinaldo, although intelligent and technically gifted, seems too puny to break through. That leaves Serginho, who has missed the national team's training more than once because of his constant trouble with the Brazilian justice system, due to his outbursts towards players, family members and photographers; and Carlos Roberto de Oliveira, known as Roberto Dinamite, Vasco da Gama's living legend, an extremely prolific striker with a powerful shot that earned him his nickname. Three months before the Mundial, Santana sent him out on the pitch but the goals didn't come. With him in the starting line-up, the Seleção had been booed for the first time.

Before the announcement of the definitive list of 22, Santana tries yet another card: Careca, the revelation of Guarani. The striker does not score but he fully repays the coach. His characteristics fit perfectly into the team's style of play. 'We have found the man,' Santana confidentially reveals to his collaborators from the technical commission after the friendly against West Germany. The striker from Araraquara is the last piece of the puzzle.

On 10 June, the Seleção are already in Mairena del Aljarafe, near Seville, the scene of the Mundial debut. The training match has only been underway for 13 minutes. Careca runs towards the ball, raises his leg, is about to shoot but then brings his hand to his thigh. Oscar, in front of him, understands immediately. A few hours later, the diagnosis of Neylor Lasmar, the national team doctor, becomes a sentence for him: 'Injury in the adductor muscle of the left thigh.' He will have to stay put for 20 days. It is Telê's turn to decree the definitive exclusion of the striker: 'Gilberto Tim, the doctors and I met immediately to analyse the situation. Dr Neylor's report is clear: Careca is out of the World Cup.' Some reporters are convinced that he did not resist the methods of the fitness trainer. In the previous days, Tim had made the imprudent comment about his working methods with them: 'I know my muscles. And I promise that nobody will have any problems. They can only hurt their bones.'

So Santana loses his man. Together with the CBF officials, a race against time begins to replace him. But there is a problem: FIFA regulations prohibit the inclusion of a player in the 22 list after the deadline has expired. To appease the members of FIFA's executive committee, the CBF leaders in each of their arguments use the weight of tradition of a three-time world football champion. This is not enough. They dissect the regulations: Article 19(5) validates an exception 'only in the event of force majeure'. Nélson Medrado Dias, the CBF's director of football, decides to appeal to this exception. Giulite Coutinho tries to communicate with FIFA but the two fax machines have problems. He finally manages to get Hermann Neuberger, president of the World Cup Organising Committee, on the phone. He is a supporter of the move of the 1986 World Cup venue from Colombia to Brazil. The request is granted.

Telê and Tim look at the names on their list and find Nunes and Roberto Dinamite. Nunes has just undergone an operation, so on 11 June they tell Roberto Dinamite to embark immediately for Spain. In 1978 the striker had been called to Argentina in place of Nunes, who was again injured. For the Carioca press, there is an explanation for this good fortune: the mystical influence of the player's wife, Jurema, the woman he bumped into ten years earlier on a crowded bus on the Caxias–Praça Mauá line, and from whom, against all odds, he has not been separated since. He was not yet the Dynamite, but even then he was good at arguing with life. She was nobody. For him she became everything. Widowed, with a son and six years older than Roberto, Jurema Crispim de Oliveira is now the most influential female icon of Brazilian – male – football. Like all myths, she is also entitled to a vast and colourful folklore, in which there is no shortage of allusions to her alleged supernatural powers that helped take her husband to two consecutive World Cups, thanks to the exclusion of another player on the eve of the tournament. But Jurema is also able to rid herself of slander with the necessary irony: 'If I had this gift, no one would ever commit the injustice of not calling him up.'

Beliefs aside, Dinamite lands in Spain ready to resume his first-team contention with Isidoro and Serginho: 'I came to fight for a place in the team, not to watch from the bench.' A demanding statement. The next day the tournament would start.

So, with Careca out of the Mundial, Nunes out of action and Dinamite out of training, once again, by a concatenation of coincidences, after many months of exhausting search, Telê Santana finally finds his man when he is about to enter the field against the Soviet Union for his first World Cup match: Serginho Chulapa.

THE MATCH

The Magic Square I

The nascent state is a revelation. It embraces a group of men who suddenly find themselves bound together by common hopes. But it is also a collective experience that needs contingencies. Above all, chance. The nascent state of the Seleção's famous Magic Square dates back three years before the Mundial. On 17 May 1979, the date that marked the debut in the national team of Sócrates, Éder and Júnior, at the Maracanã, Brazil presented the embryo of the team that is now enchanting at the Mundial. Coach Cláudio Coutinho's line-up for Paraguay brought together, for the first time, a constellation of superstars comparable to that of the 1970 national team: Cerezo, Falcão, Zico and Sócrates were now individually acclaimed as unquestionable elements in their home teams.

No one yet considered those four players as the vertices of a square and the official photo taken before the match did not yet show the midfield that would be called 'Magic' (Toninho Cerezo would have entered at the start of the match replacing Paulo César Carpegiani). And, in any case, it was not then the real 'square' that now forms the midfield of the national team, since one of the 'top' players, Sócrates, played in the middle, as a legitimate centre-forward, a position in which he stood out in Ribeirão Preto's Botafogo. Five months later Cláudio Coutinho left the bench and, with the arrival of Telê Santana, many players lost their place in the national team. Among them was Falcão, who played just the first training session of the Telê era before leaving for Italy and being forgotten. It was contingencies that came to Santana's aid. At the beginning they appeared as negative but the long path of the case started from far away and would lead him to unthinkable solutions.

On 22 February 1981, Brazil's easy victory against Bolivia in the World Cup qualifiers left only one blemish: the red card unfairly given to the immovable Toninho Cerezo. Peruvian referee Henrique Labo's report made matters worse and FIFA decided to punish him heavily with a three-year ban. The World Cup was only a year away, with two official matches (against Bolivia and Venezuela) still to be played before the event, the rest being friendlies. Cerezo was thus certain to have played his way into Spain's World Cup but that free place would become the first immobile engine of a mechanism that would bring into play, under the doubtful eyes of Santana, all the possible pretenders.

On 11 February 1982, Telê Santana goes to the Santiago Bernabéu stadium in Madrid to spy on Brazil's future Soviet opponents. After the match, while waiting to catch his plane to Brazil, the coach spends the evening in the flat of journalist Castilho de Andrade, who has been in the Spanish capital for a month as a correspondent for the *Jornal da Tarde* and Radio Globo to prepare for the World Cup coverage. Castilho shows some clippings from Spanish newspapers that talk about Dirceu, a starter in the 1978 World Cup, who is the only Brazilian playing in the Spanish league. Dirceuzinho is going through a good phase at Atlético Madrid. He plays cleanly, commits few fouls and shows respect for his opponents. Qualities dear to the Seleção coach. Castilho has received fundamental contacts from Dirceu for his work, so he owes him a debt. 'A professional with a good knowledge of football in Europe could prove very useful for your national team.' Telê Santana has not yet closed the door: 'I will take the suggestion into consideration.'

The Magic Square II

On 12 April, Telê announces the first names to earn their passport to Spain: Cerezo, Renato, Serginho, Waldir Peres, Paulo Sérgio, Carlos, Edevaldo, Oscar, Juninho, Luizinho, Edinho and Pedrinho. 'I've gone along with a criterion of justice,' Santana says to justify himself. 'It may even have a margin of error, but I've tried to summon who I consider best.'

Forty-eight hours later, Telê Santana falls ill with pneumonia, collapses and is rushed to the cardiac clinic in Rio de Janeiro. Some take advantage of the occasion to insinuate that Telê's sudden illness

THE MATCH

is due to the curses cast by Leão, Mário Sérgio, Roberto Dinamite and Jorge Mendonça, who have been left off the list.

Three days later, the coach, from his hospital bed, makes a statement that takes everyone by surprise: 'We are interested in Dirceu, a player who has already participated in two World Cups and who plays in the country where the next one will be held.' Until then, the Seleção coaches had never considered players (such as Falcão or Dirceu himself) who had chosen to play abroad. Castilho de Andrade's advice turns out to be Dirceu's ticket to his third World Cup. The journalist can be sure that he has returned the favours received by the player in the best possible way. But in May, with the first training tests, the midfielder's enthusiasm clashes with the working methods of the fitness trainer Gilberto Tim: 'I came more than charged up, but his exercises made me burst. He who is talking has great reserves of energy.' When Dirceu joined an infantry regiment in 1970 at the age of 18, he took part in the military championships in the 1,000, 5,000 and 10,000 metres. In the first event, he set a world record. In Brazil he was nicknamed 'la formiga' (the ant) because of his high level of endurance. And to this day he still runs continuously, covering every inch of the midfield. But Tim works in line with Santana's tactical philosophy and the coach wants a team that is dynamic to the extreme. In a friendly against Switzerland, Dirceu is left out and the Swiss secure a draw. Telê does not like it: 'It was an abnormal game, the worst since I arrived.' In the next friendly, the last before the Mundial, against the Republic of Ireland, Dirceu comes on in the second half and, with him on the pitch, Brazil score five goals in 24 minutes. Santana's option for the Cerezo jersey.

The Golden Cage

Millions of Italians have chosen to glue themselves to the television in order to forget, at least for a few days, the news stories, the plots of terrorism and finance. However, the climate of the first weeks of the World Cup remains hot. Three days after the arrival of the

THE GOLDEN CAGE

Italian delegation at the Pontevedra retreat, the Israeli army invades Lebanon; 24 hours pass and, in Rome, under the Flaminio Stadium, two police officers from the Villa Glori police station are executed by the subversive group of the Nuclei Armati Rivoluzionari. The day after the Azzurri's debut, Great Britain defeats Argentina, ending the conflict that had broken out over the Malvinas/Falkland Islands, and on the day of their second match, the banker Roberto Calvi is found hanged under Blackfriars Bridge in London. But the Spanish competition is also threatened by ETA (Euskadi Ta Askatasuna), the terrorist organisation for the independence of the Basque people. To deal with it, King Juan Carlos deploys 22,000 agents to defend its World Cup.

Having grown up with the label of a bumbling monarch, a puppet parachuted on to the throne to continue serving the interests of the dictatorship (by making him his heir, Franco was counting on leaving everything settled and well packed), he has instead become, with Suárez, González and Carrillo, one of the Fab Four of the transition. The Mundial is the inaugural party of the 'España' brand. Suffocating in the cradle the ambitions of the military coup d'état that wanted to turn back the hands of the post-Francoist transition, moving calmly, with institutional wisdom and a few twists, Juan Carlos is making the crown an anachronism that works, and of Spain a kind of 'monarchublic'.

The eyes of the whole world are now on his 17 green lawns, and inconvenience is not part of the plan. This is also why a pact of non-belligerence has been signed between the kingdom of Spain and ETA. But the precautionary measures taken to protect the Casa del Baron, the three-star parador (3,900 pesetas for full board, 50,000 lire) built four centuries earlier on the plan of a Roman villa, which Italy requisitioned in January by stealing it from Peru, remain equally impressive. The Italian Embassy in Madrid, following the state of tension that has spread through the country due to the sentences handed down to the protagonists of the failed coup of 23 February 1981, has asked the Fuerza de seguridad del Estado to intensify

195

surveillance of the national team. The team finds itself living in a splendid but at the same time gloomy hotel. A golden cage. A retreat, in the words of Oreste del Buono, that would have succeeded in eradicating any residue of will even in Vittorio Alfieri.

Before the arrival of the Italian delegation in Pontevedra, all the surrounding houses were scrupulously inspected. The 620 tenants were interrogated, filed, removed or put under special surveillance. Until Italy leave the hotel, the four sharpshooters assigned to surveillance from above will not move from the roofs of the buildings closest to the retreat. There are 120 gendarmes of four corps, Policía Nacional, Policía Secreta, Guardia Municipal and Guardia Civil, alternating outside the blue retreat 24 hours a day, while eight plain-clothes inspectors of the superior police corps are stationed inside the hotel with P38s in their holsters, sleeping in front of Bearzot's room.

He has been assigned room number 101, the one where Generalissimo Franco spent his nights when he went up to Galicia, but also a young Juan Carlos, before he became king of Spain. He probably also slept there one night in March 1956, a few days before another Italy vs Brazil match, which ended 3-0 and was played in Milan, before reaching Villa Giralda, his parents' residence in Estoril, where, on the evening of Holy Thursday, after playfully pointing a revolver at his brother Alfonso, unaware that the gun was loaded, he shot him in the forehead, killing him. The gun was a gift from General Franco.

The Great War

Embedded between the inlets of a bay beaten by the Atlantic, Pontevedra is a bored city that no longer expects anything from the future, not even from this championship that it watches with increasing detachment. Far from the euphoria of the Mundial, within its walls it has a few shops, a few restaurants and just three cinemas. But the Azzurri are not interested: they are banned from going out and they have brought their films with them from Italy – 33 tapes. They seem like an immensity but whoever chose them did the calculations: from 2 June to 5 July, which means getting through the first round and leaving at the end of the second – 33 twilights and then everyone goes home. Right after the match against Brazil.

On the first evening at the Casa del Baron, the head coach shows his boys Mario Monicelli's *La grande guerra* (The Great War). Perhaps not by chance: those soldiers, Oreste Jacovacci and Giovanni Busacca (portrayed by Alberto Sordi and Vittorio Gassman), initially considered to be two bumblers, end their exploits as heroes in the conflict that unites the country for the first time. Victory, for the moment, does not seem within reach for the Azzurri and Gassman himself, the Busacca of the film, joins the chorus of pessimists: 'I don't see how this Italy can worthily represent us.'

A few days before the call-up for Spain, Bearzot was still in the midst of torment. His attacking duo was Bettega and Rossi, who had done wonders in Argentina. But the former had suffered an injury a few months earlier and had not yet recovered. The coach had waited for him like a patient father, questioning him until the very last moment. Two days before the call-up, Bearzot called him to offer him the chance to go to Spain as non-playing captain, a way of showing his gratitude (in Argentina Bettega had been one of the team's driving forces), but the striker, although flattered, declined. Thin and out of training, Rossi had two years of ban behind him and barely a handful of matches. The coach brought him in anyway. The press wanted Altobelli and Pruzzo. Bearzot, together with Rossi, called the former and instead of the latter chose Selvaggi. It was a strategic call-up: if Rossi had not worked, no one would have accepted him as a substitute. But the journalists rose up again, wanting Massaro.

Before the start of the World Cup, the Azzurri play a training match in Portugal against a local team, Sporting Braga. For them it is little more than a practice match, for the reporters it is a dress rehearsal. Italy win only 1-0, Massaro disappoints, the return of Rossi disheartens and the team does not push. The World Cup is just around the corner so it would be crazy to get injured, but the journalists do not give the coach a chance. Bearzot is almost scandalised: 'The conditions of great warriors are checked at the time of the battle.' So, four days before the World Cup starts, the national team is still in the midst of chaos.

The president of the FIGC, Sordillo, the institutional figure who in theory should defend it, makes inflammatory statements: 'If this is the national team then it was better to stay at home.' Then he adds, 'In 20 years of football, I have never seen anything so mortifying.' Bearzot replies calmly to all the heated criticism launched by the Italian press: 'Those who live in football know how to interpret the relative value of certain friendly matches.' Some of the journalists ask the coach whether he should book a return flight directly from Vigo. 'If Barcelona had to be skipped,' replies Bearzot, 'for you it would be a story over quickly, while for me it would be something great. I would stay here alone and cry.' Such an unarmed confession is not enough to dampen the spirits and, the next day, in the newspaper *Il Mattino*, Bearzot is mercilessly defined as 'the most unpopular character in Italy after Tarquin the Proud'.

The Massacre Game

Enzo Bearzot's Italy find themselves in the initial group stage in the company of one European, one South American and one African team (Poland, Peru and Cameroon). They draw three disappointing matches but the others do no better and, in the end, in the rather shabby accounting that governed the fate of the group, Italy come second, behind Poland, at the expense of a surprising Cameroon, who leave the World Cup unbeaten. The group is considered to be the 'most ruined and flat of the Mundial' (Sergio Rotondo), the one of the 'ungainly' (Oreste del Buono), the one 'of non-play, of technical paucity, of sloppiness and sterility' (Manlio Scopigno).

In the hotel room of the *Corriere dello Sport* correspondent Antonio Corbo, dozens of telegrams arrive from Italy: 'Attack the national team.' After the match against Poland, Piero Sessarego, correspondent of the *Secolo XIX*, shouts at Bearzot, 'If I have to talk about football, I'll go elsewhere because here we play table football.' And Paolo Rossi's poor condition also horrifies Italian journalists. Giorgio Tosatti, one of the most respected, regarding the coach's decision to call up the centre-forward for Spain, wonders aloud, 'What knowledge of sport can a person have who insists on bringing a player in that condition,' with three broken meniscus, two years of inactivity, five kilos less in weight and no chance of becoming what he was in Argentina. But Bearzot is blamed for everything: his Italy have not won a match since 1981; the team is old; in order to bring in Rossi, he has left at home people such as Eraldo Pecci, Evaristo Beccalossi and Roberto Pruzzo, the top scorer of the championship; he waited until the last day for the injured Roberto Bettega, but he does not field promising youngsters such as Daniele Massaro and Giuseppe Dossena; his staff has three coaches (apart from himself, there are Azeglio Vicini and Cesare Maldini) but only one doctor, Professor Leonardo Vecchiet, and not even a trainer; the friendly matches he organised (in Geneva, Braga and Pontevedra), instead of clearing up ideas, did not reveal good play; the physical condition of the team is very bad; the expedition has been badly prepared, and the choice of Alassio for the initial training camp was also unfortunate.

Bearzot has been surrounded by enemies for years and detested by almost all journalists. He is a tough coach who does not abandon his ideas and has solid morals. He is therefore absolutely incapable of putting up with the compromises of football and of adopting that eloquent, all-Roman attitude that allowed his predecessor, Fulvio Bernardini, a journalist as well as a coach, to bond with his colleagues in the press despite the mediocre results. He has almost every Italian newspaper against him and has become the favourite target of national frustration. Reporters from all over the world watch in amazement as he is crucified on a daily basis. The 150 reporters in his country are waiting for him to fail. Never in football have a national team and the press of its country put up such a ruthless battle.

THE MATCH

The theatre of war is the living room of the Casa del Baron, where players and journalists face off every day for an hour. At 11 o'clock on the dot, the go-ahead is given by Marquis Carlo De Gaudio, guardian of the Azzurri, who also acts as press relations officer. In a small room on the ground floor, with a fireplace that is always lit, Bearzot, sitting on a sofa, offers himself to his platoon armed with belligerent notebooks and impatient pens, reviewing the faces of his executioners. In the front row sits the patrol of 'armed reporters'. They are the reporters from *Il Messaggero*, *Tempo*, *Paese Sera*, *Corriere dello Sport* and *Mattino* (Roman and Neapolitan newspapers that detest the coach's actions for biasing his choices towards northern teams). On the other hand, there are the 'warrior friends' Franco Mentana, Gian Maria Gazzaniga and Carlo Grandini. Their newspapers, *Gazzetta dello Sport*, *Il Giorno* and *Corriere della Sera*, have been bringing them together for 20 years in the stadium press boxes: kisses, hugs, dinners, split accounts and man-to-man marking, but those who know they have the first fruits are willing to lie to death just not to share them with the others. In one song the great old men: Giovanni Arpino (*Giornale*), Gianni Brera (*La Repubblica*), Mario Soldati (*Corriere della Sera*) and Oreste del Buono (*Stampa*). From time to time, Bearzot seeks out their gaze and finds the same perplexity for that climate of perennial lynching. In his diary, Brera notes: 'In Pontevedra I attend a press conference and feel pity for them.' Apart from them, only a handful of journalists escaped the stoning of Bearzot: Pier Cesare Baretti (*Tuttosport*), Giorgio Lago (*Gazzettino*), Bruno Amatucci (*Avvenire*), Mario Sconcerti (*La Repubblica*) and, above all, Italo Cucci (*Guerin Sportivo*).

The press conferences turn into a game of massacre. On one side Bearzot: 'Here I am, I'm here, what do you want?' In front of him a small army of Italian journalists who come to the room every day just to fight over the bones of the national team. And when they cannot find anything to bite into, they stick to insignificant news. Or inaccurate. Or, worse, invented.

Every morning a case arises: the Conti case, the Dossena case, the Antognoni case, the Rossi case. The federal incursion in Latoya

200

becomes, for Gino Bacci of *Tuttosport*, a bet at the casino (closed that day) with huge losses. The Azzurri, who were not informed of a cocktail party organised by Cinzano, were transformed into snobs. Behind the scenes, those excluded from the starting team are portrayed by the press as eager rebels. Majorettes, models and compliant entertainers slip in everywhere. Even the historic friendship of team-mates and room-mates, Rossi and Cabrini, becomes a love story. Claudio Pea, the youngest correspondent of the *Il Giorno* troop, led by Gian Maria Gazzaniga, saw them looking out of the parador window. They have just got up, their faces are sleepy and their hair is in disarray. 'If your wife Simonetta is three months pregnant,' he shouts at Pablito, 'she won't be able to join you in Barcelona if you qualify for the second round.' He says: 'I'll just have to be happy to share my room with Antonio.' They smile at each other and exchange two more words. Those that Pea uses in the lines sent by Vigo become something else: 'Without Simonetta, Pablito now shares his room with the handsome Cabrini: always to be puritanical, let's avoid the ironic comments that have been made around this new couple of which – this much can be said – it has been officially decided that Pablito is the man and Cabrini the *muchacha*.' Words that went around the world.

But Pea's enthusiasm goes even further: 'After Cameroon, for three or four days, the Azzurri will be able to meet – as they say in puritanical jargon – with their wives in Barcelona. Provided, of course, that they get through the first round in Vigo.' Which the press is certain won't happen. 'You all make me laugh. What Barcelona of Egypt are you talking about?' shouts a reporter. 'You can all see the Columbus monument from the plane. With binoculars. So much for wives and girlfriends following the Azzurri.' The joke brought Rossi out of his silence: 'This is really heavy. In fact, you know what I'll do? I'll tie it on my finger and I'll remind you of it when we get to Barcelona. Then we'll see which of us will have made the worst impression.'

The wave of criticism is partly inspired by Italo Allodi, head of the technical sector at Coverciano. His university is churning out new coaches. One of them, Eugenio Fascetti, after the first group stage is among the harshest: 'We are ashamed to belong to the same category as Bearzot.' There is a desire for renewal. Italian football is prehistoric. The Old Man is a dinosaur. At the centre, in those days, Count Rognoni also shows up. Four years earlier, he had asked the man who dominated all the market plots to get one of his protégés enrolled in the Coverciano course. Thanks to that unknown coach, his Cesena youth team has just won the 1982 Primavera championship, despite the fact that the night before the final a scream wakes the team up. It is that very young coach, in the grip of nightmares: Arrigo Sacchi. Allodi, in his spirited pupils, already sees the light of the predestined: 'He will be the new Herrera.' In the meantime, the wind is bringing that fringe climate to Spain.

The Magic Square III

On the day of his first match, two faces constantly oscillate in Santana's head, those of Dirceu and Paulo Isidoro. The press wants the name, the coach opens his secret drawer, thinks out loud and gives his thoughts to the reporters: 'Paulo Isidoro was injured by a contusion and Dirceu was able to take the opportunity he was given. He did well, applied himself, marked, moved well on the right and even swapped positions with his team-mates. These qualities made me opt for him, leaving Paulo Isidoro for another opportunity.' He thinks he has freed himself but the torments continue to chase him and, a few hours later, in a radio interview, he declaims the formation. Surprise: Paulo Isidoro is there, Dirceu is on the bench. Then he changes again and announces Dirceu in the team. In their opening match of the World Cup, against the Soviet Union, Santana fields him on the right of the attack. Behind him is Falcão, who has never been called up in the previous two years. The two 'foreigners' have earned their place thanks to a couple of pre-Mundial friendlies.

The first half ends with Brazil one goal down. The football exhibited by the national team creates yet another certainty in Telê: he

THE MAGIC SQUARE III

must move something in the team. And the piece that is removed from the chessboard set up in Seville's Ramón Sánchez Pizjuán is Dirceu. His place is given to Paulo Isidoro. Brazil play a sensational 45 minutes, equalising through Sócrates and scoring the winning goal through Éder. Dirceu never sees his name mentioned again in the competition. His third coveted World Cup lasts just three-quarters of an hour but it is enough to put him on the top step. Three Olympic Games (1972, 1976 and 1980) and three World Cups (1974, 1978 and 1982). A record. There is nobody like him, not even Pelé. But the coach is not convinced about Paulo Isidoro either. Zico tries to defend him: 'One time in one match cannot call into question two years of great performances.' Paulo Isidoro and Falcão now have a 50/50 chance of playing.

The former has just won the Brazilian Ballon d'Or, has had a splendid championship, has contributed to the qualification and the first match of this Seleção. He has been working with Santana since the first hour; 22 matches together in two years. That place is his, he deserves it. Falcão, on the other hand, has just been called up again, he has not experienced a single page of the Telê era, neither the World Cup qualifiers nor the triumphant European tour. He found himself playing in Italy in the year of the coach's arrival and has remained far from the cameras, lenses and microphones of the Brazilian media. He himself is willing to give up his starting position: 'Cerezo is an outstanding player, he has impressive mobility and resilience. The team misses him, so if it's the case, I'll go out with all humility, I'll give him my place and I'll applaud him.'

The esteem is reciprocated. When he learns that he has been lined up to play against Scotland, Cerezo himself expresses, perhaps unconsciously, his desire to have Isidoro at his side: 'He helped Brazil win the game against the Soviet Union and frankly I don't think it's right to send him away. Obviously I am here to respect the coach's decisions, but I would prefer to play in the centre, in my real position, while Paulinho could continue in his.'

Santana will not listen to reason. He is trying to create a square in midfield and, in order to achieve this, he has decided to sacrifice one

THE MATCH

of the two forwards. He has abandoned the hallowed 4-3-3 formation to embrace a brand-new 4-4-2. His former role as a player, the right wing, is to become more and more an empty space, filled according to the course of each match by the members of his midfield, whose rotation will have to avoid giving reference points to the opponents.

On the eve of the World Cup, the choice of Telê had generated much controversy. Even a comedian, Jô Soares, had created a catchphrase, 'Bota ponta, Telê!' (Put the tip, Telê!), which had spread throughout the country. In reality, play and results had contradicted the real need for a legitimate spearhead. Despite this, Telê Santana found himself having to defend himself against an army of nostalgics and, by the time he left for Spain, his patience completely exhausted, he had decided to publicly declare the death of the spearhead in football: 'Those who need a team with fixed tips and position specialists, including those who should wear the No. 7 and 11 shirts, are already dead and don't know it. Modern football does not allow more than one fixed player in a given position, otherwise he will be easily marked by the opponent.'

So now he sacrifices Isidoro, welcomes Cerezo, confirms Falcão, leaves Serginho at centre-forward and behind him Éder, Zico and Sócrates. Paulo Isidoro is informed by some reporters: 'Surely this is a misunderstanding.' A few minutes later he realises that he is no longer the owner of the shirt. But nothing now can change Telê's mind. After Italy vs Peru, an hour before Brazil's match against Scotland, the coach calls Cerezo, Falcão, Sócrates and Zico aside: 'You four will now live together in midfield.' It is eight o'clock in the evening on 18 June 1982. The Magic Square is now complete.

Meeting the King

There is the usual grey weather in Pontevedra. The usual persistent drizzle that haunts the Atlantic coast. In training at the Estadio Municipal de Pasarón, Leonardo Vecchiet is congratulated on having guessed the change in the weather. He demurs, 'I had simply read the forecast, I didn't guess anything.' Coach Bearzot's face becomes more distracted. It is the day of Peru. The Italian journalists are crowding outside the dressing rooms, impatient to know everything about the upcoming match. 'Not only the formation of the national team,' writes del Buono, 'but also the result and the consequences, as well as the immediate future for the other life.' Bearzot removes his pipe from his mouth: 'I can't say what I don't know yet. The players must be left in peace: they are youngsters, they have the right. This is my philosophy.'

In the tumultuous crowd, Soldati eavesdrops on his colleagues that it is captain Zoff's 101st match. This is certainly not news. He already celebrated the round number during the first match. But Mariòn, as Brera affectionately calls him, has his own vision of reporting. It is then suggested that the number should be paid tribute to and that perhaps the Azzurri captain would not mind a visit from him to wish him well. But the anomalous reporter is a purveyor of rare good manners. He knows that in other people's homes it is the landlord who rules, so he looks for Bearzot, finds him and, having overcome the throng of storming scribblers, catches up with difficulty.

'Until now I have never spoken to anyone. Today I would like to have a word with Zoff, would you give me your consent?'

'But of course, just imagine,' approved the Old Man without the slightest hesitation, 'there he is, our Zoff, do you see him?'

Soldati catches Zoff on the edge of the pitch.

'He's 40 years old,' Bearzot continues, 'but in a way he's the youngest of them all. Because he has remained a boy.'

'But how do you stay young?' asks Soldati.

'You have to believe in the most beautiful ideals of your youth,' Bearzot replies in a flash. And while he is closing the gap in his thought, a tall, athletic man with a familiar expression blocks his view. And, like a good host, the Old Man doesn't miss a chance to introduce him. He is the doctor of the national team, Professor Leonardo Vecchiet.

'He is also from Friuli, like Zoff and me. Vecchiet is from Moraro, Zoff is from Mariano, I'm from Aiello, between Gradisca and Cervignano. They are villages close to each other. The Tre Campanili can see each other.'

Bearzot, who will also take to the pitch with his team in a few hours, is in the mood for hospitable talk. 'You wrote that I am serious because I am of Habsburg tradition.' A few days earlier, Soldati had portrayed him as 'an honest, serious and severe civil servant with a Central European style, as was natural to his Friulian blood and Austro-Hungarian upbringing. 'When I was a boy, I remember very well how my brothers and I used to tease my grandfather by pulling out the tricolour flag and he, between being serious and joking, would take the yellow flag with the black eagle from the bottom of a drawer.'

'Not in our house,' laughs Vecchiet, 'we were sincerely on the other side, for Italy.'

Zoff appears. Soldiers and he sit next to each other on a bench, under a faded plastic canopy, while outside, in the drizzle, the other players continue their morning training. Soldati has been in the company of the Friulian goalkeeper before, but always in passing, perhaps in the middle of a lunch or any of the Juventus celebrations. Never on his own like now. He immediately senses that he is next to 'a simple, strong, good creature, warm-blooded and alive, very human, somehow inarticulate and stupendously rocky'. The Azzurri captain listens to him, locked in a motionless pose, his hands on his knees 'like those of a sculpted pharaoh'. His luminous eyes are protected by a perpetual half-light, while his voice is low, a little slow and vibrant 'like a fourth string of viola or cello, depending on the moment'.

Zoff tells Soldati about his family, his wife from Mantova, his son, his affection for Torino, his plans for the future. All these are things that Soldati does not write about in his piece. On the contrary, he himself begins to speak. This was also noted by del Buono: 'The oldest of Bearzot's boys, Dino Zoff, sits on a bench, listening to a monologue by Mario Soldati, who is supposed to interview him. Every now and then he nods politely, and even more politely he

MEETING THE KING

smiles, in his reserved and demure way. He is right, because Soldati is always amusing.' This may be true, but the special envoy, on the other hand, almost without realising it, resumes the argument he started with Bearzot and Vecchiet: 'Those immune to this scepticism about a "prerogative of tradition" are only the people from Piedmont, Trentino and Friuli, like Zoff, Bearzot and Vecchiet.' It was at that moment that, with a rapidity that takes him by surprise, Zoff emerges from his statuesque pose, brings out his defender's reflexes and breaks into Soldati's words.

'Ah no! No! This is the way to divide Italy!'

When Soldati hears those few words spoken in a low, sorrowful tone, he feels a lump in his throat. 'I have hurt him, I have mocked the most beautiful ideal of his youth. Bearzot was not wrong in saying that Zoff remained a boy.'

The next day Soldati, with Manlio Cancogni and Antonio De Rosa, goes to La Coruña to see Poland vs Cameroon. There is a newspaper strike in Italy and they are not supposed to write after the match. On their way back to Vigo they take the opportunity to stop in Santiago de Compostela, which none of the three of them know. They arrive there by crossing the Galician plateau at sunset. After the Government Palace and the cathedral, Soldati suggests that his two companions visit the old Royal Hospital, now converted into a luxury hotel. Huge rooms, sofas, carpets, baroque paintings. After passing through the bar they arrive at the dining room. The last rays of sunlight of the day shine through the low windows. The room is almost deserted. There is only one table occupied. Three diners. A man on either side, an older man with his back to the centre. An early dinner, which is unusual in Spain. 'Who knows, maybe the three will not be Spanish.' Soldati, driven by an unmotivated impulse, steps forward to the left. He thus glimpses the man's face from the back. The diner notices his presence and turns towards him. It's Havelange. Without even thinking, Soldati introduces himself, speaking French. The king of football notices the card hanging on his jacket, stands up and exchanges a few words with him.

207

'I see that you are Italian.'

'Yes president, I'm from Turin, but I live in Tellaro, a small seaside village overlooking the Gulf of La Spezia.'

'I know the place. It's beautiful.'

'On the other hand, I envy you the writer Machado de Assis. He's my favourite Brazilian. I find him extraordinary.'

Havelange smiles. The two say goodbye, Soldati leaves, Havelange takes his place at the table with his fellow diners, probably Blatter and Dassler. Soldati does not recognise them. What matters is that he, the occasional reporter, has succeeded in the Mundial. A face-to-face meeting with the absolute master of football. Those who do not expect the unexpected will never get there.

The Other Friulian

The Big Apple of Italy was once Milan. The small metropolis was home to a skinny seven-year-old boy from Friuli, Fulvio Collovati. Far from the thousand lights of the city, his world revolved only around the oratory. A double leap brought him, at the age of 13, first to Cusano Milanino, on the same ground that had baptised Trapattoni and Oriali, then to AC Milan, where he made his way: Pulcini, Allievi, Júniores, Primavera, up to the first team. Polite, correct, never violent. Few predicted a glorious career for him. They said he was too good-natured, a deplorable defect for a defender: 'With a manner like that you won't get far, you have to make yourself respected.' The young stopper's fears were alleviated by a second father, Nereo Rocco: 'When you go out on to the pitch, Teston, you have to kick everything that moves: and whether that is a ball, doesn't matter.'

Parón lived in a boarding school with the boys. Fulvio was in the room with Baresi. For all the boys that was a difficult time. Their adolescence was the first asset to be sacrificed at the altar of football. Rocco understood. It was the others, perhaps, who struggled to understand him. He only spoke in Trieste dialect, called them all 'mona' and ate at the table with the younger ones, trying to dig deep into them. In 1980, when AC Milan were relegated to Serie B due to betting on football matches, Collovati stayed with the team. It was a difficult choice, as he risked losing his place in the national team by playing in the lower division. On Saturday he played for the Azzurri, on Sunday he played for the Rossoneri. It was madness. Bearzot, however, accepted it.

Time had thus disproved the critics. Collovati was the only defender in Italian football who had never been sent off or banned. A sign that sometimes it is worth betting on elegance and style. Spain is his first world showcase. He has only one regret, that of not being able to be seen by the man who discovered him. On 4 December 1978, at the invitation of Milan, Rocco followed the team to Manchester. On the evening of the match, Collovati was on the pitch, the ever-present Bearzot in the stands. Pneumonia contracted at Maine Road weakened the Parón and liver disease took him to hospital in Trieste. He died at 11.47am on 20 February on a cold and bright morning. His last words to his son Tito were, 'Give me el tempo,' as he used to say on the bench to Bearzot and Maldini, as the matches were winding down. Four days later Collovati made his debut in Bearzot's national team. His time began then.

The Void

Even fantasy requires sacrifice. Santana's square leaves one side uncovered. If on the left there is Éder, covered by Júnior, on the opposite side, having eliminated the right wing, there is a void. The coach's objective is the carousel, a rotation to stupefy opponents by removing points of reference. But it's not so easy to implement on the pitch.

In order to bow to his coach's wishes, Zico is forced to change roles and occupy a space that is not his own, a choice that, since the match against Scotland, leaves him with nothing but thoughts: the square made too many mistakes, he was not as creative as he should have been, the rotation on the right did not work and the victory was linked more to individual play than to the football he showed. When he finds out that the formation will be maintained against New Zealand, he sharpens his tongue: 'I will play on the right, giving up my real role, just because it is a tactical imposition necessary for the team and because both Falcão and Cerezo failed to adapt. But that doesn't mean I will play the part of saviour of the country. No one can perform at their best outside of their true position.'

The good results obtained do not reassure him. Brazil are suffering from the absence of a real striker. For this reason, Zico goes so far as to publicly demand the end of the midfield square. One of the four champions – Cerezo, Falcão, Sócrates or even himself – has to go to the bench. The target, indirectly, is the latest arrival: Falcão. 'When things get complicated nobody wants to end up on the right side. But when they get easier, because the opponents open up the defence for us after taking a couple of goals, everyone wants to be there. So it's easy! I think the game against New Zealand is the last test we can do regarding this square. After that, if it doesn't work, Paulo Isidoro is the most suitable to occupy the position, because he has been playing since his first call-up, he knows that position more than anyone else and he can hold his own.'

He may be the latest arrival, but Falcão no longer feels like a fish out of water: 'We all have to adapt to the plans of the alliance manager. Ours is asking us to have someone, in rotation, on the right. But it happens that, because of their characteristics, Zico and Sócrates play in their area without the obligation to mark, while Cerezo and I have to stay behind and help the defence in the early stages of the action. It would also be easier for me to play on the right, only I wonder: who would cover Luizinho and Oscar? The really difficult thing is to play at the back and then attack.'

Telê Santana is not even touched by the controversy involving two of his best players. What he is interested in are his convictions. And that includes the four geniuses in midfield. A choice that also leaves room for Éder, Júnior and Leandro. As a good Mineiro, he throws water on the fire. 'The one on the right is a sector that does not worry me, especially for the goodwill that Zico is showing. I didn't ask him to stay there permanently, he has freedom of movement, but the others must understand that that side of the pitch cannot remain uncovered and it is important that when Zico is not there, there is always someone among his team-mates. It can be Cerezo, Sócrates, Serginho, even Leandro. All except Falcão, who is more used to advancing in the centre than playing on the right. It sounds like a cursed position, but it's like any other.'

The victory against New Zealand, the third in a row at the Mundial, puts an end to the contrasts. Coach Moracy counts every single play: 'We had 584 passes. With the Soviet Union there were 383 and with Scotland 415. The error rate was 8 per cent. The lowest since Telê.' For the second time in the history of their 12 World Cup appearances – the other was in Mexico – Brazil have won all their first-phase matches. The coach is beaming: 'The rotation on the right has worked in an exemplary manner.' Controversy buried. This is one of the reasons why his Magic Square will decorate the Sarriá midfield against Italy.

Deus é Brasileiro

The battling atmosphere leads the more cautious Azzurri to retreat to their rooms, deserting their appointment with the press. A few courageously offer their chests. Among them is Causio, one of their heroes of Argentina. He has known the Vecio all his life. He has called him that with affection since he was 16. Bearzot was assistant coach of Torino and Causio was training at the Filadelfia for a trial with the Granata team. It was there that he met Bearzot for the first time, who was then Nereo Rocco's deputy. It seemed as if it was a done deal, he had already chosen the room in the pension where he would go the following year. But instead, Rocco said, 'He's not fit enough.' Years later, Bearzot threw it back in his face. One day he showed Causio the reports he had written. They were all excellent. The rejection had come from above.

THE MATCH

Then Bearzot came across Causio again with the youth national teams and finally with the senior national team. At 33 years old, he is still one of the greatest interpreters of a role invented by Italian football, that of the full-back. He always wears a suit and tie, and he moves with elegance on the pitch. The nickname 'Barone', which was first given to him by Fulvio Cinti of the *Stampa* newspaper during his debut years in Turin, fits him like a tailor-made suit. But since he dribbles with Carioca fantasy, Vladimiro Caminiti of *Tuttosport* finds him another nickname, 'Brazil', for his South American flair, his tightrope-walking technique, and the pleasure of feinting. After his glory years at Juventus, he has found a home in Udine. It is not the end of the line, as many think. Causio does not feel finished and brings out the best in himself. Pride plays its part. But the strongest stimulus was Bearzot's words: 'Go to my land, behave yourself. Know that I'm following you. Maybe I won't call you right away, but if you do well, I'll take you to the World Cup.' *Brazil* pulled off a Guerin d'Oro championship. The Vecio calls him up: 'Conti is the starter, the hierarchy is clear. But I want you to come anyway. Even if you do not set foot on the pitch you will still be valuable. Are you up for it?' Il Barone immediately says yes. So, 19 months after his last meeting with the national team, Bearzot has kept his word.

The Vecio welcomes him to the Alassio training camp, spreading his arms: 'Hello Barone, old man from the provinces! You've also lost a bit of hair.' Causio shrugs his shoulders and replies, 'You know, I'm not used to so many people anymore, it's affecting me.' Bearzot says, 'Then I got it all wrong, I called you because you're a veteran.' And as a veteran, in fact, three days before the first World Cup match, he appears in the press room with a severe air, rising to the defence of his team-mates: 'What are you complaining about? You wrote that we went to the casino and it wasn't true, that we were with the *majorettes* and it wasn't true, that Rossi and Cabrini had an affair and it wasn't true, and even that our wives are the prize for the passage of the round. But I refuse to consider my wife as a match prize. The

212

players you write about have every right to shut their mouths because you lack loyalty. And that is the most serious thing.'

Bearzot is on the side of his boys and talks for hours in their place, allowing himself to be hammered relentlessly in order to entertain the journalists and leave the players with their heads clear. He has forbidden them to read Italian newspapers, which he strictly avoids circulating throughout the hotel. But the news does arrive. Often it is the worried wives who call from Italy asking for confirmation. After Il Barone's speech, that same day, in order to show a more relaxed atmosphere, the photographers prepare a table with a chessboard and invite the president of the FIGC, the lawyer Federico Sordillo, and Bearzot to take their places, simulating a game. After the first uncertainties, Sordillo seems to accept, but Bearzot freezes everyone: 'I don't play chess and these scenes are not to my taste.'

In Vigo, the other target of the press, Paolo Rossi, has not been seen for days. One morning, to their general astonishment, the journalists see him coming down the stairs. They immediately question him on his athletic condition, the kilos he has lost, his mood and his diagnosis. He becomes impatient: 'I needed to be alone, to collect my thoughts, no controversy.' Thin, pale and taciturn, reporters always portray him as sad. The period of inactivity has significantly reduced his muscle tone. Professor Vecchiet treats him with electrostimulation, but it takes time. 'I just have to play, play, play. I was stationary for two years, remember?'

He does not feel like talking, but in a corner of the piano bar, near a staircase, he finds himself facing Sconcerti. They were once close friends. They come from the same land, the journalist's house and the footballer's house only a few kilometres apart, and when they were young they even had the same coach, Enrico Orioli, a man from another era who taught them to love their opponents. Sconcerti met Paolo when he was a boy, when he came to Coverciano for the convocations of the national youth team. He still remembers all the scouts from the professional clubs who came just for him. At the time he played on the right wing, skipping past opponents to the left and always managing to get away on the wing. Even then he was beautiful to watch. He was clearly different from everyone else. He was light, fast and very skilful. Sconcerti was a young reporter.

They then met here and there in Italy, one a journalist, the other a player. When he became the first Rossi, the one from Vicenza and Argentina, Paolo gave him a couple of exclusive interviews that allowed him to take important steps in his career. The betting scandal divided them. In his newspaper, Sconcerti was among the guilty parties.

They met again the winter before the World Cup, Sconcerti trying to hide his embarrassment, Rossi pretending not to. They had lunch together in a restaurant where the player was cradled as if at home. Only then did Sconcerti realise that Paolo Rossi had survived. Now he has the distinct impression that he would gladly stop and talk to him, so he stops being a journalist and asks him to help him understand what a World Cup is. 'It's something immense. I've done nothing but score goals in my career, but I'm Paolo Rossi only for those three goals I scored in Baires, do you understand, Mario? I will only be Rossi for what I can do here. If I fail, I will no longer exist in the world. This is a World Cup.'

While Vigo finds itself out of the matches, far from the Mundial, shrouded in wind and controversy, on the opposite front, in Andalusia, on the Mareina sports field, 30 kilometres (19 miles) from Seville, Brazil, led by Telê Santana, improvise an off-season carnival every day. He opens his doors wide to everyone and any training session, even the most insignificant, becomes a party with Leo Júnior playing the pandeiro, singing 'Voa, canarinho, voa', the anthem he has recorded for his country, while Éder, acclaimed by millions of female admirers, scores from midfield barefoot to entertain the 11 Sevillian models accompanying the Seleção. It is no coincidence that the Brazilian team have their first three matches on Andalusian soil. From behind the scenes, the managers of the CBF have gone to great lengths to facilitate Telê's work. In order to get Brazil to stay in Seville, a city at sea level, whose temperature in the European summer is similar to that of Rio de Janeiro, Giulite Coutinho, the president of the Brazilian Football Federation, travelled to Spain four times and invited the Spanish national team to Brazil, together with Raimundo Saporta, president of the World Cup Organising Committee.

The fans' enthusiasm is through the roof ('Bienvenido Mister Futbol' banners announce). There is one 24-year-old, Ramon, who, to see his favourites, set off on 26 November, travelling 26,000 kilometres (16,000 miles) by bicycle, carrying only a rucksack and $120, as well as all his optimism. Brazil do not disappoint their supporters, winning all the matches in their group, against the USSR, Scotland and New Zealand, scoring ten goals, all of them cinematic, and conceding just two. Zico's imagination, Éder's power, Cerezo's funambulism, Júnior's cheerfulness, Serginho's arrogance and Sócrates's class have enchanted spectators and reporters all over the planet. Seville has been invaded by 15,000 fans, all in regular yellow kit. On sleepless nights they beat drums, dance the samba and speak only of a *Brasileira* victory. And they pray. Because, for them, even God, yes God, is Brazilian.

The Stopover of Shame

That evening in the summer of 1960, he stepped boldly out of his metallic blue Dino coupé – with a Fiat body and Ferrari engine – in front of the entrance to the Canottieri in Naples. In the hot weeks of the Rome Olympics, the Campania capital was the chosen venue for the sailing competitions. He had already been through a lot but the sport was aware of his existence at that moment. He was the man of reference, the host, and in the halls of the club, which *L'Équipe* had just described as 'the largest nautical complex in Europe', in an unreal atmosphere, a ball was being held that would go down in history. Halfway through the evening, Carlo De Gaudio, a 30-year-old Mediterranean, eternally tanned, not tall but athletic and overflowing with sympathy, sat down on the terrace overlooking Vesuvius to enjoy his first moment of pleasure. He noticed a nonchalant young man inviting a slender woman with a shy and austere look. He was Juan Carlos, the future king of Spain; she was Sofia of Greece.

Their first meeting had taken place six years earlier, during the famous cruise of kings organised by Queen Frederika with the aim of reviving Greek tourism, but in reality with the secret aim of encouraging a royal marriage. The eldest son of the Count of Barcelona, pretender to a throne momentarily frozen by Generalissimo Franco, was just over 16 years old and did not seem to notice his Greek peer. The princess, on the other hand, immediately noticed the young Bourbon. She found him likeable and, as a good girl, she was terribly fascinated by his wildness. Everything separated them: character, origins, friendships. He frequented Orléans and Savoy, she English royalty and German princes. Nothing happened during the cruise and Juan Carlos did not even ask her to dance. What young De Gaudio watched spellbound was their first dance, which would unite their destinies forever.

Now 22 years later, it is De Gaudio who finds himself 'in the house' of Juan Carlos. Two years after the Neapolitan ball, the young man married Sofia and was now the ruler of Spain. De Gaudio, on the other hand, is in Spain as diplomatic adviser to the Italian national football team. His is an unusual figure, strongly preferred by FIGC president Sordillo. The legacy is a heavy one, left by Gigi Peronace, a generous and tireless discoverer of talent, who played a decisive role in the election of Artemio Franchi as president of UEFA and in the appointment of Enzo Bearzot as technical commissioner, before dying in his arms one night in 1980.

De Gaudio has inherited not only the role but also the joviality of his predecessor. Officially he is in charge of relations between the Azzurri delegation and the press, but in reality he is a sort of guardian of the Azzurri. He is the guardian angel, the buffer, the filter between them and the outside world. There is no real spokesman. Bearzot speaks for everyone, he speaks to everyone. De Gaudio knows the real feelings between journalists and players and is usually good at preparing in advance. He has been through a lot and his affability has always saved him.

The necessities of war had brought out unexpected gifts in De Gaudio. With little desire to study, without a father, and the eldest of seven siblings, he soon had to put his friendliness to good use and by the time he was 16, with the Americans in Naples, he had managed to get away with supervising the unloading of goods from ships. Twenty-five lire a day, which was fabulous then. One day a baker asked him whether he could get him some flour. He knew of a mill, so he hired a carter to transport it. The route was long, the load heavy and the danger of attack very real. De Gaudio made a job of it, became a pasta merchant, reached Gragnano and became the manager of a pasta factory. Wheat was his gold mine but he wanted to go big, so he went to the source in Argentina, where he discovered a greater resource: meat. He bought 500 quintals of meat and sold it to Simmenthal in Italy. His biggest business. He put it to good use by creating the only industry in the south capable of regenerating waste polyethylene. He became the man of disposable bags. A revolution in waste collection – until then, jute bags had been used – which led him to create Polisud, Iplar and Policolor.

Before gaining prestigious positions in football, De Gaudio had two great loves: swimming and water polo, with Canottieri Napoli. He went into football as a referee, like Franchi and Klein. It was a dangerous profession where he was from. They offered him the presidency of Napoli, but he refused, preferring to found a second city club, Internapoli, which played at Vomero. He found Giorgio Chinaglia at Massese, who he later sold to Lazio for 200 million lire in promissory notes. He was entrusted with the organisation of the four matches in Naples for the 1980 European Football Championship. Sordillo then made him the diplomatic adviser of the national football team.

And now, on the eve of the match against Cameroon, 'the Marquis of Vomero' is sitting at a table to govern the fate of a team terrified of a possible defeat. Even if he does not believe it, he must anticipate it. If Italy lose, everyone goes home. So here is a comeback plan that smacks of escape. The first proposal he considers will take the Azzurri from Vigo to Madrid, from there to Paris and on to Ciampino airport in Rome, which is closed to civilians. He chooses another option. Landing in Nice and a night bus to Milan. The news leaks out. The label is ready: it will be 'the airport of shame'. It is not put into practice: the Azzurri go through without even winning a match, while Cameroon go home without losing. The Marquis breathes a sigh of relief.

The Treatment

In 1965, when Paolo Rossi was nine years old, cardiologist Leonardo Vecchiet became the youngest head physician in Italy. Three years later he would add to this title that of doctor to the Italian national team. For some time he has been preparing a detailed programme for the Azzurri, studying every potential problem in detail. He knows that the World Cup takes place in the most diverse places, where it is easy to create extreme situations that can negatively affect the physical activity of the players. Mexico, Germany, Argentina, now Spain. Each country has its own climatic conditions. This time the problems to be faced are twofold: heat and humidity. From the moment Italy achieved qualification they have had his obsession, so he started to look at the average temperatures and humidity levels of all the venues where the matches would be played. When he discovered that Italy's initial destination would be Vigo, in the coolest part of Spain, he found that the closest Italian venue to those climatic conditions was Alassio. So a tactical manoeuvre began, carrying out preparation in the Ligurian resort in order to avoid any stress with the transfer to Spain.

Now, in Barcelona, there is a different air. Playing in a hot climate means accumulating heat. Vecchiet therefore has to help the Azzurri disperse it. But sweating creates a decrease in their physical capacity. Each player can lose two kilos in training, three during the match. His aim is therefore to rebuild the emptied tanks. He has staked everything on this. They use food and medical help, while masseurs Giancarlo Della Casa and Luciano De Maria continually supply the players with water. To help the lads recover more quickly, Vecchiet also lays out small ampoules of creatine at the table, a simple supplement but useful in combating the heat.

But it is not enough just to keep them physically fit. Psychological support is also needed. This is Bearzot's prerogative. The coach works constantly on human relations. He speaks sincerely with every single player. If he does not play someone, he explains why. Vecchiet and Bearzot have been friends for a long time. The coach has full confidence in Vecchiet's scientific preparation and believes deeply in this relationship. Vecchiet is the part he lacks. Humanist and scientist. Psychologist and doctor. When Paolo Rossi underwent a series of tests on the eve of the Mundial, Vecchiet had all the data to understand that he would make it: 'He is underweight and still out of shape, but he will regain his competitive tone.' A few matches would be enough, he told Bearzot. He did not need anything else.

On 14 June, in Vigo, Rossi takes the pitch in the first match, against Poland. It is a pale result and colourless player. The press leaves pity at home. 'He doesn't stand, stumbles among the daisies and struggles to get up.' For the match against Peru, Bearzot confirms the same formation as in the first match, including Rossi. Naturally, the coach is not spared: 'Only imbeciles could think that a player who had been out of action for two years could regain the chance to play in no time at all,' 'He insists on playing him,' 'Sending him out is blasphemy.' Rossi plays badly, he is unrecognisable – 'He's a corpse,' 'He makes me cry,' 'He's pitiful.' Gianni Brera calls him an 'ectoplasm of himself'. Marco Bernardini of *Tuttosport*, at 6.16pm on Friday, 18 June, admits that he believed that 'the myth of Pablito has crumbled like a sandcastle'. After 45 minutes Bearzot has no choice but to sub him, with Causio coming on in his place. The curtain should be closed there but in the dressing room Bearzot makes the umpteenth act of faith. Rossi's team-mates are about to go back on to the pitch, while he is bent over on the bench. With one boot on and one boot off, he thinks: 'It's over.' But before closing the door, Bearzot looks him straight in the eye: 'Get ready for the next game.'

The Club of the Cuckoo Heads

In the meantime, *La Repubblica* is exceeding 400,000 copies in circulation. Eugenio Scalfari is gloating, transforming himself, according to Brera, into the most inveterate fan. The power of sales. His two pens, Brera and Sconcerti, are in a group with Mario Soldati, Oreste del Buono, who proclaims himself president of the club of imbeciles, sometimes with Gianfranco Giubilo of *Tempo* and Manlio Cancogni, correspondent of *Globo* from New York, sent by his newspaper to Spain to report on the World Cup.

In Vigo, in order to keep their distance from Bella Napoli, the night-time headquarters of the reporters, the 'writers', for 20 nights, meet at the table in the Los Garavelos tavern of a Galician socialist, Roberto Romero, who keeps the place open after hours so that they can play scopone until late. The fourth person in the card game is sometimes the painter Antonio De Rosa, who comes with Mario Soldati. The four of them viscerally detest each other without showing it too much. Brera has a sort of physical dominance over them, he is the strongest and toughest, Soldati is the most defenceless and the oldest. He travels every night with his car and driver. Twice he reports the theft of his suitcase, wandering around the hotel in his vest so that there are no doubts. During the game he sometimes goes into catalepsy for a couple of minutes. The cigar at the side of his mouth follows the beating of his heart, then he wakes up and picks up the game where he left off, breathing the breath of a thousand lives.

On the last evening before Barcelona they drink all the Italian wines that the Galician host has found for them. On the way back, Brera lays a hand on Sconcerti's shoulder. The night becomes beautiful and the air smells of the sea. When the lights of the hotel appear, Brera stops: 'You are a good boy, really. You're going to be a good man.' Sconcerti looks at him: 'Gianni, I'm already a man.' Brera shakes his head: 'Not yet, when you become one you will be a good man,' and bids him goodnight, leaving him wondering what he is at that moment, just five hours from Barcelona.

Silence is Golden

'Someone has added that the Azzurri of Italy will earn 60 million each if they are promoted to the Barcelona round, 95 if they reach the semi-finals and 180 if they are champions.' It is 2 June, the day of the departure for Spain, two weeks before the first match of the national team. The stone is thrown by Tony Damascelli, in the *Giornale Nuovo*. A few lines that begin to trigger an underground word of mouth that then, on the occasion of the passage of the first round, explodes. This is not the first time the journalist has used the formula of inference. The technique is tried and tested: it is enough to attribute a fact to generic third parties with the syntactic complicity of undefined pronouns and impersonal plurals. Heaps of approximate forms (it seems, it seems, it is said, it is thought ...) turn out to be very useful to get rid of the responsibility of certain statements. In this way one can also invent, since the fandom is of the unknown.

When, 20 days later, the Azzurri enter the second phase, the Socialist deputy Ermido Santi, the Christian Democrat deputy Publio Fiori, the senator, his namesake, Giuseppe Fiori of the Sinistra Indipendente (Independent Left), and the president of the Constitutional Affairs Commission of the Senate Antonino Murrnura present, one after the other, a parliamentary question to Prime Minister Giovanni Spadolini and the Minister for Tourism and the Performing Arts Nicola Signorello to verify, judge and prevent the payment of those millions considered excessive, offensive and morally unacceptable on the very day when the government announces to parliament new sacrifices for Italians. Spanish television also ridicules the national team: 'In Italy there are factories closing and players about to earn six million pesetas.' The report, broadcast during the night by the daily column *TeleMundial*, also reaches the Azzurri. It is the final straw that makes them say enough. Rossi and Cabrini, the casino, the young ladies, the table football, the sponsors, the wives, the insults, now the inflated prizes.

The night brings the recommendation of silence. On the morning of the departure for Barcelona, an internal commission composed of Zoff, Tardelli, Graziani and Causio meet. The agenda: relations between players and journalists. Never easy, never happy. 'We must think about playing and not defending ourselves.' The decision blossoms unanimously: from now on, no player will answer the reporters' questions. Only the captain, Dino Zoff, will be entrusted with this task. He, the most taciturn of the Azzurri. Press silence. The first in the history of football, an unprecedented initiative. Bearzot invites them to reflect: 'When you are certain that you are on the right side of things, it is a mistake to condemn yourself to silence.' The Azzurri does not retract. The coach respects their decision.

The departure is scheduled for 4pm. The players, having left the retreat that has hosted them for 22 days, are in the small airport of Santiago de Compostela, with their mouths shut and their faces dark. There is still an hour before boarding for Barcelona. Bearzot is sitting at a table in the bar. Gianni Brera approaches him. The coach is smoking a light pipe made by Enea Buzzi, which Brera himself had given him in Braga.

'Does it pull well?' asks Brera.

'Yes, I am very satisfied,' replies Bearzot.

For the first time since the start of the Mundial, the two find themselves talking intensely, alone, protected by a cloud of cordiality penetrated from afar, only by the attentive eyes of Mario Sconcerti.

'Why are you so obstinate in keeping Rossi in the team?'

'Because he needs to play.'

'But he's in a very bad condition.'

'He's getting better.'

'And Antognoni? He doesn't see the game.'

SILENCE IS GOLDEN

'The others always fear him. And then he can score.'

'Wouldn't Dossena be better?'

'He's still young, but he will work his way up.'

'No offence, but in yesterday's game you seemed to agree.'

The veins in Bearzot's neck swell. 'Are you kidding me? Never in my life would I do such a thing!'

Repenting, Brera feels obliged to give him courage. 'You will see that it will be better in Barcelona.'

'I'm sure of it. We feel free, we are reborn,' Bearzot surprises him.

'But Argentina and Brazil are no joke!' suggests Brera.

'We know their game by heart.'

Brera squints.

'I'm sure we'll have fun,' adds the coach, 'but don't tell people that.'

Brera nods.

'We are here to serve you,' says Bearzot.

'Navarro, you'll see that Rossi comes out,' whispers Brera on the plane to his neighbour. Navarro is the name he has given to Sconcerti. It was born on the day of departure for the Mundial, during the stopover in Madrid on the Milan–Vigo flight. Brera had turned to an Aviaco stewardess: 'A ticket for my friend Cordobes.' 'Why Cordobes?' she had asked. 'Because he's dark like the ones from Córdoba.' Sconcerti is dark and has long hair in a pigtail. The woman had laughed: '*El señor es palído, un hombre del norte: es un Navarro.*' Pamplona, the bulls, Hemingway. Sconcerti approves. He has been Navarro ever since.

'What did Bearzot tell you?' says Sconcerti.

'That he will play with his men. He doesn't have any others.'

'But now Italy has everything to gain, don't you think?'

'I think that if you trust the Italians, you will always be disappointed.'

'Guicciardini?'

'No, it's mine.'

During the flight to Barcelona, Brera writes a conscious invocation to the 'catenaccio saint', because when the Italians are afraid they play at their best. 'Rossi is improving and I would give a finger of my left hand to see him score a goal against Brazil.' But, absorbed in his brooding, he does not notice what is happening on the plane. The reporters following the Italian expedition start from the back, cross the aisle, skirting the many rows of passengers that separate them from the Italian delegation. The footballers in the first rows have long faces and low stares. The first to turn back with his cap still on his pen is Antonio Corbo of the *Corriere dello Sport*.

'What's going on?' his colleagues ask him.

'They wouldn't answer me.'

'And why?'

'They don't talk. It's a blackout!'

Sconcerti stops talking to Brera for a moment. 'Black what?'

'Mario, these people don't talk anymore, they keep quiet.'

The news spreads quickly among the seats on the plane. Some people are smiling, others are incredulous, but slowly panic begins to grow: 'What are we going to do now?' Attempts are made to appeal to friendship, sympathy and support, but there is nothing they can do. When the plane is about to land in Barcelona, it is Beppe Dossena's turn to give the dreaded confirmation to Roberto Renga of *Paese Sera* and Giuseppe Rossi of *Gazzetta*. 'I'm sorry, but we've decided not to talk to journalists anymore. From now on it will only be Zoff who will act as spokesman for the team.'

'And why?' they ask in chorus.

'Ask Zoff.'

In Barcelona, the group is divided: silent players here, furious reporters there. The general opinion among journalists is that within a few hours this news will pass. This is not the case, but in the evening even the press silence becomes a topic of discussion and therefore the subject of an article. The greatest curiosity is the search for the reason.

The answer comes at 11.30am the following day in the cool garden of the Hotel El Castillo, on a hill overlooking Sant Boi de

SILENCE IS GOLDEN

Llobregat, with Zoff's first press conference. The thermometer stands at 37 degrees. The captain addresses three journalists elected as representatives of the envoys accompanying the national team: Angelo Pesciaroli (*Corriere dello Sport*), Gino Bacci (*Tuttosport*) and Giuseppe Maseri (*L'Unità*).

'We have decided to have no further contact with you. The reasons are closely linked to what has been written about us so far.'

The national squad do not receive newspapers. A sealed envelope collects daily telexes with unwelcome headlines from Rome. But when the envelope arrives at De Gaudio, it is already late. The players are informed by phone calls from their families with all the imaginable emotional implications.

'We know we won't gain anything from this action,' explains Zoff. 'On the contrary, we will lose out, but the guys got tired of reading ambiguous statements or sarcastic comments that made us look ridiculous. How can we accept provocative, tendentious and ambiguous questions every morning?'

The person who has suffered most in these days has been Paolo Rossi. His crisis has been emphasised and an enormous burden of responsibility has fallen on him.

'It's not true,' continues the Azzurri goalkeeper, 'that we will receive a lot of money, and having written that we have already earned 60 million, you have not only told a lie but you have presented us as people who live in another world, on their own island, as if we didn't realise the difficult moment our country is experiencing and ignored the fact that so many workers are at risk of being unemployed. We are in your hands and you have painted us in such a way that we have lost the sympathy of the Italians. Every team needs supporters and the press, we don't think we are so strong that we can do without them, but because there has been no goodwill we have taken this decision, in the hope of regaining some peace of mind. I hope that this matter will be concluded quickly, because I will soon tire of talking. Democracy is also the right to remain silent.'

'What conditions do you set?' asks Pesciaroli.

Zoff finds himself in the role he also plays on the pitch. 'This is not an attacking manoeuvre, it's just an act of defence. You're making spirit out of our skin, that's why we're here, forced to defend the tranquillity we need.'

The most desperate Italian journalists turn hopefully to De Gaudio, who takes his time and reassures them. 'Don't worry gentlemen, it won't be long.'

Even France and Germany, even Spain, who have had disappointing results, have tense relations with the press, but not like Italy. The most forthcoming with journalists is Brazil. Darwin Pastorin is gloating. In Seville he has managed to wring every confession out of each of his myths and cannot believe his ears when he hears his colleague Marco Bernardini, who follows the Italian national team, on the phone: 'Darwin, it's hell here. Nobody talks. Every day I have to invent the thoughts of Rossi, Conti and Tardelli. Come to Barcelona and you'll understand.'

The following day, Saturday, Bearzot goes to the hotel hosting the journalists in Barcelona to spare them the discomfort of the trip and offers them the customary press conference. It is a sign of détente. But around him the music does not change. The Old Man has no fear and remains in the front row. 'Do you want to know how much I earn? My contract is filed with CONI.' The more audacious ones discover that, compared with Serie A, the coach is the lowest paid in Italy: he doesn't make 80 million gross a year, or 50 net.

An hour later, in the hall of the Princesa Sofía hotel, Federico Sordillo provides the exact figures. The World Cup brings in huge sums of money (from television and radio rights, commercial exploitation, advertising and match receipts), which are then divided between FIFA (10 per cent), the organising committee (25 per cent) and the various federations (65 per cent), who get their share in relation to the matches played and the passage through the rounds. After the first round, Italy will receive a share of the FIFA proceeds. The players will receive a legitimate share of around 40 per cent of that total, from which all travel, accommodation and organisational expenses will first be deducted. 'Each player will therefore receive no more than around 20 million, a gross figure subject to tax deduction.'

No federal president had ever announced the size of an award. It is a turning point in the customs of Italian football. But the newspapers are full of polls: 'Do you agree?' Among the celebrities, writer Camilla Cederna and journalist Enzo Tortora are against it; athletics champion Pietro Mennea and industrialist Silvio Berlusconi are in favour. They are joined by writer Enzo Biagi: 'The World Cup is a spectacle that makes billions of dollars and it is only fair that some of these should end up in the pockets of its protagonists. Why aren't questions asked about how much comedians earn? If they fill the cinemas, there must be a reason for it.'

What the politicians and journalists do not realise is that the federations are autonomous organisations: when they award prizes they do so using the proceeds of the events and not public contributions. Moreover, the Azzurri's prizes for passing through the rounds are among the lowest of the Mundial. Sixty per cent of the takings will go to Argentina, while France and England will receive 35 million, Spain 120 million. And to Brazil?

For winning the World Cup, the Brazilians claim $120,000 (20 million cruzeiros) for each player. Enough to buy a three-bedroom flat at the Jardim Paulista in São Paulo or the Leblon in Rio de Janeiro. 'We started from the 1978 prize, which had been $35 million for third place, we applied the currency correction and world inflation,' Sócrates reasoned. Giulite Coutinho countered with a third of the value requested by the players, $40,000: 'Five thousand for each stage won. Since there are four stages, passing all of them would earn each player $20,000. We have also proposed 20 per cent of the fee that the World Cup promoters will pay to the CBF. That way, another $20,000 comes out for each one.'

The final meeting takes place nine days before Brazil's first match, in the Hotel do Guincho, in Portugal, where the Seleção is in training. Before the meeting, the requested figures are leaked to the press. The leak puts the players in a corner, in the gaze of public opinion, and at that point there is nothing left but to submit to the CBF's diktats: the negotiation is closed at 10 million cruzeiros, about $60,000, just over 80 million lire, for each player. Zico admits that the players only gave in so as not to be branded mercenaries. The value of the prize paid to the group in the event of the title would still not reach 10 per cent of the turnover envisaged by the CBF: about 1.3 billion cruzeiros, $8 million. From FIFA, as a participation fee, the federation will receive more than $3 million; from Topper, the company that supplies sports equipment, $1 million; another 500 million cruzeiros from the Sports Lottery instalment; in addition to the advertising revenue from sponsors (Gillette, Hering, Chicletes Adams and IBC) and shares in the broadcasting rights of the matches. A few days before the match against Italy, Sócrates vents to some friends: 'We were summoned as if we were an army that had to defend the country. It's not like that. This is just a sporting competition. It was exhausting work for nothing. I don't want to talk about this ever again.'

The Group of Death

The mechanism of the World Cup has purposefully been constructed to get Spain, the hosts, into the semi-finals, along with West Germany (the reigning European champions and the country of the president of the FIFA organising committee, Hermann Neuberger), Argentina (the reigning world champions, protected by FIFA vice-president, Rear Admiral Carlos Alberto Lacoste) and Brazil (the most loved and followed team and home of FIFA president João Havelange).

Football, however, as Telê Santana said, is a mine of unforeseen events and it is on this uncertainty that its secret lies. And, in fact, the organisers see all their plans come to nothing on the pitch. In the plans of Saporta, Neuberger, Lacoste and Havelange, the semi-finals should be Brazil vs Argentina on one side and Spain vs West Germany on the other. Argentina, if they had not failed in the first round against Belgium, should have won their group, thus avoiding

THE GROUP OF DEATH

Brazil in the second round. The same applies to the hosts, who were beaten by Northern Ireland, despite complacent referees and penalties given away.

The most beautiful World Cup in history has so far been distorted not only by refereeing scandals but also by a grotesque mechanism whose consequences, in this second phase, are there for all to see. The disproportion of the quality in the four groups that have been created is appalling. The six top seeds of the Mundial have found themselves compressed into just two groups (Argentina, Brazil and Italy on the one hand and Germany, England and Spain on the other). In Group C, Italy's group, there are the teams that came first, third and fourth at the last World Cup; Group D, which hosts France (who have not passed this round since 1962), Austria and Northern Ireland, is, on the other hand, impressively modest. The Irish, who landed unpredictably in the second phase, do not even have a hotel in Madrid.

In any case, although born of a resounding surprise, the Barcelona group of death is now sending the world into a frenzy. All eyes are on the Catalan capital. The moment the Azzurri ended up in this hard group, the press began to consider their adventure in Spain over. Fabrizio Cerri (*Il Popolo*) already speaks of 'presumably the end of Bearzot's national team'. Gian Paolo Ormezzano (*La Stampa*) writes of a 'decline by now ascertained'. They are not the only ones who do not believe : 'It is too difficult a grouping for Italy,' Franz Beckenbauer rages, 'and the team has too old players.'

The theme of the eve of the first match is 'knowing how to lose'. The newspapers seem to be a chorus: 'If we have to say goodbye, let's at least leave a good memory' (*Corriere dello Sport*); 'At least let's save face!' (*Il Messaggero*); 'It would be enough to know how to lose' (*Corriere della Sera*); 'Lose, perhaps, but with joy' (*Il Giorno*); 'You have to at least lose well' (*La Gazzetta dello Sport*). Oreste del Buono has bought the latest book by Gabriel García Márquez, struck by its pessimistic title: *Crónica de una muerte anunciada* (Chronicle of a Death Foretold). 'Italy, if it really goes to its death this time, well, it will have a glorious one with Brazil or Argentina.'

THE MATCH

In Barcelona, however, Italy breathes a different air. And not just because the sun is finally shining. The spirit of the players begins to change. The Azzurri seem reborn. They are aware that their condition is no worse than that of other teams. Austria and Germany have qualified after a shameful staging that condemned Algeria. In order to stigmatise the farce, *El Comercio*, a newspaper in Gijón, moves the report of that match from the sports pages to the crime pages. The headline is self-explanatory: 'Forty thousand people swindled at the Molinon stadium by a gang of Germans and Austrians'.

But even an indecent Spain, booed by its own public, were only able to beat Yugoslavia or the surprising Honduras thanks to the penalties offered by generous referees, although this was not enough to prevent them from losing to ten-man Northern Ireland. Not to mention the Russian referee Miroslav Stupar, who went back on his decision after the sensational negotiation with the Sheikh of Kuwait, Al Ahmed Al Sabah, president of his country's football federation, who has carved out a place in history for having gone on the pitch and convinced the referee to disallow the fourth French goal scored by Alain Giresse. Even the Brazilians benefited from the referees' complicity in their first and most important match.

Fortunately, the commission chaired by Franchi restores credibility to the tournament by eliminating four men in black: Lamo Castiello, who favoured Brazil by denying two penalties and cancelling a goal to the USSR; Luis Barrancos, accused of giving a non-existent penalty to Argentina against El Salvador; Henning Lund-Sørensen, who helped Spain by inventing a penalty against Yugoslavia; (in all three cases the referees were assisted by Spanish linesmen); and, of course, Miroslav Stupar.

Italy arrive in Barcelona with a stutter, on tiptoe, but they are there. And they have no one to thank for getting through the first phase. Even if they are the only team to have qualified without having won, they still obtained three positive results and are among the six teams that have arrived unbeaten in the second phase.

THE GROUP OF DEATH

Four years earlier, Italy were only team to qualify with a 100 per cent record: three matches, three victories, six goals. Now, however, they have a great opportunity to change the tone of their World Cup and none of Bearzot's boys want to waste it. Yes, the air has changed. The physical condition has improved and the team have regained form. The fear of not making it, of failing the minimum objective of qualification, has disappeared. The climate, the humidity, that unseasonable cold of Pontevedra have allowed the team to store up useful energies to resist the stifling heat of Barcelona. There is the stimulus of playing against two great national teams, one reigning champion and the other unanimously considered the winner of this Mundial. Finally, there is the charge that comes from feeling alone against everyone. Now it can become an extra weapon.

Italy do not enter Brazil's thoughts. Attention is elsewhere. The second round makes Santana more concentrated but not worried. The Brazilian press also travels calmly. Brazil 'won all three games', praises the weekly *Placar*, 'scored ten goals, conceded only two and is, more than ever, the favourite in the competition. Not only because it achieves the best performances among all the candidates aspiring to the title, but because it is the only team to show, in addition to enviable individual talent, an airy, modern, offensive, almost irresistible game plan.' Italy are not a concern. *Placar* leaves aside the nuances: 'Looking back at the history of the Italian national team, there is nothing to fear ... we have all the conditions to overcome it without great difficulty.' The director Juca Kfouri's words of confidence go hand in hand with this: 'There is no denying that Italy is not scary. It is an old team and plays football without any grace or creativity. The question is: until when will we be champions only three times?'

Predictions, statements, journalists, even the president of FIFA, the Brazilian Havelange ('It is a shame that Brazil and Argentina are playing for access to the semi-final in a stadium like the Sarriá'), completely ignore Italy. Argentina prove to be an unstable team in Spain, capable of losing without a fight against Belgium, scoring against modest Hungary and finally going through against unfortunate El Salvador, thanks to a bad penalty decision. But the team is composed almost entirely of champions to whom they have added a sumptuous reinforcement: Maradona, the best player in the world. On 7 May 1979, Osvaldo Soriano wrote to Giovanni Arpino: 'Friends tell me that in a small club in Buenos Aires, Argentinos Júniors, there is the salvation of Torino. His name is Diego Armando Maradona, he is 18 years old and is, according to journalists and my friends themselves, the greatest player (even though he is short in stature) of the last 30 years. He scores two goals a game (his team is miserable but they are first) and is already part of the national selection. Of course, all the big players, and Barcelona, want to buy him: he costs, I think, five million dollars. If Torino have that money they're safe. They say that compared to him, Sívori is an energetic man. And don't say I didn't warn you.'

Because of the great rivalry between Brazil and Argentina, it is expected that this will be the closest match. Santana is also convinced that it will be the Argentines who will give his team a hard time, not the Italians: 'It is certainly not likely that someone will show, in the most difficult moment, qualities that they have not shown in less complicated times. It is an innocuous national team, dull, probably because of the campaigns directed against Bearzot and his players.' Carlos Maranhão, the correspondent of *Placar*, does not hold back: 'My team is going through a very good moment, today I am not afraid to say that we are among the best in the world and that nobody can make fun of us. I foresee a wonderful spectacle against Argentina and I admit that Italy's forwards could also react. But I don't venture a prediction. This round is difficult and only one national team will be ranked. But I have full confidence in my team.'

Announcing the landing of the Seleção at the festive airport of El Prat in Barcelona, the local newspaper *El Periódico* sums up in a headline the feeling that pervades Spanish fans: 'The greatest football spectacle has arrived'. The Brazilian national team has settled 40 kilometres (25 miles) from Barcelona, in the Mas Badó hotel, a farmhouse that, between 1929 and 1944, had been an important sanatorium for the treatment of tuberculosis. Before arriving there, President Giulite informs the team that each player will receive a Sharp television and video recorder. Compared to Seville, the daily rhythm is different for them. The matches of the second phase are held in the afternoon. On Thursday they get to know the Sarriá pitch on which they will play against Argentina and Italy. Sócrates notes in his diary that day: 'The stadium is battered but the pitch is as good as the one in Seville. For those who play the important thing is this.'

The Brazilians' first training session in Catalonia is at the Centre d'Esports Sabadell stadium, about 30 kilometres from their hotel. The fitness trainer Tim is meticulously supervising the execution of the exercises. Next to him is the assistant coach, the world champion Vavá. The Brazilians are surprised by the silence of the Italian press: 'We also talk in training,' says Éder. And indeed, even then there is no shortage of statements: 'Brazil plays football in constant movement. It is the football of the future,' Zico says. 'Italy, on the other hand, still uses man-to-man marking. Sad football from the past. In this century it's ridiculous. The Italians can be satisfied with getting through the first phase. But I still can't believe that they weren't able to beat Cameroon.' According to Sócrates, 'Antognoni is the best Italian player and one of the best in the world.' Then, smiling with his pensive air at the bewildered faces of the Italian interviewers, the captain asks: 'But is the story of Rossi and Cabrini true?' and starts dribbling head-on with Dirceu again. The two bend down on their knees, lie on the grass and the ball insists on going back and forth from one to the other, as if magnetised.

At the same time, 45 kilometres away, Giovanni Trapattoni and Giancarlo De Sisti, the coaches of Juventus and Fiorentina, respectively, are watching the Azzurri's final training session from the sidelines of the Deportivo Gavà pitch. They are the helmsmen of the first- and second-placed teams in the just-concluded Italian championship and feel the urge to huddle with their boys. Trapattoni is staying in a hotel on the Costa Brava, 80 kilometres from Barcelona, De Sisti on the outskirts of the Catalan capital, in the luxurious

Princesa Sofía hotel in Plaza Pío XII. Both have Brazil in their history. Trap scored on 12 May 1963 at the San Siro stadium when the Azzurri crushed the reigning world champions 3-0. Picchio De Sisti, seven years later, played against the Seleção in the final of the Mexico World Cup, starting for an Italy team that, on the evening of 21 June 1970, surrendered due to fatigue only 24 minutes from the end. 'I still remember how my heart was pounding as I listened at attention to Mameli's anthem.' The awarding of the Jules Rimet Trophy was at stake and the Azzurri were playing on equal terms against the strongest on the planet.

At the end of the training session, each coach is joined by his players. It does not take long for Trap to realise that Paolo Rossi is just sick with mistrust, too burdened with the responsibility of leading an entire team. De Sisti reminds Graziani, Antognoni and Massaro of the glory of Mexico: 'We too started badly, in a group without glory, qualifying with one goal, but then we exploded and went all the way.' Talking to the boys, both discover with amazement that the tactic of silence is bearing fruit. In front of the two coaches there is a group that is finally calm and determined. It really looks like another team.

The Sarriá

The fate of the most spectacular group, the one that includes Argentina, Brazil and Italy, will be decided, ironically, at the Sarriá, the small stadium of Espanyol, Barcelona's lesser-known team, with a capacity of just 44,000 compared to the 98,000 of the Blaugrana's splendid Camp Nou. The organisers wonder how it is possible to play Argentina vs Brazil, a match that could easily be the final, in a stadium with such a small capacity. It is a lost opportunity, a waste of money. What is more, the matches have to be played at 5.15pm, an unfortunate time to have thousands of spectators to watch the event. For these reasons, the organising committee officially proposes changing the venue and time. The idea comes

THE SARRIÁ

from the German, Hermann Neuberger. Havelange takes it up and considers it logical: football is a business and there is no reason why we should have to give up 50,000 spectators. The proposal is in everyone's interest because the 12 remaining teams will share the global takings of the second phase and therefore full stadiums will benefit everyone.

But it only takes one rejection to blow the idea up. And the refusal comes from Belgium. Along with Poland and the USSR, they feel they deserve to play in the main stadium in Barcelona, with a 9pm kick-off and they do not want to surrender this. A luxurious setting, early evening and cool weather. Who would want to give that up? In fact, the president of the Belgian federation, Louis Wouters, who has been dreaming of breaking Havelange's eggs in the basket since the draw in January (when his national team, runners-up in Europe, were denied the chance to be included with the top Mundial teams), has no intention of giving up such a tasty piece of cake: 'We are outraged at the very idea. If that ever happened, the team would leave Spain or play the remaining games in black. Black is the colour of mourning but also of shame.'

This is not Belgium's first protest. They wanted to be one of the top seeds, they wanted to play in Italy's group, they wanted to replace the injured Vandereycken, who was brought to Spain already convalescing. But this case is the only one in which they are successful. Coach Guy Thys comes down hard: 'First they played smart by manipulating the groupings and now that they have fallen into their own trap they would like to redo everything for money reasons. But we are against it.'

Even the directors of Espanyol, the hosts of Sarriá, dispute the possibility of an exchange: 'We've got Argentina, Brazil and Italy and we want them here.' A few days earlier, the Rolling Stones were supposed to perform in that stadium, the flagship of 'Cultural España 82' (30 million pesetas' worth of tickets had already been sold), but the club's owner, terrified of the vandalism of the crowd, said no. These three matches are too important.

235

The Estadio de Sarriá is therefore the unique theatre in which the destinies of the three teams are decided. It is a dilapidated stadium – the foundation stone was laid on 31 December 1922 – in the middle of a pile of residential buildings, on the western edge of the city. According to Oreste del Buono, 'It looks crooked, distorted, it is in any case ungainly and cramped. It looks a bit like the old Flaminio and the houses around it are bristling with illegal spectators like in Marassi. The right setting for this meeting of the Latin group.' More than 400 million pesetas have been spent to redevelop the ground and expand the initial capacity of 40,000 souls, but it remains a cramped and fiery stadium. There are no more than two metres between the pitch and the beginning of the stands. An ecstasy for the torcida.

The Eve

The centre of the pitch is a region of the soul, reflecting the identity of its occupants. It can be inhabited by shape-makers or lung-blowers. Fantasy or race. In Bearzot's ultra-modern Italy there is a man who represents the point of conjunction between the two categories. The coach, contradicting decades of catenacciari and counter-attacking clichés, has entrusted that region to him, because he knows that only on the pitch can he find his peace. The eyes burning with perennial restlessness, reflected in his neurasthenic thinness, should not deceive. He is perhaps the most universal player that Italian football conveys. A bundle of nerves capable of accelerating, neutralising, recovering and scoring.

On the turf of Deportivo Gavà, Marco Tardelli runs more than anyone else. His galloping at breakneck speed has given him a nickname he does not like: 'Schizzo'. For him, growing up thin and frail in 'serene poverty' in Capanne, perched on the Apuan Alps, running has always been a game. In the oratory football of peasant Italy he was a street kid. He spent his time stealing the ball from his opponent and the plums from the trees. As well as moving his 59kg (9st 4lb) from table to table in the hot summer months, working in a

THE EVE

bar. Like that of 1970, which crossed two destinies, the other being Dino Zoff, goalkeeper of the national team, European champions, in a training camp with Napoli, who was sitting at a table in the Ciocco bar in Garfagnana. Marco Tardelli, 16-year-old full-back in the Pisa youth team, recognised him instantly and, with trembling legs, went to take his order.

Now everything has changed, but perhaps nothing has, as captain Zoff continues to give his orders but now from the goal line. Tardelli is now 28 and at the peak of his maturity, but has not forgotten what sacrifice is.

Tuscany is a land of rivalry and parochialism. The Sienese hate the Florentines, the Florentines hate the Pisans, the Pisans hate the Livorno inhabitants, the Pistoians hate the Prato inhabitants and so on. The grudges between Florence and Pisa date back to the time of the naval battle of Meloria, in 1284, when the former overruled the latter in favour of Livorno. And the destinies of three Tuscans representing three cities linked by atavistic hatred move around the Gavà lawn: Sconcerti (Florence), Tardelli (Pisa) and del Buono (Livorno).

Gentile and Dossena invite to the stage a RAI radio commentator, Ezio Luzzi, known to the Italian listeners of 'Tutto il calcio minuto per minuto' because, following the Second Division, he has the habit of interrupting the Serie A radio commentaries of Enrico Ameri and Sandro Ciotti, with the futility of the cadets. In front of him, they pretend to finally make an intervention. In reality they move their mouths like fish. For them it was a way of playing down the situation and lightening the tone. Luzzi plays along and laughs. The Florentine Mario Sconcerti does not think so, in the stands together with other colleagues gathered in the common anxiety.

'You are making fun of people who are here to work.'

'Come here!' shouts Tardelli.

But the reporter does not stop.

'You can keep what you want to say to yourself, I don't care that you're talking now!'

The other journalists listen, a little dazed by the heat. Oreste del Buono, also sitting in the stands, is tempted to intervene. But then he gets caught up in his own enlightenment: 'What if this anger is useful?' Del Buono, from Livorno, sees in Tardelli from Pisa a desperate and heroic will to react.

Tardelli approaches the stands, Sconcerti the pitch. The duel takes place under the astonished eyes of spectators and the press. They look each other in the eyes, offended, insult each other and are about to come to blows when someone stops them.

'It's undignified here,' states the journalist. 'If we have to fix it, let's take him outside.'

Pause. Second act, outside, the courtyard in front of the changing rooms. Opposite each other. But the quarrel has become artifice. And instinct gives way to reason.

'We are doing theatre,' warns Sconcerti.

'Come on, we're smarter than we're showing.'

They shake hands. For the press it is yet another unpleasant episode. For del Buono it is a sign. It is the rage of wounded pride. And even if officially the fear of speaking up has not been abolished, they have exchanged a few words, in short, the silence continues in the Italian way, which means that it is no longer silence. As in a lovers' quarrel. And so that handful of words gives the illusion that a bridge has finally been lowered. The sentences were certainly not spoken in the name of détente. But some journalists rejoice – after all, contact seems to have been re-established.

The First Ballet

It is the turn of the Azzurri to open the second stage of matches. On Tuesday, 29 June, the first dance, with Argentina, who are already sure to impose their tango: 'Italy is the most undisciplined team in the World Cup, also because they are 50 years behind.' Bearzot cannot believe that César Luis Menotti uttered these words. They have known each other for a long time. They made a pact on the occasion of the 1978 World Cup: if they found themselves against each other, they would not hurt each other. Then the Argentine coach goes against his word and Italy punish him. Menotti has always lost to Bearzot, even when he faced him as coach in Argentina vs Rest of the World. 'Teams are *squinternate* [mad] depending on the results they get. One day they are, another day they are not. Menotti knows these things, just as he knows that judgements made before a match are susceptible to change, even radically, once you get on the pitch.'

Bearzot is mysterious with the press: 'The men I have at my disposal are all suited to this match.' The rules allow him to make his line-up public one hour before kick-off. 'I'm confirming the 16 from the first games,' he hisses, just to keep the reporters happy. For the journalists it means: Marini returns, Oriali is on the bench, Dossena in the stands and Tardelli on Maradona. The reporters returning from Alicante, where Argentina played their last two matches of the first round against Hungary and El Salvador, insist on giving Bertoni the left-back position. 'And I still don't believe it,' retorts Bearzot. 'Menotti won't be so naive!'

It's a chess game. The coach is convinced that in the end Diaz will go on the right, Bertoni in the centre and Kempes on the left, with Maradona up front. For him, the important thing will be to get the right midfield pairing in order to play. His Italy do not intend to defend to the bitter end. They want to impose themselves, despite newspapers such as *l'Unità* and *La Repubblica* having stabbed them beforehand by deciding the quarter-final calendar: Tuesday 29th, Italy vs Argentina; Friday 2nd, Brazil against the loser of the first match; Monday 5th, Brazil against the winner of the first match. Title: *Italy on court Tuesday and Friday.*

At 11.30 they deliver a telegram to Sordillo. The president opens it immediately:

The Azzurri, winners of the 1934 and 1938 World Cup titles, offered their old hearts to the Azzurri team Stop.

THE MATCH

Eight legendary signatures follow: Borel, Ferrari, Ferraris, Foni, Locatelli, Olivieri, Piola and Rava. Filled with emotion, Sordillo slips it into his pocket, takes it to the Sarriá, goes down to the dressing room and, just before the start of the match, reads it to Bearzot and his boys, the only ones left to believe in it.

The Old Man jealously guards his cards until the very last minute. Menotti tries to shuffle the pack: he moves Bertoni away from Cabrini, assigns Maradona the position of centre-forward to make it difficult for Tardelli, his traditional adversary, and inserts Diaz on the right. The aim is to drag Collovati on to the flank and Cabrini away from his position but in doing so he heads straight into the net that Bearzot has silently woven. In response to Menotti's moves, the coach hands over Bertoni to Collovati and Diaz to Cabrini, both left in their area of competence to exchange marking. He moves Oriali to Ardiles, entrusts the task of Maradona to Gentile and diverts Tardelli to Kempes, thus allowing him to build with Antognoni, Oriali and Conti a very mobile midfield pivot that prevents the adversary from thinking.

The Azzurri are lined up in a formation with precise tasks: once they arrive at the edge of their own area they have to take the opposing player who appears in their own space. Oriali is the half-back in charge of maintaining the distance between attack and defence; further forward, Antognoni, who is the director in charge of the actions towards the unmarked player, can move with great freedom, together with Tardelli, who will have the task of inserting himself in the opponents' area. Rossi and Graziani's attacking play also includes the incursions of Cabrini on the left and the lightning-fast dribbling of Conti on the right. Having clear protective duties, the team is always prepared to completely turn the game around once the ball is regained. With Cabrini, Conti, Antognoni and Tardelli, it is a counter-attack that involves getting to the opponent's half quickly, then opening the play for a free team-mate. Bearzot sets up a safety net on Maradona. If Gentile loses him, there is first Oriali, then Scirea.

THE FIRST BALLET

But Bearzot does not want to play a defensive game. The day before he goes to see Tardelli: 'I need an extra player in midfield, someone who goes into the box. I'll entrust Maradona to Gentile.' The move proves to be decisive, the whole plan perfect, the match a tactical masterpiece. Bearzot has not made one mistake. By stopping five Argentina players he neutralises the entire team. Gentile chains himself to *El Pibe de Oro* (the Golden Boy). Tardelli scores with a counter-attack manoeuvred by Cabrini, continued by Conti, illuminated by Antognoni and finished by Tardelli. Cabrini doubles the lead (thanks to a deadly feint by Conti). Passarella reduces the scoreline (with an irregular free kick, while Zoff was setting up the wall). Argentina are on their knees. When the referee blows the whistle for the end, Bearzot is excited and upset. He feels a special thrill, as it is his first victory at the Mundial in Spain. Criticised to the point of derision in the first phase, his form has found consecration against the reigning world champions. Something tells him that against Brazil he will play the real final.

After the match, the director-worker Cucci and the lawyer-president Sordillo meet at the stadium, both with tears in their eyes. Without even realising it they find themselves embracing. It is a pacifying victory. Sordillo believes that the telegram, still in his pocket, was important: 'With the heart, as well as with technique, he won.' The more malicious reporters, however, point out that referee Rainea allowed Gentile to nibble away at Maradona one piece at a time until he had eaten him all. A Spanish reporter counted 21 fouls by the defender on the Argentine, also noting with anatomical fussiness 'three elbows from dentures, two ear bites and an unchecking knee'. President Pertini, on the other hand, justifies the Italian goalscorer in the name of patriotic love: 'Football is a sport for rough people, not for ballerinas!' As it happens, at the end of the match, while the Azzurri are enjoying their first success of the tournament, the dressing room is invaded by a group of euphoric FIGC managers. But the Old Man, without a moment's hesitation, rushes towards the door: 'Everyone out, this is a victory that the boys and I have to enjoy. Alone.'

THE MATCH

The Revolt of the Excluded

Bearzot closes the door to the world. He does it to protect his boys. Never before as in these weeks have the Italian newspapers created issues and oppositions, risking to ruin the harmony of the group. Oriali against Marini, Tardelli against Massaro, Conti against Causio, Graziani against Rossi and other fratricidal clashes. Nothing could be further from reality.

The two Inter midfielders have a great relationship. Theirs is the story of a family derby. Oriali and Marini, brothers 'against' each other for one shirt. The latter plays against Poland and Peru, the former against Cameroon and Argentina, leaving the last quarter of the match to his partner. One reflective and silent, the other open and cheerful. Two sides of the same coin.

Their relay began two years earlier when Italy sat at the World Cup qualifying table. Oriali was the starter. Ten years earlier, after marking his majesty Cruyff in the European Cup Final, he found himself, as soon as he came of age, the most important man in the new direction of 1970s football. However, he watched the World Cups of that decade – 1974 and 1978 – on his television set. Bearzot gave him his debut shortly after the Argentina World Cup. The boy did well and deserved his place in the squad at the European Championship of 1980. But then he was injured. Bearzot chose Marini: he was generous, almost 30 years old and had breath to spare. Marini apologised to his partner and went to fill his role. Bearzot racked up three victories.

At the Mundial, Oriali returns as a starter in the match against Cameroon, taking the place of his partner, suffering from a groin strain. 'No problem,' says Marini, 'Lele is a friend, he and I are the same thing.' Now, he and Marini find themselves in their first World Cup but also in their last round. For both of them, however, the risk of losing their only chance and ending their careers on the bench is not something that will sour their friendship.

After the interchange between Tardelli and Massaro in the match against Sporting Braga, on the eve of the Mundial, rivers of ink were spilled over their alleged antagonism. In those days Tardelli was not yet at his best. Massaro had little experience but energy to spare. There was only one place at stake. It was young Massaro who told us how things stood: 'Tardelli was the first to give me advice on how to stay calm and take to the pitch with peace of mind.'

The same story for Graziani and Rossi. It was the former's goals, together with those of Bettega and Antognoni, that took Italy to Argentina in 1978. But 'Ciccio' Graziani had two misfortunes: he found himself ill just on the eve of the World Cup and behind him was the most in-form player of the moment: Paolo Rossi. Convinced that you cannot always be first in life, he swallowed the bitter pill and cheered for Pablito. But it was tough. At the start of the Spanish Mundial, with the return of Rossi, his place becomes shaky again. If Bearzot uses Causio on the left and Conti on the right, the only forward will be Rossi. Graziani risks becoming the centre-forward of two World Cup qualifiers, without playing a single match in the finals. The press pounces on this and asks him whether he feels he is being denied the role once again. He does not flinch: 'I'd do it again. Like four years ago. I hope to play alongside him, but I'm also ready to give up my place to him.' Without controversy. In the days of Vigo, during an afternoon training session, sandwiched between the match against Peru and the one against Cameroon, an Italian fan armed with a megaphone shouts: 'Rossi sei comico!' Graziani himself replies: 'If you've come here to annoy me, why didn't you stay at home?'

Yet another dispute created by the press is that between Conti and Causio, the greatest representatives of the so-called 'Italic tropicalism'. In reality, the two have never been rivals. On the contrary, Causio has helped Conti a lot, becoming his private advisor. Il Barone already has two World Cups behind him, and in the 1978 one he met Argentina and Brazil. But if the latter is now a different team, the Argentina side has not changed much. So, a couple of days before the challenge against the reigning world champions, Causio draws on his memories and makes some suggestions. Tarantini is to be Conti's direct opponent. Il Barone had driven him crazy in Buenos Aires and knew how to mock him: 'Muzzle him, make him feel that you don't pull your leg back in tackles either. Stay in the three-quarter area, outmanoeuvre him at speed, stun him with dribbling; you'll also risk a few kicks, but you'll see that you'll deprive Zoff and the defence of a good risk. After a while he'll stick to you, he won't want to go looking for luck in attack.' Then he shows him dozens of examples on videotape of Passarella's slips ('If he touches your ankle in his way, you're done for') and Fillol's style of coming out of his goal: two fundamental technical reasons for someone like Conti, who works above all at speed and with crosses.

Conti has never hidden his admiration for Il Barone, indeed he has always stressed how proud he is to wear the No. 7 jersey of the national team, the same as Causio did in Argentina. Causio has always been his idol: he was the one who inspired him and it is to him that he owes much of what he has learned to do on the pitch: the tight dribble, the stop, the change of pace, the running cross. To find him next to you, after following him so many times with your eyes wide open, is an unforgettable experience. He is also sitting next to him on the bus that takes the Azzurri to the stadium for the match against Argentina. Conti fidgets in his seat, smoking nervously. Causio snatches the cigarette from his fingers and forces him to calm down: 'You know who you're playing, who you're up against, what's at stake. There's no point in getting angry now, do it on the pitch.'

When, at the beginning of the Mundial, Marco Bernardini of *Tuttosport* asked Causio who of the two should have that jersey, he did not hesitate for a moment: 'It's right that Conti should play, it's just right!' The same response was given to Angelo Pesciaroli of the *Corriere dello Sport*: 'Conti is starting and that's fine with me.' His loyalty was reciprocated by his team-mate: 'If only there were more honest rivals like him. It would be nice if Bearzot made us play together!' And the coach did play them together for a while against Peru in the match that, by a strange coincidence, saw Conti score his only goal of the tournament. But not even this was enough to calm the spirits of the Italian reporters in the capital city.

The Brancazot Armada

The lair of the Roman conspirators resides in Via del Tritone, on the fourth floor of an early-20th-century building that was once the Select Hotel. This is the space where the sport section of *Il Messaggero*, Bearzot's sworn enemy, is housed. There, from a little cage, the head of the sports services, Gianni Melidoni, nephew of an admiral, commands his ship. He has chosen the parts of his crew one by one. He has given Lino Cascioli, a cheerful, jovial reporter, ready to joke, with flair and intelligence to spare, a precise task: mark Bearzot like a man, leaving him no respite, until he is exhausted. Cascioli has executed this order. During the 1980 European Championships he attacked him for neglecting Bruno Conti, this time for leaving Roberto Pruzzo at home. Both played for the capital city team. When the coach drew up the squad that would go to the World Cup, the choice of players became 'a scandalous mistake'. He did not care whether Cagliari, Fiorentina, Udinese and Roma were represented in the Italian team. Bearzot had acted 'with total disregard for the technical heritage of the teams from outside the Po Valley. But that's how the coach is, take it or leave it. We would leave him at home. But it's too late.'

On the eve of the Mundial, Cascioli goes to spy on the Italian retreat: 'It would be enough to film the movements to understand the abyss of sporting ignorance into which Italian football has fallen.' The portraits of Bearzot endorsed by *Il Messaggero* always portray him as a foggy and confused man:

> We have been able to learn that before taking on the high position of coach of the national team, Bearzot spent his days sitting in the café overlooking the square in Aiello del Friuli and when hesitant drivers passed by and stopped to ask which way to go, the future coach hurried to teach them the right

way, for which he was unanimously recognised as a teacher. Then you know what happens to those who, without being endowed with a robust balance, have the good fortune to pursue a dizzying career: they easily lose their heads.

It is actually Cascioli who has the power to make the coach lose his head. All it takes is one question from him, asked with the seraphic detachment of someone who knows he is on the other side, and Bearzot catches fire.

In the fiercest moment of the critical campaign, Cascioli leaves Vigo to follow the events of Brazil in Seville and Malaga, leaving the national team to Giuseppe Rossi and his chief of staff Melidoni, who, in 'homage' to the coach and his boys, prepares to invent a derogatory label that immediately makes history: 'The Brancazot Armada grew up in the image and likeness of its bony leader, whose shady, uninspiring, monotonous game, stuck in outdated patterns, materialises characters that are not ours and do not belong to us because they belong to Bearzot, who for only ten kilometres was not born on the other side, in Yugoslavia.'

Melidoni has been raging since the eve of the Mundial: 'We are where we were. Bearzot's stubborn work is now collecting its failures, which are the worst of the worst and do not represent the real, even if mediocre, national possibilities … Bearzot wanted to go all the way, that is, all the way to the bottom.' In the following days he intensifies his ruthless campaign until, not satisfied with the victory against Argentina, he crushes any possible enthusiasm: 'We are celebrating a Pyrrhic victory, a damned cheat that has perhaps once again postponed the necessary awareness.' In short, Italy 'cannot' and 'must not' win against Brazil. If they do, what will become of the entire group?

The War of the Pens

The controversy in the Italian press widens the circle, or rather narrows it, and the battle becomes fratricidal by means of ink-stained

THE WAR OF THE PENS

tussles between the journalists themselves: the *Corriere dello Sport* pokes fun at the *Guerin Sportivo*, which in turn criticises *La Gazzetta dello Sport*, which is too pro-federal; editor Giorgio Tosatti argues with editor Italo Cucci; reporters accustomed to blood and dust like Lino Cascioli (*Il Messaggero*) and Mimmo Carratelli (*Mattino*) rail against the 'old carcass' of Mario Soldati, stationed in Galicia and sent, with three-quarters of a century on his shoulders, on behalf of the *Corriere*, 'to Spain and not Spain as we all do'.

Exempt from the duties of reporting to which other correspondents must be subjected, Soldati, who for the first time finds himself dictating his articles on a daily basis, is only required to write colour pieces. And this is why the rancorous acolyte accuses him and his category of writers descended on the Mundial of 'confusion' and snobbery, to which, among others, the eclectic intellectual Oreste del Buono also belongs.

It is Giovanni Arpino who rages against the specialist press, defending the category of novelists who occasionally lend themselves to football: 'Those who are truly familiar with the pen look at the man and the facts, they do not let themselves be polluted by tactical preconceptions and chronicle poisons.' And if he does not, at least for the Peruvian writer Mario Vargas Llosa, another outstanding correspondent, he certainly aims to form new legends. 'Football criticism is a formidable myth-making machine, a fabulous source of unreality for the thirst for fantasies that large crowds have.'

On the day of Italy vs Cameroon, the match that marks the passage of the first round, the situation degenerates. Pietro Calderoni, a 26-year-old correspondent of *L'Espresso*, approaches Cucci and asks him, just to provoke him, the meaning of the word 'criticonzi' that appeared in the *Guerino* about the journalists against Bearzot. Cucci replies: 'Critici stronzi' [bastard critics] and is immediately punished in the pages of the weekly magazine. Calderoni himself reports Lino Cascioli in the press box in Vigo, intent on celebrating the equalising goal scored by Cameroon by hugging Gianni Melidoni. Cascioli writes a letter to Nello Ajello to point out that he was hundreds of kilometres away, but in reply he sees the following published: 'Evidently this is not a repentant journalist.'

On that same day, Alfio Caruso, a correspondent with Arpino for Indro Montanelli's *Giornale* (they have been friends since 1975 and working side by side for three years), headlines 'L'Italia di Ridolini va avanti' (Ridolini's Italy goes ahead), arousing the ire of his fellow writer, who never speaks to him again from that day on. Not to mention the fratricidal war between Arpino himself and Brera, once drinking buddies, now enemies in the name of Bearzot. They probably know that they are the two heavyweights of Italian sports journalism, but they are passing into the history of this Mundial also for their literary friendship that mysteriously ends in hatred.

The Grangiuàn

He has had a bearded face ever since he realised one morning in the countryside that he had not brought his razor blades. 'I should have thought of that before, it's much more comfortable,' he tells himself, 'and then I look better.' The hair hides the cheekbones he inherited from his Hungarian grandmother and the scar from a kick received from a horse. Solemn and chubby, like Joyce's Buck Mulligan, perpetually dissatisfied to the point of bordering on frustration, in the senatorial bedlam of the Mundial correspondents, Gianni Brera is well aware of his cultural superiority. He loves life and attacks it like a Hemingway character: he writes, goes hunting, fishing, hangs out with painters and poets, drinks and smokes. But being a character does not mean being its author. And Brera would like to be Hemingway. He has the possibilities and the gifts but he lacks the time; his profession has inexorably overwhelmed him. The ambition to live as a writer has been trampled on by the need to earn money: 'First the steak, then the Nobel Prize.' However, he suffers from the feeling that he is part of a second-class journalism, knowing that in the US, sport has been covered by the pens of Erskine Caldwell, Francis Scott Fitzgerald and Hemingway himself. The

THE GRANGIUÀN

trouble for him is that 'in our country, sport is either dealt with by Greek professors, who are bigmouth and pain in the ass, or by sloppy amanuensis, who are fanatical'.

And if the author of *Fiesta* found peace in bullfights, he sees a hint of meaning in football. He has coined a barrage of neologisms, thus ennobling sports journalism, but deep down he is aware that he has been wasting his genius writing about matches. He confides to Roberto Gervaso that he feels snubbed, yet he tries to find a meaning in the luxurious shelter he has carved out for himself: 'I think it is better to be a good tailor than a bad writer. I make plush underwear that I then adorn with lace, just to show that I also know how to embroider.' 'L'Arcimatto', the column he wrote in the *Guerino*, was for years his cathartic refuge, the only place on paper where he managed to redeem the vein of a thoroughbred writer, creating, philosophising, playing and inventing. A territory in which not everyone understood him. But Brera has always had little interest in this. He does not write for others, but for himself. He cultivates to eat. The son of a tailor but with a degree in political science, because a piece of paper would have given him a piece of bread; he is not a farmer, he has never held a hoe, but he is one in his language, in his proverbs, in his humour, in his table manners. He is one of those Italians who has carried on his shoulders a language as big as a country, capable of being read, understood and admired in every city. This is his effort. The Italian language is the land where he breaks his back. And in sport, as he literally said, the lexicon swells like a muscle.

A heavy drinker, intolerant of advice and a lover of life, Gianni Brera is the journalist who understands most about football in Italy. Even the players hang on his every word because he is able to show them what they have unwittingly done on the pitch. No journalist before him has ever managed to exert such power over the world of football. The coaches phone him on the sly and he amuses himself by getting them to change the players' roles according to a logic that no one has ever thought of. But with time, it is fantasy, combined with writing, that takes hold of him. Drawn in by the beauty of his own words, he begins to see the matches only in his head, losing all sense of reality. He is also the protagonist of the dialectical feuds between the two academies that dominate the sports press: the 'Lombard League' and the 'Neapolitan School', both of which have opposing visions of football. He naturally belongs to the former, along with Gualtiero Zanetti and Gian Maria Gazzaniga, different pens but united by the common banner of anti-reverence and catenaccio. Gino Palumbo and Antonio Ghirelli belong to the second, the 'Dioscuri del Sud' – Southern Dioscuri – as Brera calls them; 'people who resolve sport on a sentimental level', lovers of the attacking game, spectacle and goals.

Brera's school of thought remains defensive in its beliefs, even in Spain. It is in good faith even if it is brutal in all its things and its truths are always dogmatic. Above all, Italy is a nation incapable of attacking, of creating a game. It can only play the counter-game, that is, play in and for the counter-attack. According to Brera, Bearzot, with the men he has, is wrong to hope to set up a team that can create play. He is always among those who come to have a chat in solidarity with the head coach, regardless of whether he agrees with him on a professional level. Every time he can, he accuses him of not being defensive, indeed of opposing defensiveness, the only possible model for the Italians; but he is careful not to enter into details that have little relevance to the sport. The judgements expressed about the coach are, to say the least, merciless. They say that he steals the salary, that he only works one month a year or that he has lost his mind. And on every occasion Brera reiterates an absolute certainty in Bearzot's honesty, as a man and as a professional. Bearzot knows this, and when Brera intervenes in his defence he is grateful.

When Bearzot became head coach, after studying him for a while, Brera coined the motto: 'Bearzot preaches bad but raises good'. According to him, in fact, Bearzot pretended to be a modernist, to be inspired by the Dutch school, but in reality he played a strictly Italian style. It was not like that, and the coach explained why: 'It's true, ours is an Italian style module but it's made up of eclectic players and no longer of specialists in the various roles as had been the case up until today.' There was also the attempt to go beyond the departmentalising, and all these ingredients put together led to a football that was no longer one of waiting but one of initiative. On the eve of the Mundial the coach put some statistics in front of Brera from which it emerged that in his national team everyone, except Zoff, had scored goals. Brera gave up and it was that day that he gave him a pipe.

In Spain, Brera is getting to know wonderful, kind-hearted and open-minded people – from the host in Vigo, Roberto Romero, to the Catalan host Agut d'Avignon – nowhere in the world does he feel as at home, fraternally understood and thoughtfully loved as he does here, but he has before him the 'pointed and annoying' horns of a dilemma that trouble him. Hanging over the first is a polemical thesis: 'These poor scorpion fish dear to our hearts deserve the preventive reprisals of those who think they know very well that they will be bitterly disappointed.' The second horn of the dilemma is the one imposed on him by sentiment: 'Their shames are mine, their faults are mine.' Therefore, that minimum of optimism that his heart invokes must be supported by reason.

He does not consider Bearzot to be a genius but neither does he consider him to be dishonest; he considers him to be naive, deluded that he can always put his good intentions into action. According to him, the coach has tried to react to the dominant defensiveness of the Italian school and, unfortunately, he does not have the men to demonstrate its inadequacy. 'Let's go with Bearzot,' he had written in his darkest moment, 'because at this point not even Jesus Christ would save us.' Yet he knows that the coach understands football; he only needs to find comfort in a reality that he denies for matters of the heart: 'How much nicer it would be if our coach recognised the limits of our nursery and on these limits built the least dangerous and most profitable module!' From the top of the stands where he also sits, he gets lots of names, all of them for Brera equally poor in one way or another. His thesis is mercilessly pitiless: the national team's nursery is poor, 'it has gradually become impoverished due to the defection of the small and middle classes, who have discovered that football is not socially useful. Only the fourth and fifth states have remained faithful to their country, full of poor people who have inherited the hunger and the inevitable, and therefore natural, ugliness of their ancestors.'

The Big Chill

Giovanni Arpino is a long-time friend of Bearzot. He even dedicated a novel to him, *Azzurro tenebra* (Blue Darkness), a melancholy chronicle of the ill-fated 1974 World Cup in Germany, giving him the role of the protagonist, the Old Man. In those very pages he showed that he had already understood everything about his environment, dividing journalists into two categories: those always on the lookout for scandal and malice (the Jene) and those placid and patriotic (the Belle Gioie). And then he added a third, Gianni Brera, who wrote about football but delivered literature, and every time he said something everyone listened, for better or worse. Arpino always went to the stadium and, when Alberto Ronchey, the director of *La Stampa*, invited him to pry into the world of football, he immediately understood that he could not do it half-arsed. And he never went back. When he was asked to do a story on Muhammad Sadat, he replied, 'I prefer Causio, he is closer to my reality.'

The *Guerino* noticed his golden pen and invited him to court. The definitive engagement seemed a done deal but at the last moment (3 September 1969) the writer wrote to Il Conte:

> Dear Rognoni, my splendid friend, something new has happened at *La Stampa*, strictly with regard to me, and I am afraid our agreement must be set aside, at least for the moment. I was very keen to collaborate with you, with Brera, with the *Guerino* and, furthermore this collaboration would have been less tiring and rusty for me than on a

sporting page that is variously difficult and archaic. But today new things are maturing, and I can't close my eyes. Besides, if I left right now, I would consider myself defeated, and that is neither good in itself nor useful. Can we put everything off for another time? And keep both my wishes and your beautiful proposals in abeyance? I would be very grateful. Believe in the friendship and warmest regards of Giovanni Arpino.

That 'something new' was actually a historical event. The death of Vittorio Pozzo, coach of the national team, two times world champion, who became the first name of the Turin newspaper after the war. Paolo Bertoldi, head of the sports pages, undecided between two colleagues – Bruno Perucca and Giulio Accatino – ended up choosing the Piedmontese writer as heir to the throne. Arpino thus won the fame and money that his fabulous books had not yet managed to give him. It was only sports journalism that greeted him with mistrust, indeed they ate him alive. He did not bat an eyelid: 'I'm the only one who doesn't understand football in Italy, I confess ironically, so I can make a couple of Roman journalists happy.'

Yet, in the 1960s, Arpino, an established writer, was already writing about sport in *Europeo, Epoca, Tempo Illustrato* and *Guerin Sportivo*, where his first association with Gianni Brera began. They became colleagues, friends, travel, holiday and table companions. Arpino, while working on *Delitto d'onore* (Honour Killing) and *L'ombra delle colline* (The Shadow of the Hills), assiduously attended the gastronomic academies of Brera, Dario Fo and his companions. For a month, in the summer of 1970, they were side by side following the Mexican World Cup. They became infatuated. Brera dedicated an 'Arcimatto' to him, Arpino reciprocated with a 'Fuorigioco'. Those couple of hours stolen from the afternoons at the San Siro, spent inventing footballing homelands to sublimate the real ones, were no longer enough; they became friends of the night, to ask their glasses what they would have been if they had not become what they are. They went further: Arpino first named the protagonists of the novel *Randagio è l'eroe* Giuan and Olona (like Brera and his adored river), then he made him appear in the guise of himself in *Azzurro tenebra*, while Brera publicly defined him as 'my private Nobel'. They were now climbing partners. They fell in love to the point of wanting to be each other. The writer who wanted to be a journalist and the journalist who wanted to be a writer. Both in search of their own greatness as men before becoming literary men. But with time they transformed. Arpino's chronicles became more and more lucid, Brera's more sloppy. The latter was always fascinated by the former because he could see things differently, but if on the one hand he suffered from his success as a writer, on the other he could no longer tolerate the progress of his pupil. Joke after joke, the two began to dislike each other.

It was the Bearzot era that consecrated the rupture of their idyll. The clash took place in front of everyone's eyes, live on TV during a *Domenica Sportiva* in 1977, when Brera ruthlessly attacked Roberto Bettega, who, together with Paolo Rossi, had dragged Bearzot's Italy to the World Cup the following year. Arpino then publicly criticised Brera. On the one hand there was the anger that needed no explanation, on the other the logical reasoning. They were two opposite worlds that had attracted each other up to that moment. Brera was sanguine, divinatory, overbearing. He knew everything and understood everything. Always. The rest, the others, did not count. Arpino moved decisively but on tiptoe, perennially careful not to hurt people with his judgements. Brera defined Arpino as 'any old Maletto, the last of the reporters'. Arpino replied, 'I wish you to end up like Falstaff.'

Arpino and Brera faced each other for years from their respective lead columns. 'Is there anyone who still believes that to talk about football it is essential to quote Brera?' asked Arpino. 'I don't think I have anything to fear from him, as a sports journalist, what has he given us?' replied Brera, again with the rhetoric of a question mark. Arpino could no longer stand that 'arrogant, poorly documented journalist, with a verbal violence devoid of politeness that has been successful because we are a people of poor reading and we let ourselves be impressed by those who shout'. He criticised him for having acted for years by giving erroneous advice to commissioners, presidents, centre-backs and goalkeepers, for having 'zero in coherence, hundreds of contradictions and an inhuman use of the cut-throat regarding almost all the protagonists'. Brera, for his part, did not get a single prediction right (even though he was the first to say that only those who make predictions get them wrong): he prophesied that Bearzot's Azzurri would not have got through the Strait of Gibraltar in 1978 and the second round in Spain; that the Italian group would be won by Peru; that Belgium would shine at the Mundial, together with the eastern group of Czechoslovakia, the USSR and Hungary.

Then, three years before the Mundial, a twist of fate meant that the two most influential pens in football ended up under the same roof: Indro Montanelli's *Il Giornale*. The director was incredibly astute in never letting them cross paths in the editorial office, not even by accident, but this was not enough to calm the hot spirits. 'I won't write about sport as long as that Gianni Brera is here. I'm waiting for him to leave before I start again. On the contrary,' Arpino confided to a colleague from the *L'Espresso*. 'I'm waiting to meet Brera to smash his face in. I'll make him swallow his teeth with my fists, if only he comes within range.'

The ballet lasts until a few days before the World Cup, when the number one of Italian sports journalism leaves Montanelli's *Il Giornale*, which had launched the Monday edition just after having hired him, yields to the flattery of Eugenio Scalfari, to whom Giorgio Bocca and Enzo Biagi had also suggested his name, and moves to *La Repubblica*, the third daily newspaper in Italy, in co-ownership with *L'Espresso*, and Arpino becomes the first name of *Il Giornale*.

The news that the figurehead is to leave *Il Giornale* triggers an unprecedented buying campaign. Willy Molco, a friend of his, flies to Gaspare Barbiellini Amidei to say that Brera is available for the *Corriere della Sera*. At the same time, he is also being courted by *Il*

THE MATCH

Giorno ('You are a Pavarotti from the Po Valley, you must sing in your own theatre'), but his friend Guglielmo Zucconi is told no this time, which is the fourth time. Moreover, there he would have found Gian Maria Gazzaniga (between him and the Grangiuàn, both immolated to sarcasm and tavern, there is no longer good blood), a name that he does not spare himself to say to Giorgio Rivelli of the *Guerino* on the eve of the Mundial, 'has made my ideas his own and every time I come back he has to go back one place'. Gazzaniga's polemical pen, which makes every line he writes so peppery, immediately replies in kind: 'I am not Zarathustra, he is pontificating on another channel!' Brera is also contacted by *La Stampa* of Turin through Oreste del Buono. The director Giorgio Fattori is an old acquaintance of his. He declines. Until, less than four months before the Mundial, Scalfari calls him: 'A carrier pigeon gave me the news from Paris. Would you like to come to *Repubblica*?' The pigeon is Mario Sconcerti, the first to understand that the love affair between Brera and Montanelli, also due to Arpino, is over.

Just a week earlier, on the Alitalia charter flight taking the Italian national football team to Paris for the friendly match against France, Sconcerti and Brera are randomly assigned two seats next to each other. Separated by a 30-year difference and an armrest, they discover they are linked by a common passion: history.

They find themselves at nine o'clock, together with Cancogni and Soldati, in the Rue de la Harpe discussing Lombards and Romans until late into the night. When they take their leave, Brera lets slip something that Sconcerti catches right away: 'I'm very happy to have met you, I'd like to team up with someone like you, but instead I have to work with people who put their hands on me from behind. Even my boss, Alfio Caruso, uses me to make himself look good.' Sconcerti gets the message and, as soon as he lands in Rome, he knocks on Eugenio Scalfari's door: 'We have a chance to get the number one.' The editor collects signatures, thinks about it for five days, then on 2 March, at 1pm, he makes up his mind: 'Rolando,' he says, pressing the button on the intercom guided by Montesperelli, 'call me Brera.'

Paolo Rossi (Italy) scores the opening goal

Zico surpasses Gentile in the lead-up to the Brazilian equaliser

Brazil's Socrates celebrates with team-mates after scoring his team's first goal

Rossi and Cerezo

Zico, with Junior behind, screams at Cerezo after the mistake that caused Paolo Rossi's second goal

Brazil's Zico complains to the referee Klein after his shirt is ripped by Gentile in the Estadio Sarria

Falcao scores for Brazil: 2-2

Rossi scores the third goal

Rossi's exultation after scoring the goal

The last action of the game

Dino Zoff, the captain of the Italian team

Claudio Gentile and Enzo Bearzot, head coach of Italy, celebrate the victory

Italy manager Enzo Bearzot smokes his pipe before the match

The next day Brera has lunch with Fedele Confalonieri, into whose hands he delivers his final farewell. In his diary he had noted: 'Accept my resignation with a certain relief, even if he regrets … for clumsiness in front of the readers.' Before taking the leap, he confides in Bocca: 'Your newspaper is almost totally lacking in news items.' He gives him his usual dose of sarcasm: 'And where are the reporters anymore? Come to us Gianni, you'll be fine. As long as you don't take orders from those sports lunatics.' The following day Brera is in front of Scalfari. A generous offer, a quick agreement. The figurehead has found a home.

The editors of *La Repubblica* are very sceptical about the contribution that the sports pages, and in particular those dedicated to the World Cup, will make to sales. Up until a few months ago, sports news appeared infrequently, usually in the Sunday issue and on Tuesdays (the newspaper was not published on Mondays). They had only become daily on the occasion of the World Cup. Scalfari wants to give the sports news a cultured connotation, so he puts his money on the country's best-known sports commentator.

During his Spanish days, Arpino is forced to read an interview with Brera by Mario Soldati (the two people, together with Oreste del Buono, whom he detests most) in which the Grangiuàn has no problem saying that 'Arpino's articles are like a cocker's piss'. Arpino, who has won a Strega and a Campiello prize, has never met either Brera or Soldati since he has been in Spain. By now he detests everything about them, the Tuscan cigars and above all the rants against Bearzot, who instead continues to be for him the stray hero of his *Azzurro tenebra*.

The Azzurri coach feels responsible, is a friend of both and tries in every way to make peace with them. But he does not succeed. The two writers, however, although they love this Italy and although they esteem the human nature of the Old Man, do not bet a penny on Bearzot's boys. Brera, who detests Brazil's excess of ease, the scant respect lavished on that honest and virile athletic effort that is football, mumbles aloud in *La Repubblica*: 'I don't know how much

I would pay for them to lose.' For him, Telê Santana is to football what Metastasio is to poetry. Frivolous, fatuous and contemptuous of the honest toil of others. Brera is so convinced that Italy are not going to make it that he is thinking of daring to make a crazy bet with his readers. For Arpino, too, the Cariocas possess values too obvious to be doubted. They manoeuvre with gleeful skill, express sudden bursts, dazzle the opponent's defence, exchange the ball with an ease that borders on that of conjurers. Even though they dredge up repetitive legends in which a David can take down the Goliath of the day, they know that reality is much rougher than the myth. 'A rectangle of grass with a ball to kick leaves very little room for these legendary tones. Even a ball has its own logic,' Arpino admits, 'and a Mundial, after various twists and turns, always ends up imposing it.'

The Farewell Waltz

Nally is sitting in his Spanish office set up in a suite at the Eurobuilding Hotel, a stone's throw from Madrid's Bernabéu Stadium. He stares into space. He feels lost and can no longer follow the course of the Mundial. Inside his head there are too many doubts. Is he really doing his job? Has he managed to represent the best interests of Coca-Cola, Canon and his other clients? Or is he only working to help Horst Dassler and his Adidas? He knows the truth. The one who is getting the most financial benefit from this World Cup is FIFA. And the person who is manipulating it for his own ends is Dassler. The picture of the two visionaries is becoming blurred and Nally starts to get the impression that he is living in someone else's dream.

He is not the only one. A year before the Argentina Mundial, Helmut Käser, FIFA's general secretary since 1960, also realised that he was now in the wrong place under the wrong president. He is a well-balanced, competent man of integrity. A punctilious lawyer, he speaks five languages and has never missed an engagement. He has worked in football since 1942, when he became secretary of the Swiss Football Association. He has always loved travelling, photography

THE FAREWELL WALTZ

and, above all, skiing. These activities have enabled him to maintain an envied physical and mental agility, even now, as he enters his seventies. Havelange has always appeared suspicious to him, from the very first moment. When he took office in 1974, the new president had lured him into the job by increasing his salary considerably. That was not enough to control him. Käser demanded compliance with contracts, rules and statutes, promoted transparent accounting and showed no tolerance for the new management's ambiguous approach. Havelange therefore put him under increasing pressure. The Swiss lawyer realised that he needed support. He approached Rolf Deyhle, the entrepreneur who had made it easier for Havelange to locate FIFA's headquarters in Zürich.

Deyhle is a businessman with fingers in many pies (including a cartoon studio in London) who is working on operations close to those of Dassler and Nally. He thinks he can combine his interests by creating a cartoon starring a footballer. So he turns to a Hungarian artist who creates Sport Billy for him. It is a three-step plan. First, he wants to give him a life of his own through an animated series. Then he wants to make him the FIFA mascot. Finally, he wants to organise the sale of the rights to use the mascot image. Armed with preparatory sketches, he rushes to Villa Derwald, FIFA's headquarters in Zürich. He is warmly welcomed by Käser, who is working with two sleepy dogs under his desk. Havelange is away on business. They have free rein at headquarters and after the first pleasantries they get down to business. 'I don't like Havelange's cronies. We have to fight them.' For Deyhle it is a wedding invitation. He knows that the only way to do this is to take a piece of the cake away from Dassler's SMPI.

Käser offers him the contract to manage the marketing rights of the FIFA emblems for the next 12 years (until 1994). The contract includes both the use of the mascot and the FIFA emblem. The emblem was designed by Deyhle himself – the two faces of the planet inscribed in a ball. Two diamond globes that Deyhle hastily sketched on a napkin on his way by train from Stuttgart to Zürich to see

Käser. The agreement makes both parties happy. Käser has Dassler (and therefore Havelange) in his hands, Deyhle the worldwide marketing of football. As a sign of gratitude the shy secretary offers an unexpected gift to his protector.

At FIFA headquarters, Deyhle is enchanted by the sight of the cup. In contrast to the Jules Rimet Trophy, the original cup is only 'lent' to the winners for the time needed for the award ceremony and is then immediately replaced by a replica. At the moment the trophy, after the names of Germany and Argentina have been inscribed, has 15 free spaces at its base, which means it will be usable until the 2038 edition. FIFA's decision to keep the original trophy for itself came after it had been damaged during various 'custodianships' in the past. The winners, and only they, receive an exact replica.

Until now, therefore, there are only two other trophies in the world, one in Germany and the other in Argentina. The only original FIFA World Cup, 36.8cm high and weighing 6.175kg, created by the Milanese artist Silvio Gazzaniga, is resting on a shelf at the Zürich headquarters. When he sees it, Deyhle is dazzled: 'Helmut, I must have it!' To please his ally and, officially, as a token of his gratitude for his contribution to building FIFA's image, Käser has a third replica prepared for him. Deyhle thus becomes the only man in the world to own a FIFA World Cup. However, he gives to the federation another trophy. From the 1982 World Cup onwards, thanks to Deyhle, the FIFA Fair Play Trophy, awarded to the most sporting team in the tournament, will no longer be a diploma but a real gold trophy with the silhouette of his Sport Billy.

When Dassler and Nally learn about the agreement they cannot believe their ears.

'João, I thought we had a safe agreement with you!' Dassler says.

'It's Käser's fault,' Havelange justifies himself, 'he signed the contract without consulting me.'

This is a big problem. Dassler and Nally are in charge of World Cup emblems, while Deyhle has FIFA emblems. Both can run

THE FAREWELL WALTZ

businesses that take revenue away from their respective competitors. Not only that, but from that moment on, the two teams have to constantly confront each other to make sure they do not breach their respective contracts. Dassler is furious. He already has his own marketing plans for FIFA from the 1982 World Cup onwards. He tries in vain to buy off his rival. So he passes the ball to Havelange: 'You have to sort this out.'

The FIFA president informs Deyhle that the marketing rights have been terminated. The recipient of the communication makes an injunction to the Swiss court, and wins. For Dassler, however, it is his first defeat. He and Deyhle are thus forced to work together, two oversized personalities destined to clash again and again. When Dassler and Nally manage to persuade Coca-Cola to invest heavily in the 1982 World Cup, Deyhle approaches Pepsi about selling it the rights to use the FIFA emblems. These events convince Dassler that Havelange needs a new partner: 'Käser has to go, no matter what.'

Horst asks his friend André Guelfi for help; the man has contacts within the intelligence services: 'You have to think of a way to eliminate it.'

'Don't worry, if he refuses to leave, we will make his life impossible.'

When signing the contract for the marketing of the World Cup, Dassler, out of prudence, prefers to use another of his companies, ROFA, rather than SMPI. Käser, who proves to be an uncomfortable character during the negotiations, is surprised to find that name. He has never heard it before. And he's right: the agency has only just been set up. Käser complains to the head of the German Football Association, Hermann Neuberger. He expects his support but he doesn't get it, so he begins to investigate. He discovers that Havelange is imposing strict conditions on the insurance contracts for the 1982 World Cup: 20 per cent must be transferred to the company Atlantica Boavista Gruppe, based in Rio de Janeiro. Käser takes note of this name. It reminds him of something. He goes looking for Havelange's CV that he had handed out to everyone during his election campaign in 1974. He finds the name under 'F'. The director of the insurance company, Atlantica Boavista, is Havelange himself. In the accounting papers he finds two payments of $30,000 and $50,000 for rent and costs of the Rio office, deposited in a dollar account in New York. And he comes across other anomalous figures, such as the 103,000 francs for Longines watches, or 100,000 francs for the Café do Brasil. He writes it all down.

But he is also under observation. The general secretary is spied on even inside FIFA. Someone makes copies of his papers and sends them to Havelange. Guelfi prepares the attack. Käser receives a report accusing him of being 'a non-transparent general secretary who is not to be trusted'. He is later accused of having received houses and horses from Deyhle. However, one of Guelfi's men then makes a fatal mistake. He sends the information he has gathered to the persecuted instead of the persecutor. Käser meets with the Frenchman in Zürich and Guelfi apologises. According to the results of the investigation Käser is clean. Dassler also agrees to meet with Käser but Havelange has to take care of the rest.

In May 1981, during the FIFA executive meeting in Madrid, his dismissal is engineered. The meeting turns into a classic in the art of intrigue. Havelange sentences the fate of the general secretary, using his alarmist predictions about the future of FIFA. He then confesses to his executives that the federation, at the end of his second term, will be bankrupt. A final report on Käser's failings proves decisive. Käser realises he is lost. Guelfi whispers three words to him: 'Head held high.' Better to abdicate with your head held high and pocket a golden redundancy than to be kicked out. Käser bows his head, retires, as it is written in the FIFA annals, and accepts 300,000 francs until 1986. 'If you need more detailed information about severance packages,' Havelange tells him, 'go to Mr Blatter.'

The indication reveals the design. Joseph 'Sepp' Blatter is appointed in Käser's place. Two months later Blatter marries Barbara Käser, the 20-year-old daughter of the man whose place he has taken. On the day of the wedding Käser stays at home, crying. The same despicable man has stolen his future, his job and his daughter. His humiliation is complete.

But the trinity is now perfect. The Swiss is smart, even if he lacks Havelange's charisma and Dassler's vision. The German continues to manoeuvre him like a puppet, giving him orders to be fulfilled. When the three of them get together to eat, Blatter looks at Horst as if he were a god. He knows perfectly well that without him he would have had no chance of occupying that position in FIFA. And perhaps Mario Soldati, on the day of Santiago de Compostela, manages to catch that look of veneration.

In the meantime, Havelange tries to arm himself further. He knows that Italy wants to bid to host the World Cup in 1990, so he assigns the unsuspecting Franchi to FIFA's finance committee. The manager finds himself in an impossible position. He discovers expenses, squandering and corruption but cannot reveal it. He understands the Brazilian's manoeuvre; he knows that if he denounces these actions, Italy will never again be in the running for the World Cup.

Shortly afterwards, ROFA sells the rights for the commercial exploitation of the Mundial to SMPI, which turns them over to West Nally, who in turn sells the rights to the Maeght Gallery in Paris. Meanwhile, for the use of the mascots and symbols, IberMundial is created, made up in equal parts by West Nally and Real Federación Española, which then trades its uncertain 50 per cent for a more solid fixed sum. Following this retreat, noting the obvious Russian doll of sublets, José María Riera, Partido Comunista de España deputy for the city of Barcelona, tries to lift the lid by publicly denouncing that 'West Nally seems to be a front for other companies'.

The alarm raised by the Spanish parliamentarian, added to the fights with Deyhle and the humiliation of Käser, together with the actions of Horst, who has locked him up in one of his many Chinese boxes, lead Nally in the middle of the Mundial to decide to stop. The time has come to part ways. Their business connection will dissolve at the end of the Mundial.

Horst does not even take time to feel the blow. He is already setting up a new company in Lucerne, International Sports and Leisure Marketing (ISL), which will take over all of SMPI's sports marketing. Its new partner will be the Japanese company Dentsu, which will take 49 per cent of the company. In 1979 the Japanese company had begun building a relationship with Havelange to manage and market the World Youth Championships in Japan. Buoyed by its success, it tried its hand by proposing to manage the marketing of the 1982 World Cup, which FIFA had entrusted to SMPI as usual. It thus threw itself into the management of the rights to the 1984 Los Angeles Olympics. The Japanese agency has been trying to get into the German's good books for years. He knows about it but has always kept it secret from Nally. Clients such as JVC or Fuji Film had been reached by Nally himself through Hukuhodo, a direct rival of Dentsu. He was certain that Dentsu would sign a deal with him with its eyes closed. This time, however, at least at home, Horst wants to do things properly. He's going to let his family know about his marketing activities and split the ISL shares with his sisters. But now there is Brazil, a match that can change marketing plans.

The Flop

Spain is in the middle of the Mundial vortex. Having completed the first phase, the longest, it is now waiting to see the four semi-finalists who will emerge from the second round. The country, however, which expected a cascade of gold from this historic appointment, is now seeing all its illusions fall. The average stadium attendance is the lowest a World Cup has seen since the one held in Chile in 1962. Spectators have deserted the matches as a reaction to speculation about entrance tickets, which cannot be found in official sales points but are available on the black market of scalpers.

Even Naranjito, the cheerful mascot of the World Cup, has his days numbered. It has been put on the market in all sorts of ways and has gone from being the lucky charm of a blockbuster that was supposed to make a lot of money to a melancholic symbol of failure. The figure of the smiling orange, which had emerged three years earlier from the imagination of two publicists, José María Martín and María Dolores Salto, had managed to supplant that of 600 other projects. The two creatives seemed destined to be enveloped in fame and glory, as well as a million pesetas to be shared with the agency. Thirty-six months later, the Mundial has forgotten about them, the money never arrived and, in the meantime, María Dolores also lost her job.

Naranjito has not brought good luck either for the traders who pinned their hopes of profit, as well as their investments, on the Mundial mascot. Eight multinationals and 84 Spanish companies bought the rights from IberMundial, a company set up on 20 May 1979 between the West Nally Group, the Spanish federation and FIFA for what was to be the most commercially oriented Mundial of the century. According to projections in the hands of Dispansa 82, the company in charge of the production and distribution of the Mundial symbols (stickers, ashtrays, matches, ties, suits, glasses, pipes, piggy banks, hats and T-shirts), Spaniards would spend an average of 1,000 pesetas per head (12,000 lire) per year on Naranjito-branded items. Now, halfway through the Mundial, once the boost phase has run its course, the average has consolidated at 50 pesetas, 5 per cent of the forecast. Warehouses and stores are overflowing with unsold items. Mundimar 82, which has a licence to produce pottery with Naranjito, still has 35,000 of the 50,000 pieces in wooden crates. Nobody wants them. *Sal Y Pi Menta*, a Spanish satirical magazine, candidly admits: 'We are not as dumb as they thought.'

Achilles' Heel

Bearzot's impossible mission starts three days before the match against Brazil. Friday, 2 July at the Sarriá, in the stands. The coach forces the entire squad to watch Brazil vs Argentina live. His lads are not crazy about the idea of crowding under the sun, in the bedlam of

THE MATCH

the stadium, when they could easily watch the match on television. But the coach wants them to have a total vision of this Brazil, at any moment and in any sector of the field, with all its movements, its manoeuvres and also its weaknesses.

The Brazilian captain wakes up early that day, has his coffee and goes back to sleep, only coming down to the lobby for lunch. There he finds trainer Tim, Oscar and Dirceu discussing the upcoming match against Argentina. When they bring him into the conversation he immediately pulls out, 'How can you talk about football when you are awake after a month of just football?'

Shortly afterwards, a telegram arrives at the Mas Badó hotel, Brazil's headquarters:

I'm better, I'm rooting for you. Good luck, Careca.

Two hours before the match, the Azzurri receive a visit from Prime Minister Giovanni Spadolini. He had promised it in Italy and has kept his word. Twelve minutes in the midst of 22 anxious players, with their heads in the Sarriá, were enough for him to celebrate the victory over the Argentinies with anecdotes: 'I was in Brussels for the meeting of the heads of government of the European Community and discussions about the World Cup were on the agenda. The forecasts were not in Italy's favour and Mrs Thatcher, pointing her finger at me, ordered me to beat Argentina at all costs, as if I were the Italian team. I replied, "Madam, we'll do everything we can to beat them, but with a different spirit from yours."'

Then, addressing Bearzot: 'They compared my game to yours. They wrote that we didn't know how to maintain or improve our positions.' But that was before Bearzot beat Argentina, a victory that shook the country and that also seems to have benefited the government. During a meeting with the trade unions, when he opened the window, Spadolini was applauded by the cheering crowd: 'And so, thanks to you, I got my share of applause. I felt that those cheers had broken the threatening shroud hanging over the country.'

And while the Azzurri are already on the bus, he says goodbye in his own way: 'I hope to pass on to you some of the good fortune that is often attributed to me.' Luck that would now require a draw between Argentina and Brazil: at that point a draw with Brazil would be enough to go through. Better still would be a victory for Maradona and his team-mates.

Confined to a section of the Sarriá stadium that has been stormed by Brazilian fans, the Azzurri are trying to get to grips with their next opponents to the rhythm of the samba. Thirty players and staff are crammed into the last two steps of the stadium, behind the left-hand door.

Ninety minutes to find the heel of an Achilles from the other world. Argentina play their game but it is Brazil who impose their law. In total bedlam, while an inextricable band marks the success of Santana's men, Zoff and his team-mates have a significant foretaste of what they will have to endure to try to stem the green-and-yellow wave. It ends 3-1 to Brazil. Goals by Zico, Serginho and Júnior. A result that for Italy smacks of condemnation. A few days earlier, FIFA had issued an official communiqué reminding us of the main rules that govern qualification for the last phase of the World Cup. In the second round, the rules state that the first-placed team in each group will go though to the semi-finals. In the event of a draw, the difference in goals is decisive. In the group, both teams beat Argentina, but Brazil score one more goal, so a draw is enough for the Cariocas.

That goal imposes a precise delivery requirement on the Azzurri: to go through, they have to win. Brazil, on the other hand, can choose the best approach: wait for Italy to strike or attack immediately. They know how to do both things very well, thanks to a midfield that rotates continuously. Bearzot does not have four men to devote to this completely unless Cabrini is also involved, but this means making him abandon the left wing. If Oriali or Gentile are sucked in by Éder returning to his own half or spreading wide, who will counter Júnior's attacking jaunts?

THE MATCH

Bearzot leaves the Sarriá in a great hurry, while the Carioca fans pour into the streets of Barcelona, singing their unstoppable joy. The Italian coach has a few words to say:

> Argentina favoured the Brazilians' game, leaving too many inviting spaces for the opponents. But playing against the Brazilians is very difficult because every time they fight to the best of their ability. Also today nobody demerited and this confirms that a very difficult task awaits us. Against Santana's men we must adopt the same type of game that allowed us to beat Argentina. So we have to attack them immediately, without giving them a break.

That's why he wants to adopt a mixed approach: 'We'll play man-to-man, but not all-out.' The reporters warn him: 'Grazing in Brazil's vegetable garden can only lead to trouble.' But Bearzot has no doubts: 'We have to be aggressive from the start, never allowing the opponents any space.' Antognoni will have to take care of Cerezo, without giving up finishing assisting Rossi, and Graziani, with the support of Conti, will try to stop the offensive incursions of Júnior. Bearzot knows well that the Seleção is a well-oiled machine but suffers from tight marking, as happened in Montevideo in the Mundialito final against Uruguay. Therefore an excellent athletic condition is needed.

If with Argentina it was 'enough' to stop Maradona, with Brazil there will be many men to keep an eye on. *'El Pibe de Oro* is the whole of Argentina, but Zico is not the whole of Brazil.' The threat comes from Júnior. Lins da Gama Júnior, or more simply Leo Júnior, known as 'O Capacete' (the Helmet) because of his Black Power hair, is a full-back only because the midfield is full. Santana cannot do without him. He defends, attacks, crosses beautifully and can also score. His was the last goal for Brazil, the one that has forced Italy to win.

But even if they have the advantage of a draw against Italy, the Brazilian team will keep their usual offensive formation. Telê Santana has decided to play on the attack, despite the possible absence of

Zico. He is convinced that Bearzot will play with man-marking but is prepared for possible variations on the theme: 'We are ready to face any defensive system.' The *Folha de S. Paulo* headlines on the front page that Brazil attacks and Italy hopes for a miracle. A reporter lets Santana know that Bearzot is thinking of playing both zonal and man-to-man. But Zezé Moreira, one of his 'spies', reassures him: 'He'll never do it. It would be practically impossible. It would be one or the other.' In any case, even though Zico may not be on the pitch against Italy, coach Gilberto Tim does not think that the team's power will be reduced: 'We will always play with eleven men.'

'It's true,' confirms Bearzot, 'all the Brazilians are capable of bringing themselves dangerously towards our goal, but I'm sure we'll be able to repeat at a high level.' His deputy Cesare Maldini confirms and subscribes: 'We have already studied the right counter-measures to face them. Brazil will not have an easy life. Reason does not give the Azzurri a chance, but the coach has a precise plan in his head so that the miracle can take place.' Since the first match of the Mundial he has identified the weak points of his adversary, but Brazil, with their jumping to the rhythm of the samba, are good at hiding them; however, an elegant game is not enough to win a real battle.

The Vecio's Plan

In Bearzot's conception of football, knowing your opponent is indispensable to avoid or minimise the scope for surprise. It is not enough to follow the matches of the national team to be played, it is also necessary to know who the alternative pawns are, the emerging players, those who can be brought in, and to study their characteristics well. Sudden trips, disguises, hiding, official missions. Bearzot is a scholar. Solid classical elements still circulate in his Friulian blood. He stubbornly believes in a handful of forgotten values that lead him, alone against everyone, to trust in method, sacrifice, perseverance, trust, patience and rebirth. And he strives to understand in the deepest way anyone he has to face, from the last of the reporters to the most inoffensive of reserves. He has always done so. Franco Mentana, the *Gazzetta*'s star reporter, who has been following him on his endless trips around the world for over ten years, knows this well. The coach studying football, the envoy studying the coach.

Mentana is not on Bearzot's black list, the index of journalists who have gone so far as to offend him to death, not only as a technician but also as a man and a father, accusing him of being 'mentally confused' and having suffered a 'brain short circuit'. He is now a constant target. The technician asks for time but they do not give him any and, during a flight, he confides in Mentana:

'I am alone against everyone, I only have the players.'

'That's not true, Enzo. There are many people who respect you.'

'But in the end it's only my boys who believe in me.'

'And the others?'

'You see it too, they stab me in the back.'

'You know how our trade works.'

'Of course, I know the play of parts.'

'Journalists must criticise.'

'And I accept technical judgements. But not insults.'

The Rosea – a nickname for *Gazzetta dello Sport* – reporter has the impression that the coach wants to ask for help but is too proud to do so explicitly. Bearzot continues to constantly seek the warmth and understanding of others, trying to reach out to have a dialogue, to be understood. But to no avail. Mentana has known him since the time when the coach, then deputy, travelled on behalf of Valcareggi, analysing the opponents that Italy had to face. When Bernardini arrived, things changed. 'Fuffo' preferred to rely on the knowledge of journalists, ignoring the reports of his coach. Bearzot did not mind, he continued to study football for himself, noting down the forms of play and the characteristics of the teams. While waiting for Italian football to do so, he broadened his horizons, a knowledge that became an asset.

Once he had become the national team's coach, when he became aware of the 1978 World Cup qualifying calendar, he was not worried about England, the biggest opponent in his group, nor about Luxembourg, condemned to the usual buffer role. He focused his attention on modest Finland, not so much because he was afraid of failing to beat them as because he realised from the start that goal difference would be decisive in that group. Whoever scored the most against the Finns would go to the World Cup. Finland became his concern first and then his obsession. Bearzot went to see them everywhere. He hid, suffered the cold and was laughed at. He even went to watch them in Ankara against Turkey. He knew that the visa for Argentina would start from that match. And the facts proved him right. With England it was 2-0 and 0-2, absolute parity. But Italy went to Baires, thanks to the nine goals by which they beat Finland.

The Vecio's prescience took him to South America in the spring. Officially to study Peru, the future opponent in the first round of the World Cup. But then the coach flew to Rio de Janeiro to watch Brazil vs West Germany because something told him that the paths of Brazil and Italy could meet during the Mundial. So now, in light of his knowledge, he decides to change the defensive approach he used against Argentina. It is time to show that his boys can be eclectic. He imagines a modern game organisation that would combine the tradition of man-marking with the new requirements of covering the pitch. A couple of fixed points and all the others arranged in zones. With Brazil, given their unpredictability, it would be foolish to set up a static strategy.

In order to counter the Brazilian team's play, he considers a relay on the flanks. On the right Oriali and Conti will counter the advances of Júnior, on the left Cabrini and Graziani will contend with those of Leandro. In this way he creates a mobile barrier, a zone, to stop both the outside attacker and the advancing full-back at the same time. When the Brazilian players turn to the centre or diagonally, they are taken into custody by the midfield. Tardelli and Antognoni, in fact, will have to exchange the marking on Sócrates, Falcão and Cerezo and then offer themselves in attack. The Brazilian midfielders' assaults will be cut off by Conti and Graziani, before leaving them to the defence. Only Rossi will have his head cleared of defensive commitments. In defence, Gentile, Oriali and Collovati will have to deal with Zico, Éder and Serginho. Cabrini, in the absence of a Brazilian right-winger, will have the task of guarding the territory by taking charge of whoever comes forward between Zico and Sócrates. Scirea will be the extra man in the defensive and set-up spaces, a complete player capable of coming out from the back and advancing head-on into the Brazilian half when his team is in possession of the ball.

Eclecticism allows the Azzurri to perform at their best in any match situation. In the first weeks of the Mundial, Bearzot continues to keep close tabs on Telê Santana's team and notices that their game is based on vertical moves. In that stellar midfield there is an obligatory pass for all offensive actions. Zico, Éder, Falcão, Sócrates and even Júnior always use the same player as a backup to come in and wreak havoc on the opposition's defences, but happily leave themselves uncovered at the back: 'If the game succeeds, we find them in front of us and we have no chance; if we manage to anticipate them, we catch them uncovered while they are advancing and we conquer all the spaces we need to hit them.' The key man for him becomes Collovati: 'When they try to pass to him, you must always be there. If you anticipate him, it's us who become dangerous.'

With Brazil vs Argentina, the confirmation comes directly from the stands of the Sarriá: 'Guys, the game is resolved in midfield.' 'But how, coach?' his team shout to him amid the deafening cheers of the torcida, while an entire band is punctuating the play of Santana's men. 'When Brazil attacks,' explains Bearzot, 'it pivots on one man. He is the least gifted of them all, but he never goes offside, he manages to give depth to the team and it is therefore from him that all the others ask for the ball to launch themselves towards the goal. You see?' and he points to Serginho.

Serginho

His World Cup should have been in 1978. In Argentina he could have put on a show. In the Brazilian championship of 1977, Serginho was the best player of São Paulo and the second-highest scorer of the tournament, with 15 goals. He was the right name for that World Cup but he ended up missing the chance to play. On 12 February 1978 in a match in Ribeirão Preto, against Botafogo, São Paulo were losing 1-0 when Serginho scored in the 90th minute. Referee Oscar Scolfaro observed the indication of linesman Vandevaldo Ranger and disallowed the goal for offside. Serginho, beside himself, broke the flagpole and, according to the referee's report, kicked the linesman's left leg at the level of the shin, causing a gash about ten centimetres long. Serginho denied it with all his might, as he claimed it was a stone thrown by the crowd that caused the injury. Two weeks later he was sentenced to a 14-month suspension, later reduced to 11, for assault. Never before had a player been suspended for so long in the history of Brazilian football. He lost everything: the championship final, the title, which São Paulo won without him a few days later, and above all the World Cup.

Once again, with only a few days to go before leaving for the 1982 tournament, after having to deal with established goalscorers, such as Roberto Dinamite, Nunes, Reinaldo and Baltazar, not to mention Careca, Serginho risks blowing it all up. His ex-wife, Nancy de Jesus Madeira Bernardino, who demands the payment of alimony for her daughters, has reported him for beatings and ill-treatment. The trial was to be held in the 22nd section of the criminal court of São Paulo, but they have postponed the hearing to allow him to participate in the World Cup. Before leaving for Europe, the President of the Republic of Brazil, General João Baptista Figueiredo, even tells him: 'Serginho, my boy, be sensible. Don't do anything stupid. Take care of yourself because we need you.' The centre-forward promises to leave his impulsiveness at home. In Brazil, he also abandons Nicole Puzzi, the 24-year-old actress and star of the 'pornochanchada' (the soft porn genre born in the middle of the military dictatorship, strongly influenced by Italian-style sexy comedy), with whom he has been having a rumoured love affair for a couple of years.

Sérgio Bernardino, also known as Serginho or Serginho Chulapa, has scored 20 goals in the league with São Paulo, the team of the city where he was born. Perhaps this is why Telê Santana has brought him to Spain almost 'dry': in the national team he has played just three full matches in three years, and before this Mundial only once for the full 90 minutes, in a friendly against Portugal. Yet in Spain he has already scored against New Zealand and Argentina. He has a strong head, starts off well on the dribble, even if he then stumbles and loses the necessary coordination. But he knows how to fight.

Two years earlier, coach Gigi Radice had flown to Brazil to bring him to Bologna, but he was injured. Now São Paulo, thanks to his goals, will not let him go. The Brazilian girls voted him the most attractive player of the Seleção. In reality, he looks wooden on the pitch but he is six feet tall and his size helps him to open up spaces easily. That is why his team leaves him in charge of the ball.

However, he is unloved, with many wanting the more technical Paulo Isidoro in his place, but Santana listens to no argument – he has great faith in his giant. He may be a little untidy in his handling of the ball but he is decisive in the heart of the opponent's defence to back up his team-mates coming from behind.

Despite his reputation as a provocateur, brawler and troublemaker, Telê supports his call-up, and so far has not regretted it. He never wastes an opportunity to praise the centre-forward's dedication to making his scheme work: 'Whether Serginho scores goals or not is a detail. What matters is that the team scores, as has been the case so far. If a scheme depended on a certain player, it would be enough to cancel him out and everything would be more difficult.' His attack is, indeed, unpredictable but, when all is said and done, it often goes through one person. This can be predictable and Bearzot seems to be the only one to have noticed this. He does not consider Serginho, as many hasty reporters do, to be the weak link in this Brazil team, but a crucial strength that he must nullify.

At São Paulo, Chulapa has scored 243 goals, the best-ever goalscorer in the club's history. However, in Telê Santana's scheme he is one of the most sacrificed players. He does not have to worry about scoring, nor does he have to bring out his impetuousness. On a few occasions the attacking plays have his foot as the final piece. The two goals scored have lifted a weight off his shoulders: to let the world know that he can score too.

The coach forces him to play with his back to the goal, playing the role of pivot who opens up spaces for those coming from behind. In this way, in effect, the main opportunities for Brazil have been born. For this reason, Bearzot sees Serginho's role as one of the keys to the match. For the sports press and fans, however, Telê Santana's work on the attacker's irascible temperament is also directly affecting his performance as a centre-forward. The coach has tamed him but also distorted him. The more Serginho goes up against his markers, more or less violently, the more he tends to score. Now he is more 'controlled' he scores inexorably less. A double loss for him, according to press rumours.

There are also rumours that he and his team-mate Éder have made secret agreements with Dassler to go and cheer in front of certain billboards after a goal. Both of them have so far scored two goals each. Éder ran to the Iveco billboard to cheer after the third goal against the Scots; Serginho did the same after doubling the score against Argentina, also hugging Éder. In the other goals, it was not clear whether they wanted to favour any sponsors. They are the two hotheads of the Seleção, sometimes accused of living on the edge of legality, but they are Brazilian players, and when a Brazilian scores, it is difficult for him to think about where to cheer. He just cheers.

Controversial on many occasions, Serginho in this case is fully aware of the opportunity he missed four years ago, the path he had to travel to become a starter for the Brazilian national team and the unique opportunity he is presented with at this World Cup. In addition, he never forgets where he comes from: 'If I had not played football, I would certainly be a criminal now. For someone who was born without clothes in Casa Verde [the neighbourhood in the north of São Paulo] and is now here in Spain, everything is a luxury.'

More stoic than ever, unbelievable as it is, Chulapa is accepting his status as a wingman in a national team of stars. And, without hesitation, he has swapped a leading role for that of an extra. With an uncommon lucidity he also explains to reporters:

> I don't mind sacrificing myself. I'm not interested in being a star, I don't have a touch like Zico or Sócrates, I just want to find the right gaps for my team-mates. In a team, someone has to make the greatest effort and I know that many people won't understand this, but this is my role. By accepting it I knew people would criticise me, it's logical. Now I ask myself: who would play all the time with their back to the door without complaining? It often happens that I don't participate in the game, but I open up spaces. It's a mission and I'm fulfilling it.

Serginho is 28 years old and has a life ahead of him. For the first time in his career he is about to face Italy. The idea that this could be his last match does not even occur to him.

War of the Worlds

Do you exist to play or do you play to exist? In football, reality is at stake. Before the action there is nothing. A subject, a space in which to move, a time in which to last. The game of Brazil is proud to leave the margin it deserves to chance, because without chance there is no existence. Salvation does not lie in the reason that makes plans, in the schemes of a tactic, in man-to-man marking, but in the ability to live with lucidity, the randomness of events. It is all about finding one's own rhythm and not losing it, whatever happens. Italy vs Brazil has the harmony of great works of art. The Brazilians move like drops of paint on a Jackson Pollock canvas; Enzo Bearzot's Italy seem to follow a jazz rhythm, where each instrument develops its own design while dialoguing with the others. Fantasy versus strategy, spectacle versus logic. Whoever stops, whoever makes a mistake, is lost.

In the Azzurri's schemes there is the DNA of the Vecio and the tactics he adopts cover almost a century of football history. He asks his midfielders to defend by covering the space. On the opponent with the ball goes the closest player. In defence, he reverses the concept by implementing the diktat of Herbert Chapman, the man who changed the history of football forever at the end of the 1920s: it is not the space that counts, but the ball. It is useless to stop the space, the space is defenceless. You have to mark the man.

Italian football was born from the ashes of the Second World War. The game of football is the mirror of a country that in the space of a few years first lost the war and then its best players in the tragedy of Superga. Poor, without means and, of necessity, opportunists, Italians made an art of getting by in their own daily lives. Italian football could only be reborn as a defensive game and make catenaccio its game plan. It essentially sought to prevent the goals of the opposing team by locking up its own goal. The derogatory adjective 'catenacciaro' became his label. That of a team dedicated to all-out defence, to the destruction of the other's game and to the renunciation of constructing any kind of attacking play in order not to allow the opponent's attackers to shoot at goal. In reality, catenaccio is a much higher and more complex tactic that is not immediately understood. Not everyone realises how modern it is. Until that time, Metodo and Sistema, tactics that imposed repetitive and predictable grids, had been very popular. Italian football was the first to propose reasoning, a battle strategy that changed each time, according to the enemy to be faced. The first to adopt it, to defend his Salernitana, was Gipo Viani. He borrowed it from the fishermen.

As he walked along the harbour he noticed that the fishermen pulled up a net full of fish, then immediately behind a second one with the remaining catch. The fish that escaped the first one were trapped in the second. It was a thunderbolt for Viani: when the attackers overtook the full-backs to stop them, he had to add a last man – free from fixed marking – behind the defensive line. It was a system that caused a stir but it would dominate football for 20 years. Nereo Rocco adopted the scheme in Triestina between 1947 and 1954. The mainstay of Rocco's defence was Cesare Maldini. However, it was Alfredo Foni's Inter team that made the Italian style of play – created to compensate for the technical gap between the big and small teams – a winning one during the period in which Bearzot's life was elsewhere.

Il Vecio played for Inter from 1948 to 1951 and returned in the 1956/57 season. The years from 1952 to 1955 were those of Foni, who in that period of time created the first catenaccio built to win (two Scudetti in two years). Bearzot returned from his years at Catania and Torino without ever having met the Nerazzurri coach, but it is clear that he could still smell his scent in the air. In the midst of a boom (1961–63), the destinies of Viani as coach, Rocco as co-coach, and Maldini the captain of a Rizzoli-led Milan team that dominated the championship and won the European Cup, met. Taking all his tactical baggage with him, Rocco joined Torino (1963–67). In that team he found a midfielder in his last year of activity. He was the oldest of them all. His team-mates already called him Vecio. It was Bearzot.

The following year Rocco wanted Bearzot as his deputy, to teach him the secrets of the Italian school. He stayed there until his last season (1966/67), during which his destiny was reunited with the arrival of Cesare Maldini, also in his last year of activity. The following season Rocco returned to Milan for seven seasons (1967–74); this time it was Maldini who became his assistant (1971/72) and co-coach (1972–74).

Il Vecio was elsewhere, already in the national team, for which he began to tour the world. From playing football he moved on to observing football. When Bearzot took over the team, the objective was to close an era, that of the 'Mexicans' of 1970, and to rebuild the national team. The Azzurri were still eating bread and catenaccio, but the world was changing and he found himself in the midst of

WAR OF THE WORLDS

a revolution. Football was now 'total' and roles much less defined. The Italian school had been displaced. The offensive phase of the catenaccio, which was limited to lightning-fast restarts, with long throws towards the attacking players, was extremely limited by the application of the offside trap and zonal marking. The defensive phase, which involved rigid man-to-man marking, was displaced by the movements of the players without the ball.

Bearzot observed, studied and understood. He began to make his innovations, trying to keep the essence of Italian football intact. He could not completely set aside the old modules, given the great solidity of the Italian defensive school, so he tried to insert offensive movements into a system that still provided for man-marking in defence. He aimed to combine fixed marking of three or four elements with the control of space. In those years the vanguard was Dutch football, with versatile players capable of playing in every area of the pitch. But the Dutch module was too unconventional, too difficult to adapt to Italian characteristics. So, initially, the model became the Polish one. Still modern but less daring and more solid. On the other hand, at the German World Cup, Cruyff's Netherlands and Lato's Poland occupied second and third places on the podium, immediately behind the hosts. Bearzot's move was the first step towards the future. His DNA was complete:

Catenaccio [Sweeper (Viani+Rocco+Maldini)]
+
Total Football [Eclectic (Netherlands/Poland)]

The result was the 'Mixed Zone'. For the first time in Italian football, a coach was now implementing a flexible strategy that mixed different styles and allowed the team to be effective at all times. To implement it, he needed versatile players who could guarantee him the flexibility that modern football had begun to demand.

This is how Bearzot comes to choose eclectic players, such as Tardelli, discarding instead the stars, such as Pruzzo and Beccalossi, who are too stuck in their roles. Scirea is the guarantee of the last

THE MATCH

man, the free agent who continues the tradition but with more mature tasks. In fact, he can also act as a support for the offensive game, with his advances and throw-ins. Gentile and Cabrini are the defenders who remain in charge of man-marking but, on the left, Cabrini also takes on the task of supporting the attack, with frequent advances on the flank, becoming a fluid player. Collovati, the stopper, also remains a man-marker to all intents and purposes. In midfield, Bearzot, apart from the defensive midfielder Oriali who offers balance in front of the defence and often takes on the task of man-marking the opposing director, arranges the team in a zone: an all-round half-back on the right, Tardelli, and a more advanced director on the left, Antognoni. On the right-hand side of the pitch there is a wing-back, Conti, who usually has the task of getting past a man, going deep and crossing; a centre-forward, Rossi; and a second forward, Graziani, who switches with the central striker. It is no coincidence that six of the team come from Giovanni Trapattoni's Juventus, a mainstay of Rocco's Milan team.

The Friulian coach sets the team up with the dual intent of stopping Zico, Sócrates, Éder, Falcão and Cerezo, but at the same time always being ready to recover the ball in order to restart. The time of passive attitudes based on waiting and a long throw-in is over. The versatile talents of his lads can defend and play the game at the same time. This is the manoeuvred counter-attack.

The Brazilians are wary of Italy's game. Schemes are used by those who do not know how to play them. They are a constriction, a protection, a defence. The game is something else, perhaps, says Bearzot. The pure game may know and must move without rules but, if the aim of a game is to win, then a strategy is needed, and applying it is a sign of commitment. To mark requires study, knowledge of the opponent, analysis of the position and evaluation of the team's possibilities. Humanistic qualities. Brazil refuse tactics, avoid complications, choose linearity in the name of spectacle. Consequently, they choose a moderate speed that leaves time for technical finesse. Everything must be soft – the touch, the play, the

280

marking. Play must be instinctive, because only improvisation, if you are an artist, creates spectacle. It is a game in which, at times, individual skills overshadow team skills. This is the fault of history. The first players learned football at informal parties, far from the Western colonialists. When they were confronted with them, they avoided any kind of physical contact for fear of reprisals. So they resorted to dribbling, which was easy for them, as they were samba dancers. Surprise, vivacity and spontaneity were all already present in their most authentic spirit.

Santana has revived Brazil's footballing identity, being less tactical and tied to patterns, more fantasy, talent and individuality. It is a tradition that harks back to the culture of the 'malandro' or rascal, celebrated by Pelé's Seleção and whose most recent manifestation is the 1982 national team. Between the two eras, Brazil embraced organised play. This line dated back to the military coup of 1964 and the 'technocratic' policy that the new regime sought to impose on all social sectors, including football. In fact, the national teams of 1974 and 1978 were based on an idea of organised football, entrusted to a tactically astute system of play, a line that resorted to organisation before fantasy.

Santana's team now lines up with a unique 4-2-2-2. It would be unthinkable for an Italian player to deploy in a team that lacks width, but that is only an indicative positioning on paper. Brazil attack with nearly all their men, leaving only the two centre-backs, Oscar and Luizinho, to guard the rearmost part of the defensive line-up, which is almost in midfield when their own forwards are close to the opponent's goal. The two marauding full-backs, on the other hand, are the men that the defence sends forward like two wings in classic sabotage action: Leandro, with long gallops on the right in a strip that is purposely cleared by his team-mates, who suddenly 'open up' towards him; Júnior, from the left, with precise aims in the opponent's area for the personal goal, in which he is a true artist.

But it is above all the exceptional midfield that feeds the attacking manoeuvre to the maximum, the Magic Square: Falcão,

Cerezo, Sócrates and Zico. The position of the fantastic four does not respond to a fixed pattern, but is often dictated by inspiration and an understanding that never leads them to overlap. All the Brazilians go for the goal, including Éder, who converges from the left to explode his violent and malicious shots, and Serginho, who, as well as opening up space, is always present in crowded areas.

Even when defending, the Brazilians always aim to capture the ball, without ever throwing it away, and shorten the distances as much as possible to trap opponents in ever-tighter spaces. The Seleção has a fluidity that is capable of recreating new schemes that are always perfectly balanced, despite the constant movement of the players. But not all that glitters is gold.

The Tower Move

On 27 June Franchi flies to Italy. On 2 July the Palio of Siena is being run, and on 29 June he has to oversee the 'tratta', the matching of the horses to the competing *contrade* (districts). The operation takes place in Piazza del Campo and is attended by the mayor together with the ten captains who take part in the race. He has been the captain of the contrada della Torre (District of the Tower) since 1971 and he cannot miss it. On the eve of the draw he accepts the invitation of '96 hours of the Palio', and during the broadcast produced by the private Sienese broadcaster Canale 3 he gives his first thoughts after the passage of the first round of the World Cup: 'The championship began with 24 countries. Twelve teams went home and 12 stayed. Among these 12 there is Italy. I think that it is not bad to be in a prohibitive group, because in this way there's nothing to lose. Anything can happen. Twelve years ago, Italy scored only one goal in the first round, but then they exploded. Let's hope that it will be the same this time.'

The Palio is his life. It is a world apart, so different from football. Thunderous but also genuine. 'It has reflections of amazing humanity. There is nothing like it in anything in life that you are doing. The intensity of it is not comparable to football. And we can never get it

THE TOWER MOVE

across to those outside this inner circle.' But in the world of football, thanks to him, everyone now knows that there are sacred dates on which you cannot have meetings – 29 June is one of them. In the first Mundial calendar, compiled on 9 May 1979, that day, along with the Palio, was initially set aside for rest. But then the calendar underwent changes. And ironically, the day of the 'tratta' coincided with that of Italy vs Argentina, while that of the Palio coincided with the match between the loser of the first match and Brazil. Franchi thought he had burnt the two matches of the Azzurri. Instead, on 2 July, the Argentines will play the yellow-green team.

As a Palio man, Franchi knows that the choice of horse, no matter how closely you look at its runs in provincial races, is ultimately based on the feeling of the moment. And a few days earlier he confided his own to a journalist friend: veteran of the national team Alfeo Biagi, who reached him by phone on the eve of his departure for Spain.

'How are you, old man?' said Biagi.

'I'm starting to get a bit tired. Sometimes I think it would be time to retire, but then the passion takes over and I carry on.'

'You do well.'

'Tell that to my family. They never see me at home, the years are heavy and things don't always go the way I want them to, then the fatigue sets in.'

'Come on, you've got a big World Cup coming up.'

'I don't know why, Alfeo, but I have a strange confidence in this national team, even if I have to keep it to myself.'

'Your usual diplomacy.'

'You'll understand, I'm the president of UEFA, the one of the Referee Commission, I'm ... a bit of everything! I have to pretend to be neutral.'

'Bad thing about institutionalism.'

'But I have blue in my heart, you know.'

'I know it well. And where do you think the Azzurri will take us?'

'Look, I came close to the title in Mexico. This time I feel, and I can't tell you why, that Sordillo could do it.'

283

'I wish.'

'Don't call me crazy. I sometimes sense things first.'

The Palio on 2 July often coincides with the World Cup or the European Championship, but nothing could stop Franchi from being in Siena on those days. In 1978, during the World Cup in Argentina, as a member of the FIFA Organising Committee he had to guarantee a constant presence. But on that fateful day, he could not miss Siena because the Torre was taking part in the Palio. With a ploy, he tried to reconcile the calendar of the World Cup with that of the Palio. He flew to Buenos Aires, crossed the Atlantic, travelled thousands of kilometres and arrived on time in the Piazza del Campo. But the journey and the sacrifice were not rewarded. His contrada did not win.

In the 1982 Palio, after a long sequence of uncompetitive horses, the draw finally awards Torre with Rimini, the horse that has won three Palios and has been indicated as the favourite of the race. It is the aligning of the stars that Franchi has been waiting on for ten years. The right jockey on the right horse. On the day of the Palio, during the blessing of the horse, Rimini suddenly limps away. The injury is serious and shortly afterwards is diagnosed as a fracture. Just when it seemed close to becoming a reality, Franchi sees his dream crumble in an instant. The captain's despair becomes collective. The contrada wants Rimini to be present at the race.

Meanwhile, a thousand kilometres away, the Azzurri are sitting at the Sarriá following the Brazilians against the reigning world champions.

Franchi goes through long hours of trepidation. If he takes it to the square, the horse risks being slaughtered after the race. So Franchi makes his decision and warns the municipal authorities that the Torre will not run, thus saving the horse's life. Franchi and jockey Bastiano, without speaking, watch on television the race that they have prepared at the table. When it ends, the jockey sighs: 'I would have won this Palio, I'm sure of it.' Franchi, disconsolate, returns to Barcelona on the eve of Italy vs Brazil with withered thoughts in his head: 'Only Brazil can lose this World Cup, but at this point anything can happen.'

The Bluff

After Italy's match against Argentina, a series of strikes lead to the press suspending publication until the eve of the match between Italy and Brazil. Oreste del Buono, a literary critic who, after ten years as editor of *Linus*, a dozen books and a hundred translations, finds himself commenting on the World Cup on behalf of *Stampa* and *Guerino*, suffers this and goes to watch the match between Brazil and Argentina as a fan, knowing that he cannot talk about it. 'A newspaper that doesn't come out always misses a great opportunity. A newspaper that doesn't come out for three days, imagine that.' For him, Brazil vs Argentina was not a match between two teams, but a three-sided clash. 'There was also Italy on the pitch, of course. The blue shirts crept in, shuffled, appeared and reappeared, to reappear with capricious punctuality between the white-and-blue ones and the green ones, in a memory of Italy–Argentina and a foretaste of Italy–Brazil.' Inevitably he wondered, 'How would Zoff have done here? And Gentile? And Tardelli?' When the Brazilians, by wiping out the Argentines, mortgaged ownership of the football of the future, he remembered Tardelli, his quarrel with Sconcerti, his goal that twisted Fillol. And he lit up: 'On paper the games seem to be done, yet those blue shirts that in my hallucination as an Italian fan in tow I kept seeing at the Sarriá stadium between green-and-white shirts suggest to me, not to hope, but to be sure, sure that at least some of the Italians (the three mentioned, for example, and for me especially Tardelli) will take the field so as not to make a bad impression. Of course, a lot will depend on who will take the field.'

After the confrontation with the Argentines, Juarez Soares, the reporter on the sidelines of TV Globo, talking to the doctor Neylor Lasmar, had learned that while Batista's contusion, caused by Maradona, seemed curable, Zico's seemed more worrying in view of the decisive match against Italy. Zico, besieged by journalists, preferred to divert the topic to his direct opponent: 'While I try to make my work on the field help my team, Maradona always falls into the trap of having to prove at all costs that he is better than me.' Then, showing the marks of Passarella's blow on his left leg, he added, 'Problems like that take two to three days to resolve, so I hope to face Italy.'

Zico had received a blow to the muscle. If it had been the knee, the Mundial would already be over for him. The Brazilian journalists are still divided in their predictions: the majority believe that Telê Santana will not change the team even if he has not officially announced it. Even now, on the eve of the match, Zico still feels some pain in his left leg at the point of the calf where Passarella's foot landed. He was trying to dribble past him when the blow came, but the Brazilian forward never accused him of intentional misconduct. It was late in the match and fatigue was clouding his reflexes. Even before receiving the Argentine's treacherous kick, he had already been training to evade the Azzurri's close marking with many backwards and lateral movements on the offensive front to make room for Sócrates, Falcão and above all Éder, on whose powerful shot Brazil rely heavily. In reality, the Argentine's entrance served to spark a war of nerves. The Seleção agreed to confuse the ideas of Italy. On Friday, Sócrates wrote in his diary: 'Zico will play, but the Azzurri will only know when he enters the field.'

Hotel Majestic, Room 427

The last fuse of rancour is lit in the final training session. Coming out of the Sarriá, after stopping Maradona, Claudio Gentile had let out a liberating shout, perhaps sent to his opponents or to those who did not believe him: 'Bastards!' For Cascioli, of *Il Messaggero*, that shout has become a pretext. 'More than an insult, it was a stone thrown at the press box.' When the last training session in Gavà ends, on the eve of the match against Brazil, Gentile and Cascioli

HOTEL MAJESTIC, ROOM 427

find themselves facing each other. The anger of the blue defender shatters the blackout for a moment.

'You're a liar!'

'I heard very well.'

'Then you are a liar twice over!'

Cascioli calls Bruno Bernardi, correspondent of the *Stampa*.

'He heard it too! You told us bastards!'

Gentile is furious. 'It was an instinctive outburst after a tense game, I didn't address it to anyone in particular.'

The guardian De Gaudio arrives. But the gentleman from Vomero this time cannot face the wrath of the reporter. Cascioli has poison for everyone. 'We come here to prostitute ourselves and you are constantly putting us on trial! Here you want to criminalise the press!'

Bearzot enters the scene. He points at Cascioli, the man who has ridiculed him mercilessly for months in the pages of the Roman newspaper, and he pours all his fury on him. 'No shouting in our house! I'll tell you what you are, a scoundrel! You have done nothing but offend me and the national team!'

The two almost come to blows. Players (Causio and Antognoni) and officials (De Gaudio and Vantaggiato) stand between them. Roberto Renga of *Paese Sera*, wanting to act as peacemaker, nudges the coach with his leg. Photographers and cameramen film the scene, the other reporters remain astonished. The silence is broken by a threat: 'Bearzot, this isn't over. I'm going to sue you!' Cascioli signs it. The fatigue, the stress, the grudges, the fears, the tiredness, the tensions. There is less than 24 hours to Brazil. For the Azzurri there is no peace, not even in the most delicate hour.

Del Buono flies into the room to attach himself to his typewriter:

> The latest news from the dressing room is encouraging. The Azzurri's nervous tone remains high: they have once again quarrelled with the Italian journalists in tow, by now their usual sparring partners. And this time, to the delight

THE MATCH

of both Italian and foreign TV stations, Coach Bearzot generously entered the fray. All for one, one for all. The national team is the only Italian affair that I don't think is allotted by the parties.

Mario Sconcerti, on the other hand, listens without a word to the merciless condemnations of his colleagues (only a few whisper in dismay: 'Not you, Bearzot!'). He feels out of place and he would like to be somewhere else. The clamour of the previous days has given him the measure of the general breakdown and loneliness into which Bearzot, 'a man of great defects and nerves as steep as the wrinkles that dig into his face', is falling. A man of the frontier, a fighter of life, who likes to feel at the mercy of everything and lead an eternally uphill existence. It sees him afflicted by fixations and persecution manias, but he is a real man, authentic, never a dancer, willing to follow himself even at the bottom of a paradox.

For the correspondent Sconcerti, he is the most intractable Bearzot he has ever known. For 13 years now they have been going around the world together. He has always valued the person, less the technician. He has watched him during the 'morning wars' alone, besieged, harried, but always ready to retort with all his fury. When, after the match against Cameroon, he heard him say that his team had played a smart game, he stood up and attacked him harshly. The next day, however, he apologised. For the form, not the substance. Shortly afterwards he reconsidered: 'Maybe it's true, Italy played with intelligence, it was important to pass the round. And then it was the only one to risk beating the North Africans.'

Sconcerti, the reporter from *La Repubblica*, is making his World Cup debut. He has got there thanks to three impeccable moves. First came the scoop of the hot summer of 1974, when he found himself travelling around Italy in the car of the new coach of the national team, Fulvio Bernardini, and managed to report live on the purge of the entire old guard (Rivera and Mazzola above all) and at the same time the birth of the new Italy. A blow that earned him a transfer to Rome

288

to the head office of the *Corriere dello Sport*, which he joined when he was only 21 years old. Five years later, he had to move again, but he only had to move down two flights of the same building. At the age of 31 he was given the task of founding the sports pages of *La Repubblica*, in Piazza Indipendenza, where the newspaper occupied the first two floors of the building. Eugenio Scalfari's newspaper, which had been created three years earlier as a 'second newspaper' for a public that had already read the day's events, had initially renounced the obligation of exhaustiveness, leaving out most of the news and sport.

The second move, the turning point, came during the other Mundial, the one in Argentina. It was Saturday, 10 June 1978. Scalfari, affectionately nicknamed 'Barbapapà', had organised a dinner on the terrace with the elite of Roman culture. Suddenly he was alone at the table. He got up and found the guests in front of the television. It was Italy vs Argentina. The next day he approached Gianni Rocca:

'Why do we give so little space to the World Cup?'

'Because sport is not on the agenda of your newspaper.'

'Let's devote two pages to it from today.'

The sport of *La Repubblica* was born there, at Scalfari's house. On the top floor of a 1930s building on the Nomentana.

On the eve of the Mundial, comes the third move. This was to get *La Repubblica*'s director to buy the doyen of sports journalists: Gianni Brera. And now he is in Spain on behalf of his newspaper together with Brera, of whom he is technically the head of service but for whom, in fact, he carries information and suitcases. He gets up every morning at eight and goes to bed at two, coordinates the work of the correspondents and writes an average of three pieces a day. In the afternoon, when Italy are not playing, he goes to see Brera. Sconcerti knocks on room 427 at the Hotel Majestic. He finds the figurehead in boxer shorts and a vest, long socks and moccasins, with a handkerchief against the sweat resting on the front between the straps of his vest. It is suffocating inside the room. Brera keeps the windows closed and air conditioning off. He loves the heat. No one has ever seen him outside without a jacket, not even in the 40 degrees of this Catalan summer.

He left for the 12th World Cup with the unpreparedness of the ignorant tourist. For Brera, Spain is a southern country that is barely separated from sun-baked Africa. All he packed in his suitcases were cotton shirts and light clothes. The moment he landed in Vigo he had to revise his assessments. 'In June, Galicia has a Norwegian climate. The people who live there are of mixed race, Iberians and Celts have merged their blood, and in fact they are called Celtiberians. I look at their faces and find them very similar to ours, of northern Latins.' The discovery mortifies him ethnologically, historically and climatically.

In the torrid heat of Barcelona, it is the Majestic that does not excite him. Too cold for him. After visiting the bar on the ground floor on the first day, he has vowed never to go back, because of the air conditioning. He hardly sleeps. He has moved the thermometer to 25 degrees. The air is impregnated with the smell of the Tuscan cigar he always keeps in his mouth. He sleeps in a room with two double beds, in one of which he rests, while on the other his two suitcases are camped out. They look old, poor and flimsy. To Sconcerti they remind him of the immigrants' cardboard suitcases. In reality, they are made of hard, precious and resistant material, like the bark of their owner. In one are clothes, in the other medicines. Nobody knows what he takes, he has no obvious health problems and does not talk about them, but he travels with a small pharmacy in tow, like all those condemned to nomadism.

It has been a long day for Brera, travelling over 100 kilometres (60 miles) with Mario. He has watched France vs Northern Ireland on television and will soon be organising himself to watch Poland vs USSR. Afterwards, it has already been decided that he will go to eat with Sconcerti and Soldati at Rancho Grande. He already regrets the Galician nights. He finds no peace here. He has visited the Picasso Museum and the great Gothic basilica of Santa María del Mar. Evenings have been spent with Soldati and Cancogni, the last ones in a bad atmosphere. Cancogni, due to the cold, has lost his voice and can no longer contain the irrepressible Soldati.

Brera ends his piece with the words: 'With this little bit of Brazil, the present Italy can only try to avoid a thrashing without unworthily scarifying and losing face.' He also invokes Our Lady of Tibidabo and, in the event of grace, promises to wear the habit of the flagellants to follow the procession of St Bartholomew in August in his country. He makes Sconcerti read what he has written but does not want to talk about it. Sconcerti sees the matches on the pitch, Brera likes to scrutinise them in his head. They have been like this for years, travelling the world, Sconcerti looking for news, Brera commenting on it. Only now, however, have they started to do it together. For each other.

Back in his room, Sconcerti relives in his head the clash between Bearzot and Cascioli and leaves on the paper what he thinks could be his Spanish testament. The epilogue of a personal chronicle dedicated to an ailing Italy. The last thought before the end: 'It is the sign of a worn-out army on the threshold of the last battle.'

The Last Session

For Brazil, the dress rehearsal before going on stage is over. The last training session to the rhythm of samba. After the final test, Santana encourages his team.

'Tomorrow you play as you know how. That's all you need.'

He then approaches Falcão: 'You know them. Is there anything you want to say?'

The Italy-based midfielder is the most concerned. 'They will stay in defence and play on the counter-attack.'

His comrades sneer.

'Paulo, it must have been easy for you to earn a living in Italy!'

Falcão smiles, but then seriously turns to Santana: 'Italy is not what we saw in the first round. It is a team that can be dangerous. Wouldn't it be better to change our tactics tomorrow?'

Telê is cutting. 'Do we want to qualify by drawing? Brazil always plays to win.'

The euphoric chorus of comrades follow the technician. 'We play so well like this, if we change and lose then what could we say? The friendlies went well, the first round games went well, we beat Argentina. Why do that if everything is going great for us?'

The meeting ends like this. Everyone takes a shower. Only Oscar approaches Santana. 'Telê, let's think about it, won't it be a risk to launch an attack against the Italians?'

Santana reassures him. 'Don't worry, we win 4-0. No problem.'

At that precise moment, Space Shuttle *Columbia*, which left Kennedy Space Center on 27 June, returns to Earth. After 4.7 million kilometres, 113 Earth orbits, seven days, 1 hour, 9 minutes and 31 seconds, it brings home pilot Henry Hartsfield and his commander Ken Mattingly, both of whom woke up that morning to the patriotic song 'This Is My Country'. Mattingly is no ordinary man. He was the capsule communicator, the man who maintained contact between NASA's control centre and the Apollo 11 astronauts. A few days later, on 6 August 1969, he was appointed command module pilot for the Apollo 13 mission. On the eve of the launch, however, it was discovered that the lunar module's backup pilot, Charles Duke, was suffering from rubella. When it was discovered that Mattingly had never contracted it, he was replaced to avoid the risk of him falling ill during the space flight. He did not fall ill, but saved the astronauts on Earth.

This time, waiting for him and his companion on runway 22 at Edwards Air Force Base in California – the first concrete runway for a shuttle – are President Ronald Reagan, in a cream suit with white shirt and brown regimental tie, and his wife Nancy, patriotically wrapped in a red skirt under a white shirt and blue scarf. Both with their hair pinned back as if the jet of an engine had just hit them.

The news of the return of the shuttle fills the American front pages on 5 July. On the other hand, there is almost no mention of the World Cup in the newspapers, not even in sport. If Europe does not

THE LAST SESSION

understand baseball, the United States reciprocates with football. One person who does understand it is Lawrie Mifflin, one of the nation's first female sports journalists. She came to the world's attention with her coverage of the 1976 Montreal Olympics in the *New York Daily News*. Since 25 April, she has been writing for the *New York Times*. The newspaper has been devoting paragraphs with some continuity to the unknown World Cup. Warren Hoge, who has been working for *The Times* in Rio de Janeiro for three years, wrote: 'This is a little-known phenomenon in the United States.' Perhaps from there he is able to get a better understanding of what is happening in Spain, where in recent days 'at least 24 nations, including world powers, have fallen under a spell'.

On the day of the Sarriá match, Mifflin, intrigued by US indifference, is on the phone with Jim Spence, vice-president of ABC Sports. Their conversation is not about the challenge of the day between Italy and Brazil. For the first time, an American network is planning to televise the World Cup Final, live from Madrid on Sunday, 11 July at 1.30pm, Eastern Time. Full cable coverage of the event is offered only by the US Spanish-language SIN National Spanish Television Network, which, in agreement with Mexico's Televisa, acquired the broadcasting rights for 1.5 million Swiss francs. The 1966 (NBC), 1970 (ABC) and 1974 (CBS) editions came only through clips of matches. The last World Cup, in 1978, had no English-language coverage on American television.

'It's a very special event,' Spence explains to Mifflin, 'it's the most watched event in the world and it fits perfectly with our "Wide World of Sports" philosophy of showing only the most important international events.' ABC is not doing this for commercial reasons, its executives do not expect exceptional revenue from this choice. Spence no longer wants to broadcast the North American Soccer League's Soccer Bowl as he has for the past four years because the ratings have been too low. If the network embarks on such a venture, it is only for a matter of prestige. Even if there is no shortage of problems.

THE MATCH

When ABC applied in February to rent satellite for the final, they realised that camera positions were not as easy to obtain as they would be for any American sporting event. Giving each country additional cameras separate from the main feed provided by Spanish television is impractical. ABC are baffled. They know that the Spanish network will tend to offer wide shots to accommodate the viewpoint preferred by football viewers, that of the centre stand, while American sports fans are used to a more spectacular view, where wide shots alternate with close-ups. For the moment, the channel has only been granted two unobtrusive positions: one in the stands, to film their announcers as usual, and one high up to show an overview of the stadium. The other problem is related to advertising. Unlike foreign networks, ABC will interrupt the broadcast for commercials. 'Each time we'll have two 30-second commercials in a row,' Spence explained. 'But what if there's a goal right during a commercial?' asked Mifflin. 'During North American Soccer League games it has rarely happened.'

The final is six days away and, on this 5 July, the ABC managers are not paying attention to the match that is about to be played at the Sarriá. In those same hours, however, Mifflin has realised something that escapes them: 'A football match,' he writes in his editorial, 'is like theatre, with a main story that also includes smaller, personal dramas, between players who face each other step by step. Losing a piece of dialogue in a play is not the same as missing something decisive, but it means losing an essential part of the story just the same.' To walk away from the pitch for a commercial, even without missing a goal, is to frustrate the true football fan.

The Brazilian spectator, on the other hand, needs only one thing to be satisfied: to win. Even the Americans know this. In the same columns of *The Times*, George Vecsey writes: 'Brazil will play against Italy in the small Sarriá stadium for the right to move into the semi-finals next Thursday. The Brazilians would advance in the event of a draw. But Telê Santana, Brazil's coach, said: "We will not play for a draw. We will play for a win."'

294

Quelli Che il Calcio ...

'Francesco Graziani holds more interviews than Robert Redford at the Cannes Film Festival.' To understand how and why someone could sign, with the RAI stamp, this mocking statement, we must first go back in time.

The grandfather of the reporter in question, twice married to wealthy ladies, was the Lord of Contursi, a town in the province of Salerno not far from Naples. Beasts, men, houses, land and mountains. It was all his. All it took was one evening and one hand of cards to lose everything. Everything that was his, that would have belonged to his children, and his children's children. The Lord of Contursi also lost his life shortly afterwards. He had claimed he could eat 60 hard-boiled eggs, for a bet. He won. It was the only time. His son Mario, on the other hand, lost two wives, the first to pneumonia, the second to heart disease. Otherwise, he was just like his father. Elegant, perfumed, generous. And, of course, a gambler. There were 12 brothers, all ruined by horses. Mario's son was not yet born when he first came to the San Siro racecourse. He lost and had to walk home with his nine-month-pregnant wife because he had gambled away the tram fare.

With this DNA he came into the world on a Thursday at the end of October. They called him Giuseppe. Then Peppi, Peppino and finally Beppe. When he turned 12 and his father left him, his sister and his mother to move to Caracas, he thought: 'He did well to dance on his horses. If he had left me some I would have done it, maybe at billiards, where among other things you can hardly breathe because of the smoke.'

Grateful to his absent father, he damned his mother. He went to school reluctantly and when he read in the final papers 'Viola Giuseppe: rejected' he commented, 'But they don't even know me. Missing, they had to write.' It was at that point that his mother's benevolent diktat reached him: 'Find a place and may God help you.' His god had a name: Vito Liverani. He was a photographer

THE MATCH

by profession and about to set up the Olympia agency. Tired of seeing Giuseppe in the way, he recommended him to the director of Sportinformazioni, the news agency (where he himself rented a room that he used as a photographic studio), which acted as the Milan correspondence office for the *Corriere dello Sport*. The director was Luigi Ferrario, known as Babbone, because he had compromised himself in the midst of the Republic of Salò, the Italian government between September 1943 and April 1945, by taking over the editorship of *Gazzetta dello Sport*, which was bought at that time by the Gruppo Editoriale Partito Fascista. He was a huge and severe man who aroused awe in everyone. Except for him. The agency was a training ground for fresh minds. They worked at breakneck speed, three folders in 15 minutes with no margin for error – Ferrario did not tolerate that. The journalists wrote directly on a matrix, which then printed bulletins that were distributed to newspapers every two hours.

Sometimes editors walked into a phone booth with three notes on a piece of paper and dictated articles to the newspaper, up to five pages long, including punctuation and spelling. Always a good start. Not at all intimidated, young Viola first entered as a collaborator and then was hired at 30,000 lire a month, including Sundays, nights and all the other holidays on the calendar. On the day of his mother's death, at seven o'clock in the morning, Babbone went to his house, two hours after the event, to comfort him: 'Look, dear Viola, all you need to forget such great pain is work. Come to the agency and you will see that everything will pass.' Viola followed the advice. Among his young colleagues he became a name. 'Beppeviola' was a brand that began to make people talk about it. So much so that when Babbone died he inherited the management of the agency.

A few years earlier, Ferrario had come to an agreement with Aldo De Martino, his counterpart at Agisport, the other Italian sports agency, to merge the two titles under the aegis of the newly formed Editoriale Sportiva Lampo srl. De Martino, while retaining his capital share in Sportinformazioni, began working shortly afterwards at the Milan headquarters of RAI, within the experimental television section, which debuted on 3 January 1954, becoming shortly afterwards head of the television sports editorial office. Perhaps it was thanks to this hook that Viola, from the agency, began to take his first steps in RAI. He found himself in room 341 on the third floor, together with Adone Carapezzi and Ivo Fineschi, an unusual trio that lived in harmony. During his exam to become a professional, Enzo Biagi asked him: 'In your opinion, is Fanfani right-wing or left-wing in this DC?' 'It depends on the day,' he replied. Promoted.

The final contract with RAI in 1966 allowed him to marry Franca, the girl from upstairs in the building that marked the apex of the triangle in which he had pitched his tents since birth (Piazza Adigrat, Via Sismondi, Via Lomellina) in a Milan overwhelmed by a new energy, hungry for change. His life was spent at the hippodrome, where he drew inspiration from one bet and another, at Bar Gattullo, where he devoured huge sandwiches, then a popular comedy show and cabaret, where he combined the two by writing the lyrics for his accomplices. He wrote everywhere and worked a lot because he had a family and gambling debts, because of horses. But genetics cannot be resisted.

And if it turns out that Graziani gives more interviews than Redford, it is because Beppe Viola is the RAI correspondent who knows most about the life and soul of these Azzurri. And he does not think twice about being ironic about it. He is a print journalist, radio commentator, commentator, author, scriptwriter and even an actor. His face is unflappable, his complexion pale, his tone monochrome, his eyelids heavy, his smile contagious; he is eternally dressed in a short-sleeved Lacoste shirt, mostly burgundy, and always sweating. With it on, he slyly rides his ideal of unconventional journalism, cultured and popular at the same time, certainly far from epic, commonplace and stardom. Seemingly unconcerned, at work he has an intransigence that does not allow for deviations. He is Gianni Brera's perfect sidekick on TV and Bruno Pizzul's sidekick at scopa (an Italian card game).

Always prone to jokes, he conducted an interview with Gianni Rivera in tram number 15, he decided not to broadcast on *Domenica*

Sportiva the long-awaited report on the Milan derby because it was so unwatchable ('we'll broadcast last year's, at least it was football') and, forced to comment on the winter games, he candidly confided to viewers, 'You'll be surprised that I compromised myself with such an event, but I'm a RAI employee with daughters to take care of.' Perhaps this is why he is not much loved at RAI. His 'other' way of being a sports journalist is marginalising him from the lanes that count: 'I'm holding out to beat, modestly, the world record for non-career failure.' All he gets is a lot of fake compliments, no promotion and even less money. After the Argentinian Mundial he sent a 'Letter to the Editor', which turned out to be a masterpiece of dramatic comedy:

> I'm forty years old, I have four daughters and I feel like I'm being taken for a ride. A few days ago the editorial secretary told me that I have no right to the newspapers. On my word, I have never stolen pianos or expense accounts. I have not harmed the virtues of the numerous ladies and young ladies who circulate on the third floor. I have never received or taken a beating in the course of fights. I do not think I have ever 'disturbed' the careers of colleagues who are more culturally prepared than I am. I have always tried, in my modesty, to look after the interests of the company that I love like a mother, a stepmother I would say. At this point, however, I leave TG3 to others, to those who are intellectually better equipped and have more goodwill. I am going to London on the next 10 January. Marx and Mazzini did it, I can afford it too. To learn English at my own expense.

They loved him so much at RAI that someone denounced him with the accusation that he was taking money from 'those of the crocodile'. Close investigation and no responsibility ascertained. Only a reprimand with the obligation to wear a shirt and tie. 'So I would have sweated more and better.' But at the Mundial it was too hot and he took refuge in the cool comfort of his standard issue Lacoste shirt. With it on, light and free, he X-rayed the players' insides.

When he interviewed Graziani at the Azzurri's training camp, he first flattered him ('Take off your glasses, you're more handsome'), then unleashed his typical blows, calm but incisive: 'How do you get by without love for so long? Are there homosexuals on the national team?' Beppe Viola is like that, with an unmistakable personality. He is not afraid of the powerful. Like when he managed to stop Luca di Montezemolo at Monte Carlo: 'So, tell us, Libera e bella,' taking inspiration from his long hair. 'What do you mean, excuse me?' the executive replied astonished. 'But yes,' he explained, mimicking a well-known shampoo commercial, 'free of hair and beautiful in dandruff.' Montezemolo glared at him: 'Go away.' Or when he responded to a request from a general of the Carabinieri Corps for 'exemplary punishment' for a film crew that had forced a checkpoint to film a fire: 'With regard to your request for an exemplary punishment, we inform you that the three protagonists of the crime – driver, journalist [him] and cameraman/phonic – were executed at dawn in the courtyard of RAI in front of the lined-up workers.'

And he is on the side of the last in principle. Like when, on the eve of the Mundial, he discovers and covers for an aspiring reporter, not even 18 years old, hiding in the hedge of the Alassio retreat. His name is Fabio Fazio. Maybe he wants to be a journalist, but in the meantime he works with a radio station in Savona and has managed to obtain an accreditation that is only valid for the morning. But the conference has been moved to the afternoon so, when the gates closed, he decided to hide for four hours while waiting for the time to meet the Azzurri. 'Water in the mouth, you didn't see me here,' implores the young Fazio. 'Seen who?' replies Viola, winking.

Viola has not been tender with Bearzot in recent weeks but his irony is diffuse, not targeted. The Vecio, however, looks at him with suspicion and, when he returns to the Puerta del Sol retreat in the afternoon, he does not want to talk to him. Gianfranco De Laurentiis, also a RAI correspondent, takes care of it and only thanks

THE MATCH

to his good offices does Bearzot finally grant him the interview. But Viola, instead of asking him how the Azzurri are doing or his predictions for the upcoming matches, asks him whether he does not feel a little worn out. On the eve of the two matches of the group of death against Argentina and Brazil, he manages to be once again ironic, critical and confident at the same time: 'Our team faces the challenge with the conviction of being supporting players but the Azzurri, at least it is hoped, are also used to sudden heroics. For example, dumping the journalists and enjoying the hours of freedom among the tourists, hand in hand with the most loyal fans.' Irony that results in the certainty of 'spending another four years in the group of mediocrities'.

Viola leans towards the Brazilians. He compares them to Picasso. He does not want to pigeonhole them ('To define Brazil as just a football team is reductive to the point of insolence'), preferring instead to focus on the 'Bearzot Band'. If the Brazilians 'arrived in Barcelona singing', the Azzurri are consumed by 'nervousness, petty rivalries and controversies'. A madhouse, according to him. And he gets his hook from the context: 'They work in a small town where, among other things, there is a nursing home for mental illness, so they told us when they took us in a taxi. Maybe they were making fun of us, maybe the image of our team at the moment suggests such an idea. As usual, the field will verify this. If we get something decent out of it then we're crazy. It's better than being whiny and anonymous.'

On the day of his debut against Poland, RAI forced Viola to conduct, together with Daniela Poggi, 'Azzurro', a singing event invented by Vittorio Salvetti to bring luck to the Azzurri of football. At the Petruzzelli Theatre in Bari, Franco Battiato sang 'Cuccurucucu' (the song that the Azzurri always sing on the bus in Spain), Vasco Rossi 'Splendida giornata', Loredana Bertè 'Non sono una signora', Marco Ferradini 'Teorema', Fabio Concato 'Domenica bestiale', Riccardo Cocciante 'Celeste nostalgia', while Lucio Dalla and the Stadio sang 'Grande figlio di puttana'. But there were also Antonello Venditti, Franco Califano, Alberto Camerini, Roberto

300

Vecchioni, Peppino Di Capri, Enrico Ruggeri, Milva, Fred Bongusto and Gianni Morandi, captain of the winning team.

Tired of feeling atypical, he and some colleagues (including Gianni Mura) set up Magazine, a news agency based in a small villa in Via Arbe. Personalities such as Giovanni Trapattoni, Gianni Rivera, Jean-Louis Trintignant, or budding talents such as Giorgio Terruzzi pass through it. He calls it the *Marchettificio* and supplies all that cross-industry publishing on sport, entertainment and customs that he, as a family man, needs to raise funds to last the month. Above all, it could allow him to say goodbye to RAI after more than 20 years of mutual tolerance.

In the meantime, he has already packed his suitcase in Barcelona. He has only left a white Lacoste shirt out. The one he will wear the next day at the Sarriá.

The Night

It is night. In the Mas Badó retreat, the phone rings. The call is for Telê Santana. On the other end is Brazilian president João Figueiredo: 'You have done a great job, tomorrow I'm sure you will complete it. Best wishes!'

At the El Castillo hotel all the lights are off. Only four eyes are excluded. They belong to Tardelli and Conti. Bearzot knows this, he has renamed them 'Coyotes'. They are the ones to whom he has to tell fairy tales to accompany them at dawn.

The first to fall asleep is Gaetano Scirea. The serenity he radiates on the pitch accompanies him even at night. He is one of the strongest free agents in the world and he is performing his role with absolute naturalness, on tiptoe, conceding little to the spectacle. He has never been sent off, yet he plays in defence. All he needs is class and a clean match, his head held high, his elegance, his purity of touch that is moral clarity. He has modesty of words. He will not shape his era because he makes no noise, but his is a silence that carries weight.

THE MATCH

He began his career playing up front. One day, Scirea took on the role of libero without enthusiasm, almost thinking of it as being demoted. But, accustomed to respect, he honoured the role, until fate paved the way for him: the usual starter broke his leg and he became Gaetano Scirea. One day, in Bergamo, the journalist Angelo Caroli approached him: 'You played a wonderful match.' Scirea lowered his eyes. He moved on to Juventus. Achille Bortolotti, president of Atalanta, said to Giampiero Boniperti: 'Gaetano, I'll take him to Turin. Because this boy is different from all the others.' During the World Cup in Argentina came his technical explosion. In Mar del Plata, the venue of the first two elimination rounds for Italy, who had just beaten France and Hungary, the same reporter told him, 'You are the strongest in the world in your role.' Scirea lowered his gaze to the ground again, but admitted, 'It's true, maybe you're right.' Caroli was stunned, then understood that the player, honest to a fault, could not lie to himself.

A difficult role. Constant commitment. The brain always on the move. Looking at everyone and no one. The intuition that precedes reasoning, but he has extraordinary qualities. He knows how to move around the pitch and can read the game a second before the others. He plays by heart with his team. When Cabrini started forward, for example, he went to take charge of the attacker who was left unguarded. And when he has the ball at his feet, he does not limit himself to freeing the area, but organises the game to get the team's manoeuvre going again in the best possible way. For him, nothing seems to be exceptional, since he has learned to measure every element of his existence with the yardstick of common sense, from his professional life as a football player to his intimate life as a father and husband. And his moral cleanliness also makes him a champion off the field.

After training he sometimes goes home at lunchtime with a group of strangers: 'Mariella, these gentlemen have travelled hundreds of kilometres to come and watch Juve and I thought they had to eat something.' He is a man who moves in peace: good, accommodating,

THE NIGHT

honest and humble, with an old-fashioned style. But he is not afraid to look old. He has the comfort of an example, that of Zoff, a man who taught him not to look back. They have always shared a room. Inside, they play cards, sometimes read; simple things, like their ideals, because they don't need a lot of rigmarole. The room they share has a name: 'Switzerland'. Tardelli gave it to them.

The other rooms see the pairing up of Antognoni and Graziani, Causio and Selvaggi, Conti and Galli, Dossena and Altobelli, Marini and Bergomi, Massaro and Vierchowod, Collovati and Baresi, Oriali and Bordon, Cabrini and Rossi. Gentile is always in a room with Tardelli. While Gentile falls asleep within a matter of seconds, his room-mate could not sleep, which is why he left for Spain laden with books. For Gentile, however, sleep and performance are inseparable friends, so Bearzot moves Tardelli to a room alone. The same thing happens with Conti. So Gentile and Galli find themselves in a room together, while the two insomniacs have a single room each.

Tardelli is reading Giovanni Arpino's *La suora giovane* (The Young Nun). Every now and then he picks up a photo and stops to contemplate it. It is that of Sara, his daughter. Conti, on the other hand, turns over in bed. A thousand thoughts dwell in his head. He pursues one of them, which takes him to the Tre Fontane pitch in Rome on the eve of the World Cup. He and Falcão, wearing the shirts of their respective national teams, are posing for photographer Giuseppe Calzuola. President Dino Viola approaches his pupils: 'When I come back, I want one of them to wear a World Cup shirt.' Falcão leaves before the championship ends. To his team-mate he says: 'You go ahead, next year I'll play it all the way, maybe as world champion.' In a few hours, he will be facing him.

In the morning, Conti sees Pato Moure, Falcão's foster brother, who has come to Sant Boi de Llobregat for an interview with Bearzot for the Brazilian broadcaster TV Globo: 'Bruno, Brazil have won four games out of four so far, while you, before beating Argentina, risked being eliminated by Cameroon. Now you face Brazil. And although the odds are all in our favour, you are not doomed from the start.' 'On

303

paper, it is true, there is no match. But none of us can swear on the final victory. That's what makes football great,' comes Conti's reply.

Conti and Tardelli cross paths in the corridor. Insomnia has kept the two awake and they will be Falcão's 'neighbours' in one way or another. Tardelli, who is to be his watchdog, asks Conti to open the treasure chest of his secrets: 'He's a modern Brazilian, he's good at predicting the game and always knows what to do in advance. Dribbling isn't his best skill and if he's being hunted he doesn't feel comfortable. He can serve a team-mate from 30 metres out and usually hits the ball with his instep. He is precise with his right foot and powerful with his left.'

It is a long night, like Christmas Eve. Doubts, hopes and confessions punctuate the time. There is no place for dreams. To make them you have to sleep and Bearzot does not sleep; to sleep you have to have digested and he does not eat. He smokes the pipe, an enormous one given to him by the boys. A Savinelli Autograph. Almost a pipe. It's so big that, if he were attacked, he could use it as a defensive weapon, so he says. The Old Man is in bed with a book in his hands and his mind on tomorrow. His centre-forward takes away his sleep. He is still lost. To the press he is a foreign body. But he believes. Stubbornly. He's growing, he needs to play. But time is slipping away. Brazil, tomorrow. Who knows?

Bearzot browses without reading. It is a red volume, in Latin, from Loeb, an English series of classics. It contains three books by Quintilian. His daughter Cinzia, a classicist, slipped it into his bag. Between the pages there is a leaflet on which some chapters are indicated: 'They might be useful for your class of champions, Maestro!' He lets himself be guided: '*Igitur nato filio pater spem de illo quam optimam capiat.*' A father must conceive the highest possible hope for a son. And Paolo is like a son to him. But will insisting in the end hurt him? Should he remove him from the team or leave him as a starter? '*Ingenia puerorum nimia interim emendationis severitate deficere; nam et desperant et dolent et novissime oderunt et, quod maxime nocet, dum omnia timent nihil conantur.*' The natural qualities of children are sometimes depressed by the excessive severity of a correction. It is because of this that they lose confidence and end up being afraid of everything, without having the strength to dare. This is the portrait of his centre-forward. '*Quatenus nullo magis studia quam spe gaudent.*' Nothing exalts commitment more than the hope of success. And in the comfort of this he places his expectations.

Marathon–Sarriá

When a victory is unexpected, the joy of those who conquer becomes multiplied. History tells us so. And Bearzot knows it well. Especially Greek history. He knows who Miltiades was, the man who was entrusted with the task of commanding the Athenian army at Marathon against what, until the fifth century BC, was the most powerful army in the world, the Persians. If it was Brazil that was invincible in football in 1982, then they were undoubtedly the equivalent of the Persian empire. Where the green-and-yellows had defeated all the teams on their own continent and even those in Europe, the Persian conquests had reached India, Africa and Asia Minor. All that remained for Persia was the Mediterranean region to feel it was the master of the world. But to achieve this, its king had to pass through Greece. Like Telê through Italy. A mere formality.

Determined to subjugate all the cities that opposed his rule, Darius, with his thick hair and curly beard, solid and plastered like a sarcophagus but as cunning and far-sighted as few others, assembled a fleet that had never before been so impressive, just like the Magic Square, and set his sights on Attica. His quarter-final was to be played on the Hellenic peninsula. Like the Seleção, his Persia had won practically everything. But the Hellas would open the doors of the West to him and thus mark the end of the West. A fate common to Telê's: the title would make his Brazil world champions for the fourth time, and therefore unreachable.

Between the Seleção and access to the final there is now Italy. The Italians have no chance of winning, like the Athenians. Persia then had its own Falcão, the tyrant Hippias, exiled from Athens 20 years earlier, who had turned to selling military secrets to the enemy. He proposed to start the music with archers: the Greek phalanx would first be targeted from afar with bows, then, towards the end would be given the *coup de grâce* by the pressure of the two cavalries on the wings. But Miltiades also knew the Persian kingdom and its military organisation. Exactly like Bearzot, he loved to study in the field, to spy on his enemies, to understand the psychology of his adversaries. He went to the plain, looked around for a few hours and analysed the situation. His game was being played at Marathon. A wide space that would allow the Persians to hit him on the flanks in the blink of an eye. Just as the treacherous Hippias had planned. So he stood there looking for a solution and, as has often happened to the underdog since David and Goliath, he managed to turn his weakness into strength.

First he had trees felled and piled up on the sides to narrow the space and give the opponents less opportunity to manoeuvre. Marathon thus became the narrow Sarriá, the pitch without sides. Then it was up to him to decide how to position his team. The only possible solution was the most daring one, but also more risky. He decided to weaken the centre to the advantage of the wings. He thinned his army to four lines instead of the usual eight, to make his extension exactly as wide as that of the Persians. From a distance, the adversary would, at least at first, have renounced lateral manoeuvres.

Like Santana, the Persian generals were counting on the Athenians to stand firm and wait for them, expecting a team entrenched in defence. Instead, Bearzot and Miltiades shouted the same command to their boys: 'Go ahead and show who you are!' When the opponents showed up on 21 September 490 BC, the Athenian army's knees started to quiver. They were just too big and too well armed for them. True demigods, like seeing Sócrates, Zico, Cerezo, Éder and Júnior side by side; 26,000 human bodies with an immaculate record on their shoulders. But Miltiades did not blink an eye. He had a plan in his head; he knew what he wanted and what

MARATHON—SARRIÁ

he had to do. Everything would be accomplished in a short time. He had taken the first step. The second was up to the Persians. The third was up to God. Or one of the many.

The Greeks listened to their commander. They moved forward. And they ran, they attacked, and attacked. Bravely, fearlessly, perhaps desperately. But they did. And as the Greek centre advanced under a violent shower of arrows, the wings moved forward and overtook it. Most of the arrows hit the ground behind the Athenians' backs. Speed and lightness won out over the experience of the Persians, and the layout of the field proved to be right. When the centres of the ranks came into contact, something amazing happened: the strong wings of the Athenians swooped down on their astonished counterparts, putting them to flight. The Brazil of arms, however, did not stand idly by; they advanced to drive their opponents back. But it was at that very moment that weakness became strength. The Greek infantry broke up, its wings, as Cabrini, Conti and Oriali might do, broke away from the sides, converging towards the centre and attacking the soul of the Persian army on the flanks. The Persian army, deprived of its defence, found itself locked in a pincer manoeuvre, to suffer what it had planned for the Greeks. Incredibly, against all odds, the surprised and frightened Persian giant was defeated.

When the referee of their destinies blew the whistle, the soldiers looked at each other in astonishment. It was gone. Persia had been beaten by a handful of peasants. It was incredible, but it was true. Miltiades had done it. He had not made a single wrong move; he had managed to combine defence and offence brilliantly, he had prepared the best battlefield and waited in cold blood for the enemy's assault while keeping control of his troops, but above all he had guessed the right moment to launch an attack. The stainless psyche of the Persians was shaken by the day. It was the first time the Greeks had ever prevailed over them in a pitched battle. The victory gave them confidence in their own destiny and marked the beginning of Athens' golden age. Beating Brazil could mean

Against the Legend

Eleven men from our home against a legend. This is how, in eight words, the director of the *Corriere dello Sport* writes about the event on the front page of his newspaper. He is sitting at his desk when he decides it. He has not moved from there throughout the Mundial. When he was 12 years old, on 4 May 1949, a tragedy turned his life upside down and changed its course, taking him to the editorial office of a sports newspaper, *Tuttosport*, instead of to university classrooms. His father, Renato, a journalist with the Grande Torino team, lost his life in the Superga air disaster. He was in his mid-twenties, and now his son is five years older. Perhaps this is why, unlike many of his colleagues, Giorgio Tosatti has always held all his world championships in the editorial office in Piazza Indipendenza, 500 metres from Rome's Termini Station.

So this time, too, he will not set foot in Spain. His role also dictates it. He loves talking about football more than football itself (he is the only Italian sports journalist in possession of the Technical Director's licence) and spends his time editing his daily newspaper day by day, headline by headline, page by page. He has made a habit of opening the first one with nine-column sweeps, as if to build up to a momentous turning point each day. The columns he chose to punctuate the stages of the Azzurri's journey to Barcelona were cutting: 'Another howler', 'Let's go back home', 'Azzurri, what a pity!' and 'End of a nightmare'. The title he has invented for this 5 July is: *Contro la Leggenda* ('Against the Legend'). The legend, of course, is Brazil. For him, the 11 men from home are instead those of a 'national team that sucks', 'fruits of the uncertainty, of the late second thoughts, of the insecurity' of its coach, author of an expedition prepared in an 'improvised and amateurish' way. Tosatti does not like frills, he gets straight to the point: the adversary of this

AGAINST THE LEGEND

Italy entrusted 'under contract to a man who makes and unmakes as if it were his personal property' is too great for its possibilities. And if you do not have the means, you cannot erase a legend.

He is not the only one who thinks so. Brazil has always represented the eternal fascination of football. No country has participated in so many World Cups – all of them, 12 out of 12 – and no team can boast such a rich achievement, marked by three World Cup titles won in 12 years, followed by 12 years of fasting. Since the 1970 final in Mexico City, Brazil have been waiting to take back the World Cup. This time the opportunity seems to be the right one: it has been a long time since the team has offered such a vivid sensation of irresistibility. Under the leadership of Telê Santana, they play formidable football, *futebol bailado*, pure spectacle. The writer Mario Soldati was enchanted the first time he saw the team at work. It seems incredible to him that each player can move without respite while maintaining the same distance between himself and the nearest team-mate – on the right, left, front and back: 'A single perfect geometric figure that moves forward, backward, undulates, expands, shrinks, with a stupendous automatism.'

By the time it comes to Italy, Brazil have not lost a match. They arrived in Spain as the big favourites. For the Azzurri, the maximum objective seems to be to bring home the skin without scratching; that is, to get a draw, to go home unbeaten. Victory is a miracle they can only dream of. A draw or a decent defeat, on the other hand, are results that would allow them to leave the World Cup with their heads held high. Therefore, everyone agrees in wishing only a dignified farewell, the press agrees to the reasonable prospect of losing with honour, advises a wise game of containment, warns the Azzurri against the insanity of facing Brazil as equals, instigating the team to disown, in the face of an objectively terrible test, the ideas considered visionary by the coach Enzo Bearzot. The adverse prediction is unanimous, *Placar*, the bible of Brazilian football, headlines: *Italianos rezam aos santos: têm medo de levar goleades* (Italians turn to the saints: They are afraid of being thrashed), but also in Italy, Gianni Brera writes

THE MATCH

in *La Repubblica* that 'by seven o'clock in the evening, King Enzo and his army will find themselves under a shower of vegetables', while the *Corriere della Sera*, through its head of sports services, Carlo Grandini, is already talking about 'the next elimination' and 'normal surrender' to this Brazil from another planet.

The football wizards are all in agreement: Italy will be out in no time. Ominous prophecies and gloomy predictions are wasted everywhere. According to the Gallup Institute, which carried out a survey in 19 countries around the world, Italy had a 1 per cent chance of success in the final, the same as Peru and Chile, while Brazil led with 24 per cent. The ideal formations that sports newspapers have drawn up after the first phase do not contain any Italian players. In the special ranking of the 24 teams that took part in the first phase, published by *El Mundo Deportivo*, Italy rank 15th. The magazine *France Football* has elected the Brazilian national team as the best in the world, followed by Germany and Argentina. There is no trace of Italy.

On the eve of the second phase, the stock exchange of the favourites for qualification to the semi-finals gave Brazil 55 per cent chance, Argentina 35 per cent and Italy only 10 per cent. Now that Argentina have been eliminated, Brazil's odds have risen to 70 per cent, while Italy are at 30 per cent.

Even the stars have warned Bearzot: Mars and Saturn in Libra do not augur well (especially for Cabrini, Gentile, Rossi and Tardelli), and this situation favours a general climate of protest with possible incidents: injuries, penalties not awarded and goals disallowed. Brazil, on the other hand, are credited with luck, intuition and the ability to score. This is confirmed by the magazine *Alien*, addressed to futurologists and cabalists ('Brazil is the team with the best chance of becoming champions'), and by the Italian clairvoyant Giuseppe 'Giucas' Casella, who is sure that the green and gold will go to the final: 'Unfortunately, I don't foresee brilliant results for Italy.' *Dribbling*, the TG2 weekly magazine, has entrusted to an electronic processor the magnificent fate of the Mundial: from Barcelona Italy will take the road home, Brazil the one that will lead them to the

310

World Cup. The clandestine bookmakers are perfectly in line: Seleção in the lead. The odds for the match are: 2/5 Brazil win, 2/1 draw and 4/1 Italy win. Nils Liedholm, the coach of the capital city team and godfather of Bruno Conti on the one hand and Paulo Roberto Falcão on the other, agrees with these predictions: 'No matter how hard I try, I can't imagine how the Azzurri will be able to get round Brazil.'

Even the weather seems to ally itself with the South American favourites. It is the sultriest day of the Mundial. 'A belt of fire surrounds Barcelona' shouts *El Noticiero*. *La Vanguardia* highlights the record: 'The highest temperature of the year.' The Azores anticyclone, a depression from the North Atlantic and a layer of hot air from the Maghreb are the main actors in the exceptional heatwave that is suffocating Catalonia. Wind flows from the Sahara have driven the hot bubble along the western Mediterranean, bringing temperatures to unprecedented levels. The spring had been stingy with water: between April, May and June, only 39 millimetres of rain fell, leaving the fields completely dry. This situation inevitably encouraged the development of fires, causing the strongest heatwave to hit Barcelona in the 20th century. During the day the maximum is 39.8 degrees, an absolute record, and at night the minimum never falls below 30. The atmosphere is boiling hot.

The sun has beaten down mercilessly during Italy's last training session while near Sant Boi, where the Azzurri are staying, 6,000 hectares are burning by spontaneous combustion and at least 20 villas in the area have been destroyed. Bearzot wipes the sweat from his brow with a handkerchief. He knows that the Brazilians are used to these temperatures, while for his own they are terrible. But he smiles in front of the journalists: 'The prospect of trying to overturn the odds is fascinating.' At the helm of the Azzurri he has met Brazil twice, losing both, in New Haven in 1976, during the Bicentennial Tournament of the United States, and in Buenos Aires, in the third-place play-off of the last Mundial. When asked by journalists in the press room how he will take this third defeat, he pierces them with a doubt: 'What if Brazil lose?'

Only in January, more research by the Gallup Institute showed the confidence of Paulistas and Cariocas in the possibilities of the Brazilian national team consecrating itself on Spanish soil. A rampant optimism that has led Telê Santana to be constantly forced to answer the same question: 'Has the Brazilian team reached the pinnacle of perfection?'

'We haven't reached it,' he had explained in January, 'but we are working on at least getting close to it.' A few days later he had been pinched again on the same subject. 'The perfect team doesn't exist,' he replied impatiently, 'and if it does, I haven't seen it.' But the newspapers kept insisting, so Telê tried to settle the matter once and for all: 'I don't want perfection, I just want them to play football, satisfy the fans and put on a show.' The statistics, however, have turned the match into a fantastic play-off: eight matches, four victories for each, 13 goals for Italy and 13 for Brazil. Outside of Italy, however, the Brazilians have the upper hand: victorious in Rio de Janeiro in 1956, Mexico City in 1970 and Buenos Aires in 1978. The only time that Italy managed to win a World Cup was in 1938.

The Corsera Crew

In Spain he is the standard bearer of the Bible of Via Solferino. Some time before, the *Corriere della Sera* headlined 'O Bearzot o il Mondiale' (Bearzot or the World Cup), revealing if not which side he was on, at least who he was against. He was joined by the head of sports services Mario Gherarducci, Silvio Garioni and Franco Melli. In his capacity as head of the football sector, Carlo Grandini did not spend a day without criticising this 'badly directed, weak of legs and heart' Italy, its game and its coach.

When, before the World Cup, Bearzot brought in Bruno Conti, he wrote that the coach had gone into a state of mental confusion, in the same way that in Argentina he had been the victim of 'mental confusion' for not having given the formation to the press. Two years earlier he had indicated to Sordillo the name of Liedholm as Bearzot's replacement. The number-one problem for him was the Vecio, a man of 'nervous fragility', who 'more often makes mistakes than he gets it right', inclined to 'transmit to the team more his own tensions than his confidence'.

Grandini has three certainties: the first is that 'the impromptu restructuring of the Azzurri's apparatus' is 'already on the important tables'; the second is that 'our football cannot stand comparison with Brazilian, Argentinian or German football'; the third is that Rossi is a finished player: 'the pale guardian angel of this grey Spanish adventure ... a sort of lonely wounded sparrow who no longer knows how to fly'.

Twelve years earlier, the Italian national team that reached the final in Mexico, after beating Germany in that epic 4-3, was then met with threats and beatings at Fiumicino airport for having surrendered only in the last 25 minutes of the World Cup, to Brazil. Grandini was one of the reporters following the national team and was therefore involved in the Roman brawl. As night fell, he was put in a police van with others, and only when he arrived at the gates of the capital and the light of the street lamps shone through the window grilles did he realise that next to him, leaning against a basket that was collecting his still soiled game clothes, was Ferruccio Valcareggi, the coach who was defeated by the Brazilians, but who was nevertheless second in the most glorious World Cup for Italy since the days of Vittorio Pozzo.

This 5 July, the same newspaper is convinced that it will go from euphoria to tomatoes this time as well. It therefore continues to suggest abandoning dreams, because 'ten Gentiles might not be enough to stop that wonderful ball machine in the yellow jersey and green shorts', since the Brazil seen so far in Spain belongs to another footballing planet.

Silvio Garioni, an elegant gastronomic rambler as well as a ruthless portraitist, supports him: 'Bearzot is probably still convinced that there was no war in the Malvinas because Mrs Thatcher forgot to warn him.' Two years earlier, the coach of the national team agreed

THE MATCH

to take a photo together with the Milanese reporters. There were Gigi Garanzini, Marino Bartoletti, Tony Damascelli, Gino Bacci, Franco Mentana and others. Bearzot was in the centre of the frame, smiling, wearing a blue cardigan that caressed a ruffled shirt. Silvio Garioni was the only one under his arm.

The Artist

It is the day. Before the Mundial, the stadium had been idle for several weeks, which allowed the turf to be in splendid condition for the three matches of this round. On the eve of the match, the maintenance team dedicate the entire day, until nine o'clock in the evening, to fixing the holes created in the battle between Brazil and Argentina.

On the morning of the match, the supervisor Tonino Fernández, a Real Club Deportivo employee hired by FIFA to act as caretaker of the Estadio Sarriá, and his team – Isidro Toribio Pavón on the lawnmower, Manolo Espinosa on the sanitary facilities, Carmelo Ruíz on the electrics – showed up on time at seven o'clock despite having had little sleep. A few days earlier, new doors replace the obsolete square woods with aluminium circular posts. They have been assembled to the exacting standards of width (7.32 metres) and height (2.44 metres) (more than 24 x 8ft). Over breakfast, Isidro explains his plan to his colleagues. For Italy vs Argentina he had drawn an ear of corn; for Brazil vs Argentina a series of concentric circles. This time he mows the grass in diagonal strips a metre wide, always respecting the 18 millimetre thickness. The cut is made by combing with the motor mower. There is not much time to decide, as the work will take at least three hours, the match is scheduled for 5.15pm and the teams will reach the stadium a couple of hours earlier. It has to be finished by two o'clock.

Isidro's architecture has already received official compliments from Ramón Glariana, FIFA's supervisor, and even Havelange. Never before has a design been seen on grass at a World Cup. Isidro's technique for the Italy vs Brazil carpet involves a play of greens. He arranges the rollers in one direction and another so that the teeth can comb the grass on one side and the other in an imaginary fringe. It is a long and tiring job that Isidro does standing up, covering about ten kilometres with his motor mower, accelerating and decelerating. There is much more to do: apply chemical fertiliser to make the field shine, water it and arrange the changing rooms.

To draw the lines, Tonino, the director, chooses not to use chalk but lime. Outlining the pitch is the task he has reserved for himself. It is his way of framing the work.

The Exercise

Six days have now passed since the first Sarriá match and the Italians' victory over Argentina is still holding sway in the press and in fans' comments. The blackout continues but it has borne its first fruits. 'Keep on keeping quiet' wrote some newspapers. In any case, above all the words, spoken or unspoken, the enthusiasm has become contagious. The city of Barcelona, suddenly tinged with blue, has been invaded by thousands of Italians hoping to take part in a celebration.

On the opposite side, in the Mas Badó retreat, the Brazilian squad attends a match in the morning between the technical committee and journalists. After the meeting, mass begins in the retreat chapel. Falcão is the first to cross the threshold but is promptly stopped by Luizinho: 'Paulo, that's not appropriate, we're in shorts.' Falcão takes his arm in a friendly manner: 'He won't mind. What counts is what you have inside, not what you look like.'

In his prayer, Falcão asks God that no one gets hurt in the afternoon match. He has always been religious – his family is Catholic, he studied at La Salle in Canoas, a college of friars, and he attends church. Believing in God gives him security. Against Italy he will play, trusting that everything will go well. He never prays to win. Victory is obtained on the pitch and not with supplications. He knows that the Italians are also religious, yet he hopes that his invocations, together with those of all Brazilians, can help the national team to count on Zico. He is very important for the team. He is the one who keeps the ball safe when he is on the right side of the pitch. Although he knows the Italians, Falcão has only played once against the Azzurri national team. It was in 1976, in the United States Bicentennial Tournament, where Brazil won 4-1, but he had to go off at half-time with a sprained ankle. He is convinced that it happened because he forgot to pray that day.

Beyond the divine appeals, the general opinion is that the match will be an exercise for Telê Santana's men. In the press room, the young Pastorin pontificates: 'This will end in a goalfest, believe me – I have seen the Seleção up close.'

He was warned by one man, his director, Baretti: 'Look, the Azzurri are on the upswing.'

Bearzot confirmed, 'The stronger our adversary, the higher our ambition.' He had already confided this to Adalberto Bortolotti during the days in Vigo: 'When it is indispensable to win, my boys know how to respond.' According to the coach, Paolo Rossi, the man who had to save this Italy but whom nobody expects to anymore, is growing. He has seen him in training, followed him in the matches, watched him with special attention, talked about him every evening with Maldini.

'He is not yet the one in Baires,' says Bearzot.

'Are you worried, Enzo?'

'We have to study a more limited range for him.'

'Without defensive obligations?'

'Yes, Cesare. I feel we are close.'

'But time is not on our side.'

'I know, but did you see it against Argentina?'

'He was almost scoring.'

'The sense of displacement is intact, the timing that disorients the opponent as well.'

'Even his jerk a little bit at a time is coming back.'

'We are close, Cesare, I can feel it.'

After lunch, the journalists staying at the Majestic start moving. The Sarriá is just two kilometres away. Pessimism is rampant among the press. Before leaving the hotel, they all pack their bags. Without the Azzurri, the World Cup is over for most of them. They are finally going home. One of the reporters is so certain that he has put up a sign in the lobby:

3.30 P.M. DEPARTURE OF THE COACH
FOR JOURNALISTS WISHING TO ATTEND
BRAZIL'S TRAINING SESSION AT SARRIÁ.

The Doubt

As soon as the sun rises, the dread of an unthinkable elimination crosses the mind of *Placar* reporter Alberto Helena Jr. And the closer the match time comes, the more this unpleasant feeling grows. On the way to the Sarriá stadium the bad omen receives a further boost from his colleague Maranhão.

'Telê's Brazil have only had one instance of man-marking in front of them so far,' he says behind his inseparable pipe. 'It was against Uruguay, remember?'

It was the final, lost, of the 1980 Mundialito, the only blemish for Santana's Brazil.

'More or less,' replies Helena. 'It wasn't exactly Italian-style marking but, in any case, it was similar.'

However, he is heartened by the fact that, in the end, if Italy rely solely on individual marking, if they persist only in resisting Brazil's constant sieges, what can they achieve? 'Only a huge zero-zero on the scoreboard,' he says to himself, 'while we would be left with the gift of beauty and this, until now, has made us unbeatable.' But then why this strange feeling, this grey premonition?

When he arrives at the Sarriá, he sits down and tries to find himself an answer before the match starts. 'Italy, heck, it's Italy, two-time world champions. And today they will play free, without any responsibility.' He then remembers the sentence he heard from an Italian journalist after their victory over Argentina: 'Italy are more afraid of facing a team considered small than the world champions.' 'It is possible,' he thought. 'This happens with all Latin teams: they are more afraid of shame than of the strength of the opponent.'

So, here lies the essence of the match: everything is expected of Brazil, as nothing is expected of Italy, despite their success over Argentina. And yet, thanks to that victory, the Italians can allow themselves the luxury of entering the pitch calmly. Their only obligation is to avoid a thrashing by what everyone considers the best team of the World Cup. So, if they have nothing to lose, why not win then? This is where Helena's doubt creeps in. If he looks into it he can find his fears. They have all escaped from a word that has been inviolate until now: danger. Brazil may be in danger of dropping out of the World Cup.

Maranhão, next to him, has cold eyes. Santana's words dance in his head: 'We are not unbeatable.' Whatever happens, he thinks, this match will go down in history. It will be a marvellous display of technique and courage. On both sides.

Lettera 32

Sconcerti and Brera make their way to the stadium well in advance. They are full of papers and typewriters. They sweat to light a match. Brera in his suit and tie snorts when he realises that the police barriers force them to walk the last kilometre. His heaviest weapon is a portable Olivetti Lettera 32; it is 35 centimetres by 34 centimetres, 10 centimetres high, less than a pen, weighing barely six kilos.

The old Sarriá, where Zamora and Schiaffino played, is already as full as an egg. The Brazilians, with their yellow shirts, colour it in. The 20,000 or so Italians dress as they come, and it is a miracle that they are there at all. Sconcerti is well aware that at that very moment, in at least three different parts of the world, six armies are standing in front of each other. But he cannot believe that there is not some history being made in this sweaty corner of Barcelona, where some 20,000 people are trying to identify themselves as Italians.

They sit in their usual spot, a palm away from the curve of the Brazilian cologne. From his hippopotamus-skin purse, Brera takes out his tools of the trade and pleasure to place them carefully in front of him. Tuscan half-pipe case, pipe and tobacco, cigarettes, stopwatch, notepad, three biros, mini field pharmacy in the guise of anonymous blister packs of pills. And the inseparable diary. This year's diary is branded Piaggio. When he opens it, he sees himself projected back two weeks. Eight pages before his present. 20 June: 'Vigo. Raining. Melancholy. Nothing to do. Still here for 25 days. What a bore, ouch.' He arrives at 5 July. He finds the note from the morning: 'Hot sun' and then, just below the centre:

'Brazil-Italy (Jesus).'

He takes note of the man-marking and the zone of competence with notarial precision, but when the curtain rises the fan in him will wake up. Since he has been at *La Repubblica* his life has become more comfortable. The newspaper does not go on sale on Mondays, so he has plenty of time to reflect, re-read and re-think before composing his piece. Nothing like the life he used to lead with *Il Giorno* and *Guerin Sportivo*: 20 folders thrown on to paper in a few furious hours with an inversely proportional relationship between quality and time. He would finish at almost midnight, get out of the car and go to Riccione in Milan, where he would find three jugs of Barbaresco and the warmth of his friends. The five pages of *La Repubblica*, 30 lines of 61 characters, he wrote at the Mundial, at the end of the match, tapping 9,000 times on the exhausted paper (double extra strong), in the wake of the notes jotted down in his notebook.

The Azzurri are gathered in the hotel lobby waiting to board the bus, a Pegaso 6100S Mundial-82. Presented at the Salón del Automóvil in Barcelona in May of the previous year and supplied to the 24 nations taking part in the championship, the World Cup buses are painted the colour of the teams; the Italian one (registration number M7242R4) is tricolour, the Brazilian one yellow-green (called Verdão); they have a 300hp engine, 32 reclining seats, a meeting area for seven people, a bathroom, a bar, a hi-fi system and two colour televisions with video recorders. On the way back from the match against Argentina, everything happened on the Carioca bus – 45 minutes of winding roads and unbridled samba, culminating in a shaving foam war in which Cerezo and Isidoro got the worst of it.

Among the Italians about to leave the retreat, on the other hand, there are few words and much concentration. The most cheerful is Franco 'Spadino' Selvaggi. To boost the team's morale, he gives tactical orders, pretending to be Bearzot: 'Gentile, stay on the right; Cabrini, break through on the left; Tardelli, insert yourself unexpectedly.'

He is the one who helps his team-mates relieve the tension. But there are also those who cannot relax, such as Conti, who sits in a corner and squashes his thoughts with Octopus on his Game & Watch.

It is time to leave for the Sarriá. Fifteen kilometres separate the Azzurri from the stadium. Half an hour, traffic permitting. The bus crosses the river, goes along the Autovía del Nordeste and, once on the Autopista, goes straight on along Avinguda Diagonal, until it turns into Avinguda de Sarriá. As it enters the last stretch, Tardelli shouts, 'There it is!'

Below the Sarriá, the Azzurri's coach stands next to the Brazilian one. The players watch each other through the windows. The looks of the Italians are tense, concentrated, perhaps frightened. The Carioca group is singing happily. The match is just one lap of the second hand away.

The coaches have to announce their starting XI. Bearzot has lined up for Italy: 1 Dino Zoff (captain), 4 Antonio Cabrini, 5 Fulvio Collovati, 6 Claudio Gentile, 7 Gaetano Scirea, 9 Giancarlo Antognoni, 13 Gabriele Oriali, 14 Marco Tardelli, 16 Bruno Conti, 19 Francesco Graziani and 20 Paolo Rossi.

On 21 May, in Alassio, the head coach established the criteria for assigning the shirt numbers. The goalkeepers would be assigned 1, 12 and 22, all the others in departmental order (defenders, midfielders and forwards), and then in alphabetical order. If Bettega had come in, Pablito would have been assigned the 'Argentine' 21 and his team-mate the 20, but with the arrival of Selvaggi the 20 goes to Rossi.

Santana, on the other hand, assigns the first 11 numbers to the starters. The hole left by the No. 7 shirt reveals the lack of confidence in Paulo Isidoro, who is replaced by Falcão.

In particular, the coach is counting on: 1 Waldir Peres, 2 Leandro, 3 José Oscar Bernardi, 4 Luizinho, 5 Toninho Cerezo, 6 Júnior, 8 Sócrates (captain), 9 Serginho, 10 Zico, 11 Éder, 15 Falcão. Zico is there.

Half an hour before the match, the teams come out on to the pitch for a warm-up. Pastorin approaches the net that separates the pitch from the lower stand. He sees Edinho Nazareth Filho, the Fluminense libero bought by Udinese. 'Are you confident?'

'No, we don't trust them. We saw the Azzurri against the Argentinians, they were perfect.'

'You'll see, you'll make it.'

'I don't know, there's something weird about it.'

He then notices that, a little further on, Claudio Gentile is staring at the pitch in seclusion. The two are friends, as a reporter (who follows Juventus) and a footballer (who plays for Juventus) can be. He asks him, 'Gento, who are you going to mark?'

Gentile for once, for a friend, breaks his silence: 'Éder, the one with the scar on his arm.' Before going to Spain, he had asked the journalist for a favour: 'During the World Cup I would like to read a great book, give me a title.' A few days later, the reporter had given him *All Quiet on the Western Front* by Erich Maria Remarque. 'Hey, Darwin,' shouts Gentile towards the stand, 'that book shocked me.'

Pastorin smirks. 'They should have it read in all the schools.' And in the silence that greets them a moment later, they both think back to the pointless fratricidal struggle that has been created between journalists and players. Well aware that the real wars are fought elsewhere.

The Killer

RAI correspondent Gian Piero Galeazzi skirts the pitch in search of the Azzurri. Tito Stagno, 'the man from the moon' then head of the sports editorial office, has convinced him to do interviews on the sidelines. The technique has been studied at the table: he has to physically block the player without letting him go until he has finished his hot commentary. His range of action is wide. He starts in the coach car park, where he collects the players' predictions, at half-time he moves to the grandstand, where he meets personalities and VIPs waiting for interviews, and finally, to try to get the last great truth out of the players, he shows up at the exit of the pitch. Like a killer. This is how he prepares his personal report on which Beppe Viola then sews the text.

It is his first World Cup. In truth he was ready for Argentina but at the last moment Stagno left him in Rome, at the court of Paolo Valenti for *Novantesimo minuto*, where, a couple of years later, he made the coup of his life. On 23 March 1980 he had just ended his link-up from the Stadio Olimpico for a Roma vs Perugia match when he was informed by Claudio Ferretti, the radio correspondent, that the dressing rooms had been blocked by the police. He asked Valenti for the line again and, without knowing it, found himself to be the only witness to the first blatant act of Totonero, a scoop that gave him a call-up to the 1982 World Cup.

When Claudio Villa, chosen by the Spanish organisers to sing the World Cup anthem, arrives on a Guzzi motorbike, he goes straight to him because every Roman needs his points of reference. Galeazzi's point of reference in Spain is Giacinto Facchetti, commercial manager of the company Le Coq Sportif. The former Italian international has a flat at the Grand Hotel Princesa Sofía and access to the Real Club de Barcelona to play tennis. Galeazzi does not let Villa in: 'I am an

THE KILLER

Italian journalist.' Nothing. 'I am an envoy from RAI.' Still nothing. Try in Spanish. 'I am the famous Italian TV journalist Gian Piero Galeazzi, please can you practise a little bit of tennis?' Silence. 'My friend is Giacinto Facchetti, great champion of Inter Milan.' Prego señor. From that moment on, he lives the life of a great gentleman.

It is always raining in Vigo. Galicia, the land of seafood and *pulpo a feira* (a traditional Galician dish of octopus), offers no pasta of any kind, so, in full abstinence, Galeazzi and Enrico Ameri force the restaurant Bella Napoli to prepare spaghetti with *angulas* (baby eels) for all the reporters. In Barcelona he has been reborn. The players are ghosts, the news is scarce, and there is plenty of time to relax. The fun stops when the wives of the Azzurri arrive. For the day of freedom of the players, he decides to choose to send a report on this to the evening news. He places a video camera at the entrance to the Princesa Sofía lifts and records all the movements of the players in the company of their wives. In and out. The aim is to time the length of their stays. The record is held by Selvaggi (entry 13.45, exit 16.45). But Rome objects to the contents and the report is not aired.

He works in tandem with Beppe Viola. He is sent every morning to Bearzot's conference and now, well in advance, to the Sarriá. Viola acts as his big brother. Galeazzi worships him. Following his instructions, he arrives with the cameraman before the advertising banners. Outside the gates he is overwhelmed by thousands of Brazilian fans. Once inside, he pulls up to the edge of the pitch. He finds Paolo Rossi, talks to him in the past tense. But this time it is the centre-forward who stops him: 'We'll take stock at the end.'

A few metres above them, in the tribune d'honneur, are the minister for the Cassa del Mezzogiorno, Claudio Signorile, the minister for health, Renato Altissimo, and the minister for cultural and environmental heritage, Vincenzo Scotti. Nicola Signorello, minister for tourism, sport and entertainment, the only one holding the relevant post, has remained in Rome to watch the match from the offices of his ministry. Next to them sits Luca Cordero di Montezemolo, CEO of Italiana Edizioni. There are also, of course, the advisor, Carlo De Gaudio, the CONI president, Franco Carraro, the president of the World Athletics Federation, Primo Nebiolo (who left Indianapolis four times to be at the Sarriá) and the UEFA president Artemio Franchi. Together, of course, with the president of the Italian Football Federation, Federico Sordillo, accompanied by his wife, and Antonio Matarrese, who has been president of the football league for just four months.

In the stands are the coaches, Giovanni Trapattoni, Sandro Mazzola, Picchio De Sisti, Carlo Mazzone, Rino Marchesi and Antonio Valentín Angelillo. There is also Felice 'Farfallino' Borel, world champion in 1934, guest of RAI and *Radiocorriere*. Of the four past world champions still alive, only he has taken the plane to go and suffer with the Azzurri at the Sarriá: Schiavio is not in good health, Ferrari attended only the opening match between Belgium and Argentina, then returned home, while Pizziolo has to stay with his sick wife. Borel has seen the matches in Vigo and is optimistic: 'The four teams of the first round all played not to lose, so it became difficult for the forwards to find outlets in the area. Now Italy have regained game and morale, because they are meeting teams that are not only concerned about defending. We'll score again,' says the two-time top scorer of the Italian championship (1933 and 1934), 'and it will be the revenge of Italian football.'

The Future, Now

The ball in the centre of the Sarriá, the referee over it, the players on the pitch, the perimeter of the advertising around them, the stands framing them. Behind every atom of the stage there is a story. Each element of this glimpse of reality is orchestrated by men who move the destinies of the Mundial. Havelange, Lacoste, Blatter, Samaranch, Nebiolo, Deyhle, Franchi and Saporta. They are the most powerful men in sport. But it is Dassler who is making their fortunes, along with that of footballers, managers, heads of state television, presidents of federations and Olympic committees. The puppeteer who pulls the

THE FUTURE, NOW

strings of world sport now has the power to get the president of the IOC or a world federation elected. He is also able to steer the choice of cities that will host the Olympic Games or the World Cup. Since Havelange, all the key figures have been the direct emanation of his will: Juan Antonio Samaranch, president of the IOC and Miembro de Honor of the organising committee of España 82; Primo Nebiolo, president of the IAAF; and Joseph Blatter, who was inducted into FIFA as his man.

In the year of grace of the Spanish Mundial a huge river of money is beginning to flow, rushing into the coffers of the federations thanks to television rights and sponsorship contracts. The audience can no longer be neglected. The presidents of the world's three most important sporting bodies have realised that the time has come to support a major project linking sport to television. A sponsorship programme using companies to promote the image of football and its champions. The future, now.

The Match

Why

On 5 July 1982 there was to be no match. At the Reunión de la Comisión Organizadora de la Copa Mundial de la FIFA held on 17 May 1979, the calendar provided for the opening ceremony on 16 June 1982, a first group phase of four matches a day until 25 June, followed by a second group round between 27 June and 4 July. Then 5 July was to be the rest day and nothing was to happen during this afternoon. But Dassler's thoughts, when he saw such a compressed schedule, immediately went to television rights. Overlapping so many matches meant halving the possibilities. So here was the correction, which arrived on 22 March 1980. The Mundial would open on 13 June and, starting on 15 June, there would only be three daily matches in the first phase. The second phase would be held from 28 June to 5 July. The future, then, now.

The ball lies motionless on the disc, waiting for the hour to strike. It is, of course, the official ball, the Tango España, created by Adidas and contractually imposed on FIFA. As early as the 1962 World Cup in Chile, the federation realised that it was no longer possible to delegate responsibility for the balls – which usually deflate or get lost – to the home team. Dassler was happy to meet this need. Adidas undertook a study into lighter, better-performing balls until, at the 1970 World Cup, they presented Telstar, the first ball of the modern era made of waterproof leather. Featuring 32 panels – 20 white hexagons and 12 black pentagons hand-sewn together – and inflated by air. The result was an almost perfect sphere, the archetypal football. The alternating black and white colours were designed for spectators, especially those who watched the matches from home (the first televised FIFA World Cup in Mexico). Hence the name 'Telstar': television star. Then came 'Chile' in Germany 1974 and the other 'Tango' in Argentina 1978.

THE MATCH

In front of the ball is Klein. His choice is the fruit of Artemio Franchi's good intentions. His kit, like that of all his World Cup colleagues, is signed by the house of Dassler, and the FIFA logo that stands out above his pocket is one designed by Deyhle. His feet are wearing a prototype of the black boots that Adidas is planning to launch for the next Olympics in Los Angeles: breathable uppers in nubuck and nylon, with a wide mesh, and a Polyair midsole that makes them lightweight and flexible. There are also three white, red and blue stabilising plugs, with a cylindrical section, applied to the midsole, which regulates the rigidity of the sole and acts as a shock absorber according to a mechanism called the 'Vario Shock Absorption System', which allows better performance depending on the terrain, running style and weight.

Adidas's signature is also on the boots of Tardelli, Cabrini, Oriali, Gentile, Graziani and Luizinho. And also on Falcão's. His feet actually wear handmade, hand-stitched boots to alleviate the pain caused by his bunions. But Adidas has contractually obliged him to add the three white stripes. They are badly painted, but you cannot tell from the television. And that is what counts.

The Azzurri are tucked into their Le Coq Sportif kits. The rules prohibit them from displaying the brand name, not allowing any kind of propaganda on the shirts other than 'figures representing national symbols'. That is why they keep their white tracksuit jackets on during the anthem. FIFA, however, allows the coat of arms sewn on to Brazil's jersey to pass. Not everyone realises that it contains a secret.

On the blue shield that houses the golden image of the Jules Rimet Trophy, definitively handed over to Brazil after their three victories (symbolised by the three green stars above it), an amphibious amulet has been improperly placed. It is a white disc containing a stylised green plant with three red berries – the coffee plant. The federation sold it to the press as the image of the Brazilian symbol, but it is actually the logo of the Café do Brasil company.

Around them, the posters of Coca-Cola, Gillette, Canon, Iveco and JVC condition Spanish television direction according to Dassler's contracts and wishes.

In the tribune of honour, the personalities are applauded. Havelange, Nebiolo and Franchi in different ways all owe something to Dassler. The first the power, the second the chair, the third the respect earned by the team of his country. Not to mention the fact that the FIFA president's team (Havelange) and the UEFA president's team (Franchi), the man everyone is pointing to as his next successor, are facing each other on the pitch. In the 1970 final in Mexico City, they faced off against each other. Havelange was president of the Brazilian federation, Franchi of the Italian one. Two titles each. An immense amount of money was at stake. The biggest cake football had ever offered. The third definitive Jules Rimet World Cup title. Havelange won it. For Franchi, today there is a thirst for revenge.

The Chairmen

The two most important figures in Italian football also sit in the grandstand. They scrutinise the pitch. They do not look at each other; they do not love each other. Between the head of the league, Antonio Matarrese, and that of the federation, Federico Sordillo, disagreements have been the order of the day. However, they are able to take credit for the victory against Argentina in which, however, only the latter believed.

Matarrese belongs to a powerful family from Andria that has built half of Bari. He began his political ascent with the presidency of his city's team. An instinctive and dangerous blunderer, he went over the top when, commenting on the first outings of the national team, he came out, galvanised by the same journalists, with a boomerang phrase: 'I would kick all these Azzurri in the arse.'

Sordillo is a different kettle of fish, from Pietradefusi in Irpinia, with a degree in law from Naples, who landed full of hope in Milan at the dawn of the economic boom and quickly became one of the most authoritative legal advisors to companies and industrialists and the most listened to advisor to the best and most influential families in Lombardy. A million miles away from the archetype of the southern lawyer, he is a rigorous modern professional whose only weakness, they say, is that he considers himself a great joke-teller. He knows football well, from his days at AC Milan: he was president, Nereo Rocco on the bench and Gianni Rivera on the pitch. His reference figure has always been Artemio Franchi, whom he succeeded at the helm of the FIGC in 1980, after his spontaneous resignation following the football scandal. A fate that risked repeating itself.

On the threshold of the Mundial, Italy were about to present themselves in Spain with a federation without its main representative. The resignation of the lawyer Federico Sordillo was ready, the day already decided. That of the last federal council, before the friendly match in Geneva with Switzerland. Personal crisis, moral weariness, difficulty in holding the reins of both professional and federal life. Then he remembered that in his life he had never left things halfway, so he moved on.

The World Cup had been described as terrible, but the reality far exceeds the imagination. Controversy at every turn, problems and difficulties of all kinds. More than once Sordillo has witnessed the organisational collapse of the federal staff. The World Cup is now a monstrous event and he feels that there is a need for managerial figures. De Gaudio, for example, is doing everything he can, but in his eyes he is still a 'federal'. In his head there is also an office for sponsorship linked to the FIGC. He is tired of seeing players wearing boots from one house and shirts from another. Sordillo is already an innovator: he has introduced sponsorship in Serie A and widened the borders to the second foreign player. In this adventure, Bearzot's team has finally given him great satisfaction.

Someone had advised him to detach himself more from the national team clan and especially from the players. He could not do it. He is a fanatical president, he wants to maintain a constant relationship, he wants the Azzurri to feel that he is close to them. He has tried everything possible to encourage them to play a good World Cup. He has praised, encouraged and even criticised the team. Yet, on the eve of the first match in Spain, after his unexpected remarks, when he crossed the threshold of the Casa del Baron to enter the dining room, no one stood up. No one greeted the president. All heads remained bent over their plates. A silence that led him to turn and leave: 'I am not welcome here.' His remarks had probably been misinterpreted and had affected the pride of his boys. It was at that moment that Bearzot realised that his men were just as wounded as he was, that in their blockade to the outside world there would be no place for the others and that from that day on they would have to find the strength to fight on their own.

Three Men and a Pipe

Three men burn their thoughts in the bowl of their pipes. President Pertini is in the car, in Paris on an official visit. He has just left François Mitterrand at the Elysée Palace and advises his driver to 'fly' to the Italian embassy so as not to miss the start of the match. Bearzot has only been criticised for one choice: 'He shouldn't use those pipes. Now I'm going to give him a proper one.' The president is a connoisseur, who owns over 500 of them. He used to smoke only English-cut ones, preferably Dunhill or Barling, comfortable to hold in the mouth. Later, his role and his pride made him embrace the reason of state, and he now testifies to the made in Italy brand, with large and showy pipes, even if they are unmanageable. However, he hates it when they are given to him as gifts, preferring to buy his own. He recognises the hard work and art of the great masters and, when the opportunity arises, he loves to export their skills abroad.

Unlike the president, Brera no longer buys his pipes. He receives them directly from Enea Buzzi da Brebbia, then distributes them to those who deserve them. Bearzot was one of the recipients, who thus added his gift to the usual Peterson and Castello. In the locker room of the Sarriá, however, clenched in the teeth is the Autograph of his boys. Hosted, as always, by Borkum Riff in bourbon whiskey. From his dark green tobacco holder, instead, Brera, sitting comfortably in the stands, takes a mixture composed of Dunhill 965, Three Nuns and Antico Toscano. For Brera, the smoking habit is of divine origin: it must serve the lungs for the forced gymnastics to which they are subjected before the breathing exercise. I wonder how the Pope would take it.

Karol Wojtyła is also a football fan. In his heart, perhaps, he hopes that Italy and Poland come out 'miraculously' unharmed from their rounds to find themselves in the semi-finals. On the eve of the match against Brazil, during the Sunday Angelus, he entrusts to the 10,000 faithful in St Peter's Square ecumenical words full of spiritual institutionality: 'In these days the attention of millions of people is focused on the World Cup taking place in Spain. I would like to send cordial greetings to all the players, along with the hope that sport will help to strengthen the sense of universal solidarity and the common commitment to peace and harmony among all peoples.' In the meantime, this hope is about to give way to more earthly passions. It is time to extinguish the pipe of peace. In a few minutes it will be battle on the field.

The Gentleman

He has been everything. That is perhaps why he is loved by everyone. Pacifist, war hero, lawyer, socialist, exile, painter and film extra. He created Europe's first free anti-fascist radio station (set up after selling a family farm), organised, with Adriano Olivetti, Turati's escape to Corsica, was a military leader of the Resistance, an SS prisoner, escaped from Regina Coeli death row, was sentenced to 14 years, including life imprisonment and confinement, for a tip-off, but then saved the lives of those who had him locked up. Out of a principle of justice, always refusing any form of compromise.

When Alessandro, known as Sandro, Pertini became President of the Chamber of Deputies after the financial scandal involving his

THE GENTLEMAN

party broke out (it had emerged that for years the Italian Oil Industry Union had paid 8 million lire to party cashiers, including the PSI, in exchange for favourable measures), he caused the palace to tremble. 'My friends,' he vented in an interview with Nantas Salvalaggio, 'I will not stay a minute longer in this chair if my conscience rebels. I will never accept becoming the accomplice of those who are drowning democracy and justice in an avalanche of corruption.'

The party crisis, superimposed on the economic crisis, had thrown the country into a state of deep malaise. The balance was precarious but Pertini, at the cost of blowing up the entire system, did not even want to consider covering up for a dishonest man, even though he was his party companion: 'I don't give a damn about the system, if it agrees with the thieves. I've already told my Carla: "Have your bags ready, I might just drop everything." They say that a modern party must "adapt". But adapt to what, holy Virgin Mary? If adapting means stealing, I won't adapt. Better, then, to have a party that is not adequate and not very modern. Better our old clandestine party, without neon offices, without long-legged secretaries and ultra-shiny nails.' He speaks like this because he knows the greatest trap for a politician. That of falling in love with power. 'A man who is afraid of losing his seat, his influence over other men, his telephones, the artwork on the walls, the state limousine, well, he is a lost man.' The antidote? 'Always have your suitcases and letter of resignation ready. My Carla knows this. We have a small flat in Corso Vittorio, there's no problem with giving up.'

He has always spoken without fear. He has no currents, interests, banks, industries or alliances behind him. His exclusive wealth is his past as a free man, as a gentleman. Shortly before, he had refused to sign the decree increasing the MPs' allowances. 'But how, I say, in a serious moment like this, when the father of a family returns home with his pay reduced by inflation, do you give this example of insensitivity? I will not sign with these hands.' And he is committed. He does not even dream of giving his wife a car to go shopping. The wives of under-secretaries and ministers all use the blue ministerial

335

cars to go shopping: 'When these poor provincial girls realise that their husband has made a career, they all feel like Poppaea.' His wife, on the other hand, takes the bus. 'Carla would be ashamed to go to Campo de' Fiori to buy salad or pears in the ministerial car. It would be a slap in the face to poor people, an abuse of power, a theft.'

A few days after his election as President of the Republic, Pertini woke up with a start, clapping his hand on his forehead: 'Of course! How the hell did I not think of that before! He's fine: he's good, honest, and he knows about sport too.'

Carla was startled: 'Sandro, what's up, who are you talking about?'

The president had found his spokesman (and only he could make such a choice). Antonio Ghirelli, a sports journalist, the author of *Storia del Calcio in Italia* (The History of Football in Italy), the director of *Corriere dello Sport*, the leader, together with Palumbo, of the Neapolitan School so opposed by Brera. This partnership was broken off two years before the Mundial, in Barcelona.

Pertini inaugurated the custom of intervening directly in the country's political life, which was a novelty for his role. Instead of a strictly 'notarial' interpretation of presidential powers, he preferred an unconventional approach and participation in the main events of national life, both happy and sad. He never missed an opportunity to make Bearzot feel all his closeness. They share the same character, rigour, pipe and zodiac sign (which they share with half the team: Rossi was born on 23 September, Tardelli on the 24th, Pertini on the 25th, Bearzot on the 26th, Gentile on the 27th, Cabrini on 8 October, all Libras). Both are accused of being direct, stubborn, grumpy, sometimes unbalanced. Both choose men over the jersey they wear. Bearzot, a Granata inside, summoned half of Juventus to the national team; Pertini, a socialist, chose his predecessor's Christian Democrat as his special secretary. When they asked him why he did it, he jumped up in his chair: 'What in God's name are these questions? If an official is doing his duty, why do I have to change him? Of course, many of my people are at war with me. They say, "Well, you could have taken a comrade and you didn't!" In short,

I've never liked the Mafia. I choose people for what they are worth, not for the label or the recommendation they carry.' And in the name of his beliefs, he has also chosen his side in football.

After the 2-0 victory against modest Luxembourg (with a team deprived of Rossi and Giordano due to bans, Cabrini and Graziani injured, Antognoni and Causio sent off), Bearzot was subjected to an unprecedented psychological lynching by the journalists, and went to Sordillo: 'President, if my presence harms the national team I am ready to resign.'

'Forget the hysterical criticism,' Sordillo reassured him, 'just listen to the constructive ones.' 'Then I'll stay,' replied Bearzot, 'because I believe in what I'm doing, even if I realise I'm alone against everyone. We desperately need moral support.'

And it came, from on high: 'Keep doing your own thing, Bearzot!' It was Pertini's.

The Epic Poets

RAI journalists are on strike for the renewal of their contracts. The announcement reaches the ears of the young correspondent Carlo Nesti while he is in Madrid. He greets it euphorically. It could enable him to make a sensational change of plan. Since the beginning of his professional career in 1976, he has not had the chance to be a fan and to mix with the crowd. The opportunity is once in a lifetime, so after catching a Madrid–Barcelona flight and joining a group of friends arriving from Turin with an Italy vs Brazil ticket for him too, he finds himself in the stands of the Sarriá next to the Azzurri fans.

Sitting as usual in his seat is Nando Martellini, the timeless voice of Mama RAI. He started 38 years earlier. He was then little more than a boy, played the drums, knew five languages and wanted to pursue a diplomatic career. But sport was his true passion. A good report card had convinced his parents to give him a trip to Berlin to see the Olympics. By train, third class, sandwich in a bag. And

THE MATCH

Jesse Owens, an experience that left its mark. When he joined RAI, he alternated between foreign politics (the Christmas of the Italian prisoners in the Suez Canal), news (the funerals of Luigi Einaudi and Pope John XXIII) and sport (first radio commentary in 1946, Bari vs Napoli; first TV commentary in 1958, in London, England vs USSR). One day, Vittorio Veltroni, the head of the news services, took him under his arm: 'If you keep reporting the matches and then the Pope's blessing, people will imagine him with the ball under his arm. Choose: either the news or sport.'

He chose sport. He followed everything: the World Cup, the Olympics, the Giro d'Italia and the Tour de France. In the 1960s he was the main voice of the radio programme *Tutto il calcio minuto per minuto*. He made the leap to football commentator during the 1968 European Championships. A golden debut: the Azzurri won them for the first time. He returned to the bench behind Nicolò Carosio (he reported on the World Cup won by Pozzo), but a sensational gaffe by the latter opened the door to the match of the century: Italy beat West Germany 4-3. The extra time exhausted Italy, who then collapsed in the second half of the final against Brazil, and that defeat in the last straight left him choking on the cry of 'world champions'. Now, 12 years later, he can still hear it in his throat.

His voice is polite, warm and reassuring. Never intrusive, almost detached. And yet so familiar to Italians. Emphasis does not belong to him. He does not want to drug his audience, but to accompany them with grace and sensitivity, with a taste for the essential.

While waiting for referee Klein to blow the whistle, he rereads the cards and goes over the names. It is up to him to tell the story of the 90 laps of the clock that will bring Italy to a standstill. Thirty-two million spectators are ready in front of the television screens. Only half of them will be able to watch the match in colour.

Far from the moderation model of the Italian commentator, but equally adept in his role, is Luciano Valle, Rede Globo's Brazilian reporter, who, tucked into his short-sleeved white polo shirt, is ready to narrate the exploits of the Seleção, together with commentator

THE EPIC POETS

Marcio Guedes and the two journalists Juarez Soares and Pedro Rogerio, coordinated from the studio by Fernando Vannucci.

Italian radio is also ready. Enrico Ameri is about to receive the line. He is not an admirer of the Italian coach: 'As a technician he has always been modest, as the selector of our national team I judge him to be a foolhardy, reckless person. Sometimes, as you know, modesty goes hand in hand with luck and this is the hope that remains when talking about Enzo Bearzot.'

There is another reporter waiting for the match to start. He is not an official voice and receives no salary for doing so. He is the journalist Michele Plastino, who, together with his trusted cameraman Valentino Tocco, left Rome armed only with a camera, a tape recorder and a microphone to report on the World Cup from the stands. A true pioneer of local television broadcasting, three years earlier, in the semi-clandestinity of the newborn channels, he occupied a space that had been deserted until then. He arrived in Barcelona with the same corsair attitude and romantic intentions, in order to capture what RAI cannot broadcast: the heart of the match, the mood of the fans. Moments forgotten by the control booths of the worldwide filming but sometimes more heartfelt than a goal.

A few weeks earlier he convinced Tocco and Giorgio Stagno to go with him to the World Cup to shoot some images. But his father was ill, so to start organising the work he sent them ahead. The camera, however, did not pass through customs and the two were sent back. In the meantime, his father passed away. Shipment failed, camera blocked, he grieved. Plastino was devastated: 'I need something strong. Let's start again. Even without a camera, without anything. We will find something there, in Spain.' They arrive a few hours before Italy vs Brazil, grab a phone book and look for a rental company. They just walk through the gates of the Sarriá without accreditation, with a huge camera on Valentino's shoulder and tickets found at the last minute. To be in the stands, in the middle of the crowd. At the controls they look at them with suspicion, but they wave, smile and pretend not to understand.

Against the force of any adverse storm they are now inside the belly of the Sarriá.

Italy, Make Us Dream

The transition to the second phase has attracted thousands of Italians to Spanish soil, even if the organisation has done everything it can to make life difficult for them. Betting everything on mass madness, Mundiespaña, the group that obtained the exclusive contract for the management of hotels and tickets during the Mundial, after having sold 50 per cent of tickets abroad, has ignobly imposed the purchase of the ticket together with the hotel (after having tripled the price of the rooms and extended the minimum stay beyond that needed), with the result of discouraging tourism, so there are unsold tickets, cancelled hotels and half-empty stadiums. Forced to book in advance and pay a high price for packages, many fans have decided to watch the World Cup on TV or perhaps to opt for charter flights with a same-day return. Marconi Tours proposed a package with departure at 8am from Bologna, arrival at 9.30am in Barcelona, a short tour of the city, lunch in a typical restaurant, transfer to the Sarriá stadium, numbered central stand ticket, then return at midnight. All this for 380,000 lire (roughly £160, equal to £500 in 2022 prices).

For Spain, this is a colossal economic fiasco, which the hoteliers are desperately trying to remedy by distancing themselves from Mundiespaña and lowering their tariffs, and the organisation itself by recovering the tickets and pouring them back into the domestic market, which, because of this ill-advised strategy, has found itself with far fewer tickets than demand. Those who bought, at very high prices, a stay in two-star hotels, offered by agencies affiliated with Mundiespaña, have the worst seats at the Sarriá stadium. The best seats have not yet been sold and are in the hands of touts charging extortionate prices. This is not the only theft. Italian fans arriving in Barcelona suffer robberies of all kinds. The consulate general in Calle de Mallorca 270, open three hours a day, is swamped with the work of issuing temporary passports. On the eve of the match, José María Rodríguez, one of the managers of the Seguridad, reassured the fans: 'Don't worry, we have the biggest security system we have ever seen.' There are 30,000 employees, 3,500 inspectors, 22,000 agents of the Policía Nacional, 6,500 of the Guardia Civil – the Sarriá is manned day and night.

In contrast to the misadventures of the 10,000 Italians who arrived with a ticket obtained on the black market, there is the courtesy of the Catalan people, a cordiality that the fans reciprocate at the ground. The Spanish press praises them: 'They are an example of warm and civilised support.' The Italian fans who are about to crowd the Sarriá are a disorderly, genuine and spontaneous crowd, who have not planned their visit to Spain in any way. The fans are funny and colourful. They wear tank tops, plastic bags or tricolour sheets. To protect themselves from the sun, they tie a handkerchief over their head, make a painter's hat out of a sheet of newspaper or wear floppy fishing hats. They do not use choreography, uniforms or organised choirs. If they have to shout something they do not have an original repertoire; a vehement 'Forza Italia!' is enough and when they sing it is always 'Fratelli d'Italia' or 'Volare', the institutional anthem and the popular one. And of course 'Alé-oó'.

For Del Buono, who saw them in the first match at the Sarriá, the fans of the Azzurri are a 'race that will be studied in sociology textbooks'. However 'tired by the trip to a foreign land, they found the strength to solemnly sing the national anthem at the start of the game. *Fratelli d'Italia, l'Italia s s'è desta* … they attacked and then stopped. It's hard, even for football maniacs, to sing stuff like Scipio's helmet with which Italy has girded its head. The rest of the anthem was sung with the mouth closed in the supreme yearning of passion. But the mouths opened wide later.' And the Italian euphoria infects even the most detached critics. There is a banner that, first on the stands in Vigo and then on the front page of the *Gazzetta*, accompanies the Azzurri on their way; it simply says 'Italia facci sognare' (Italy, make us dream). It is a heartfelt invitation which, as Grandini writes in the *Corriere*, 'even the most detached reporter finds hard to resist'.

According to Brascopa, the organisation that deals with the flow of Brazilian tourists in Spain, the yellow-green fans at the stadium will be more than 20,000. They all dress like their players, yellow jerseys, green borders and the advertisement of Café do Brasil, which pays $5 million to the national team. Topper, which produces the shirts, is giving another $2 million. The commercial manager, Paulo Nalon, explains that they have sold 60 million shirts. A frightening number. In the streets they sing *Esta chetando a hora*, the time has come. It seems that they have already won. Everywhere the surdo, the tanborin, the reco-reco, the pandeiro, the ripinique are played. Barcelona is like Rio. One of the fans waves the *Jornal do Brasil*, with the front-page headline 'Now it's Italy's turn'. All those yellow shirts have been jumping and dancing non-stop since 14 June, leading some to suspect that they do not know how to do anything else.

Leading them is Pacheco, the acknowledged leader of the torcida. His real name is Nathan Pacanowski, he is 40 years old and in real life works in the marketing department of the Brazilian Gillette. Born as an advertising invention on the tables of the Alcântara Machado agency at the end of 1980, he became first a puppet and then a cartoon. In the run-up to the World Cup, Gillette decided to humanise him into a good-natured, slightly overweight official linked to the sales office, who had attracted the attention of the directors. Invested by the general manager ('Nathan, you will be the Pacheco who will go to Spain') Pacanowski now lives in the Seleção's entourage after Gillette formalised his role as mascot with the CBF.

In the midst of the Brazilians is Finnish photographer Juha Tamminen. He is 25 years old and got into football by watching Nottingham Forest in the English Second Division with his grandfather. His first passion was actually horse racing. He used to go there as a kid with his father until he was able to gamble, then when the law tightened up on minors he took up football. He travelled to

Nottingham to go to the stadium to watch the matches. To escape the cold of his own country, however, he flew to South America in the winter of 1981 to watch the Mundialito. He thought it would be a once-in-a-lifetime trip, but now he is back in a Latin country. He has not been accredited, he has come to the Sarriá as a fan. In spring he bought a Canon A-1 camera, a 35mm/f2.8 lens and a 100-300/5.6 telephoto lens. Then he bought a ticket from the Finnish federation. Now he is at the top of the stand, behind a Swiss fan, right under the huge yellow-green sheet that covers the torcida.

At the end of the match against Italy, a big party is already planned in the Plaça de Catalunya, and nobody wants to think of having to give it up. In the meantime, the Sarriá is already getting drunk with the sounds that the Carioca orchestras are playing in a haunting rhythm of drums. For days the *fiebre amarilla* (yellow fever) has infected the whole city of Barcelona. It is now the last delirium of the white nights on the Ramblas.

A Soul Split in Two

He arrived in Spain with his military discharge in hand: destination Seville, to follow, for the first time as a correspondent, the matches of Brazil, on behalf of *Tuttosport* and *Guerin Sportivo*. It was Arpino, with great generosity, who pointed him out to Italo Cucci: 'I'm sending you a boy. He's good, his name is Darwin Pastorin. He's so good that he couldn't find work in Turin.' It was shortly afterwards that Pastorin met Bearzot. Italy were in their retreat at Villa Sassi and Cucci sent him as a challenge: 'Let's see if you can interview the national coach knowing that he doesn't talk to us.' At the time, the weekly magazine was attacking the coach. Shortly before, Cucci had published a sarcastic cover: an angry King Kong beating his fists on his chest and shouting: 'I vote Bearzot.'

'Mister Bearzot, there's a Darwin for you.'

He said: 'There's always Darwin and Freud.' The coach was immediately friendly: 'I shouldn't talk to a newspaper that is always attacking me, but you are so young and with a clean face, how can I deny you an interview?' And he told him about his love for Latin classics and Turkish poetry.

Pastorin is imaginative, dreamy and romantic: the perfect reporter to recount the exploits of the Cariocas. Brazil is the national team of his passion, his myths and his memories. In his support for Brazil there is romanticism, provocation and an ancient bond. He has not seen his São Paulo for 21 years but he loves it madly. It is the home of his childhood and therefore of his dreams. For him, Brazil is more than ever the favourite of the competition: 'Not only because it has produced the best performances of all the teams aspiring to the title, but because it is the only one to have shown, in addition to enviable individual talent, an irresistible offensive game plan.'

He has just sat in the stands at the Sarriá reserved for reporters. Italian head, Brazilian heart. The one soul split in two.

The Game Is Not the Same for Everyone

The Corporación de Radio y Televisión Española (RTVE) is ready to link up. Just a couple of years earlier it would have been impossible. Spanish television was not able to cope with a World Cup and had to make an incredible effort to modernise its technology so that all locations could send the signal in colour. Although Barcelona, along with Madrid, was the only city capable of doing so, it did not have the technical infrastructure nor the facilities needed by TV correspondents from all over the world. Land in San Cugat was used to build the new RTVE centre, with an investment of 700 million pesetas.

To bring the international signal to the main broadcasting points, RTVE then built in Madrid in record time – 13 months, at a cost of 3.5 million pesetas – the Torrespaña, a telecommunications antenna, reaching a dizzying height of 232 metres, designed by the architect Emilio Fernández Martínez de Velasco and jokingly nicknamed 'el Pirulí' (the Lollipop) due to its long and slender shape. It was

THE GAME IS NOT THE SAME FOR EVERYONE

inaugurated in the nick of time a month before the first match, on 7 June 1982, in the presence of João Havelange.

Thanks to the mast, the live broadcast coordinated by the Spanish director can interpret the space and time of the match in its own way. The fate of the former is in the hands of the director, the location of the cameras and the choice of shots. The observation point is in the centre of the stand. It is there, on that camera front, that any television viewer will ideally be seated to follow the match along a single horizontal axis. Seven cameras have been positioned at the Sarriá. There are three in the stands, the first to cover the entire pitch. This is the main camera, the one that will always follow the ball, whatever happens. It will be able to catch passes, throws, formations and movements of the two teams. Its wide vision will encourage the spectator to participate. The second camera, for the narrower pitch, will enhance duels and marking but also the expressions of individuals or individual technical gestures. The third camera is for close-ups. There are two cameras beside the pitch, one fixed and one shoulder-mounted, facing the benches. Behind the goals, in the upper part of the curve, there are two more for replays.

Live broadcasting forces television to follow the timing of the match, denying it the possibility of organising the succession of events according to a narrative convention. Suffering, euphoria, trepidation and beauty will be variables dependent on the match itself. The direction will observe the instructions agreed at the beginning of the Mundial, without excessive personalisation, following an austere and unspectacular line. The grass must never be lost sight of, even in the case of aerial play. Close-ups of running players are discouraged. Anything that is not part of the action should not be shown. Only in the case of dead time, when the ball is off the pitch, may close-ups of players, coaches or fans be shown. If there is a goal, the sequence is always the same: the action seen on the wider-range camera leaves space for the close-up of the jubilant player, following him in his embraces with his team-mates, while the narrower angle goes to the reaction of the goalkeeper to follow the psychological image of the protagonists. The first replay starts from behind the goal, with the graphics of the scorer's name superimposed. This is followed by the second replay in wide field, then the reactions of the fans and possibly the reactions of the benches. But there can also be other replays. There is no longer an absolute view. The match created by the Spanish host broadcaster, thanks to the satellite, can be customised or supplemented by the broadcaster showing it in their own country. Therefore, Spain, Italy and Brazil will not always see the same images. The match is no longer the same for everyone.

Tom Clegg's cameras are also in the ground. He played the part of grappler Tashtego in John Huston's *Moby Dick* and directed half a dozen episodes of the science fiction series *Space 1999*. He is currently shooting material for *G'olé!*, the official film of this year's World Cup, commissioned by FIFA and produced by Tyburn Film Productions Limited. The eyes behind the camera are those of the Samuelson brothers: Michael, Sydney and David, three sons of British film pioneer George Berthold 'Bertie' Samuelson. The first of them will, in five years' time, organise Britain's biggest charity appeal. The second, in 13, will receive a knighthood from Prince Charles. The third, in 22, will win an Oscar.

The Last Words

Just a few minutes to go. The Azzurri are sitting on the benches in the Sarriá dressing room, the ones on which Espanyol have spent 21,098,000 pesetas. The dressing room assigned to the Azzurri is large and spartan, 147 square metres usually used by the home team. No lockers, just wooden benches, shelves and hangers. An unreal silence envelops the room. The 11 Vecio boys are about to meet the strongest team in the world. Bearzot rests his cotton jacket on his shoulders. He had seen it in Milan in a shop window in Corso Buenos Aires, and it was love at first sight: 'Uniforms for everyone.' The press was already prepared for the funeral and he said to himself: 'This little waterfront jacket will remind the world that we go to Spain to

THE LAST WORDS

play.' In that nautical blue-and-white uniform he now stands in the centre of the dressing room. He looks for the right words, finds the perfect ones: 'Guys, be calm. We are not weaker than them. I know, they are Brazil. But if they are as invincible as everyone says they are, then it will not be a disgrace to be eliminated. So what have we got to lose by trying? The pressure is all on them. Let's make them feel it. This could be our last game. Let's play it all the way. Whatever happens, I'll always be proud of you.'

The marking is as established. Collovati on Serginho, Oriali on Zico, Gentile on the right on Éder, Cabrini on the left on Sócrates. To Rossi, pointing at Oscar and Luizinho, he recommends only one thing: 'They are the last safeguard, every now and then they get distracted, they always make a few mistakes: when it happens you have to be there.' Bearzot still has a doubt in his head. He gnaws on his pipe in search of answers. He confers nervously with his deputy Maldini. In the tunnel, the players of the two teams find themselves a few metres away from each other, ready to enter the field of play, separated by a net that prevents physical contact but not the exchange of glances. Just before climbing the stairs, the head coach shouts to his team, 'Guys, let's go back!' Once back in the dressing room, he announces decisively, 'Sit down and listen to me. Claudio, you're going on Zico.' Gentile does not bat an eyelid: 'Just him or also Éder?' It is a meaningless question, dictated by adrenaline. 'You take care of Éder, Lele. Oriali on the right flank and you, Claudio, only on Zico. Is that clear, guys?'

Captain Zoff, in his forties – the oldest player in the Mundial, even three coaches are younger than him: Carlos Alberto of Kuwait, Mancio Rodríguez of El Salvador and John Adshead of New Zealand – will have to confirm the confidence he needs in the entire back line. Gentile, at right-back, after having nullified Maradona, now has the task of blocking Brazil's most dangerous man, Zico. On the opposite side, Cabrini will continue his forward thrusts, while Scirea remains the impeccable libero, with the solid agility of Collovati at his side. One step ahead of them, Oriali, as well as looking after Éder, will link up with the rest of the midfield made up of Tardelli, Antognoni and right-winger Conti, ready to serve the forwards Graziani and Rossi.

Everyone now knows what they have to do.

The Italian

The green glare of the grass floods the hungry irises of the players. Lined up like soldiers, 22 men stare in silence at the splendour of the grass. Zoff has 104 blue defences on his shoulders and a pennant in his hand. The eyes of a Brazilian are fixed on him – Oscar. The Azzurri captain's name is Dino, like his father. He is Italian, like his family. He is a goalkeeper, like Oscar used to be. He loved to jump. He loved being in goal. Then one day they put him in defence and from then on he abandoned the goalposts. Now, if he leaves his area, it is only to head into the enemy's goal. Flying is a matter of timing, like his role. He has been taught that a full-back has to get to the ball at the same time as the attacker, to scare him off. He chooses the moment, catching the ball cleanly, because 'he who is violent cannot play'. He has never been sent off for a bad foul. As he watches Zoff on the edge of the pitch, the memory of his debut suddenly emerges. There was Pelé on the edge of the box. He was his myth. He would have been his opponent. He could almost touch him. He wanted to ask for his jersey, but shame stopped him. Pelé was the king and Oscar was a boy.

The day before he was a simple youth footballer at Ponte Preta. A year before, he did not even want to play football. He had started kicking just to imitate his older brother. Selector Mário Juliato had to work hard to keep him going. Oscar did not want to know. 'I don't want to be a footballer!' He was consumed with fear. He just wanted to stay with his family on his grandfather's farm. He did not feel ready to leave Monte Sião for Campinas. The city scared him a lot. It was too big, too far from home, too far from his family. Encouraged by his parents, he decided to attend the call. During the journey, Oscar had already planned what to say: 'I thank you but I don't feel like it.'

THE ITALIAN

When he turned up, Juliato asked him, 'Where is your suitcase?' He was about to open his mouth when his father interjected: 'It's here.' Oscar turned sharply to the luggage rack as if a torpedo had pierced the defences. But if he was trembling, his father was firm: 'You're here to stay.' Oscar stayed.

Over the next few days, he hoped to get injured and even prayed that he could go home. But staying turned out to be the best choice, for everyone. The coach left, Juliato took his place and Oscar became a starter. He began to enjoy the pleasure of the beautiful game, enjoyed his talent and found peace. That afternoon he enjoyed his leisure time sitting in front of the stadium. After his match, Oscar usually ran home to his mother. The next day, however, Ponte were playing against Santos: 'I want to see Pelé.' The No. 10 had decided to retire from football, so this was a unique opportunity. Mário Juliato, his coach, approached him: 'Italian, I think I need you tomorrow.' Full-back Araujo had not yet renewed his contract. 'If he doesn't, can I count on you?' Oscar doubted that Juliato understood. 'In the meantime get ready, sleep with the professionals tomorrow.' Araujo did not renew his contract and Oscar took his place.

He made his debut against Santos as Pelé scored his last goal in a Paulist league match. It was 2 October 1974. A few months earlier, Dino Zoff had been on the cover of *Newsweek*. Oscar, on the other hand, asked to finish his studies, graduated and enrolled at the Pontifícia Universidade Católica de Campinas to study physiotherapy. It was not easy. The university forced him to miss training and football forced him to miss classes. But he made up for both by training on his own and doing his internship at the hospital. When he graduated he was diverted to Giorgio Chinaglia's New York Cosmos in the United States. It was hell for him. He played little, suffered from a cyst under his femoral artery and missed his family. He first brought in his father, then his brother, and finally a friend who could cook. American soccer was not followed, so Oscar had disappeared from the media and from the eyes of Telê Santana. Until he accepted the offer from São Paulo. If he had not, he would not be here.

THE MATCH

Fratelli d'Italia

The Azzurri emerge from the dressing room wrapped in white, wearing their tracksuit tops. The Seleção already emanate light in the golden glow of their shirts. In the middle, a trinity, the officials. The Bulgarian linesman Bogdan Dochev has already refereed Italy against Cameroon. His counterpart from Hong Kong, Chan Tam-Sun, has already met Brazil, in their match against Scotland, where he was second assistant. Klein nods. Zoff stares at the void opening up before him and takes a step, just one. The gaze of Sócrates, the other captain, engulfs him. The players appear in the lap of the Sarriá. Around them a pile of buildings crammed like crates on the dry plain of the Ciudad. There is no shade, no wind. The stadium is bubbling with euphoria. Flags wave. The Brazilian flag represents the Amazon rainforest, the gold reserves and Rio by night, together with a positivist and militaristic motto, 'Order and Progress'. The Italian tricolour, the symbol of the Renaissance, immortalises the green of the meadows, the white of the snow and the red of the blood of the fallen.

Assembled side by side, the 22 men stand motionless on the Sarriá pitch. It is the moment when it is easy to believe everything, that of the anthems. The photographers crowd into the centre. Only one of them moves to the left. He does it to frame the silhouettes in yellow. It is the demigods who stand out in the frame of his Nikon. The reporter, however, is the Italian Calzuola, one of the 15 Italian photographers accredited for the match. The day before, Cascioli told him, 'Peppe, listen to me. I've seen the Brazilians play, they're a team from another world. Take photos directly of them and tonight prepare your suitcase. Tomorrow we're all going home.'

So he did. In the small hotel that has hosted him these last few nights, his luggage is already packed. He has paid for the hotel himself, as well as the flight, the meals and all the journeys. Al Sarriá wears bib 47/441. With it on he can move as he likes. He already knows that behind the doors are the most quoted agencies: Ansa,

350

Associated Press, Olympia, Efe. It is up to them to stop the networks. He looks for the man. The character, the look, the movement. To capture them, he wears three Nikon F3 cameras around his neck, all loaded with rolls of film containing 36 shots. Two in black-and-white, for newspapers, and one in colour. And it is with this, during the Brazilian national anthem, that he takes aim, pointing the lens at the Brazilian deployment.

Eleven golden statues nailed to the anthem stand to attention. Éder, Serginho and Waldir Peres are lulled into silence. Falcão, Zico, Oscar, Luizinho, Júnior and Sócrates sing the 'Marcha Triunfal', the one that Francisco Manuel da Silva composed in 1822 on the occasion of independence from Portugal. 'Brazil, an intense dream, a vivid ray of love and hope… you are beautiful, strong, fearless colossus and your future reflects this greatness. Adored land among a thousand is you, Brazil, O beloved country!' The author of the music died before these verses, composed by Joaquim Osório Duque-Estrada, could rest on his notes. The two never met but were united forever by their people.

The captain of the team that now represents them, along with Leandro and Cerezo, has his hand over his heart. Applause. Silence. The next introduction begins and Cabrini turns instinctively towards the Gol Norte, the curve that gathers the Italian fans. He swallows his saliva and brings his hand close to Tardelli's. He plays 'Fratelli d'Italia'. He attacks 'Fratelli d'Italia'. Giuseppe Garibaldi considered it the most enthralling warlike victory song after 'La Marseillaise'. A handful of stanzas to evoke the history of Romanity. The heroic helmet of the Roman general Publius Cornelius Scipio, later known as Africanus, the man who defeated Hannibal in the battle of Zama in 202 BC; the trimmed hair of the slaves, the legionary cohorts. Victory, heroism, Italy. The words were written in Genoa in the autumn of 1847 by the young poet and patriot Goffredo Mameli, who a few months later would find himself, with the rank of captain of the *bersaglieri* (riflemen), at the head of 300 volunteers to fight the Austrians on the Mincio. There he would collaborate with Garibaldi and, like him, be wounded in the leg. That 5 July in 1849 would be his last day. The following dawn he would consign to immortality those five verses and his 22 years, the same age as Franco Baresi, who now sits in the stands waiting for the world to discover his talent. Bearzot's national team, however, cannot hear those verses. What is played in the stadium is an instrumental version of the 'Canto degli Italiani', with only Michele Novaro's notes. The words run through the players' heads, mixed with fears and hopes. The last ones. It is time for the showdown.

In the Middle of the Pitch

A roar breaks the lines. The last remnant of silence is swept away by thousands of trumpets. Tardelli and Gentile take off their tracksuits. In the middle of the pitch, two friends meet in opposing kit. Falcão's arm is on Conti's shoulder, as if to shake off the dust of an old friendship. They left Rome with a promise: should they find themselves against each other, they would eventually exchange shirts. 'Whatever happens, Bruno.' They are joined by Tardelli and Cabrini, direct opponents in the Italian championship. Handshakes and friendly smiles. Then the Brazilian returns to his friends' eyes.

'May the best man win, Paulo,' Conti whispers to him.

'*Que ganhe o melhor,* Bruno,' Falcão replies, chewing a cigarette butt incessantly.

They reach out their arms to caress each other's cheeks. Their last gesture of affection. For 90 minutes they will be rivals.

The gesture is immortalised by Calzuola. He could miss it. It is a story that began in Rome and that he created. Before leaving for Spain he had Conti and Falcão pose with the shirts of their respective national teams. He has a special relationship with the Brazilian. In Rome, they both live in Monteverde, a stone's throw from each other: the reporter at the Orti di Trastevere, Falcão at the Hotel Villa Pamphili. But apart from not having a house in the capital, Paulo does not even own a car. So every now and then he calls Calzuola:

'Peppe, I'd like to go to the seaside, will you drive me to Fregene?'
He picks him up, takes him to the beach and maybe even takes
some photos. For the pre-Mundial one, Conti, who has known the
photographer since 1976, had no problem finding the blue kit, while
Falcão had never yet worn the new yellow-green jersey, so Calzuola
then asked his colleagues for help. 'Peppe, don't worry,' Massimo
Tecca of *Paese Sera* reassured him, 'I'll get you one.'

The shot was taken on a bright May morning at Tre Fontane,
the Giallorossi's training ground. The two players posed side by
side. They did not know yet that they would be up against each
other. And the shirts were not exactly World Cup ones (Conti wore
a long-sleeved winter shirt, Falcão an old jersey with a Korean collar
that Tecca recovered). The socks were also makeshift. Together
with them posed Liedholm and Viola. Having taken the photo, the
Roma president turned to his two protégés and asked that at least
one of them bring him a World Cup shirt. 'It would be nice,' thought
Calzuola at that moment, 'if we really played an Italy–Brazil game.'
The hope has now become reality and at this point the reporter
is only missing the end of the story. 'If at the end of the match I
photograph the exchange of the jerseys, I will magnificently close
this circle.' But for the moment it is the two teams who pose for the
ritual photo.

Meanwhile, Brazil has come to a standstill. All activities are
paralysed. Post offices, banks, shops and schools have decided
to cease operations an hour before the start of the meeting. The
institutions agree that nobody would dream of doing anything else
during a match like this. 'Robbers don't steal and ghosts don't haunt,'
wrote Brazilian playwright Nelson Rodrigues. 'There are no crimes,
no deaths, no adulteries. Everything is postponed until after the
game.' Even churches stop services and factories stop production. It
is pointless to leave workers on assembly lines, knowing that they
will all be watching the Seleção. Rio's Getúlio Vargas Foundation
has estimated that while Brazil plays Italy, the country will lose $225
million in production. But despite the recession, sales and rentals of

television sets have exploded. 'With the loss of purchasing power, even middle-class people have lost their self-esteem,' explained the Reichian psychoanalyst André Luiz Gaiarsa, 'and in this sense football becomes a salvific element for the sensation of taking part in a collective enterprise as rich in emotion as it is distant from a daily routine that one despises.'

'So depois da Copa' (only after the Cup) is the standard response to all deadlines, including institutional ones. 'From this moment on,' Minister da Justiça do Brasil Ibrahim Abi-Ackel declares on 14 June, 'political concerns are secondary.' It takes only a few hours to realise that the intention has also been taken seriously by the Ministro chefe do Gabinete Civil da Presidência da República João Leitão de Abreu: 'Today was a happy day. In addition to Brazil's victory over the Soviet Union, we also had a ceasefire in the South Atlantic.'

Mr Tim's Certainties

The bench is sunk into the grass like a trench. For coaches, doctors and substitutes it is time to dive in. Bearzot has chosen a replacement for each role: a goalkeeper, a defender, a midfielder, a defender and a striker. The cavern of white lime then swallows the bodies of Bordon, Bergomi, Marini, Causio and Altobelli; for Brazil, those of Edevaldo, Paulo Sérgio, Paulo Isidoro, Fonseca and Renato. Together with them, on the South American bench there is the fitness trainer Gilberto Tim, who sits on a rock-solid certainty that he has never hidden: 'The dream will come true, Brazil will beat Italy and we will become world champions.' The reason for such ostentatious confidence lies in the seriousness of his work.

Authoritarian and intolerant, Tim is clear about the Seleção's physical preparation. Instead of focusing on agility and speed, he has concentrated on muscular endurance in Spain, using methods that have not always been well received by the players. On the other hand, he does not tolerate lazy people and has a special cure for waking them up with continuous sprints of 200 and 400 metres. On the eve of the tournament, when, due to their status as the absolute favourites, the Brazilian national team seemed to be living a moment of grace. Nothing too serious had disturbed the members of the technical commission during the run-up to the World Cup. With the fitness preparation in the hands of Telê Santana's trusted man – assisted by doctor Neylor Lasmar, auxiliary technicians (world champion Vavá and Paulo César da Costa) and masseur Abílio José da Silva – the players had only complained of muscle aches, slight bruises or minor ailments. Until a series of unfortunate incidents struck Tim's certainty.

Sócrates had been seized by a malaise that he himself, a medical graduate, was unable to explain. 'I feel a strange physical tiredness and I don't know what to attribute it to, it could be an organic decompensation caused by the loss of mineral salts,' he had said in making a self-diagnosis. Then it was the turn of Careca, who could not cope with Tim's sessions. However, the only one to speak out was Dirceu, openly complaining about the working methods and training rhythms imposed by Gilberto Tim, and getting into a dispute with the physical trainer and even Lasmar for hiding a contusion on the eve of the friendly against Switzerland: 'I came here very excited, but the tests made me burst. The training sessions wouldn't stand up to a boy of 15, let alone someone like me of almost 30.'

Gilberto Tim then replied, 'My players have to get tired in training so that they don't get tired in the game, and the team has to be mobile to the extreme on the pitch.'

Oscar, on the other hand, is at one with Tim. If the coach has a cult of physical preparation, the defender loves to work. He feels the need for it, he has to be in perfect physical shape to be able to play well, otherwise he cannot have confidence in his abilities.

On Saturday, Tim only trains the players who did not take part in the match against Argentina. Thanks to the rest and the diet established by Lasmar, the team has recovered all its energies and is at the Sarriá in top form.

THE MATCH

Zoff's Gloves

Klein places the ball on the centre spot of the pitch. It is the Adidas-branded Tango, one of the 5,000 made in the ball factory in Caspe, a stone's throw from Zaragoza. It weighs 420 grams and has a similar design to the Tango Riverplate of Argentina '78 but its leather is much more flexible. The seams with which its pieces are joined are handmade, and waterproofed using a polyurethane bath. It has excellent contact with the foot, is abrasion-resistant, does not deform, bounces beautifully and is fast. They say it can fool goalkeepers with long-range shots. Waldir Peres, who missed the first such shot, knows something about this, but that mistake turned into a moment of unity, camaraderie and solidarity. At half-time, the whole of the Seleção team gave a lesson in humanity. On that day Santana wrote in his notes: 'Everyone makes mistakes, whether it's me in the formation or the striker at the moment of scoring. The problem is that when the goalkeeper makes a mistake, it's a goal.'

The one person who knows that he can do no wrong today is Dino Zoff. That is why the Azzurri captain has not neglected the coverings on his hands. Grey on the back to recall the jersey, fiery red on the palm to pay homage to Spain. Zoff's gloves mark a boundary in time, between the past and the future. When he started out, goalkeepers' gloves were mostly made of wool. Some, like Ivano Bordon, Zoff's deputy, preferred to play bare-handed. Or they used the inside of ski gloves, or rope gloves, whose outside was covered with the rubber of table tennis bats. The 1960s were a time of experimentation. Gloves were considered a luxury and clubs did not invest. Goalkeepers struggled to find the most suitable material to improve grip, protect their hands from the cold or rain. Some glued rubber strips on to leather gloves, at the fingers and the palm, to increase their thickness and thus their resistance to ball impact. But when it rained, the grip was poor.

The defining moment was the change of identity of the ball. From leather to plastic, a transformation that made the game more spectacular but also made it more difficult for the goalkeeper to catch. Leather balls had such thick seams that they turned the fingers into claws. Plastic-coated balls, on the other hand, had definitively imposed the problem of gloves on to goalkeepers. It was time to find a solution. The speed of the ball and the goalkeeper's ability to stop it were the new issues to think about. So from wool, to leather, to rubber, we finally reached the point of no return. Latex. A complex and almost secret emulsion of rubber in water. With it, the first manufacturers appeared. In search of the first rudimentary sponsorship contracts, they went to summer training camps to show their gloves to goalkeepers. If they liked the goods, a handshake was enough and the exchange was done. Use in exchange for visibility. Both free of charge.

The most fortunate of these manufacturers were Messrs Allegri and Montescani from Fiorenzuola. Their black glove, made in Switzerland by an obscure craftsman, unimaginatively called A/M and sprinkled with latex pieces on the fingers and palm, quickly became the object of desire of the number-one players, and therefore also for Zoff. Shortly before his departure for the 1974 World Cup, he saw them on his Cesena colleague, Lamberto Boranga, and instructed masseur Selvi to find out where they could be found. In the end it was Mr Allegri himself who handed Zoff a supply of A/M gloves. Three pairs and a Piacenza cup. This was the contract.

Other gloves made by Italian craftsmen began to appear, such as those created by Due Lupi. And the search went on, until Uhlsport arrived in Italy. It was founded in 1948 in Balingen, south-west Germany, when its founder Karl Uhl began producing studs for football boots. But in the 1970s he became increasingly aware of the importance of gloves for a goalkeeper. The ones Zoff is wearing against Brazil – Uhlsport model 040 with Velcro fastening – usher in the season of Supersoft, of bright colours, of thin, soft and secure grips.

First Half

Rossi, the most discussed character, the most criticised player, came out of the Mundial with little glory and a lot of trouble, which he never experienced as a protagonist.

Fabio Vergnano,
La Stampa, on the eve of Italy vs Brazil

The Kick-Off

The first deal is a promise of happiness. A fast, spinning ball as it caresses the entire crescent of the green-and-yellow midfield. Four touches are enough to paint that smile on the Brazilians' faces. They close in on the feet of Júnior who, from the left, is the first to decide to cross the line. It is to him that the first note of the match falls. He sends the ball deep towards Serginho, but Collovati anticipates Chulapa and ends the opening move of the match in textbook manner: Brazil forward, arrival of the Azzurri stopper, relaunch of the first Azzurri action. Bearzot approves with a nod of the head.

A little time passes and the ball disappears over the Italian byline. Éder, driven by generous energy, goes towards it anyway, picks it up and throws it to Zoff. That same ball then passes nervously from leg to leg, from team to team, until it arrives in midfield between the legs of Paolo Rossi. Once, twice, three times in three minutes. But Falcão denies him any chance of recovery.

The first real orchestral movement of the match, however, is Italian. In the middle of the Sarriá, while Antognoni and Cabrini triangulate quickly, Conti, Graziani and Rossi stretch out. The passes are quick notes. The ball swirls from one side of the pitch to the other, sewed into a double thread on the grass, returns to the feet of Cabrini, passes over the defence with a lob and is hurled by Tardelli towards the centre of the penalty area. It lands at Rossi's feet. In front of him, Luizinho and Leandro leave a hole. The goal is open.

The Italian chooses the volley. It becomes a swing and a miss. In an attempt to try again, he takes a shoulder bump from Leandro and falls to the ground once more. Four minutes, four balls, four falls. It is impossible to understand what a player with three meniscus, five kilos less weight and a two-year fast of football is doing in the middle of such an important World Cup match. Perhaps the only one who might know is Bearzot.

The P Point

The start is a backline, that of Italy, and because of a back, that of an Azzurri player. Rossi's mistake gives Brazil the ball, which accidentally hits Conti's kidneys before sliding inexorably towards the goal line. Ineluctably it is crushed by Collovati's quick leap that avoids a corner, which seemed almost certain. The ball is still in motion and history changes. The manoeuvre becomes Italian. Scirea gets the ball to the flank, where the recipient is Conti. In front of him, the dishevelled dance of Serginho, shirt out and legs together. Conti feints to the left and passes to the right, in an instant. Cerezo moves in to confront him. Conti turns on himself, feints, counter-feints and burns Cerezo.

He pushed a wheelbarrow, young Bruno, in his first job as a bricklayer. He delivered gas cylinders on a bicycle during his further training. He trained on the sly, eventually, in the crystal shop where he later went to work. Lessons in balance and dribbling imparted by life. Conti now crosses the halfway line, approaches Éder and goes past him. Falcão watches his friend. Oriali does not cover Conti's advance, so Júnior abandons his line. But, at that very moment, Conti looks up. He realises, he alone, that on the opposite side he has been followed by a free blue shirt.

Bearzot had wanted to see Conti perform before packing his bags for Argentina in 1978. It went well: 'I'll take you to the World Cup.' To Conti, who was not yet 21 years old, he gave the first official Azzurri shirt in the first match of that World Cup. He never took it off again. From that day on, 'Bell'Antonio' – a Brancati label that has never excited him – started running down the left corridor and never stopped.

Cabrini has moved from the area he is called upon to defend and dares to go as far as the weak side of the Magic Square, the right one, which nobody wants to watch over, with a gamble in his head. In that instant an entire line finds itself in the middle of a drama. Seven players are involved, seven points that form a straight line. Luizinho, Júnior, Rossi, Cerezo, Graziani, Oscar and Leandro. A perfect image: two pairs of Brazilian defenders on either side, the two Italian strikers in the middle and a Rio midfielder in between them. The five Brazilians turn suddenly towards the Azzurri full-back, as if seeing him for the first time. The ball is in the air. The Brazilian line immediately begins to move to the right. Graziani and Rossi rush forward in an opposite movement. Júnior, the only one to have raced towards Conti, finds himself a step behind and desperately looking to get back. Falcão starts to close the diagonal in place, then stops. He does so to centre himself, but thus leaves a hole behind Luizinho.

Conti's pass makes just one bounce, the second is controlled by Cabrini. Two steps, a glance into the box and the movement of his left foot. The Brazilian line observes, astonished, while Cabrini's ball flies outstretched to trace in the air the only line passing through the P. Graziani leaps into the area, while the same trail of glances now points to that suspended ball. Rossi watches the ball come towards him. Waldir Peres moves towards the woodwork. Rossi takes two steps forward. And yes, like a man who is so light, Pablito lifts himself from the heaviness of the world, approaches the ball and presses it against the suspended void with his forehead. The Brazilian last defender finds himself unbalanced, on his left foot, with his right leg raised and his arms open. Pablito opens his mouth wide. There is still his imprint in the air. Waldir Peres turns with an expression of terror and watches the ball slip behind him. Time stands still.

The Fleeting Moment

Behind the Brazilians' goal a flurry of clicks break the silence before the roar. Calzuola sits to the right of Peres's posts. He surveys the mirror of the small area that welcomes Rossi, Júnior and the last defender. He presses his index finger on the release button and winds up the roller. Press and wind again. And again. A shiver runs through him as he follows the fate of the ball from his little window overlooking the pitch. Cesare Galimberti, sports photo reporter for the Olympia agency, sits in the best seat, in the middle of the goal. Cold as a killer, he has already pressed his finger to his Canon. His 38 years have not taken away the nickname 'Cesarino', which he has carried with him since he found work at Vito Liverani's when he was only 14, just like Beppe Viola. It was 1958 and, a couple of years earlier, Vitaliano, known as Vito, had opened the first agency specialising in sports events. When it came time to christen it, Gianni Brera was his godfather: 'Vito, don't put the usual banal names with the word "Press" in front of them, in 1960 the Olympics will be held in Rome, so ...' And so it was Olympia. Or rather, Fotocronache Olympia. Even if his wife didn't like it because that was the name of their concierge. The year before the Mundial, he sold it and with the millions he made he founded Omega. But Galimberti stayed at Olympia and the agency that has been his home all his life is now offering his views. He knows that after every click he has to reload the machine. He has one bullet, he cannot waste it. His brain has to move faster than his technique. And his brain says: 'Now!'

Nihil potest homo intelligere sine phantasmate. Nothing can be understood without images. A gesture that freezes the movement, making it eternal, impresses our eyes and mind even before the film. History is a choral display of representations that speak to us without mediation, in an ever-open narrative. To photograph means to recognise a fact and organise the forms in a fraction of a second. To place head, eye and heart on the same line of sight. To stop time, to create space, a space, one of the thousand spaces we can live (and see) among all possible spaces. The eye, the head, the finger are obliged to be attentive, precise, quick and capable. Ready to grasp the fragments of a visual discourse. The fruitful union between intuition and luck, in defiance of distraction, in glory of curiosity.

'We feel that something must be happening,' wrote Robert Louis Stevenson, 'we don't know what it is, but we go looking for it.' And

THE FLEETING MOMENT

the search stops there. When Peres squints his eyes, clenches his teeth, a dry suction drags across his mouth, stretching the muscles of his neck until his jaw stiffens. A grimace that only a reporter from the Spanish photo agency Efe, lurking behind the door, manages to stop forever. Everything moves. Everything flows. Perhaps it is because of things like this that man goes through existence in a constant search for the absolute. But the truth is hidden in the moment.

The world is a totality of facts. Facts exist through interpretations. Interpretations are formulated by the mind. But there is no one interpretation that resembles another, because each mind has its own view. Therefore every truth is relative. But a goal is a goal. For everyone, forever. It is the absolute. It contains the before of the action, the after of the exultation and a central, unique, memorable, eternal moment. The fleeting moment finally stopped, grasped, immortalised. Like the cinematographic fixity of Giotto's frescoes. And the instant captured by the reporter.

Rossi and Peres are facing each other, in the same moment and in the same symmetrical position. Waldir Peres is immortalised in the act of falling to the ground. Sweat trickles down his jugular, his jaws creak, his left arm is weighed down on the grass, his right arm, still raised, carries the echo of an attempt. He has just turned around and in his eyes there is all the fear of the earth, in his clenched jaw the awareness of having lost a duel. Paolo Rossi is in front of him. The spirited eye, the wide-open mouth. He too has only one arm raised, his left, but he is raising it to the sky in exultation, as if in front of a mirror. Equals and opposites. Striker and goalkeeper. Rossi exulting in front of Peres falling. Just as in morals, evil clings to good, so in the reality of a match the ferocity of a joy can only sink its nails into a pain.

It is a goal. Rossi, after 777 days in limbo, instinctively runs towards the goal. Antognoni embraces him, Graziani goes towards him. Conti brings his hands to his face. Júnior's run ends inside the goal. Falcão instinctively looks for an anchor to his right. He makes a gesture towards the linesman, but it chokes him inside: Dochev's flag points inexorably towards midfield. It is a goal. A 60-second-long action, carried on from one end of the pitch to the other by six Azzurri – Collovati-Scirea-Conti-Oriali-Cabrini-Rossi. Triggered by a mistake by Rossi and finished by Rossi himself. In the fifth minute of the fifth Azzurri match, on this scorching 5 July, his header from five metres gives Italy the lead. It is only 5.20 in the afternoon. An hour that sculpts the numbers of this minute and of Pablito's shirt.

O Galinho

One-nil. Ball in the middle of the goal. Júnior sadly bends down to collect it from the net. Serginho and Zico, as five minutes earlier, find themselves staring at it, motionless in the middle of the pitch. Telê Santana chews his inscrutable gum as he packs his very own 'Puta madre!' for the planet. It sounds like a signal. The Brazilians resume their earlier dance, although their spin is confused and the ball creates closed rings in the ground. When Cerezo spots Oscar in the area he chooses a twisted spin and thus hurls the ball into absolute emptiness. Italy start again: quick passes, a ball lost and regained, Conti, Rossi and Graziani happily triangulating, a shot off target. Zico interrupts the umpteenth Azzurri phase, rips the ball from Antognoni's feet and hits it long for Serginho, but it is a mere formality for Zoff.

On the stroke of ten minutes, Sócrates crosses the halfway line and heads the ball towards Serginho. He is hunted down by Collovati, tries to turn, but Cabrini is also on his back. The ball, however, bounces off the full-back and back to him. His march is disjointed but inexorable. Scirea tries to stop it but the ball moves to Zico's feet before bouncing back to Serginho. Zico looks at his team-mate with the face of someone who has just been mugged. He has. A few days earlier, against Argentina, both men had pounced on a ball that had spun into the box, and Zico had stolen the joy of the goal from his team-mate. Now Serginho controls the ball on the edge of the penalty area with his right instep, takes two steps, reaches the penalty spot and stands alone in front of the Azzurri goal. Only

O GALINHO

Zoff is between him and the goal. He lifts his right leg and takes aim. Zoff stretches out his six-foot frame on the grass but his fingers do not touch the ball ... because the shot does not find the target. It goes out of play. Serginho stops in disbelief, turns around, feels the weight of millions of eyes on him and touches his nose for a moment as if to hide his embarrassment. Until he smiles. Zico looks at those lips, thick with greed. 'What the hell are you laughing at? You can't miss a ball like that!'

Zico had already lost a World Cup four years earlier without his team ever being defeated. That is why before starting the Mundial he whispered to his team-mates: 'Don't worry, there will be no ghosts in this Cup.' Arthur Antunes Coimbra, known as Zico, is the man who in this championship contends with Maradona for the prize of the best player in South America, if not the world. His physique is certainly not imposing and his short stature is compensated for by his flexible muscles and excellent technique. He is a champion built in a laboratory. Light as a twig, he had no chance. But young Arthur's aches and pains were entrusted to José Francalacci, a fitness trainer of Neapolitan origin, who imposed gruelling gym sessions on him every single day. And after four years, Zico, 13 kilos heavier, was ready for the Flamengo first team. He went on to become, behind Pelé, Brazil's most famous player. Not for nothing after 'O Galinho' (the cockerel), did he earn himself a precious nickname: 'White Pelé'.

He is now in an incredible state of grace: in two years he has been top scorer and best player in the Copa Libertadores, best player in the Intercontinental Cup, top scorer in his league and the newspaper *El Mundo* has awarded him his third South American Golden Ball after 1977 and 1981. He has arrived in Spain after scoring over 300 goals in official matches. But he prefers the effectiveness of team play to the preciousness of superstardom. Maturity has brought him closer to humility and it has taken his hands off the desire for fame. It is the result that counts. So solidity has become his best weapon.

O Doutor

His reputation as a philosopher precedes Sócrates. In Spain it has served to accentuate his aura of imperturbability. In reality, if there is a bohemian player at the Mundial, it is him. Opposed to intensive training, he leads a life on the fringes of football, among writers and artists. He smokes to think better, drinks to chat with friends, until late at night, but he does not speak English, because 'it's the language of imperialism'. On 17 May, in the middle of the national team's meeting in Toca da Raposa, he and actors Paulo Gracindo and Lima Duarte filmed an episode of the television series *O Bem Amado*: 'I've never denied it: I like to make forays into the world of the arts. After all, the telenovela is a type of theatre. And playing football is also an art. At least that's how I've always seen it.' A month later, on 23 June, in the middle of the World Cup, on the day of Brazil vs New Zealand, he took to the stage in Seville to duet with his friend Raimundo Fagner, a well-known singer of Brazilian popular music.

The Seleção's fitness trainer Gilberto Tim forces him to cut down on smoking and alcohol and puts him on a programme to increase his muscle mass. Thanks to this he has gone from his usual 71 kilograms to his current 86, his thoracic perimeter has increased and with it his lung capacity. In other words, greater stability, more breath and greater endurance. He does not rely on speed or strength, but on intelligence and intuition. His feet are the last repositories of the beautiful game. Unreal progressions, as if he were floating in the air. His speciality is the backheel. For the Brazilians it is *O calcanhar que a bola pediu a Deus*, the backheel that asks God for the ball. Pelé says he plays better from behind than others do from the front.

Off the field he is a man of few words. For discretion, shame, shyness. Inside, he transforms: he shouts, directs the team, stimulates his team-mates, and everyone obeys. 'I talk for 90 minutes. The rest of the time I prefer to listen.' The shout creates a force inside him, offering him the certainty of victory. At the end of the first half against the Soviet Union, 1-0 down, Telê Santana spoke to the team.

O DOUTOR

Sócrates watched him without saying a word. Walking up the steps to the pitch with his head down, he called out to Falcão: 'You go ahead and I'll stay behind. This role is more suited to you today.' Falcão followed his advice, and Brazil won. In the next match the same script. Scotland scored, he shouted to Zico: 'Let's stop running and get the ball rolling more.' And the Tango began to slide docilely. This was exactly what the coach wanted when he chose him as captain. He had thrown him the armband, saying only, 'Turn around!' Nothing more; it was not necessary.

He is almost 30 years old and at the peak of his career. The only Corinthian called up, he came to Spain with the responsibility of leading one of the strongest Seleção ever to a fourth title. At home he has left his ideals, his two beloved books – Kafka's *The Trial* and *One Hundred Years of Solitude* by Gabriel García Márquez – three children and a wife, Regina, who is about to give him Mariana. He confessed to Falcão: 'I hope he is born after the final, so he will already be champion.' Even before the match against Argentina he had already expressed his blind faith in the Seleção: 'We may not be the champions, but the team is already the best of this World Cup.' After beating them, on the eve of Italy vs Brazil, he confided to the most intimate reporters: 'You know, I can already see myself lifting the cup.' An imprudence that did not surprise his interlocutors in the least. 'I'm not overly optimistic. I simply believe that no one can take the title away from Brazil.' Fair statements that if uttered by any other player would be seen as overbearing.

But O Magrão (the Magrone, as the fans call him) is no ordinary player. He is in danger of playing a significant role in his country's politics. In fact, perhaps he already has one, and he wants to make it clear that, if Brazil are world champions, the government should not benefit from this victory: 'Brazilians today are well aware that football is only a sport and this cannot serve as support for any political campaign. Even if our team wins the cup, the voter should not see the title as a victory for the government, only for the players. We are here to play football and nothing more.

If we win it will be great, if we lose it will not be the country that will be defeated.'

Although he plays in the same national team, he feels he does not have much in common with his team-mates. His colleagues think about earning a lot of money today so as not to have to work tomorrow. They want to win their own corner of peace, protected from the evils of the world. He does not want to lose his critical spirit. Economic attractiveness is secondary, the important thing is to follow one's own path. 'For sure this will be my first and last World Cup,' he vented to the newspaper *O Estado de São Paulo* on the day of Italy vs Argentina, 'also because I don't expect to play until 1986.' He wants to hang up his boots to devote himself entirely to the poorest and most marginalised in society. His future lies in social medicine. He dreams of building a villa to live in as a community with all his friends, and a hospital to work alongside his former faculty colleagues. But he knows this is utopian. And for an idealist like him, an Olympics would have been better: 'It was a terrible frustration to take part in a World Cup.' He dreamed of cultural exchanges, of meeting people from other countries: 'It would have been nice to be able to discuss our problems with them, but we were isolated from each other and only met on the pitch.' It is a disappointment that distances him from an ideal of sport. His own.

The 12 Steps

Brazil know how to chase. They were down against the Soviet Union and again against Scotland. In both cases the response was relentless. Every action can be a good one, even one that starts from a throw-in. Leandro throws the ball in to Sócrates just before the halfway line. The Doctor plays the ball between Antognoni and Cabrini into Zico. Gentile barks but does not bite. A lightning-quick touch with a soft outside edge of the boot and the ball goes back to Sócrates. The Doctor takes six steps before catching up with the ball and another six before shooting. When he lifts his head he sees Zoff at the near post. The goalkeeper stares into those two Homeric eyes buried in a parchment face but he cannot interpret them. Sócrates keeps his shoulders straight, remains in possession of all his elegance, holds his breath, leans forward and, in a split second, decides to shoot into the gap that has been created between the goalkeeper and the post. Desperate to get to the ball, Scirea slides over the lime line drawn by Tonino Fernández, reducing it to dust. Sócrates's right-footed strike is a pool shot. A cunning bullet that slips low to the ground exactly between wood and leg. The ball goes in the hole. It is 1-1.

Zoff is sitting on the ground with his legs open, almost dazed. Scirea, lying on his stomach, looks up. In front of him is his companion of a thousand battles. It is a dialogue with the eyes. Brazil have equalised and did so with impressive simplicity. A couple of men and three touches. Sócrates raises his hands to the sky. For a moment he betrays a childlike expression. He is then submerged by the bodies of Éder, Júnior and Falcão and the Gol Sur grandstand is in awe.

Sócrates and Zico's one-two stunned the Italian defence. Those 12 strides of Sócrates sent the Italians back. Twelve years after the final in Mexico City, Italy have again bowed to the easy will of Brazil. It is the 12th minute.

The Clown

Sevilla's Benito Villamarín Stadium, one minute until Brazil vs New Zealand. The green-and-yellow national team is lined up on the edge of the pitch for the traditional photograph. Something is wrong. Seven players are standing, only four kneeling, with a symptomatic absence on the right. Usually Cerezo or Falcão pose in the top row. Sócrates turns to them: 'Is one of you thinking of coming down from there?' Not receiving an answer, he moves to the corner and leaves the space reserved for the right half-back open. A little reluctantly, Cerezo comes down and the photographers are finally able to activate the shutters of their cameras. It is a small act, emblematic

THE MATCH

of a controversial decision: to play two star players with seemingly irreconcilable styles side by side.

'I think Falcão should play in a suit and tie,' joked Éder, 'while Cerezo is dressed as a clown.' The elegant Falcão calling for the ball in a whisper. The sprung Cerezo shouting, 'To me!' in a shrill voice. 'And he doesn't ask,' Sócrates points out, 'he runs past and demands the ball.' 'They are so different, but inseparable,' Santana justifies himself before facing Italy. 'They each play in their own way to pursue a common goal.'

Cerezo is a Mineiro from Belo Horizonte. His father was a clown in a circus. This is how he got into football, by chance, playing *Futebol de Salão*. His long legs attracted the attention of an observer from Atlético Mineiro who took him to the club's trainer. It was Telê Santana. It was his good luck. The coach has always been his greatest admirer. Even in the Seleção, Antônio – known as 'Toninho' – Carlos Cerezo is his amulet, he must always be there on the pitch. His circus background and unusual resemblance to the actor Richard Pryor should not be misleading. The only thing he has in common with the clown figures is his melancholy. While he can put on a show on the pitch, he has a closed character, loves fishing and hides away with his wife and two children on the banks of a river in Mato Grosso as soon as he can. At the Mundialito he was elected best player of the tournament but, due to the heavy suspension imposed on him by FIFA on the eve of the World Cup, he lived days of anguish at the possibility of losing his starting status: 'After the match against the USSR, the team will be ready and Telê will not change it at that point. I have no doubts.'

The CBF hints at the possibility of an amnesty. 'I don't believe it,' he replies dejectedly, 'the truth is that I'm out of the first match, probably out of the World Cup.' No one can blame him, the possibility exists, and even when journalists ask what will happen if the team wins without him, Zico replies lucidly, 'It depends on how we play.' And during a simple training session in Lisbon, in his eagerness to be seen, he risks being out of the match again: an impetuous entry to

THE CLOWN

stop the Amora defender causes him a contusion on the back of his right foot. At this point he closes in on himself. He continues to fight alone. In the training camp, he only complains about not being able to fish. He does not even take advantage of the one free day before embarking for Seville. He prefers to stay in the hotel, resting his foot, with his shoe untied, to ease the pain.

'Let's go for a walk, Toninho,' Falcão invites him.

'You know I can't, I have to train,' he replies, sticking the St Anthony and St Gerard medals between his teeth.

The exchange of jokes does not escape Carlos Maranhão of *Placar*. It is he who, as Cerezo walks away, picks up Falcão's confidences: 'This man is one of the four candidates for the title of best player in the world.'

Without having heard his comrade's opinion, Cerezo is joined by Maranhão. 'Telê is coming, he sees everything. I kill myself in training, spit blood, run, free, push, attack and defend. I have an insane will to succeed, I have tremendous faith that I won't lack strength and inspiration to go a centimetre further, to stretch my leg a little more, to arrive in the best condition when the ball appears, to score one of those goals that no one will forget.' In the exercises led by Gilberto Tim he is last in line, but no one stretches his legs or arms back with more energy than him.

With Dirceu, the Brazilian national team lost the first half of the match against the Soviet Union. With Paulo Isidoro they overturned the result. With Cerezo, the expectation is one of spectacle. Cerezo, in reality, does not exhibit the refined talent of Sócrates, does not perform the staggering dribbling of Zico and does not possess the elegance of Falcão. He is the antithesis of the superstar. But paradoxically, for that very reason, he is a champion. With his dangling run he flies tirelessly around the pitch, and it is through him that the talent of others shines. His presence is therefore out of the question.

'Cerezo is very important for the team today. He is one of the best Brazilian players. He didn't play against the Soviet Union only because he was suspended,' Telê Santana cut in on the eve of the Scotland match. Without a doubt, he is the missing piece.

'What a nightmare I've been through lately,' he sighs with relief when he sees himself in the starting XI. 'All they talked about was Falcão, who has international prestige, Zico, who is from Rio, and Sócrates, who is from São Paulo. They had simply forgotten about me. I was just an injured Mineiro boy, who nobody wanted to interview.'

On the Friday of the match against Scotland, Antônio Carlos Cerezo shaves in front of the mirror. It is the ritual that for him means only one thing: today we go on stage.

The Running Man

The pre-Socratic philosopher Democritus would have considered only three concepts to justify the evolution of a football match: players, movement and vacuum. Players moving in a vacuum. Every event revolves around individual players. Provided, however, that the void between them is acknowledged. Without the void, there can be no movement. And in a football match like this, everything is reduced to a mechanical phenomenon that can only find its basis in itself. There is no need to question divine intervention, blindfolded goddesses, saints and blesseds, fate or destiny. The empty spaces on the Sarriá pitch are no less real and less decisive than the plays of Sócrates or Tardelli, because it is only thanks to them that the players are able to move. And if Gentile suffocates all of Zico's spaces, if Cabrini uses up his flank, if Antognoni chooses the free corridor, Paolo Rossi perpetually moves his gaze in obsessive search of that space. His task is in that uninhabited space. Inside that absence he must meet the ball. When the space and time of his necessity turn out to be perfectly aligned, he must present himself at the appointment. Without missing a fraction of a second. Moving swiftly into that emptiness before others can think of doing so.

For ten minutes the teams face each other relentlessly. When Italy go forward, Brazil suffer. Falcão is forced to mow down Tardelli five metres from the penalty area. Klein blows for a free kick. Antognoni's shot is deflected by Oscar, ending up in the goalkeeper's arms. Waldir Peres holds it tightly against his chest, safe. He cannot imagine what is about to happen.

Peres throws the ball out and Leandro chests the ball to Cerezo. Three Brazilians are in line, between the penalty area and centre line. Leandro, Cerezo, Éder. Behind, are two defenders, a little further ahead, Falcão. Rossi and Graziani retreat to their own half of the pitch, the others stand and watch. Cerezo raises one leg and receives the ball on the inside of his boot. He waits for the ball to touch the grass, raises his head to see his team-mates and barely twists to place the ball towards his left. 'If he had a good foot, he would score a lot of goals because he always gets to the ball and he knows how to get out of the way, but he shoots badly,' Santana admitted on the eve of the match, 'but he does a lot of other things and when he is there I am calm.'

Anyone in his place would feel calm. If Pelé's Brazil had managed to codify the game of football according to classical harmonies, Santana's men have learned those codes by heart and now know how to bend them to their liking, in a perfect tension between rule and licence, where ease of execution goes hand in hand with mannered play. *Maneira Brasileira* thus translates into inventiveness and refinement, but also into artifice and refinement. Brazil continues its dance. But dance, as we know, creates movement. On the left, the line was no longer closed by Éder, who had slipped just ahead. Cerezo's pass becomes a dramatic assist to nowhere. For the second time in the space of a few minutes, Toninho has passed into the void. The circus, the fear, the bad feet. Everything comes back. The ball rolls between Falcão, who is two metres ahead, and Júnior, five metres behind. The players watch the ball travel across the Sarriá grass, towards who knows where. A sudden silence takes over the pitch. But no amount of breathlessness can stop the ball from continuing on its inexorable path. Falcão, Júnior and Éder are rabbits in the headlights and they miss the moment. Time stands still. It expands. For all but one.

THE MATCH

The world, says the first syllogism of Ludwig Wittgenstein's *Tractatus logico-philosophicus*, is everything that happens. It is the totality of facts, not of things. A man running towards the ball is a fact. And as such, the 'running man' comes from nowhere. He is the man who has understood everything before everything can take shape. He is infinitely further back than the Brazilian line he is now about to break. Stealing the ball from a Brazilian is not just a chore, it requires imagination. Because genius, as Perozzi said in *Amici miei* – the film that Mondadori and Scalfari talked about the night *La Repubblica* was born – is imagination, intuition, decision and speed of execution.

When the ball starts from Cerezo, the 'running man' turns his back on Brazil's goal, intent on returning to his own half. But as Cerezo starts to play the ball, writhing like a dancing maenad, the 'running man' turns around and observes him. 'Every now and then they get distracted, some mistakes they always make. When it happens you have to be there.' Just as the ball is about to come off Cerezo's right boot, the 'running man' decides to stop his retreat and to turn back. He glances at the ball and follows it. In an instant, the one who escaped the Brazilians understands that that ball travelling in the void can be his. That this could be his moment. That superhuman Brazil are finally about to make a mistake and that he must be there. If time were stuck on this frame, no one would bet a lira on the 'running man'. There are three Brazilians around the ball. And Falcão would only need a couple of paces. The 'running man' is out of the game. He occupies a space of forgetfulness. But the 'running man' is Paolo Rossi and he knows it is his ball. So he runs, runs, runs. He passes the golden statues of Falcão and Luizinho, picks up the ball and raises his head. Waldir Peres sways as he stands in front of him. Júnior awkwardly rushes at the ball with his legs open. Júnior dodges it before caressing the line of the box. Waldir Peres is off the mark. Rossi unloads all the violence of his words on to the ball. The ball goes past Peres. And from 25 yards out it goes into the goal. It is 2-1. It is only the 25th minute.

The Defence with a Moustache

Peres crawls along the goal line like a fly with just one wing. In the middle of the pitch Cerezo is paralysed. Zico and Júnior look for him, find him in tears, shout at him. 'If you don't stop crying,' barks the former, 'I'll hit you. This is a game for men!' He does not realise that he is saying the same words that Obdulio Varela had addressed to Schiaffino in the fateful match in 1950. He is echoed by the second: 'Toninho, if you are afraid, have the courage to come out. Now!' Cerezo says nothing and walks with his head down towards his position. Falcão watches Rossi with a strange feeling, as if he has turned into a butterfly while he looked away. The second goal also rattles a bell in Klein's head: 'Maybe we're making World Cup history here.'

He, Zico and Serginho are for the third time on the centre spot. Brazil's assault resumes. Gentile stops Zico on the edge of the area. It is a fair fight. Zico gets up and shakes his hand. Two nights before the match against Argentina, Bearzot had knocked on Gentile's door: 'Claudio, would you feel like playing against Maradona?' Gentile did not let a second pass. 'Mister, what's the problem?' Perhaps he imagined it would be Tardelli's turn, as usual. Instead Bearzot, smiling, handed him the task: 'Well, then go and study it.' He watched the images on the video recorder and realised that he had only one way to stop him. Smother him. Maradona was itching to show his tricks but Gentile's grip cancelled him out, sending him into a rage.

Zico has been assigned to Gentile this time, but he knows that, compared to the Argentine, Zico is more inclined to play for his team-mates. He must never let him turn. If he does, he'll never get him back. He therefore plays in anticipation and tries to take him out of the Brazilians' game as much as possible, so that his team-mates have difficulty serving him and he serves them. He applies a golden rule: be heard, but not seen. Become his shadow. He follows him everywhere like a wet nurse, even in midfield. That's where Klein stops him. In return for his protests he presents him with a yellow card. This means goodbye semi-final. That is, if Italy ever get there.

Gentile grew up braving the sun in the dusty streets of Sant'Antonio in Tripoli. Every afternoon after school, emigrants against Arabs. Even though he was born in Libya, this is how the child Claudio first learned the tricks of the trade. In addition to hitting the ball, he had to watch his back. Smart opponents ready to strike with their bare hands. Or bare feet. Football matches turned into battles. Ask the dust. The only possible world. Without even knowing that in a Nordic elsewhere a young man named Pelé was being crowned king of Sweden. He has a surname that clashes with his rough manners and a nickname he detests: 'Gaddafi'. Vladimiro Caminiti gave it to him, thinking he was doing him a favour. An odious label that he has to accept. Libyan mother, Italian father. An indissoluble bond that unites him to the other side of the Mediterranean Sea.

In Libya, the only son of two poor, illiterate Bedouins always took the family camels out to pasture on his mother's property. He had brutal ways but she let him be. He was Muammar Gaddafi. In 1961, the air was changing. Mr Gentile, 'Libyan' since the age of one, realised this in time. He took eight-year-old Claudio and the rest of the family, packed his whole life into a suitcase and left Tripoli for good. That same year, while Saporta went to Brazil, Darwin Pastorin took the opposite route and arrived in Italy. The two children, both torn away from their homeland, found themselves in an Italy eager for growth. It was the same Italy where a young reporter, Italo Cucci (for whom Pastorin himself would work), first set foot in the *Guerin Sportivo*, the newspaper that was about to extol the exploits of the Milan team of Rocco, Viani and Maldini, more than half the DNA contained in Bearzot's tactical blood cells.

Mr Gaddafi was far-sighted. At the age of 27, the gruff neighbour became the youngest head of state in the world, expelled the 20,000 Italians living in Libya and mercilessly dispossessed them of all their assets.

In 1976, when Bearzot was beginning to take charge of the Nazionale, Fiat sold ten per cent of its shares to Colonel Gaddafi's

Libyan central bank in exchange for $415 million. 'We didn't need this money,' Gianni Agnelli justified himself in front of an oval table in a lounge on the eighth floor of Corso Marconi, the headquarters of the Turin company, 'but it's a good rule that capital should be found when it's not needed.' This was not true. Fiat was in desperate need of a breath of fresh air. Its chairman knew this. Perhaps Claudio Gentile did too. And out of respect for the lawyer, he kept his nickname. In spite of everything.

His team-mates prefer to call him 'Gento', after the Real Madrid winger. For Brera he is Saladin. Even his moustache, which he grew before the Mundial as a bet. At the end of the last training session in Alassio, he challenged four journalists: Luca Argenteri (*Corriere dello Sport*), Tony Damascelli (*Il Giornale*), Silvio Garioni (*Corriere della Sera*) and Franco Mentana (*La Gazzetta dello Sport*): 'You keep writing that we'll be home soon, but you'll regret it. Want to bet that we'll still finish in the top four?'

In front of the reporters' laughter, Gentile launched his provocation: 'You don't believe me? Fine, from today I'll grow a moustache. If we don't finish in the top four, I'll keep it for another four years, until the next World Cup.' It was not a joke. From that day, for the first time in his life, Claudio Gentile, followed by Oriali, started to grow a moustache. His wife Laura saw him in a RAI report: 'Claudio, cut it off, you look like a travelling salesman!' He was always confident. In January of the year before, during the symposium organised by Adidas in Nuremberg, he was asked the name of the two finalists in Madrid. 'I'm sure it will be Italy and Germany.' Laughter and disbelief. Again he looked ahead and reassured his wife: 'I'll cut it off as soon as we get to the semi-finals.' This could be the last day.

The Right Choice

'I want three!' Zoff's shouts are directed at his midfield. The free kick is for Brazil. Conti, Tardelli and Oriali form the wall. In the area, Collovati collapses to the ground under Klein's eyes. The match is

THE MATCH

stopped. Bearzot sends on Professor Vecchiet. The Azzurri stopper drags himself in tears off the pitch, behind Zoff's goal. The match resumes with Italy down to ten. Éder is over the ball. The most spectacular goals for Brazil come from his shots. Here in Spain he is one of the great revelations: he scored the winning goal against the Soviet Union, stunning goalkeeper Rinat Dasaev with one of his trademark volleys from outside the box that suddenly dropped just metres from goal. His lob against Scotland is already part of Mundial history: the whole Benito Villamarín stadium jumped to its feet as if enjoying the end of an opera. His weapon is technical mastery. He strikes with the lower part of the outer left boot. His shot starts as fast as a thunderbolt. 174kph (108mph). The ball explodes, floats in the air and catapults downwards.

This time his thunderbolt bounces off Tardelli's shin. Cerezo then sends the ball back into the box, Sócrates heads towards goal, but Zoff gathers low down on the line. A few seconds later Collovati gives up. He has sprained his left ankle. After just half an hour, Bearzot's plan has collapsed. The coach remembers the words of Hesiod: 'The right choice of moment is the most important factor.' He turns to the bench and speaks to the last man who thought he would be called upon: 'Boy, it's your turn, warm up.' The boy was not even supposed to be here. Thirty-four days earlier he was supposed to be in Barletta for his military service. Spain seemed a chimera. Then he managed to unravel the puzzle. And now Giuseppe Bergomi is about to step on the green grass of a World Cup. It's minute 34.

Lo Zio

To look older the year before, he grew a moustache, like his brother. For everyone he is 'Lo Zio', namely 'The Uncle'. The half-back Marini was responsible for such a nickname. On his first appearance in the team, after checking him out, he said: 'And you are 17? You look like my uncle!' After all, Giuseppe Bergomi had never been a boy. He could not. At the age of 16, he left for Leipzig with the junior national team while his father Giovanni was undergoing surgery. As soon as he arrived, he called home: 'Mum, how did the operation go?'

'Well. Take it easy.'

After a few hours, however, the phone rang in his room: 'Come home immediately, Beppe, daddy didn't make it!'

He suffered a lot but reacted like a man. At that point, football had to become a future in a hurry. And Bearzot, who also lost his father while football kept him away from home, two years later gave him his debut in the frame of a small existential revenge. The Leipzig match that fate had made him miss. He only knew the Azzurri shirt that one time, in a friendly against East Germany, playing the final 29 minutes, but now it is a different story.

Now 18 years and 195 days old, the youngest Azzurri player ever, he crashes into the Mundial in the most important match, against the strongest team in the world. No emotion escapes his face, not even when he receives a caress from Cabrini: 'Courage Beppe!' Having taken his position, Gentile turns: 'Go on uncle, this is the right moment.' He does not reply but his gaze is enough to reassure his team-mates.

In the stands the journalists mumbles: 'Bearzot is in big danger. That boy has too big a task for his age.' But the coach had no doubts: 'You take over Serginho.' He knows he can handle even worse situations. Bergomi glues himself to the Carioca tower. A few minutes later, the first test. The manoeuvre is Brazilian. Júnior plays in Serginho, Bergomi slips in between man and ball and the danger flashes away. That is his opening move.

The Last Fires

The last grains of time slip away. Zico, fed by Sócrates, heads into the Azzurri area. Gentile grabs him under the arm. Zico looks up and unloads his right, slips and ends up on the ground. Zoff blocks and the ball bounces into the box. Klein whistles. Zico looks at his side. There he finds the bite of a shark. The Galinho trusts in a penalty, the Azzurri in Klein. The referee in the linesman, Chan Tam-Sun, telling him to raise his flag. Offside. Zico flaunts the gash on his shirt. Klein is practical: 'You can change it if you want.' Zico continues with his bare skin showing.

If yellow is nevertheless enveloping the Brazilian's chest, it is because the colours of the national kit were not immune to the *Maracanazo*. The defeat of the 1950 World Cup, in which the Seleção played as usual in a white jersey with a blue collar, led the newspaper *Correio de Manha* to hold a competition to design a kit that would erase the blinding whiteness of the desecrated colours of the national flag: blue, yellow, green and white. More than 300 professional graphic designers took part in the competition, including Nei Damasceno, who designed the poster for the 1950 World Cup. As a joke, a 19-year-old illustrator from Jaguarão, on the border with Uruguay, Aldyr García Schlee, also sent in his sketch on a piece of paper. On it was sketched a yellow jersey, a colour that for him represented the exotic par excellence, with green cuffs and collar, blue shorts with white stripes, white socks with green and yellow piping. He did not have the same colour blue as the flag, so he chose the one he had on his hands, a cobalt. The Brazilian Fine Arts Association judged Schlee's sketch to be the most harmonious and chose it. The green shirt proposed by Damascene ranked just behind him.

Schlee's jersey, which made its debut on 14 March 1954 at the Maracanã against Chile, became the world's best-known sports kit thanks to its evocative colour. Underneath it is a faithful reproduction of Schlee's cobalt blue, exactly what he had in his hands that day. He, who created Brazil's new visual identity, is a supporter of Uruguay, the very country that provoked the need for a new shirt. On the afternoon of the fateful final, Schlee had crossed the Mauá International Bridge to go to the Cine Rio Branco, in Uruguayan territory. In the middle of the film, the lights came on and a voice solemnly proclaimed: 'Attention, we have the honour to inform you that Uruguay is the new world champion!' At that moment euphoria took over the hall and the audience stood up to sing the national anthem.

THE LAST FIRES

Italy, too, began in white but soon abandoned it. This happened during the epiphany of 1911, when they met Hungary in Milan. The reasons for the blue are many and blurred. The sea and sky of Italy, the colour of the Savoy family, the mantle of the Virgin Mary (to whom the family was devoted). It had snowed that day and the fog would have confused the light colours, so perhaps it was also the result of chance. Or a hasty choice. But blue it was, and blue it remained.

Graziani on one side, Éder on the other: they are the last fires. On a scramble following a corner kick, Oriali clears the Italian penalty area and Klein whistles for the end of the first half. Thirteen minutes each of ball possession. Brazilians devoted to attack, Italy never giving up. It's 2-1 to the Azzurri. Nobody would have bet on it, not even Klein. When he found out that the Azzurri would be Brazil's opponents, he was not at all excited: 'The Brazilians will win easily,' he told the linesmen before entering the pitch. 'No one will remember this match in three months' time.'

Half-Time

In truth, I tell you that on Tuesday we will pack our bags and go home reasonably satisfied.

Gianni Brera, *La Repubblica*

In the Grandstand

The press box is a deluge of noises and chattering. Violent and heated. For Brazil there are 610 accredited places: 164 print journalists, 220 radio-telephonists (public and private), 40 photographers, 44 assistants, 104 technicians, 7 administrators, 15 managers, 16 cameramen. Italy's army has 304 taking part in the Spanish World Cup, half the number from Rio de Janeiro. The Italians have 160 journalists, 32 photographers, 40 RAI reporters, 32 technicians, 16 administrative staff, 8 managers and 16 cameramen. Overall, the press box and the pitch-side area has 1,600, almost four journalists for every hundred spectators.

In the last quarter of the first half, Soldati leaves the stand to go for a drink. At that moment he ponders whether or not to leave the stadium. He does not feel like suffering any more. But then he remembers the commitment he has made and now he is back in 'the journalists' seats'. Giuseppe Calzuola also moves away from the edge of the pitch to approach his colleagues sitting in the press box. From there Sconcerti sees him run across the pitch with some difficulty. Calzuola is out of breath but breathing the happiness of the craftsman who has fallen in the biggest event in the world. He is already thinking about how to move after the final whistle. His problem is to get the films to Italy as soon as possible. At the end of the match, he and other colleagues will have to go to the airport – 'you can always find someone to go home' – to deliver his work into trustworthy hands. The Mundial organisation provides ready-made packages. The photographers have to write down the addressee, fill them with rolls and hand them over to the staff to be loaded.

Gianni Brera looks at the pitch at the Sarriá. He still sees the players there. The Italians who came down from Mars take him back

THE MATCH

to the Uruguayans of the 1950s and the inferiority complex that grabs 'black players by the throat when they are not called Pelé'. He rereads his notes: 'Sócrates slyly runs with a kick in the butt detachment'; 'Falcão beats the hell out of defensive recoveries'; 'Serginho blinks like a fool to see Collovati leave with tears in his eyes'. He reflects out loud with Sconcerti: 'Three of the Azzurri's top players are not playing in the best condition. So it is unthinkable that the Brazilians will let themselves be cheated as they did up to the 45th minute.' Then he goes on to write in jest. Like Bearzot's Italy, his stubby fingers find an unexpected agility as they tap on the mechanical keys of the Olivetti Lettera 32. He scans the dances of the *futebol bailado* in evocative hendecasyllables, impressing his illuminations on extra strong sheets of paper curled up in the roller. Two, to prevent the paper from tearing due to the violent impact of the metal characters.

When he has finished writing, he picks up his Montblanc and proceeds to correct it. When he looks up at his compatriots in the stands, all he sees are dark faces. Disconcerted by the scoreline, Melidoni and Grandini still have a poisoned pen. If it were to stay that way, for Italy it would be a dream, for them it would be trouble. For Alberto Cerruti, at his first Mundial as correspondent of the *Gazzetta*, it is a family affair. His sister is about to get married. Months earlier she asked him which date to choose: 'Book for the end of June. Italy can only go so far.' She set the date for 10 July. 'I'll be back home anyway.' But Cerruti is still in Spain. He knows that if Italy win he will not see his sister get married. It is a long shot. However, Cucci, his deputy Adalberto Bortolotti of the *Guerino*, and Baretti, the director of *Tuttosport*, the only two newspapers that support Bearzot, blindly believe in it.

Pier Cesare Baretti, known as Pierce, met Bearzot in the courtyard of the Filadelfia. He was a young student from a good family with a passion for sports journalism. When he arrived at the stadium in a red Spider, the Old Man looked at him with suspicion, but he soon realised that the young man really wanted to understand in depth how a team, a dressing room and tactics worked. Always fair, professional

IN THE GRANDSTAND

and loyal, he had started working thanks to Antonio Ghirelli and, by dint of delving deeper, had found himself editor of *Tuttosport*, one of the few newspapers that now keeps out of the game of massacre. Since February, he has sided with Bearzot's choices. When the entire sports press began to rise up to see Beccalossi and Pruzzo in the squad, he was one of the few to follow the coach's reasoning. He had understood that someone like Beccalossi, an unquestionable but atypical talent, could not fit into the coach's plans. He could already see the precise features of the team: the only possibility would have been to insert him as a wing-back, a role already guaranteed by Conti and, in the event, by the previous starter Causio. Alternatively, he could have been used as a finishing midfielder, a role that already belonged to Antognoni.

Some people have ended up in the Brazilian section of the press box by mistake. This is the case of Roberto Renga. Spain is his first World Cup. He is 36 years old but for *Paese Sera* he has already covered the Italian European Championships in 1980. With him are the more experienced Mimmo De Grandis, head of news, and Gianni Ranieri, 'the violinist'. Before the match against Argentina he bet against *Il Messaggero* triad Melidoni–Cascioli–Rossi and two colleagues from *Paese Sera* that Italy would win with a goal from Tardelli. 'Are you crazy?' the others had laughed at him. Before this match he stopped Falcão, asking him what precautions the team would take. 'None. We only play one way, like this.' Half-time finds him more confident than ever. 'If Rossi also scores from outside the box, anything can happen.' He is impressed by the shouting. The Azzurri on the pitch are shouting like crazy, including Zoff. He can hear them clearly from the stands. They charge among themselves to frighten the opponents.

Even the director of *Placar*, Juca Kfouri, notices this. As he stands up, he glances at his colleagues and twists his mouth. A few days earlier, at the moment of greatest euphoria, he had paused to reflect: the only thing Brazil had lacked in the previous World Cup was courage. They had not shown their game or imposed their style. And

THE MATCH

yet, coming out undefeated, they had almost won. Telê has returned the magic that Brazil had forgotten. And Kfouri wrote fearlessly: 'We may not win the World Cup, but the most important thing has been regained.' The beauty, the finesse, the magic with which the Brazilians made football a mysterious art for most of the world. 'Our spell is back, definitively restored, to pay homage to those who, first and foremost, love a green field, full of people around, a ball and 22 artists trying to win, looking for this supreme instant called a goal.' A beauty to be preserved at any cost: 'Reflect, friends, while we wait for the title to come. Is it not better to lose like this than a treacherous victory?'

Next to him, Helena saw Zico escape, before his eyes, Gentile's steely pursuit and, with incredible skill, Sócrates pierce Zoff's net by penetrating from the right, just as Santana had predicted. He is not convinced by the teams. He thinks Leandro is struggling on the right as well as Éder on the left. Credit to the Italians. Steady in their marking, they have in Scirea the impeccable sweeper to cover the holes that the individual talent of the Brazilians opens when they enter the penalty area. Brazil now have to overcome the barrier of nervousness and break the Italian wall. Helena takes advantage of half-time to move. She finds a more uncomfortable place, but closer to the field. He sits two steps away from Gata Mansa, the Seleção press officer. Between them a Spaniard who, understanding his pessimism, cheers him up: 'Brazil can't lose, man. Because if they do, everyone who loves football will have to cry.' Helena looks at him, smiles benevolently and thinks: *May God hear you, my new friend, because in here I keep thinking that injustice has already been perpetrated.*

Meanwhile, in Rome, 33-year-old Paolo Samarelli is locked in his house in Via Nizza. It is hot, the windows are open, not a fly is flying outside. The Mivar television is on. During the first half he has taken quick notes, sketches with a biro on a large pad. He is preparing the frames of the drawings that he will complete after the match, going over them with Indian ink. The *Guerin Sportivo* promised to send him a video recorder. Some time before, he had sent the weekly magazine some of his 'moviole'. As soon as he saw them, Italo Cucci rushed to call him at home: 'Come to Bologna on Sunday.' He picked him up from the station in a black Volkswagen Beetle and together they rushed to the Comunale. It was raining. After the match, they went straight to the newsroom. It was there that Cucci made his proposal: 'You score all the goals of the day and I'll pay you every Sunday.' And it was there that Samarelli began to become Samarelli. He was no longer (only) a graphic designer or the illustrator of the crime news as in *Paese Sera*. He was an artist, the man capable of fixing the moment. From grass to paper.

He can be very fast – he is used to it, all the goals on Sundays he has to do in three hours – but at the same time he is very accurate. His drawings are the closest thing to the essence of football. They capture the breaths, stop the movements, because he knows how to bring players to life like no one else. Even though they are drawn, his men are not imprisoned in a static state, they move on a wonderfully precarious balance, they are always 'about to': falling, moving, snapping, surrendering or shooting. And this makes them alive. His compositions have married a complexity that is a great lesson in harmony. The perspective cut, the solids, the voids, the spaces, the frames. Everything is composed with a perfect dosage. In addition to talent, there is another reason: Samarelli plays football. The matches and the pitches show him the real prospects. He recreates the gestures and postures of the players within himself with the experience of his own matches.

He has always enjoyed drawing movement, but football is never an easy matter for him. A stationary footballer or ball is just one category, but if it moves it becomes something else. A bad goal conceded is not really a mistake, just as a goal scored is never really a feat. His drawings collect the series of circumstances that occur and that when added together lead to what others call a technical gesture. He is obsessed with the right proportions. He knows that the Sarriá goal as seen from the pitch is enormous, that the penalty area in front of Zoff has a vastness of its own that the television view sometimes alters. For Rossi's first goal he chooses a lateral viewpoint so as to use the edge of Peres's area as the diagonal of his illustration. The studied width of the spaces allow him to depict the three crucial touches: Conti's pass, Cabrini's cross and Rossi's header. Until Peres's dive, which is stopped just moments before he hits the ground. For the double, however, he chooses to stand behind Rossi to show the curve of his shot, Júnior's awkward slide, the vast area flooding the box and the goalkeeper's vain flight over the horizon.

The drawings of the match's goals will be sent the same night by 'fuorisacco', the service dedicated to the press that has absolute priority over ordinary mail. To do so, he will have to cross the deserted city and leave them at the post office in the San Lorenzo railway station. From there, with the last possible train, they will arrive around 9am at Bologna station, where a clerk appointed by the newspaper's secretariat will be ready to collect them. At that point, that collection of moments captured by Samarelli will be imprinted forever on the pages of the *Guerino* and in the memory of Italians.

The match is about to resume. In the Azzurri dressing room it is time for the last recommendations. Bearzot speaks to the team. Without shouting. Calmness is his strength, a legacy of his education, his extraction, his tradition. He was accused of having isolated the national team, but the team needed to be protected, defended from all the interests that could infiltrate from the outside world. He and the Azzurri created an island, so they survived. Only one half separates them from glory. Bearzot knows that it will be endless: 'It will be long, but rest assured, you will make it. Now they will attack us, but we will be faster.' It is the moment to go out, to show the world who they really are.

The Backup Plan

The tireless Horst is closely following Italy's progress. He has taken note of the resounding victory of the Azzurri against Argentina and is waiting to see who will prevail between Bearzot's and Santana's teams.

THE BACKUP PLAN

There is much more at stake than a football match. Italy, like Argentina, wear his kit but Brazil move other money: that of the sponsors. If Santana's team were to lose, Brazilian industries would disappear from the scene. After the second group phase there are two matches left: semi-final and final. Brazilian companies, sure of the presence of their champions, have opted for the most ambitious spaces, as Casas Pernambucanas, Staroup jeans, Doril painkillers, Vitasay polyvitamins, River 90 cigarettes and Caloi bicycles are doing at the Sarriá. But if Italy were to go through, even though they are represented at the stadium (Zanussi appliances, Annabella furs, Irge pyjamas, Ellesse clothing and, above all, in full view, Iveco vehicles), there would be a hasty retreat, with the real possibility that, beyond the indestructible JVC, Seiko, Canon, Gillette, Winston, Coca-Cola, Sport Billy, Fuji Film and Metaxa, empty spaces could be created. A plan B is needed.

During half-time, Horst calls Gabriele Brustenghi, the lawyer of Leonardo Servadio, patron of the Perugian sports company Ellesse, his direct competitor (which, however, covers sectors not saturated by the German company, such as tennis, skiing and surfing). In the last year its turnover has grown from 75 billion to 107 billion lire. Servadio has a score to settle with both Horst and the FIGC, for more than one issue. The most serious is that relating to the kit of the Italian national team. In Argentina, the players went around with the Ellesse brand, appearing on television and in every photo with the sponsorship in exchange for which the company had granted ten million in prize money at the end of the World Cup. The tops worn by the Azzurri generated one million pieces produced and sold. A resounding success for Ellesse. It was inevitable they would attempt a repeat performance in Spain. In this World Cup there has been an auction to dress the national team. The Perugia company won it with an offer of 4 billion lire for four years. Ellesse sent the leisurewear to the FIGC in the belief that it was the only one to have competed in the tender. But the federation contracted on 28 October 1981 with the French company Le Coq Sportif – a troubled sponsorship that was only accepted by the Azzurri on 20 May – and a few days later

393

delivered to the players Ellesse's clothing with the Le Coq Sportif brand name stitched on.

Ellesse sent a telex to Sordillo in which it complained about the attitude of a federation that had excluded an Italian company in favour of a foreign one: 'We do not want reasons other than those governing tenders to be involved in the inexplicable decision of the FIGC.' On 9 June Gabriele Brustenghi flew to Vigo to represent Ellesse, a man who knows the mechanisms of the new football like the Hail Mary. He is the man who brought a provincial team, Perugia, to within a hair's breadth of the Scudetto, who brought in Paolo Rossi the following year, and who invented sponsorship on the shirts. Brustenghi was co-opted by the company in 1975. He took care of Ellesse's paperwork but Servadio had a soft spot for him and asked him for advice on 'communication'. A word that was worth at least four: marketing, advertising, promotion and external relations. Brustenghi, who played tennis, immediately succeeded in approaching Corrado Barazzutti. It was a stroke of luck because Italy won the Davis Cup in 1976 and the Italian became the first international tennis player to take to the court with a sweatband (branded Ellesse, of course) on his forehead.

Brustenghi was closed but determined. Few words but big ideas. One of them above all: 'The company must produce an image.' A year before the 1982 Mundial, using Servadio's niece, Titti D'Attoma, and Susanna Masci as leverage, the lawyer set up Ad-Link, a company to manage Ellesse's advertising operations independently, without informing Servadio. Its function was ambiguous: it was the advertising link between the company and sporting events, an executive arm of Ellesse. Faced with his complaints, Sordillo first raised his arms ('I'm sorry, I don't know anything about it'), then tried to patch things up, badly ('The auction took place but it wasn't perfect'), and finally shifted the responsibility on to others ('The affair was badly handled by some federal manager'). Brustenghi tried to see the players, but De Gaudio prevented him from doing so. A few days later, Ellesse's lawyer made fiery statements: 'Now I understand everything: it is clear that at the time there was an agreement at a later stage, and certainly not clear, with the company Le Coq Sportif.' No one wanted to give an answer. Or could not. The matter was then buried.

In any case, Servadio did not limit himself to acquiring promises from the national team, but also guaranteed access to the stadium posters. In August 1981, Ellesse made a deal with SMPI and, for $400,000, secured the exclusive supply of clothing for all the personnel involved in the Mundial. All those involved with the team and all the service staff, including the hundreds of ball boys. It also included the right to be present on the stadium billboards, although not in prime TV positions. Those spots were taken by those who had moved with impressive means and well in advance: the main sponsors, companies of the rank of Fuji, Gillette, Coca-Cola and Canon. After all, since Servadio has just opened a factory on Iberian soil, at Ellesse, which parades on the most hidden edge of the pitch, barely touched by television footage (between a door and the corner, where Irge is also located), it may be fine to be noticed by the Spanish public alone.

The unpleasant surprise received from the FIGC meant that the Spanish mission got off to an uphill start, but it has also led the Ellesse ambassadors to redouble their efforts. Almost improvising, the girls of Brustenghi's team manage to set up stands outside the stadiums and provide tops to Italian and foreign journalists. Endless queues form in front of the stands and even the best-known correspondents turn up several times with a thousand excuses ('I've lost it', 'It's been stolen from me', 'It's for my colleague') just to get another free item. For Ellesse, this is a lucky moment: the sensational discovery of the love story between Princess Caroline of Monaco and tennis player Guillermo Vilas, both close to the clothing company, has made the headlines (Vilas is the official testimonial, while the princess even appeared on the cover of *Paris Match* in 1978 wearing an Ellesse hat). In this World Cup, however, Dassler, with Ellesse, has created, unmade and reworked pacts that seemed consecrated, even on billboards.

THE MATCH

On the opening day, a Robe di Kappa banner is placed in the centre of the pitch. A breach of contract for the agreed exclusivity. Brustenghi is indignant. Servadio is arriving in Barcelona. He talks to the employees. There is nothing more to do, as the stadium is now completely in the hands of the army deployed in anticipation of the king's arrival. Brustenghi returns to the hotel furious. A gentleman of 50 appears in front of him, looking apparently insignificant. He holds a roll of paper under his left arm. The man puts out his hand: 'I am Horst Dassler.' Brustenghi is looking at the most powerful man in sporting business. But he is also guilty of serious misconduct, so he scrutinises him with detachment. 'I heard that my men did something wrong. I am here to put it right,' says Horst. He spreads the scroll out on the table. It is a map of the advertising presence in the stadium. 'At this point, it's impossible to remove the Robe di Kappa banners, but there's still time to move your banners behind the goals. Are you satisfied?' Brustenghi is tense and excited. He nods his head, but reiterates: 'The unfairness we suffered remains.' Horst, irritated, rolls up the plan and throws it into the bin. The lawyer, aware that he has gone too far, tries to speak, but Dassler has already disappeared from his sight without a word.

Brustenghi sits in the lobby for three hours without watching the match. Then a phone call comes from the reception desk. It is Enzo Gentili, the factotum of Ellesse: 'Gabriele, you don't understand, the Robe di Kappa posters are gone and ours were behind the doors!' Dassler has made the restorative gesture. He has been loyal. Tears of gratitude flow down Brustenghi's face at the news.

Now Horst, seeing how Italy are going, senses Servadio's desire to gain further visibility. So he thinks to offer him the possibility to put his brand in evidence on the sidelines by emphasising it with TV zoom shots. 'If Italy goes to the final, how much money can you spend to get close-ups?' Brustenghi replies: 'I have $300,000.' Dassler takes his time to see the outcome of the match: 'Let me think about it.'

Second Half

I stared at the crowd, at my team-mates, and felt a deep bitterness inside. Now you have to freeze time, now, I told myself. I would never experience a moment like that again. Never again in my whole life. And I felt it slipping away. It was already over …

Paolo Rossi

The Second Act

The second half begins without any further changes. Bearzot and Santana still rely on their starting XIs (apart from Bergomi). These are the teams and they must not be touched; what has to happen happens. The curtain opens. Klein blows his whistle, Rossi passes to Antognoni. The second act of Italy vs Brazil begins.

The Seleção immediately appear rougher. Disquiet also engulfs the defence. Luizinho repeatedly tries to escape, leaves his area and goes looking for luck 30 metres further on, to participate in the attacking moves. But the man-to-man defence written by Bearzot and directed by Zoff immediately begins to work again, relentlessly inhibiting the Brazilian attackers' moves. The sense of possession still sets Luizinho's soul on fire. The ball is his again and, if he loses it, he gets it back. He chooses Éder, from whom he has stolen his role and position, and uses him as a wall. He calls for a one-two but Cabrini spoils his plans, sweeping away the ball and his ambitions in one fell swoop. A few passes later Falcão imitates him. It is now his turn to draw a triangle, which he does with Júnior. On the return pass the Azzurri's attention is elsewhere. Gentile and Bergomi are following their men – Zico and Serginho – on the other side of the area. The action is textbook, simple but effective. Twinned with the one that led to Sócrates' goal, there is also the same run made by Scirea, only with Júnior as Zico and Falcão playing the Doctor. But Zoff does want to see the same film twice and immediately dives to his right.

There is a bad rhythm in the samba of this Brazil. They have taken the field to look for an equaliser in every action. There is no time to rest, only for the big manoeuvres. Like the one that starts from Júnior, by now an added midfielder, directed at Serginho. Bergomi clears it. There's a throw-in and Brazil pick up where they left off. Magic is like dreams, it has to come true to make sense. The ball comes back to Júnior, who turns it again to Serginho, but there is nothing to be done; the move always breaks down at that point. Bergomi is there again and he anticipated the Brazilian by stepping forward with a confident stride and his manly moustache.

The music changes, the South Americans' phrasing becomes more elemental, stripped of its elegance. Júnior's shot ends weakly in a goal kick and Éder's ill intentions remain nailed on the edge of the penalty area, between Oriali's feet: there is no way through. The counter-attack begins. Conti crossed the boundless Sarriá prairies, leaving a diagonal trail on the ground. Along the way, epic signs sing the praises of Iveco, Gillette, Canon, Coca-Cola, Fuji Film, Seiko and Sport Billy. Having reached the Brazilian half, this time it is he who wants the triangle. He does so with Antognoni, who looks up and mocks two defenders with a lob, to leave his team-mate with the ball inside the penalty area. Conti sees the goalkeeper away from his the post and uses the outside of his left boot but Waldir Peres watches the ball slide wide.

The Last Souvenir

If eight Brazilian touches are enough to bring Sócrates into Zoff's kingdom, Italy need fewer to make the opposite journey and with just three touches find themselves on the opposite bank. Cabrini stops the Doctor on the goal line, passes to the midfield for Antognoni, who offers Rossi the chance of the promised land. Pablito gets off the boat and enters the area. The shore is only a few metres away, the waves are against him and Luizinho is in front of him. He unbalances him on the left to slip past him on the right. He hears Peres's breathing and begins to follow in his wake. The blue shadow points straight at the goalkeeper. He glimpses it over Luizinho's shoulder. He is there, at his post, his legs bent and arms outstretched. His shadow is already inside the goal. Luizinho, on the other hand, takes hold of Rossi's shadow. Striker and defender stick together. The same gestures, the same movements, the same millimetric pace. Until Luizinho, with the same shoulder that Rossi is using as a viewfinder, throws him into the water. Pablito drowns in the area in front of the dull eyes of Peres. Man overboard. Mars and Saturn, embedded menacingly in Libra, watch impassively. Klein follows them and decides not to stop the ship. The Azzurri cash in and move on, without much fuss. The show must go on.

Éder, Paulo Isidoro and Cerezo were his idols. Now they are his companions. Luiz Carlos Ferreira, known as Luizinho, would never have imagined this. Football is his life. And it saved him. For him, born in Nova Lima, Minas Gerais, the almost certain destination was the mine. He listened to the matches being told, the news came from the radio. There were few television sets but that was okay, his was a warm family. His father had instilled in him solid values. And he lived in a friendly town. Harmony provided quiet lives and one of the lowest crime rates in Brazil. It was the mines of Morro Velho that had the right of life and death over the locals. They could offer the Mineiro inhabitants work but at a cost. When Luizinho was eight years old, a trainload of gold ran over his grandfather, who lost a leg, and his uncles fell ill with silicosis from the dust. His family's best friends died.

His parents wanted to save him and at the age of 15 enrolled him in a mechanical assembly course. Luizinho went in the evenings. The days were for football. From the age of 12 he played in the amateur Vila Nova city championships in Morro Velho, his parents' neighbourhood. One day Baiano, the warder of Vila Nova, brought him into the youth team as a centre-forward. During a match, the full-back was injured and two team-mates were sent off. The coach Nelsinho, who had played for Cruzeiro, Vila and Bangu, turned to the bench: 'Who feels like playing full-back?' Nobody made a sound. Luizinho seized the moment and raised his hand: 'I'll take care of that back there.' And there he stayed.

In 1977 came the leap. It was a magical year: he met the woman of his life, turned professional and played in the Brasileirão. A year later, Procópio Cardosolo took him to Atlético. There they played already established players such as Cerezo, Paulo Isidoro, João Leite and Reinaldo. The team lost the championship, but were undefeated. He did not have a car, he did not earn much money. He got on the bus in Nova Lima at five in the morning, arrived in Belo Horizonte, got off at Guarani Street, took another bus and finally arrived at Atlético's Vila Olímpica. At six in the evening, when he could not catch the bus, he would ask the older players for a ride to the centre. Then he would take the bus to Nova Lima and at nine o'clock in the evening he would arrive home, where his plate was already waiting for him next to the wood-burning stove. He had time to eat it and then go to sleep before the alarm clock went off at five. All this, every day, for two years. As soon as he earned some money he thought about a car. Procópio prevented him from doing so: 'You won't get a car if you haven't bought a house for your mother first.'

Luizinho did not object: 'That's what I want too, but you have to find me a place to sleep here in Belo Horizonte.' So he lived for a while at the Hotel Bragança. Later, he managed to buy a Chavetinho (a Chevrolet Chevette), life improved and he was able to get married to Marcia, who was born a stone's throw from his home. Wife and oxen. The golden moment expanded. In 1980 he won the *Bola de Prata* as the best Brazilian full-back. He hoped to be called up for the youth national team but Santana had noticed him and called him up for the senior squad. When he read his name on the list he could not believe it. Him, very young, alongside Zico, Júnior and Sócrates. 'My God, and now?' Many fans had never seen him play: 'Who is this Luizinho?'

In the next two years he proved himself. Now he is playing his first World Cup at the age of 24. His father, unfortunately, did not get to see him on the pitch but he is also bringing something of him to the Sarriá grass. The values of his parent have remained in him and have helped him a lot. Even if he has to fight with the dark side of his game. Hand and leg fouls are part of his repertoire. Before grounding Rossi, twice in this World Cup he was pardoned in the penalty box.

In the match against the Soviet Union he had first grabbed on to Shengelia, later he hit the ball with his hand. In both cases Lima pretended not to see. For Pelé, however, it left an indelible memory. They were facing each other in one of O Rey's farewell matches. Luizinho slipped in to anticipate him, hitting his leg. Four stitches. The last souvenir of playing football.

No Truce

In the eighth minute of the second half he calmly delivers the ball to Serginho, who is held back by Bergomi. Klein sees the foul. The Italian extends a hand and lifts the colossus. The two exchange a caress. They smile. Their respective moods are not so far apart. They probably have the impression, right or wrong, of feeling a step outside their respective empyrean. Serginho surrounded by demigods of whom, according to many, he does not even possess a piece of cloth; Bergomi on his true debut, a child to whom, during the Pontevedra days, Bearzot had told him to watch and learn. 'That's what I'm going to do,' he had announced in Vigo, 'with the hope that my team-mates who go out on the pitch will teach me how to win a Mundial.' The journalists laughed. But now Italy are here and he is on the pitch playing for them.

Brazil see red and strike relentlessly. It is Zico's turn to take a free kick: a lifted right-footer, the wall is beaten, the direction is good but the trajectory too high. Then Leandro teases the goalkeeper, unloading a grenade from over 30 yards, but the Azzurri captain is there. Éder intercepts a pass from Antognoni to Oriali, then swiftly passes to Zico, who raises his head and sees a clear and long avenue ahead, leading to the edge of the penalty area. Cerezo receives the ball, with only the goal in front of him. And Zoff, of course. The Brazilian is about to climb over the fence but the captain comes out of his kennel like a beast, runs across the garden and rushes at him, snatching the ball from his feet. The ball rolls to safety. The Italian fans chant fearlessly: 'Come on guys!' Brazil are insistent, until Oriali,

THE MATCH

tired of listening to nothing but samba, lifts the needle, intercepts a ball from Júnior and puts Italy back into gear: Conti for Cabrini for Antognoni for Rossi, who sees Graziani in the area in the same spot he had been in the fifth minute. He copies Cabrini's cross that gave them the 1-0 lead and waits. Luizinho has déjà-vu but this time his forehead anticipates that of the Azzurro.

It was the dawn of a crazy minute. The Brazilian onslaught culminates in a cross from Júnior. It arrows from the left across the entire Azzurri area to find Serginho. Zoff realises, goes forward and punches it away. The ball ends up at Éder's feet, then back to Júnior, who stops, while one eye catches sight of a team-mate in the area. It is Cerezo, who knocks the ball over Serginho, who is being hunted by Bergomi. The ball bounces on the ground and Serginho, the least Brazilian of Brazilians, attempts the redemption of a lifetime: with his back to goal, he lifts his left leg and looks for the backheel. He finds it but along with the oaky body of captain Zoff. On the counter-attack Graziani, from the left, with a feint eats up Luizinho and Falcão. Oscar rushes into the area to cover. The cross goes to Rossi. Oscar feels the ball rolling behind him, tries to hook it with his backheel but misses. Peres sees the copy of the first goal, only this time Pablito has the ball at his feet. He hits it on the volley, right-footed. The goalkeeper scrambles at the post. The ball takes a different route and goes out for a goal kick. By grace received.

Brazil are unprepared for the Azzurri attack and the disadvantage has made Santana's form falter. Bearzot has studied it well. Oriali on the right and Cabrini on the left follow his dictates to the letter: 'If you linger on the outside, the mesh of their defence will widen.' In this way Rossi can have a free pitch. The defenders are, in fact, in trouble: on the one hand, Leandro and Oscar suffer the attacks of Cabrini, Tardelli and Antognoni (but also of Rossi and Graziani); on the opposite side, Luizinho and Júnior, disoriented by Conti and Oriali, are often badly positioned and caught by surprise. Thus Rossi and Graziani find themselves on the receiving end unmarked.

The Azzurri goalkeeper parries a free kick from Éder. Choral manoeuvres are stemmed in the Azzurri and Brazilian areas. Antognoni's free kick is grazed by Graziani but the ball goes wide. From a triangle with Júnior, Cerezo, on the volley, sends the ball into the side-netting. Éder surges towards the area but Oriali cuts him off. A foul. A free kick from 30 yards out. The Brazilians are phenomenal from set pieces and Zoff knows it. On the left are Éder and Júnior on the ball. The Italian wall is getting into position. Zoff shouts like a madman: 'Antonio! Antonioooo! Get in the middle!' Júnior shoots. From the dimpled bench, the trainer Alessandro Selvi, with his pipe clenched in his teeth, the masseur Luciano De Maria, the secretary Guido Vantaggiato, the coach Enzo Bearzot, the technical assistant Cesare Maldini, the doctor Leonardo Vecchiet and the masseur Giovanni Della Casa follow the trajectory, petrified. The ball smashes into the wall. The fans are shouting: 'I-ta-lia! I-ta-lia!' Paulo Isidoro warms up. Serginho sees the bench, tries three times to make his mark, but first Gentile's header, then Bergomi twice, take the ball out of his thoughts. So far he, Zico, Cerezo, Júnior and even Leandro have tried in every way. The one who has hardly touched the ball is Falcão.

The Scream of Judas

Betrayal only exists in the prison of a relationship. It is not the enemies who betray but the custodians of our trust. Falcão is the man who cannot betray Italy. When he set foot there with his mother, he was greeted by 5,000 hugs. He thought he would find managers and formalities but he was welcomed with a warmth that made him feel at home. He will not be the one to break the Azzurri's dreams. He will play the game of his life, yes, without taking it away from anyone, however.

When, under enormous expectation, the Telê era began, he was there. But four months later, his departure for Rome was fatal. Two years later, Telê, keeping faith with his pact (to also observe players abroad), remembered him. And when the squad was announced, Paulo Roberto Falcão's name appeared next to the No.15. Looking for lost time, in order to have him in the early stages of preparation, Santana asked the CBF directors to obtain an early transfer from the Roman club, two weeks before the end of the Italian championship. President Giulite Coutinho, in order to satisfy the coach and obtain the release, was forced to take out a $2 million insurance policy in the event of injury.

The unexpected choice aroused the jealousy of his colleagues. Starting midfielders such as Batista, Cerezo, Zico and even Sócrates. Each of them tried to mark their territory. The one most worried about losing his place, Cerezo, was protected by his team-mates. 'I don't think Falcão, after so long away from Brazilian pitches, will be able to fit into the team,' Sócrates hastened to let it be known before the player's arrival. Galinho also expressed his perplexity: 'Falcão will arrive in a team that has already been formed for a long time and will certainly find it difficult to adapt, because in Europe he is playing a very different football to ours.' Batista chose a more diplomatic route: 'What I do, Cerezo and Falcão don't do. What they do, I don't do. Ours are completely different styles and will be used as needed.'

The midfielder, a regular starter at the 1978 World Cup, was even sponsored by Pelé: 'I don't deny Falcão's great talent and the fact that he deserves all the fame he has. But playing with the attacking flanks, Batista is the ideal player to exercise the function of area leader, covering Júnior and Leandro and giving tranquillity to Oscar and Luizinho.' As usual, faced with the noises of the henhouse, Santana did not hide: 'Batista is good at marking, but lacks fluidity when attacking, Falcão is a player who can go forward, Cerezo is more complete, because he knows how to defend and attack perfectly, giving more mobility than Falcão to the team.'

Falcão kept his opinions to himself. He could not debate with his team-mates, as he was the latest arrival. 'I don't think they will sabotage me. Almost the whole group has played with me and I'm sure they will help me.' In fact, the reception he received from his colleagues was not so warm. He was treated with respect but also with detachment. For some he was still an intruder. After all, he had not participated in either the friendly matches or the daily training sessions of the last two years. An *estrangeiro*, as Brazilians call those who play abroad. Santana made him a starter for the first time in May. Against Switzerland and the Republic of Ireland, ahead of his debut against the Soviet Union. Falcão managed to fit into the team in just a few days without any rejection crisis. He scored two goals, against Scotland and New Zealand, and became Brazil's star player. Above all, he is the first 'foreigner' to find a permanent place in the history of the Seleção.

His expectation to play in Spain was enormous. He wanted to feel the taste of a world game. His debut reminded him of Jofre Funchal, his first coach. He was just a frail child with no future. He was studying at the São José College in Canoas, forced by Pedrinho Figueiro, his gym teacher, to undergo long training sessions before he could touch the ball. He hated gymnastics but Jofre not only gave him the ball, but also lessons, supplements and tickets for the return journey. He trained in the old Nacional stadium, in José de Alencar. He had to take two buses to get there. He sold empty bottles to pay for the trip but sometimes he did not earn any money and in those cases old Jofre took care of it. On the day of the trial for the new players, his parents gave him boots but one of the boys took them from him. Jofre bought him boots so he would not go barefoot. It was to him that Falcão dedicated the victory against Scotland. He was so confident that he did it before the match. The shirt, as always, he kept for his mother. During the last training session in Madeira a little boy asked him for the shorts from the match against New Zealand. 'I'm sorry, I've already promised them to my grandmother Angelina.' She, who already owned the ones worn in 1976, 1978 and 1979, was the daughter of Italians. And from her Paulo heard the first words of this language.

He knew both the Argentines and the Italians well but, when the second-round group combinations came out, it was the South

THE MATCH

Americans who worried him: the same players as in 1978, with Maradona added. Against Italy he knew he had to escape the tight marking. Up to the last obstacle: Scirea, the libero who locked up the Azzurri defence for good. It was the role he feared the most, but also the one that fascinated him the most. Before ending his career he wanted to occupy that position.

Telê Santana is watching him run like a gazelle. He is watching his stride, the way he moves around the pitch. Even when he is under the most physical stress, his heart does not beat more than 35 times per minute. The rate of a person at rest is over 60 beats. In the hours immediately before the match, half the team experienced a noticeable increase in their heart rate, but his showed no change, a sign of perfect self-control and an incredible ability to govern any state of anxiety.

The coach is reminded of the great Ademir, the 1950s star player who in turn inherited the talent of Leonidas. Brazilian genes that are passed on over time. *Placar* dares to call him 'the greatest player in the world'. He is living the 68th minute of his fourth Mundial match and 43 minutes have passed since Paolo Rossi left Peres lying down to contemplate, astonished, the second ball to enter his goal. Falcão was at his side.

Brazil continue to press. Cabrini marks Sócrates, who moves into the centre. Once again the right-hand channel is left unguarded. Júnior opens up the pitch. Falcão receives the invitation. His feet swim in his hand-sewn boots. His eyes run into the area, then begin to rummage around the flank. On his inside-right comes the cover of Tardelli. Cerezo, desperate for redemption, rushes forward to throw him off balance. He succeeds. His feint fools Tardelli and Cabrini. But also Scirea. A gap has opened up. Falcão glimpses Zoff. A Bernini-like colonnade is erected in the area. On one side Sócrates, Scirea, Cabrini and Tardelli, on the other Serginho, Gentile and Zico. Bergomi remains anchored on the penalty spot. The shot is fired. Powerful, left-footed. Zoff follows the ball through a forest of bodies, unbalanced to the left. He dives. The ball splashes towards the man left in the middle. Bergomi instinctively just touches it. It is a sigh in a storm, but it changes the course of history and the destiny of a goalkeeper.

At half-time the captain had promised that not another ball would get between his posts. Instead it is a goal and it is 2-2. Zoff is furious: 'Beppe, did you touch it?' Instead, the Brazilian's heart leaps like that of a crazed feline. Falcão cries out. For the Italians it is the cry of Judas. He opens his mouth wide, clenches his fists and flies towards the bench and a World Cup semi-final.

João Batista Scalco takes his photo at that moment. They call him the 'Van Gogh of the Pampas' for the excellence of his professional performance. In November 1978 he witnessed and played a leading role in one of the most notorious cases of human rights violations during the military period: the kidnapping of the Uruguayan couple Lilián Celiberti and Universindo Diaz. The following year he received the Esso Journalism Award, the recognition that publicly established him as one of the country's greatest photojournalists. In this World Cup he is not feeling well. He is only 31 years old but he is often tired. He repeatedly brings his hands to his chest. He thinks it is the heat. And it is precisely the heat of an electric shock that is imprisoned in his photo of Falcão. His arms stretched out like two light poles. Veins running from his neck to his wrists like electric wires. The closed fists. His mouth wide open. Brazil is there. And Falcão, in this instant, is its prophet. Conti watches him move into another embrace. And he thinks: 'Perhaps it is fair.'

Tiziu's Moment

His head tells him: 'Take the centre-forward out, put Isidoro in and win this match!' If Brazil play, they have to make people dream. And a draw does not bring dreams. Santana wants the cherry. The words of João Saldanha, when Serginho was substituted against New Zealand, ring in his ears: 'Now the ball is round again.' An authoritative attack, but perhaps unfair. Although crushed by the

THE MATCH

weight of celebrity, the striker has interpreted his role with dignity. If at times he appears clumsy, it is only because he is off his game. Santana has given him a subtle and thankless task: 'He becomes indispensable and invisible at the same time.'

Paulo Isidoro, standing at the edge of the pitch, is staring at the Sarriá grass. They call him Tiziu, after the Brazilian bird. Small build, great speed. Taciturn, like all minnows, he speaks with his eyes. Two black orbits suspended in a globe of milk. Until a few weeks ago they seemed to carry only one certainty: he was in great shape, fresh from a golden year, the best of his life. Santana's call-up was just a formality: 'I've been called up because I deserve it. I'm the Ballon d'Or, the best player in the league. My place can only be here.'

Isidoro was also watching the meadow that morning in 1972. He was 19 years old, the age at which his destiny was fulfilled. A few days before they had noticed him playing among the amateurs of the Ideal Bairro das Graças. Carlos César Pinguim, their president, had given him the opportunity: 'This is your chance, Paulo. There's a recruiter from Atlético out there, his name is Irineu. Show him what you can do.' When the match was over, Irineu approached him: 'Would you like to try out for us?' He summoned him to Lourdes, where Atlético had a training ground. Paulo played every Sunday on dirt pitches. He felt at home in that dust. He had never seen a real football pitch. He listened to the matches on the radio and the one time he went to the stadium he was scared.

The land had always been his home. As a child, when the cattle were grazing, he used to push away the dung with his brothers so he could play barefoot football inside the fence. From the stables to the amateurs of Cruzeirinho de Matozinhos. Until his father, a construction foreman who had settled in Matozinho to build a sugar factory, along with his wife and eight children, decided to move to Belo Horizonte. Paulo stopped studying at the age of 11. It was 1964, the year of the coup. The same year that his peer Sócrates saw his father set fire to subversive books. In that same year the Mineirão stadium was inaugurated. His family could not afford the ticket price but one day his sister offered to pay for him. He refused. 'You have to go, Paulo. You love playing football and you have to see it to know what it's like.' He went with her. It was a traumatic experience. The crowd terrified him and the fright prevented him from seeing the match.

That morning he did not have the right boots. On the way there he thought, *It's Atlético, there's bound to be a beautiful field of grass.* When he arrived he found only dirt. 'Just imagine, it's like ours.' He looked at his boots: 'These are good for today.' He entered the pitch and he played serenely, calmly, even happily. He wasn't afraid to make mistakes. The ground made him feel at home. After only 20 minutes he heard a voice: 'That's enough, boy. You can come off!' He felt humiliated. But that time was enough to convince the Atlético management: 'Tomorrow morning you come back here. And ask the warehouseman to find you some boots.'

Things didn't change when he found himself on the other side. Atlético sent him to Nacional to build him up. Every time he entered the Vivaldo Lima stadium in Manaus, the screaming crowd made his legs shake. Only with time did he manage to control his emotion, but it was not easy. In 1975 Atlético took him back for good and the coach started to play him. It was Telê Santana. Isidoro told himself it was done: 'I will give everything I can. God will help me for sure. And only he can stop me.' He started to think big. The national team, the Ballon d'Or. He wanted to win them at all costs. And he succeeded. In the national team he found the coach who had discovered him and became the star of the Seleção. The dream of dreams for any Brazilian. He arrived in Spain at the peak of his form. No obstacle could stand between him and his dream. Only God could stop him. And his God in Spain was called Santana.

The war for his jersey involved everyone. He fought it with cunning, in silence, without ever getting nervous, demonstrating on the pitch what he knew how to do. He stroked the medal of St Jude around his neck, displaying a coolness that baffled his rivals. But Telê's eyes moved faster than the ball. And at dawn, in the Parador

THE MATCH

Carmona, they came across a player who was talking in his sleep. When Telê made the call-up, amazement stole his words: 'I'm going to put in a false forward, let's say, a non-pointer, who can give freedom to the flankers.' Isidore did not understand. Then Telê approached him: 'Paulo, you have the technical and physical attributes to do what I want.' Isidoro's head was bobbing, as if to say: I'm ready. 'When the others have the ball, you will have to go back and help close in the centre.' Isidoro blinked and smiled. 'Is that what I have to do? Count me in.' The pattern worked like a charm for the whole season until the eve of the Mundial.

Leaving the pitch after the last training session, he had economised on words in front of the journalists: 'Mundialito, European tours, eliminations, friendlies: are these enough credentials?' Santana had sent him out on the pitch all the time. The role was his. The World Cup stage was preparing to welcome him. His wife Silvana had shown him an album before he embarked for Europe: 'Don't worry, my love, I'll put your champion photos in here with the No. 7 shirt.' But when Isidoro was about to enter the scene, Telê changed his cards. In the first match he did not put him in the starting line-up. Tiziu thought that Cerezo's absence implied an emergency plan but that match was fatal for him. A correspondent asked him why he had not requested an explanation: 'When Telê told me to follow his scheme, I didn't ask him why. Now that he has removed me, should I ask him? He has the right to make his own choices. He is the coach.' He was sure he would play in the next match. Instead, he was just a backup. One half against the Soviet Union, ten minutes against Scotland and a quarter of an hour against New Zealand. Always picking up the crumbs left by Serginho. His extraordinary pace, scoring ability and covering skills were no longer enough.

He still cannot explain why his coach has relegated him to the bench. He was the starter. The greatest of all Brazil. But hope has never abandoned him. The hope that keeps him going was transmitted to him by his father. He did not want his son to think he was poor: 'Remember Paulo, if we want to, we can achieve anything!' And so now. 'Am I a reserve? Next time I'll be a starter.' So far that has not happened. Against Argentina, he didn't even take to the pitch. Even though he was consumed with grief, he was certain to play against Italy. Tomorrow is always another day. And now the edge of the pitch keeps up the flame of his hope. 'My time will come. As long as I play as I know how to do in these 20 minutes. They are my pass to a place in the semi-finals and, who knows, maybe even the final.'

Luizinho brings his disappointed gaze towards Telê Santana. He would now like a defender instead of a striker, to protect the result. 'We have already drawn twice. There's no way we can win this game. Let's limit ourselves to defending, let's end it here, let's move on and win this World Cup.'

The Brazilian buoy, as he makes way for Isidoro, treads the Sarriá grass with his head held high. He leaves the field as a World Cup semi-finalist, just 21 minutes away from glory. He does not think in the least that these could be his last steps in the national team jersey.

Three to Two

Time does not exist in itself. It is the actions that create the sense of what runs through its minutes. Klein's stopwatch mercilessly gobbles up Italian hopes. And the Italian game has no choice but to present a crowd of simultaneous and extremely rapid ideas on the pitch.

A draw is not enough for either team. The Italians must win. The Brazilians want to win. But every single end can become a new beginning. Like when Cerezo races in with his head to meet a ball lofted by Antognoni. His clumsy intent catches Waldir Peres by surprise as he chases the ball to prevent a corner. He knocks the ball with his left hand like a pelota player, but Thomson Chan Tam-Sun, the linesman from Hong Kong, gives meaning to his presence at the Mundial by signalling that the ball is out of play. By an inch, but it is out. Peres pretends not to notice and returns to the goal with the ball in his arms, ready to put it back into play. Rossi comes up to him: 'Give me that ball.' Peres jokes, spinning around, juggling.

413

THE MATCH

These are the last flashes of the match. Brazil are drawing and therefore among the top four teams in the world in the 1982 championship. Even the last soldier in this invincible army is beginning to feel the thrill of the semi-final. Rossi insists: 'Do you want to give me that ball?' The goalkeeper hesitates, then his expression changes. When he sees Klein pointing to the corner flag, Waldir Peres, 31, the extreme defender of the Brazil of the Gods, makes a gesture that may never be seen again on a football pitch: he does not throw the ball to the other side, he does not leave it on the spot, he does not kick it out, he does not throw it away, he does not push it away. He does not let the attacker pick it up. He simply hands it to his opponent. He delivers the ball into Rossi's hands. It is the strongest image of the match. It is the condemned man handing the weapon to his executioner. As if to say, 'If anything happens, I want you to take care of it.'

So it is a corner, the first one Italy have won in the match. Rossi throws the ball to Conti. His team-mate catches it on the volley and heads to the corner flag on the left of Peres's goal. The Brazil area fills with life. The players are moving like ants. Tardelli watches from the sidelines. He looks for openings between the defenders but everywhere the roads are barred. All of Brazil's players are back in the penalty area. No one has ever seen them all defend the fort, gathered like ten in a handkerchief. Waldir Peres is in the centre of his goal, glued to the line. He sways, bent forwards with his hands resting on his knees. He turns his head towards Conti with his mouth half open. He almost seems to be smiling. But these are no longer his divinatory certainties. The sun is slapping him. It is the gift that Zoff decided for this moment when he won the coin toss before the match.

Conti watches the ball. He casts a glance at the crowd milling about in front of Peres. And he strikes. The ball lands high on the edge of the area. They jump up together, back to back, Sócrates and Paulo Isidoro hitting it with their heads. The ball flies up into the sky in a slow, inexorable steeple and then plunges into the midst of seven Brazilians and a couple of Azzurri. One of these is Tardelli, who turns on himself to power his left-footer. Luizinho and Oscar come at him like furious wings. To no avail. Tardelli's shot goes through them, tearing the whole Brazilian area apart. Peres looks at it. In front of him stands Graziani on the left and Rossi on the right, like sentries. Both have their backs to him. Rossi keeps his feet on the line of the goal area. Graziani a metre further on. It is the detail that changes events. Tardelli's shot was destined to slip between the two Italians and towards the goal, straight into the arms of Peres, but Graziani, in an imitation of Tardelli's gesture, began to swivel to volley the ball with his left. Rossi thought the same when he placed his left foot on the ground to unleash his right.

The image, from Peres's eyes, is this: two perfectly symmetrical Azzurri are about to hit the ball. One with his right, the other with his left. If Graziani touches it, the ball goes to his right, if Rossi touches it, it goes to his left. The choice is trapped in the metre that separates the two Azzurri. Peres is aiming at Graziani: he will hit the ball first because he is the first one who could intercept it. And so it seems for an instant. As he sees the two feet about to strike the ball, the goalkeeper takes a half-step to his right. He cannot know. He has no time to understand. Graziani misses the moment, by a whisker. And the ball goes to him again. Rossi. The ball slips through his wire. And Waldir Peres feels it on his face.

The Sorrows of Young Peres

Darkness. Peres emerges from an immense black eyelid. A failure has just occurred in his heartbeat. He seems to come out of a long absence. From a lost innocence. He has always felt the need to give his existence meaning. From the moment he found it, he felt reassured. Waldir Peres immediately plunged into the tremendous sea of his absolute beliefs. He became Christian, theocratic, millenarian and restorationist. As a Jehovah's Witness (a tradition among Brazilian goalkeepers: his predecessor João Leite, during the Mundialito, used to give a Bible to his opponent before every match, writing on it 'Jesus loves you') he swam desperately in faith, knowing that on the other side his god would be there waiting for him. Stroke after stroke he paraded on his way, proud and sure of his own sacred belief, but now that he has emerged from the holy waters to find himself standing on the white line of a lawn, he begins to lose all his certainties and starts to flounder.

Someone asked him who he looked like. 'Nobody,' he replied dryly, 'because ever since I was a child I was so good that I only wanted to look like myself.' He seems to try to hide with excesses of confidence. There are few players in Brazil who can boast of having played more than 500 matches for the same club. Waldir Peres Arruda is one of them, having always played for São Paulo.

They call him cold because he neither exalts himself nor beats himself up. In reality, his is a mask. Brazil has long since ceased to be the land of great goalkeepers and he knows it well. He envies his European counterparts because they have enjoyed a school that he has not been able to attend. Where his hands cannot reach, however, faith can. The night before Brazil's match against the Soviet Union, Waldir Peres Arruda dreamed that the ball was bouncing on a horn that had sprouted on his left forearm. On entering the Ramón Sánchez Pizjuán stadium in Seville he was still wondering what the vision meant. The answer came in the 34th minute when a harmless ball kicked by Andrey Bal hit his forearm before going into the goal, giving him a nightmarish hour until the goals from Sócrates and Éder. When Waldir was alone in the Sevilla stadium, overwhelmed by the pain of the most despicable duck seen at a World Cup, the penalties he had saved, the goals he had not conceded, the spectacular interventions that had made him part of the team, suddenly became a thing of the past.

Frango. A chicken, as the Brazilians call ducks. From the next day Waldir is 'O fragueiro'. He blamed the Tango ball, which he said was too small: 'It skidded before reaching me, it changed trajectory.' He blamed the Seleção attack: 'I hadn't taken part in the game yet, until then I had only shouted, given suggestions to my players. If I had been active, like Dassaev, that ball wouldn't have gone in.' But he then admitted: 'I think I was tense, a bit out of control, and on the one-goal shot I failed.' He vowed it would never happen again: 'Maybe it was the best thing that happened in my whole career, because I made a mistake at a time when I shouldn't and now I feel the weight of that mistake.' Since then he has often chosen the rebuttal to avoid any kind of problem.

When the public began to lack confidence in him, his reserve, Paulo Sérgio, in theory the great beneficiary of the misunderstanding, was very supportive. After consoling his team-mate in the dressing room, he told the besieging journalists: 'Yes, I want to play. But I can't assure you that, in Waldir's place, I wouldn't have made the same mess.' For this and other reasons, Waldir remains, even against the wishes of some. The excluded Leão, meanwhile, gloats.

True, Waldir's mouth curves at the corners, upwards, and he always looks as if he is about to smile. But that mouth says little about him. It is the eyes that you have to look at. He has the look of someone who is afraid that something terrible is going to happen. He has a decent build and a tanned face, but he has been losing his hair for a few years now, which makes him look tremendously older than the others, as well as giving him a decidedly earthy aura. He is not regarded as a deity, like Sócrates, Falcão and Zico, but rather, together with his opposite team-mate, centre-forward Serginho, he is seen as the weak point in the Brazilian constellation. In reality, he has always performed well in the Brazilian championship, has won the Paulista four times and therefore does not deserve mistrust. But a little bit of the role – in Brazil, and not only there, a goalkeeper is only a failed footballer – a little bit of the duck of the first goal against the Soviet Union led him to represent, should things go wrong, a potential scapegoat. He knows this and he moves between the posts devoured by fear, swallowed up by his worst nightmares, the ones that always ended the same way: with the ball behind his back and the weight of the guilt sinking in.

He knows what bad luck means and does not want to die twice. He knows the cursed fate suffered by Brazilian goalkeepers who

THE MATCH

have made even one mistake. That of Moacir Barbosa, keeper of the great Brazil of 1950, was decided 11 minutes from the end of a World Cup that had already been won. Gylmar dos Santos Neves, better known as Gilmar (from the union of his parents' names, Gilberto and Maria), considered the best green-and-yellow goalkeeper of the 20th century, the only one to have won two World Cups, was denied the chance to play for almost a year after a defeat in 1951. Seven years later, on Maurice Guigue's final whistle, a 17-year-old boy named Pelé leaned on his shoulder to cry. In 1964, Heitor Perroca managed to save Pelé's penalty. But one unlucky match was enough for fans, managers and clubs to show him no mercy. He was forced to dissipate his talents in small teams, until in despair he decided to give up football for good and converted to the Jehovah's Witnesses. Luis Antonio, after conceding five goals in 1975, was crushed by unbearable criticism and pressure. The fans ridiculed him by calling him a 'truck driver'. He was so traumatised by football that he actually bought a lorry and started to travel in the hope of never stopping, and leaving his memories far behind. In the same year, Waldir Peres won the Bola de Ouro. The best player in Brazil. Him, a goalkeeper. The future looked bright.

Now, when asked if he fears anyone among the opposing forwards, he replies solemnly: 'It is they who should fear me and not the other way around.' But he had seen Italy against Argentina and watched Paolo Rossi carefully. His was an obsession. Something or someone told him that sooner or later the Azzurri might wake up. Maybe it was a dream. Or his god. And in him he places his expectations. To save himself from everything he cannot control, he has begun to consider sacred what others call the unknown. He has always projected into the sky his fears, his hopes and above all the fear that dwells in the depths of his soul, where the demands of reason do not apply and where everything is confused in the dark night of uncertainty. His doctrine commands him to wipe out all possible eternal returns, imposing his own petty time of absolute hell. In the name of which everything is consumed. And Waldir Peres, a goalkeeper by profession, is at this moment corroding to the point of extinction the ultimate possibility of having a space and time for himself in the glory of the days to come. He can be reborn, of course. But not there. Life for him will be elsewhere. As it was for Barbosa. Because it is a network.

The Italian Sarriá fans explode. Klein whistles and runs impassively to the centre of the pitch. In his head he thinks, *It's incredible!* It is so unbelievable that the RAI commentator Nando Martellini, dimmed by the heat and tension, excitedly announces: 'And it's a draw!' Instead it is 3-2. There is a quarter of an hour to go.

The Last Quarter

It was the hot autumn of 1968. He was about to enter the pitch when a manager approached him: 'One day you will be able to say that you played in the third division.'

In the universities, student movements protested against the society of their fathers. The year before, the Pisan workers' power had been born. The boy Marco was experiencing the youthful turmoil through his brother Flavio's stories. But he was not interested in politics. It was on the pitch that he wanted to carry out his struggle. Too skinny to play, he struggled more than the others and had to train twice as hard. He was put into a package ('Either you take it,' his coach Romano Paffi had said, 'or you forget Zanni and Lucarelli') that would take him to wear the Pisa shirt, his hometown, before that of Como and Juventus.

But his initiation was that time. He played for San Martino, a local family team. On that day, his 35-year-old counterpart did not show up in the third division. Paffi told him, 'I'm missing a man, you're playing this time.' And he, a child, jumped into the fray. The opponents were men, the pitch as hard as concrete, the boots pierced by studs. His feet were bleeding, but he kept quiet and played. As he does today. Early in the match, after a clash with Falcão, he was injured but he gritted his teeth and carried on. This time, too, he held on. To the last. He served Paolo Rossi. The 3-2 shot on goal came from his foot.

He was just 14 years old that day in the third division. It was 14 years earlier. Now, as he walks off the battlefield injured, Marco Tardelli is twice as old. The back that unconsciously turns its last glance at the Sarriá has a number printed on it: 14. Now he will be able to say that he played in a World Cup, against Brazil.

A Caged Lion

He came to the World Cup with a guitar. He plays it every evening to keep the group company. Every now and then Bearzot joins in at the hotel piano. The highlight is 'Generale' by De Gregori, and he is as loyal to his coach as he is to a general. Bearzot had asked him for help during a difficult period. He had responded with total dedication, fighting stoically against the attackers from Denmark, Yugoslavia and Greece. At the time the Old Man promised him: 'If we qualify for Spain, I'll find a way to get you to 20 appearances.' A goal that was worth the gold medal of the Pozzo award, with all the advantages that went with it. Bearzot never broke his word. And now, having conquered Spain, he is keeping his promise. After defending Italy as a starter against Poland and Peru, Giampiero Marini comes on to the scene against Brazil.

It is his 15th appearance for the national team. Against Argentina, he also came on in the 75th minute to play 15 minutes of fire. The same awaits him now. He is one of the men who has to solidify the result. For the first time at the Mundial, Oriali and Marini, the fratricidal duality, are on the pitch at the same time. Perhaps due to emotion, Oriali is cautioned a minute later for a foul on Éder.

Tardelli feels like a caged lion in the dressing room. Surrounded by a silence that now seems unreal to him, he tries to chase the echo of the bedlam around the pitch. Outside the door, the stadium attendants are in front of a small television set. The Azzurro looks out but does not dare to watch. Too much emotion. He cannot bear to see

A CAGED LION

his team-mates on the pitch without him being able to do anything. So, limping, he starts to go in and out to ask them for updates. A few moments later Sócrates scores but it's offside.

Dochev points this out. Nobody, perhaps not even the Bulgarian, expected him to be called up for the World Cup, because he had always been preferred at international level by Ivan Yosifov and Welitschko Tzontschev. He is assigned only one match to referee, that of Italy against Cameroon, decisive for the passage of the round. In Sofia, where he lives, Bogdan Dochev spends his days in the administration office of an agricultural machinery industry. Sitting at his desk every day, dealing with figures and lawns to be cut, his thoughts inevitably drift to the grass on the football pitches. Rough in his dealings with players and secretive in his private life, like Cerezo he likes to take refuge in fishing. This year in the Bulgarian championship he has never sent off anyone. He is respected and feared. And Sócrates barely looks at him, without saying anything.

The Brazilians are exhausted but not defeated. The Azzurri still have breath and try to relieve the pressure with reasoned counter-attacks. Bearzot's strategy is situational. The same choice can be progressive or reactionary depending on the result and who is in front of you. His approach is a Hegelian matrix. Ideas do not stand still, they move, they contradict themselves if necessary. It is an escape from the absolute, from fixed schemes. Because his Italy manifests itself differently in different circumstances. And Brazil are once again caught off guard. Antognoni takes possession of the final minutes. It is his match; he has not put a foot wrong. He takes a free kick that Rossi sends just wide, he devours the Brazilian right flank with a tunnel to Júnior, and he smashes a header towards Peres's goal. Now, as he faces the wrath of Leandro, Cabrini sweeps away a ball that Graziani stops on the touchline. Antognoni starts from his area, begins to run, receives the ball from Graziani, goes over the halfway line and, as Rossi flies down the right, he burns Júnior, Cerezo and Oscar to serve his team-mate. Rossi sneaks into the box and looks on. First Oriali comes in and takes the ball, then Antognoni receives it, while Peres

421

runs from post to post: one, two, three, four passes. On the fifth he opens up as best he can in front of the perfect coordination displayed by Antognoni. And he dives. A roar floods the dressing room. Tardelli thinks, *It's over, they've scored.* Klein is facing the back of the net. He looks to his right and sees Thomson Chan Tam-Sun's flag raised. Antognoni is celebrating on the opposite flank but Graziani, from behind, puts a stop to his joy: 'He disallowed it.' He turns and brings his hands to his head. The goal is disallowed for offside. It never existed. It was the envy of the gods that haunted Antognoni.

The Envy of the Gods – Part One

Herodotus recounts that, among the ancient Greeks, the special qualities of a human being, such as elegance, skill in dancing or in the art of war, could arouse 'the envy of the gods' whose wrath would strike mercilessly at those they considered too lucky.

Giancarlo Antognoni has height, vision, an elegant stride and the ability to kick with both feet. He made his debut alongside an old Brazilian champion who had come to the end of a successful career: Angelo Benedicto Sormani. The Fiorentina public immediately adopted him, his surname turned into a nickname and for everyone he became 'Antonio', 'the boy who plays looking at the stars'. He seemed destined for a life of success, but instead divine jealousy fell on him with merciless constancy.

On his debut for the Azzurri, in a match for qualification for the European Championship, at the Feyenoord stadium in Rotterdam, against Cruyff's Netherlands, Antognoni had amazed. From one of his passes Italy went ahead. Shortly afterwards, from 30 metres, he exploded a right-footed shot that went into the top corner to the right of Jongbloed, who was static, but the ineffable referee Kasakov, in his last match, disallowed it. It was the first step in a long series of bitterness.

When the Azzurri met England in Rome in the World Cup qualifiers for Argentina, it was he who scored the opening goal.

A great free kick that beat Clemence after skimming Keegan's calf. But that goal, with subtle perfidy, had been stolen from the almanacs. Patience ... he would have made up for it at the World Cup. Instead, after two years of excellent physical condition, he was haunted by tarsalgia, which compromised his performance: he often played with a limp, with an increasingly insistent pain in his foot. At the moment when Fiorentina began to sink, he, who by then had become 'the captain', decided to fight until the end, taking on all the responsibilities that the role imposed on him. For example, in Pescara, where a few minutes from the end, Fiorentina, who needed to win, were awarded a fortunate penalty. Antognoni went to the penalty spot to kick the most important ball of his career, took the run-up and missed.

Bad luck accompanied him to the World Cup in Argentina. He only managed to play in the match against the hosts, which was won thanks to a move set up by him and masterfully concluded by a Rossi–Bettega triangle. The disappointment was great. Italy, who with a 100 per cent contribution from Antognoni could have fought for the title, had to be content with fourth place and he lost the opportunity to show himself on an international stage. An opportunity that, given the restrictions of the Viola society, could only guarantee him the national team.

The Envy of the Gods – Part Two

The World Cup was just over six months away. He had two dreams in his heart: to experience a World Cup Final and to sew the Italian flag on his chest. An orthotic solved the problem of tarsalgia and he knew he could count on a competitive formation. The team, entrusted to 'Picchio' De Sisti, Giancarlo's former companion in the purple jersey, was strengthened with the arrival of Graziani and the young Massaro. It was the year of truth. In the national team, however, in the last two poor draws in the World Cup qualifiers, against Yugoslavia and Greece, Bearzot replaced him halfway through the second half. These were 'contingency choices', which the northern press cartel exploited to make a case for his performance and support the candidature of Dossena from Granada. Criticism that Antognoni did not accept.

A week after the poison pens, Fiorentina hosted Genoa. The Viola captain contested the first 55 minutes, moved by a devastating desire for revenge, which resulted in technical feats of unmatched mastery. He was practically perfect. Until Bertoni set off his most seductive pass. He paraded it obliquely through six opposing bodies. Antognoni watched it travel towards him. It was inviting, tempting, just waiting for him to control it. The captain was alone, in front of him was Martina. The chance he had been looking for since the beginning of the match. The ball bounced on the chalk line and shot into the air. He jumped, got there and headed the ball, but he also found the knee of the Genoa goalkeeper planted on his forehead. A huge impact. Antognoni remained motionless on the grass, lying down, helpless, his arms hanging by his sides.

The opponents were the first to understand. Gentile from Genoa walked away with his hands on his head, captain Onofri burst into tears. He ran towards the red-and-blue bench. 'He's dead,' he shouted, pointing at him, 'he's dead!' Comrades and adversaries made desperate gestures to the doctors. The visiting team's Pier Luigi Gatto ran across the pitch. The player was frothing at the mouth. His eyes were rolling. He was no longer breathing. His heart had stopped beating. The stadium held its breath. The cardiac massage began. Professor Bruno Anselmi and the masseur Ennio Raveggi came running from the Viola bench. There was confusion. The tension caused an altercation to break out between Doctor Gatto, who was energetically practising heart massage, and the distraught Viola masseur.

Antognoni was motionless on the ground, surrounded by photographers. Anselmi took over from Gatto, who checked Antognoni's pulse. Then Raveggi switched to mouth-to-mouth resuscitation. He noticed that the boy had his tongue stuck in his throat, so with a finger he extracted it and resumed respiration.

A human dome surrounded the scene. The managers shouted to each other, 'Go! Away!' The stretcher appeared in a chilling silence. The Viola captain was loaded on to the stretcher but the doctors immediately dropped it on to the grass to resume massage. Twenty-five seconds into the darkness, Antognoni barely lifted his head. The two doctors had saved his life.

He opened his eyes again in the dressing room. He was safe but the injury was serious. Fracture of the cranial bones. He underwent emergency surgery by Professor Mennonna and recovered, but the convalescence was long. Fiorentina were fighting for the Scudetto and at the end of the season there was the Mundial. It was the season he had dreamed of for a lifetime. But the Viola fought and, when he returned, they were still on a par with Juventus. 'Antonio' could finally play in the sprint for the Scudetto that he had always wanted. However, they lost the championship a quarter of an hour from the end, by a single point, through a doubtful penalty, for a goal disallowed. Exactly like against Brazil, where a valid goal was denied by the referee, a quarter of an hour from the end. The gods are never distracted.

The Promise

'We will go ahead. And I will score a header in the last minute,' Oscar promises to the journalists the day before Italy vs Brazil. On the eve of the match against Scotland he had dreamed of a flock of birds flying high. A premonition, according to him. In the third minute of the second half he entered the box, heading for a ball in by Júnior. He rose into the air and hit it with his head. At that moment Edinho sprang from the bench with his arms raised, already sure it would go in. And it was José Oscar Bernardi himself, 28 years old two weeks earlier, who nurtured this conviction. For 53 days he had been training exclusively for the aerial game, lifting his six foot frame like a bird hunting for its prey. It was a long apprenticeship, the brainchild of coach Mário Juliato nine years earlier, in the youth ranks of Ponte Preta, in Campinas. Three days after starting, he looked like a specialist. The head is his gift. Carlos Maranhão in *Placar* dedicated a full-page photo to him under the headline: 'Oscar, a leap for glory'.

He has more confidence in his head than in his feet. He has always liked to run, he can do it all day, but with high balls he feels at home. So he has specialised. He trained every day until he was exhausted, and in order to get used to jumping higher and higher, he even wore sandbags. At Ponte Preta, the coach always put taller players in front of him. When Ponte played against Palmeiras, Oscar was faced with João Leiva Campos Filho, known as Leivinha, one of the best headers in São Paulo and Brazil. Oscar was just a kid but he managed to steal all the high balls from him, thus robbing him of the joy of scoring. For Oscar it was a confidence boost, the conviction that led him to specialise in high balls.

Santana had suggested the play against Scotland: Júnior, a left-sided player who uses his right foot, hits the ball with his left foot to the near post, where Oscar is found. Falcão said that in that match he had demonstrated the greatest quality a footballer could have: 'That of doing exactly what he knows he can do, avoiding doing what he doesn't know how to do.' Oscar, in fact, always goes back to his place if he advances for a header. He knows he cannot compete with the feet of Sócrates, Zico and Éder. He only does what he is sure he can do. So he knows that he can only hope to score if he flies at a ball through the air. He is a loner. His team-mates affectionately call him *belo* (beautiful). He reads a lot, does not drink, likes to listen more than talk. He is always attentive, kind and generous with everyone. He can joke but is never intrusive. He is terrified of making mistakes. He is always afraid of causing problems or discomfort, of saying something stupid or hurting someone. He only tries to facilitate group harmony, even taking into account the different affinities. He was originally in the room with Leandro but, knowing that he's a friend of Renato's, he left him that place: 'I'll go with Cerezo.'

It is the last minute of Italy vs Brazil. It is seven o'clock in the evening. With two touches, Brazil push forwards. In a flash Éder finds the ball between his feet, riding madly towards the Azzurri's area until he finds himself fouled by Conti. Klein awards a free kick at the right-hand edge of Italy's penalty area. The left-winger nervously claims the ball from Falcão, the last chance. Zoff moves along the line, waving his hands, trying to organise his men. Éder is ready with the ball. Conti and Oriali are the only sentries in the wall. Nearly everyone else is in the box. Eight Italians and six Brazilians. Oscar is among them. He hurriedly whispers into Cerezo's ear, his room-mate: 'Toninho, this is the last chance. We'll swap, you keep the full-back busy, I'll stay in the area and surprise them.' If he has decided to leave his area, it is to do what he is able to do.

The Blue Oak

He has diaphanous skin, a confident gaze and magical fingers that seem to follow the weave of his door with invisible threads. He has always known where to put his hands. He trained as a mechanic, three years at the school, when he was not working in the countryside for the family. His first job was at a workshop in Cormons, assistant mechanic. Four and a half kilometres from Mariano del Friuli, where he was born. Then to Gorizia: 14 kilometres there and the same number to come back, by bike or by bus, depending on the weather. He brought home his first money, 60,000 lire a month. And the owners also let him go to play football. Between the posts, of course. If he had not been a footballer, he would have ended up as a mechanic, he is sure of it.

No myth, no television either: he was a goalkeeper even before he read in *Sport Illustrato* that the role existed. He still remembers his first gloves, grey with red grommets. He was 12 years old. In 1966 he was already one of the best in Italy, but Edmondo Fabbri, who had coached him at Mantova the year before becoming technical director of the national team, decided not to take him to the English

THE MATCH

World Cup, to avoid accusations of partiality. Four years later he was a regular player. In the meantime he secured the first European title won by Italy, in 1968. However, he was robbed of his place at the World Cup in Mexico by Enrico 'Ricky' Albertosi, his reserve until the penultimate friendly match. The legendary Italy vs Germany encounter saw him on the bench. However, the place was his without question in 1974. *Newsweek* dedicated its cover to him: he was the strongest player in the world. But the goal he had to defend was that of a strong but dishevelled national team, which left the scene after only three matches. In 1978, at the age of 36, he found himself experiencing a World Cup for the first time in his life. Four shots from distance took Italy off the podium. First the Dutch double by Brandt and Haan, then the Brazilian one by Nelinho and Dirceu.

The day after the epilogue, the *Gazzetta* headlined mercilessly: 'Zoff condemns us'. It seemed the foregone conclusion of a goalkeeper who was certainly irreplaceable, but by now an old man, who lacked the most important title: the World Cup. Those goals in Argentina beat him to a pulp. In the meantime, he bowed his head and started again. Day after day he increased his training, without ever stopping. He did not speak out for almost five months, offended like a tribal chief above all suspicion. When he did decide to speak, he did so in Bratislava to the *Corriere dello Sport*: 'Those goals are not on my conscience, my professional skill has not been affected.' And he postponed the appointment to 1982, in Spain.

It sounded like an outburst but now it's reality. Medical tests revealed an impressive field of vision and lung capacity. Age is just a detail. He has not missed a league match, won his sixth Scudetto in ten years and arrived in Spain at the age of 40 to celebrate his 100th appearance with the national team in the opening match of the Mundial. But that is not enough for the press. The journalists consider him finished: a man of that age should no longer be on the pitch. They even attack him after a training match, accusing him of having made two bloopers against the Pontevedra team. The Azzurri captain is stunned by such senseless ruthlessness: 'You all seem crazy to me.' Roberto Renga closes the episode on the pages of *Paese Sera* in a cutting way: 'We don't even have to ask ourselves what Zoff is, we already know: 40 years old.'

'At 40 you can go to the moon,' says Zoff, let alone stand between the goalposts. And he has always wanted to be there. Ever since the boy Dino said to his team-mates: 'I'm going in goal.' And not because he was the last to arrive on Mariano's grass. That white strip that joins the two goalposts perhaps seemed like a frontier to him. And he, who, coming from a farming family, knew values such as sacrifice, waiting and silence like the Ave Maria, wanted that role of guardian. He has played against Charles, Sívori, Pelé, Cruyff, Maradona and Zico.

He always seems the most serious, but he is not cold. The heart comes first. Those who know him know that. But at work he cannot laugh. He grew up watching his father toil to feed him. That is why work is a religion to him. Twenty years ago he was a boy who, with his duffel bag full of used underwear over his shoulder, waited in the rain on Sunday evenings for the bus to take him home, even though he had spent the afternoon between the posts at Udinese's Moretti stadium. Through door after door he has arrived here today, captain of the national team, responsible for the destiny of an Italy that is about to achieve a remarkable feat, in the face of predictions, bets, the press and history.

Zoff's Oscar

In the evening, the Sarriá stadium magically stops chewing empanadas. The jaws stop. Silence surrounds Éder's feet. He is not yet the favourite son of the gods, but he can always become one. The penalty area is a tuna trap. Leading the blue herds is the patriarchal mantra of their goalkeeper. Éder bends down, spreading his arms by his legs. His eyes point to the penalty area. He steps back. Klein whistles. One step, two. The left-footed cross hits the ball with his instep. The ball is flying – slowly and softly – across the entire penalty area. The journey to find

THE MATCH

the far man, the one for whom it is destined. Unsuspecting bodies migrating en bloc towards the goal. Defended by one man.

Zoff's motion starts at the exact moment he stops following the trajectory of the ball. He reads the action and knows before anyone else who is going to hit it. The header that emerges from the melee in the middle of the area belongs to Oscar. He hits it cleanly, precisely: the ball heading for goal is a bullet; 40,000 sighs remain trapped. Zoff is one step ahead of the line, the ball bounces to his left, towards the post. Between him and that ball, in the imaginary triangle formed by three crucial vertices (himself, Oscar and the ball) there is a cruel, uncomfortable and infinite hypotenuse. He has to rotate, find the strength for the momentum, dive to his side and reach for an angled, strong header. There is no more time to think. The moment that Oscar's header travels the space between him and the goal, the fate of a team is now only in his reflections. The same reflexes wounded forever four years earlier at the World Cup in Argentina. His indestructible career can end or be consecrated at this moment, at the age of 40.

Zoff moves the weight on his right leg and for a long moment he coils like a spring. The ball passes like a comet under the eyes of 12 dancers: Oscar and Cabrini, Isidoro and Graziani, Júnior and Marini, Sócrates and Bergomi, Zico and Gentile, Rossi and Luizinho. The Azzurri captain dives to his left, towards his absolute moment. He widens his dramatic eyes, loosens his mouth, opens his hands and chases the ball in flight. Oscar returns to the ground with the hoped-for excitement of making history. He, an ordinary defender in a team of demigod strikers, the saviour of the country. Behind the goal, an exhausted Galeazzi, sitting on top of a German photographer's briefcase, clutches Galimberti's photographer with his heart in his throat. In the unreal silence of the stadium he clearly hears the sound of gloves on the leather ball. Zoff falls back to the ground a few centimetres from the white line, nailing the Tango to the turf. Then he remains motionless. He knows that victory is locked in his hands. And he wants to stop the moment.

THE END

Ten years earlier, on 17 June 1972, he was in the exact same position in Bucharest. The exact same minute (89th). The exact same result (3-2 to Italy). Hainal's ball had not gone in, but Zoff had brought it towards himself. The Slavic referee Gugulovic interpreted the gesture in his own way and gave the Romanians the 3-3 draw. This time a World Cup is at stake, the sacrifice of one team against all and the last World Cup of a lifetime. He thinks, *If I just make the gesture of pulling the ball back towards me, Klein will think it was in and give the goal.* So he holds the ball firmly on the edge of the line. The only part of his body that moves are his eyes. In the midst of a forest of legs, they search desperately for Klein's black socks. When he spots them, he looks up and finds his face impassive.

The referee is in the perfect position. If he makes a mistake it will be the biggest mistake of the Mundial. If he gets it right it will be his masterpiece. He also goes back in time. On a similar occasion, in Israel, he had awarded the goal. But the ball, he later discovered, had not gone in. Goalkeeper and referee are now bringing their mistakes to light. They have a chance to redeem themselves. But while Klein's salvation lies in his own gaze, Zoff's is enshrined in a decision. The Israeli is faced with the false joy of six raised arms. Sócrates, Zico and Oscar rest their gazes on him. His hawk-like vision ignores them and continues to point straight at the goal line. Dochev remains static near the flag with his arms by his sides. Klein's hands signal for play to continue. The Brazilians still think they have drawn level but Zoff suddenly stands up, shaking his index finger, and reminds them that life begins at 40.

The End

It is now 30 seconds beyond time, 22 hearts are beating spasmodically. Almost all of them beat in Zoff's area. Brazil chasing an equaliser, Italy defending the result, whatever the cost. The Sarriá is boiling. The spaces are saturated. Éder is desperately looking for one and he has to take his corner. The last one. But he is smothered by a

THE MATCH

billboard, positioned in the corner of the pitch with the best visibility. The Coca-Cola one. That is where it all started.

But now there is no more time, no more space. Éder, who seemed to exult by contract in front of the sponsors, throws the sign towards the photographers. Two Brazilian fans, along with a couple of men from the Policia Nacional, help him uproot it.

The Tango's last trip to the Sarriá is on. He is denied by Zoff with his hands and by Cabrini with his header. But the full-back is hit in the face by Cerezo's outstretched leg. It is a foul. The bench gasps. The Azzurri rush out of the trenches. Maldini is flailing like a madman towards the Italian area, as if to say, 'There's no more time!' Santana is impassive. Bearzot puts his jacket back on. At his side Altobelli and Causio. The men of the Policia Nacional rush to cover them. One of them, more docile, waves his hand, as if to say, 'Don't worry, it's done now.' But it is impossible to follow an order. Madness has taken over the bench. Zoff has the ball back in his hands. Klein looks at his stopwatch. Zoff runs the ball along the goal line. Sócrates rushes at him, but the Italian goalkeeper slips it from his feet.

The captains of this battle are at the epilogue. They are once again facing each other. Exactly as they were 90 minutes before. Different in everything. The first is balanced, the second is unbalanced. The same weight on their shoulders, in the name of democracy. For the Brazilian, the right to make his voice heard. For the Italian, the right to remain silent. He is the captain of silence. For a moment they look into each other's eyes and Zoff almost seems to say 'no' with his head. Sócrates remains stone-like, standing to attention like a Greek kouros. Zoff raises the ball and kicks it skywards. He watches it go. It eclipses the sun above the Sarriá for an instant, and at that moment he hears a whistle.

The Doutor applauds. Daniel Souza, a young Brazilian fan near the goal, hears Gentile shout at Zoff, 'It's over!' He is perhaps the first person in the stadium to understand this. Bergomi turns his gaze towards his captain. Scirea turns to Klein, then looks at Bergomi, then at Zoff. It takes a split second.

THE END

In the dressing room the attendant takes his eyes off the screen: 'Señor, el partido ha terminado 3-2.' Tardelli, overcome with uncontainable joy, rushes out. Yes, it is over! All eleven Azzurri instinctively raise their arms. Italy, considered second-best in the contest, have beaten the invincible Brazil and will be semi-finalists in the World Cup. The Azzurri technicians, reserves and masseurs break the banks and go on to the pitch. Maldini jumps happily and heads towards Scirea. He runs into the Azzurri defence: Gentile, in a vest with Zico's shirt in his right hand, and Cabrini, with their arms wide open. They hug each other mad with happiness. The coach finally finds a smile on Zoff's face. An insane joy envelops everything, hiding fears and erasing grudges.

Bergomi turns towards Sócrates and tugs the fabric of the yellow jersey. The captain pulls it off. For the young Beppe it is the first trophy. Marini turns towards Falcão and takes off his jersey, but Paulo, the most Italian of the Brazilians, replies, 'I've already promised it. With his eyes, he seeks out Bruno Conti, the most Brazilian of the Italians, who goes towards him. Before rejoicing, he chooses to hold his friend close. He does so by throwing his arms around his neck. Falcão wraps his arms around Conti's waist, looking into space. He does not have the strength to say anything. A year of sacrifices has gone up in smoke, his incredible comeback in Santana's esteem, his fantastic performances, his three goals. All vanished in a few minutes. And against the national team of the country where he plays. In front of him there is only despair. Conti feels it and does not have the courage to remember his promise. He gives his team-mate such a sad expression that he thinks, for a moment, that it is Italy who have lost. Then the Brazilian slowly slips off his shirt, like an automaton, hands it to him, receives the blue one, scampers between players and photographers and, without saying a word, enters the tunnel. Conti cannot hold him back. The day before, he had said to himself, 'It ends two to two. We save face and they go through to the final.' The photographer Calzuola, who has been running desperately towards them, manages to catch the exchange. Plastino, from the stands, is the only one to capture it with a camera.

The first person Bearzot runs to embrace is Zico. He had been his coach in the Argentina vs Rest of the World match after the 1978 Mundial. While Dochev picks up the ball and holds it under his arm, Klein looks for Rossi to shake his hand. The ritual of the shirt is consummated in a few seconds. Scirea exchanges with Cerezo, Oscar with Graziani, Antognoni with Leandro, Oriali with Éder, then he, shirtless and with a yellow jersey clutched in his fist, celebrates with Altobelli.

Zico and Gentile approach the tunnel. And it is there that the Azzurri defender surprises the Brazilian with a counter-attack question: 'Arthur, would you please give me the one from the first half?' Anyone else would tell him to go to hell. At the end of the Argentina match Maradona had run off the pitch in a rage. Zico, on the other hand, is distinguished by his gentility. He signals for him to follow him into the dressing room and enters without a word. Gentile is the only Italian who manages to sense the unreal Brazilian silence. At the start of the match he had said, 'I'll follow him to the showers.' And now he comes out with a torn jersey to return to the court. With the trophy in his hand, he hugs Causio and then clings to Bearzot. In his fervour he breaks the bar of his glasses. Waldir Peres goes straight to the dressing room. Touching the St Jude's medal, Paulo Isidoro follows him, having left for Spain thinking of achieving a dream, but instead he will have to look elsewhere.

Santana seems to have taken refuge in other times. The time has come to unfurl the sails and leave the stage in Spain. He has fought his battle and finished his race, but he has kept his faith. His men leave a meadow that no longer belongs to them. The remnants of what had been the mightiest army in the world climb 'in disorder and without hope the valleys they had descended with proud confidence'. The last glimpse of the Catalan sun sees them disappear from the Sarriá like sleepwalkers. Without speaking, while the silence of their music is filled with a euphoria that is alien to them. Brazil can always

THE END

find champions again, but not legends. And Italy have just beaten a legend.

In a magical instant, Rossi and Bearzot find themselves facing each other. The centre-forward spreads his arms and crosses them around the coach's neck. They look at each other without saying a word. Pablito smiles like a child while a tangle envelops them. A pace behind, Luizinho watches them and, instinctively, applauds them. One man. A hat-trick. Against Brazil. In the final stage of a World Cup. This has never happened and it will never happen again.

Italian flags are waving. Thousands of white hats bounce on the steps. Leaning over them are a handful of grey buildings silhouetted against the sunset. Silent witnesses of an afternoon to remember. Antognoni, Graziani, Cabrini and Conti intertwine in a single embrace. A hold that knows no frontiers, that has no more flags, that will bind them forever. It is the Azzurri team. They are not the eternal rivals, they are Bearzot's boys.

The Azzurri disperse in the general embrace, while Bearzot begins to descend the stairs leading to the dressing room. On the third step he is blocked from above. It is the RAI microphones of De Laurentiis and Galeazzi: 'Enzo! Enzo!' He turns and looks at them with a smile pulling at his face. Overwhelmed by the feat, he tries to convey what he can of his personal hurricane of emotions: 'It was an exceptional match, dramatic.' Praising his team: 'An Italy that was never tamed throughout the match. We could have beaten them four times.' Not forgetting the honour of arms: 'They played very well.' Until his head is grabbed by a firm but gentle hand and a kiss reaches his neck. Behind him, a man in a grey jersey with the No. 1 stitched between his shoulder blades walks away.

Almost unnoticed, a green-and-yellow kite falls to the ground. It flutters a couple of times like a fish on the deck of a boat, before resting limply on the grass. At that moment Klein approaches the exit. He realises that this has been his last match. He will never referee a final: 'If Brazil goes home, Havelange will want a Brazilian in my place. And Coelho is an excellent referee.' Italy's victory has condemned him, but at the same time he consoles himself: 'I close with a match that will go down in history.'

A few more steps and he will no longer be a referee, the right man at the centre of a match. A magistrate of the playing field, short in stature and of great rigour. The afternoon is beginning to slip away and at sunset even a small man can have a big shadow.

Rossi widens the corners of his face. In one poignant instant, he realises that this and only this will be the past he will always want to find again. So his incredulous eyes wander through space to collect memories. Peres, from the edge of this same moment, would like to throw himself into nothingness. His hands have only touched glory, and now ten stupid fingers of nothing hang on his hips.

The players return to the dressing room. Graziani lingers for a moment, takes three steps towards the pitch and raises his arms to the fans. He swallows the superb air of the Sarriá again, crosses paths with Causio and hugs him. The last actor to leave the stage is him, a happy blue, called 'Brazil'. Maybe it is just as well. In a moment only the grass remains. And the fans bewitched by the enchantment of his cape. The heart of the stadium continues to beat. 'Alé-oó, alé-oó.' *Tu-tu-tum.* 'Alé-oó, alé-oó.' *Tu-tu-tum.* The air fills with the sweet smells of grass. Klein breathes deeply to savour it one last time. And exits the stage.

Conclusion

I am not exaggerating when I say that Brazil's defeat against Italy was the worst and most disruptive event in my first seven years on this earth. The separation of my parents was barely a setback in comparison.

Tim Lewis, 1982: 'Why Brazil vs Italy Was
One of Football's Greatest Ever Matches',
Esquire, 11 July 2014

The Child of the Sarriá

Seconds after Klein's whistle, Brazilian photographer Reginaldo Manente looks away from the players. He turns towards the central stand to search the crowd for a face that can portray the tangle in his throat. His attention is caught by a woman. Beautiful and in tears. In her weeping he finds his catharsis. On the shelf at home are three Esso awards, the Oscars of Brazilian journalism, awarded to portraits of weeping figures: the striker Amarildo in the 1962 World Cup, a fireman supported by two colleagues and a mother who has just been evicted from her home, together with her daughter.

Tears have smudged the woman's make-up and she is now trying to wipe her face. Manente continues to keep his eyes on her, climbs over the protective barriers and starts to climb the steps to get as close as possible. He bumps into João Havelange, the highest authority in football, but does not even notice. When he is less than two metres from the subject, he stops. The light is perfect. He is about to shoot when his gaze falls on the child sitting next to her. It is her son. His name is José Carlos Vilella Jr and he is crying his eyes out. His family has been invited to Spain directly by the FIFA president. His father is Fluminense's lawyer in Rio de Janeiro, known as the 'Rei do Tapetão' for his forensic skills. His mother was Miss Fluminense. Little José is only ten years old and does not even notice the photographer's presence at the time. The woman tries to console him: 'Don't worry, José, Brazil is not dropping out of the World Cup.' The boy knows this is not true but, staring at his mother, he stops his crying. Manente comes a little closer. *If this boy starts crying again*, he thinks, *I have my picture.*

He turns his reflex camera upright and welcomes José into his lens. Through the lens he can see his black hair, his head held high

THE MATCH

and his chest puffed out with pride in the yellow jersey he is wearing. The shirt of Brazil. José inhales the air. He is about to resume crying. At that moment Manente snaps.

An ocean away, Mário Marinho, editor-in-chief of the sports section of the *Jornal da Tarde*, has a problem. He has to find a way to open the following afternoon's newspaper, when the whole of Brazil already knows about the defeat. He can't use the title 'The Seleção lost to Italy with three goals from Paolo Rossi'. *I need something different.* What he is looking for begins to appear when the *transmissor de fotografías*, the electronic device connected to his telephone line, starts to ring. It is Manente. He is sending 20 images from the Sarriá. At his side are two correspondents, Roberto Avallone and Vital Battaglia, who has just picked up José's photo. The moment he started to sob, Manente had confirmation that this was the shot he was looking for.

In São Paulo Marinho chooses that very picture. In doing so, he makes a courageous decision. He tells the printer to print it full-page on the front of the *Jornal*, without a title. His is an innovative newspaper and the editor himself encourages his journalists to be inventive, but this time the idea is daring. It is approved, however, and the 6 July page comes out with just José's photo. That sincere crying manages to interpret the suffering of a country, becomes the symbol of the traumatic elimination of the Brazilian team and causes the highest circulation in the history of one of the most important South American newspapers. The photo will win Manente his fourth Esso prize. The fourth tear in his eye.

Endings

*Excuse me, who won? I just
arrived from Italy.
No, nothing, there was a …
normal game.*

Dialogue between a fan who has just arrived
at the Sarriá and Antonio Matarrese after the match

José's Destiny

When he returned to Brazil, little José Carlos did not know he had been so famous. He only realised this four years later, on the eve of the 1986 World Cup. A family friend saw the photo on a television programme and recognised him. The presenters were commenting: 'It's a pity that the Sarriá child was never found.' At that point, his father did not hesitate. He called the programme and promoted the boy nationally through interviews and television appearances. Since then, the boy had been involved in all the re-enactments of the Sarriá tragedy.

He returned to the spotlight in 1994. Brazil and Italy faced each other in the Rose Bowl in Pasadena in the World Cup Final. The media wanted to see how he would react after 12 years, in the event of another Seleção defeat by the same opponents. His father welcomed the idea and hosted a cocktail party with journalists on the day of the match. But José, now 22, did not want to risk becoming the symbol of a country's pain again, so he sought refuge in the home of a friend and watched the match there. The journalists began a manhunt throughout the São Conrado neighbourhood, knocking on the doors of the friends his mother had pointed out. But young José managed not to be found. He only returned home after Roberto Baggio's penalty. His father did not speak to him for the whole summer.

Thirty years after the Sarriá match, the *Jornal da Tarde* closed its doors. The 6 July cover was considered the one that marked the history of Brazilian journalism forever. Ruy Mesquita, director of Grupo Estado, the company that created the *Jornal*, called it 'the greatest moment in South American journalism'. It is a moment that has remained engraved on the memory of 120 million Brazilians.

The following year, in 2013, a Visa credit card advertising campaign managed to bring together perpetrator and victim:

footballer Paolo Rossi and spectator José Carlos. It was an intense encounter, during which the 57-year-old Pablito warmly embraced the 40-year-old José, as if to return the joy he had stolen from him.

Photographer and photographed have met several times over the years. They are friends, bound forever by the image that changed both their lives. José, who has since become a lawyer, has a giant picture of that front page on one of the walls of his house. One day they exchanged the photo that made them famous. Behind each of the two prints was a dedication:

For my photographer friend Manente.
José Carlos, former crybaby
and
For my friend José Carlos, who, despite being so sad
at the time, brought me many joys.
A big hug from his former unknown friend,
Reginaldo Manente.

The Sarriá Tragedy

The defeat caused mourning and tragedy in Brazil (seven heart attacks, four suicides and a murder after an argument in a bar just after the match). It was equated with the *Maracanazo*, when Brazil lost the 1950 World Cup at home, and is now remembered as the 'Sarriá tragedy' (the label was created by a journalist from the newspaper *O Tempo*, Chico Maia, born Francisco Barbosa Duarte).

After Klein's whistle, the 54-year-old Brazilian commentator Fiori Gigliotti found himself face to face with Telê Santana: 'It's all your fault, you've made too many concessions to the players!' Telê replied that he was 'a poor old man'. When he entered the dressing room, the coach hugged each member of his team: 'Go back to Brazil in peace, the whole world is applauding you.' At that moment, coach Gilberto Tim was struck by a feeling of profound loss: 'I feel as if my dearest relative has died.' In a fit of rage, he smashed his fist through the wooden door of the changing room. Nobody said a word. Only

THE SARRIÁ TRAGEDY

Júnior tried to cheer up his team-mates by reminding them of what the team had represented in that World Cup: 'I leave here with the conviction that the best national team is leaving the Mundial just because of fate.' But hardly anyone listened to him.

At the doping controls, Paulo Isidoro and Paulo Sérgio were drawn for Brazil, along with Conti and Antognoni for Italy. Isidoro, standing in a corner and watching the euphoria of the two Italians, still could not believe it. When he was approached by the reporters from the *Jornal do Brasil*, Antonio Maria Filho, Márcio Tavares and Marcos Penido, he asked them: 'But did we really lose against Italy?' His eyes were red and his voice was hoarse. Until that moment he had kept all his disapproval inside, in the hope of returning to the starting line-up sooner or later. But now that the dream was over, pressed by journalists as distraught as he was, the dam collapsed: 'I have always been polite, I have never spoken to criticise, but inside I have a great bitterness. I haven't opened my mouth so as not to upset the apple cart, but now I have to say it: I don't understand why the coach has kept me as a starter for two years to make me a reserve right here. I have to find an explanation. I was the biggest victim in this story. So I hope you understand me, I think I have every right to vent. And I'm not saying this because we lost, I would have done it even if we had won the title.' Marcos Penido was at his first World Cup experience. The report that recounted that outburst (*O amargo sabor da derrota. A doce alegria da vitória*) brought him and his two colleagues the Esso prize.

Isidoro was tempted to stop playing and did not follow Grêmio to the World Club Championship. A few months later his son was born. The temptation to stop returned on the day of the 1984 final between Santos and Corinthians. During the interval between the first and second half his president Milton Teixeira approached him hesitantly: 'Something unpleasant has happened to your father.' He replied: 'No problem. He's dead, isn't he?' To the president's dismayed look, he replied coldly: 'I can't change the past now. I'm going back to the field. Life goes on. We must win this title.' He returned to the pitch and played the second half, trying to chase away his thoughts.

THE MATCH

It ended 1-0, with Serginho scoring with 15 minutes to go. At the final whistle Isidoro knelt down. At that moment he dedicated the title to his father. After the match he asked his president to terminate his contract. He was tired. But then he decided to return to the pitch, wearing the Atlético shirt. Thirty years after the Mundial he closed the discussion on the Sarriá match: 'We cannot say that Rossi was lucky that day. It was thanks to him that Italy won. And it is right to give him the credit he deserves.'

During the press conference after the Sarriá match, the Brazilian coach, trying to explain the fall of his team, had already expressed a similar thesis: 'Italy showed they know how to play well in defence and to be a dangerous team in counter-attacks. In order to try to draw, we were forced to leave our defence uncovered and we almost scored more goals.' The Brazilian press tore him to pieces, accusing him of incompetence. There was no reporter who stayed out of the hunt for the culprit. Santana expected it: 'Today the Seleção played better than in the match against Argentina. Yet it made a lot of mistakes. And I am happy to say that they did it individually, just look at how the Italians' second goal came about, when Cerezo sent the ball over the opponent's foot. I am not passing the buck. I have also made mistakes, we have all made mistakes, without a doubt.' When asked whether he felt he was already a champion, he did not hide: 'We were confident. After all, how could we not be? The work was good and the results even more so. We were only thinking about the final.' He closed with a burst of pride: 'We didn't want to be just a confident national team, but a bold and fearless team.' It was at that moment that Santana received the applause of the international journalists: '*Senhor Santana, obrigado pelo futebol de sua Seleção.*'

Once ready, the players left the stadium. Sócrates saw the singer Fagner in the corridor, hugged him, was moved and got on the bus. The moment he sat down he realised that the loss of the title had brought him the greatest frustration of his life. Spanish fans placed a banner on the road leading to the retreat. It has remained in the

THE SARRIÁ TRAGEDY

hearts of Seleção: 'Brazil, the best does not always win'. President Giulite Coutinho held a meeting to thank everyone and praised Telê Santana for putting together an exceptional group. On that occasion Sócrates decided to speak on behalf of the players, explaining that they had played as they knew how, in the best way possible. When he finished his speech everyone was moved. Júnior said that the tears showed only one awareness: that this close-knit group would part. Forever. And so it was.

The two coaches left the Sarriá in different moods. Back at the hotel, the Brazilian players received phone calls from their families. Few were able to say anything. Tears clogged the lines. The night was also terrible, nobody could sleep. Falcão stood at the window of his room for hours, looking out at the street in the dark: 'I tried to imagine the people who were sleeping peacefully at that moment, without any worries, and those who were suffering because of us.' Then he wrote in his diary: 'No matter how much you prepare, you are never ready for defeat. We lost a game at the wrong time and there is no explanation for that. I have never felt so sad in my life. I cried like a child and the other players cried too: the training camp turned into a wake.'

The reporter Ricardo Setti, together with his colleagues, went to Mas Badó to try to understand what had happened. Zico was the most severe: 'We didn't talk much on the pitch, that's one of the reasons for the defeat. If you warn a team-mate you can avoid conceding a goal. And that's what was missing when Cerezo had the unfortunate idea of misplacing the pass. If we had shouted, if we had warned him, perhaps the fate of the team would have been different.' Falcão was the most lucid: 'For the whole match Italy did not give us the time to set up our game, to make plans, to bend the Azzurri to our rhythm.'

Nathan Pacheco did not return with the delegation; he disengaged from the team and no longer wore the role of mascot.

Sócrates, for the first time, made a personal request: his daughter was about to be born and he asked for an early return.

THE MATCH

Towards Glory

On the evening of 5 July, the Italian squad returned to El Castell almost at dinnertime. Before sitting down to eat, Gentile went to his room, entered the bathroom and trimmed his moustache. Looking in the mirror, he finally found his look. But everyone would always remember him for the ferocious Saladin face he had had in those first five meetings.

The Italians ended the dinner without any special celebrations. Just a small toast with a glass of white wine: 'We haven't won anything yet.' The next day Bearzot was thrown into the pool by his boys. It was the only moment of euphoria.

From that moment on, Italy did not miss a beat. Rossi also never stopped: after his hat-trick, he scored two goals against Poland in the semi-finals and one in the final against the Germans. Six days after the match at the Sarriá, Italy were deservedly world champions. The six goals were enough for Rossi to be crowned top scorer of the Mundial, best player of the tournament and that year's Ballon d'Or. As he himself had predicted, confiding in Sconcerti in the dark days of Pontevedra, those last three matches changed his life forever. Everywhere in the world Italy meant 'paolorossi'. For better or for worse: when, shortly after the end of the World Cup, a flu epidemic struck Brazil, it was immediately christened 'Paolo Rossi'.

Five years after the Sarriá match, Pablito left football forever: 'I stopped playing because I felt the need to detach myself from the world of football. The desire to manage my own life was strong. For too long others had done it for me.'

Talking about that golden year, Rossi often repeated that the satisfaction in the three awards he won could never be compared to the happiness of the hat-trick scored against Brazil. 'The joy that a goal on the pitch gives you does not come from the announcement of an award. And the first goal against Brazil for me was fundamental, the most important of my entire existence.' When asked in 2019 by sports magazine *The Last Man* whether he would trade the three goals he inflicted on Brazil for six Ballons d'Or, Rossi replied decisively: 'No. Thirty-seven years on, have you ever wondered why that World Cup has remained in people's collective imagination? Because it was everyone's victory, not just that of Paolo Rossi, the top scorer, nor just that of the team. That victory is considered Italy's victory, in which everyone, no one excluded, participated in a strong way, feeling part of that Italy.'

Marco Tardelli recovered from his injury after the match and was instrumental in the final, scoring the second goal against the Germans. After scoring, he ran around the Bernabéu's pitch and performed his famous 'scream'. That gesture meant many things. It was an angry and crazy reaction to all the accusations he had suffered, but also pure joy. 'Scoring in a World Cup Final,' he explained, 'was something I dreamed of as a child and my celebration was also a kind of liberation for having realised that dream. I was born with that cry inside me and that was the exact moment it came out.' That goal was his last for the Azzurri. The double exchange that preceded it, conducted in the middle of the penalty area by a full-back, Bergomi and Scirea, definitively overturned the Italian label of defensive-style football. The image of the race was also linked to the Ellesse brand, this time placed in a strategic position. This was a clear sign that Dassler and Servadio had reached an agreement.

Bruno Conti was defined by Pelé as the best player of the World Cup. When he returned to home, he was greeted like a hero by an oceanic crowd. Marini was also gratified. Bearzot kept his word and gave the player his 20th appearance on 16 April 1983 in the qualifying match for the European Championship, against Romania.

The envy of the gods, however, continued to fall on Antognoni. After the goal annulled by Klein against Brazil, the studs of a Polish defender gave him a cut on the instep of his right foot, excluding him from the final, which he was forced to watch from the stands with the double bitterness of seeing the last great occasion slip through his fingers and the possibility of being in Cabrini's place at the moment of the penalty. The goal against Brazil would have been his first in

THE MATCH

a World Cup. Antognoni looked for it desperately in the semi-final against Poland until he was fouled, which put him out of action. 'It's a verdict I've carried with me all my life,' he later confessed bitterly. 'If Klein had not disallowed my goal, that injury would not have happened and I would not have missed my appointment in Madrid. It is a conviction that no one will ever take away from me.' He left the national team one year after the Spanish World Cup. He suffered another serious accident in the championship. He returned to the pitch 21 months and 51 matches later but too many things had changed in the meantime. The Coppa Italia he won in 1975 remained his only Italian trophy. Those won with the national team were stolen from him exactly 30 years after the Spanish triumph. These included the 14 gold medals (one per match) donated by the Italian Football Federation for the 1978 World Cup in Argentina and the 1982 World Cup in Spain, the four for the 1980 European Championship in Italy and the one for his first 20 appearances for the Azzurri. Shortly before, in 2011, Antognoni and Klein met by chance in Tel Aviv, where the former Viola champion was accompanying the Italian Under-17 national team. The elderly referee approached him good-naturedly as soon as he recognised him: 'Look who's here!' Antognoni played along. Neither of them mentioned the episode of the disallowed goal.

When Gentile climbed the steps of the Bernabéu to receive the World Cup, he crossed paths with Darwin Pastorin. Their happy embrace was immortalised in *G'olé!*, the official film of the World Cup. Zoff's arms, intent on lifting the cup ended up instead, after Zucchi's photo, on a postage stamp signed by Renato Guttuso. The Azzurri captain bade farewell to football a year after the Mundial: 'I can't cope with age.' If 82 remained a magic number for him, the same cannot be said of 83. Apart from being the year of his retirement, it was the number of the minute in which, during the Mundial, he conceded Collovati's goal against Peru, Passarella's free kick for Argentina and Breitner's flagship goal in the final against Germany.

He became an excellent coach and president until he gave up football for good. As a player, he won a European title and a world title with the national team, a feat never achieved by anyone else in Italy. He had the chance to win the European Championship also as a coach, in 2000, losing the final against France, only on a golden goal, scored by Trezeguet. The defeat unleashed the wrath of the then prime minister. 'From Mr Berlusconi,' said Zoff, 'I don't take lessons in dignity. It is not right to denigrate the work of others publicly, it is not right to disrespect a man who does his job with dedication and humility. A man and his professionalism have been insulted, a worker has been disrespected and I cannot accept this. This is not a political stance. My only policy, as you know, has always been sport.'

That day he was around a table in the meeting room on the first floor of Via Allegri in the FIGC headquarters. When he stopped talking, the journalists did not understand, until someone from behind asked: 'What does that mean? He's not resigning, is he?' He, dark in face: 'Of course. I know that this decision will cost me and that I probably won't come out of this well, but I can't not do it.' The same words as in Barcelona, at the time of the press silence.

He never had any regrets: 'I have received so much from life. I should kiss where I walk. I turned my passion into a job. I played for a long time, longer than I thought. I've been happy.' And among all the moments, the image that meant happiness for him was the kiss given to Bearzot at the Sarriá, after Italy vs Brazil: 'With that gesture I managed to scratch my modesty.' Throughout his life he has always spoken words full of affection, gratitude and admiration for the coach: 'We only won the World Cup because of him. We were all against him. Only a great leader could win a World Cup in that way.' When he turned 70 and was asked to define himself with an adjective, he replied: 'A serious person.' The International Football Hall of Fame inducted him as one of the 25 greatest players of all time, alongside Pelé, Beckenbauer, Cruyff and Zico.

With the victory in 1982, Italy became the only team together with Brazil to win a third World Cup. Before the match on 5 July,

THE MATCH

Zico said: 'Europe plays old football.' The first four teams of that World Cup were all European. Italy and Poland, two of the teams in the group deemed by journalists to be 'the flattest of the Mundial', came first and third, respectively, beating Germany and France, contradicting all the talk and rivers of ink. At the end of the final against Germany, it was Enrico Mentana, Franco's 27-year-old son, who broke the news on TG1.

Shortly afterwards, at 10.45pm, Giampiero Galeazzi for TG1, Gianfranco De Laurentiis for TG2 and Carlo Nesti for TG3, positioned themselves in front of the entrance to the RAI studio, ready to share three minutes each with Bearzot. The world champion coach appeared a quarter of an hour later, accompanied by Vantaggiato. He embraced the first two and gave them their allotted time, but when it was Nesti's turn, he got up and left. Many months later, having received a letter from the journalist, he explained to him that he had nothing against him, but that on this occasion he represented *Il processo* and Aldo Biscardi, who had attacked him so much.

After the press conference, Mario Sconcerti looked out on to the pitch to enjoy the last breath of a now deserted Bernabéu. Suddenly Bearzot appeared by him. Among a thousand questions, the journalist pulled out one that had been chasing him for some time. The most personal. 'Am I one of the good guys or the bad guys? I haven't figured it out yet.' Bearzot was exhausted but had the strength to hearten him. 'Rest assured, you are incapable of offending.'

Sconcerti made him understand that such deadly feelings were no longer of any use to a man who had become a legend. But he was immediately contradicted by Bearzot. 'I do not forget those who have offended me, I have too much respect for human values.'

'Even if they throw honey into every line now?'

Bearzot remained true to himself. 'Believe me, I drown in that honey, it disgusts me so much.'

After the Madrid final, Zoff stayed at the Santiago Bernabéu longer than his team-mates for interviews, gave his gloves to photographer Giuseppe Calzuola and returned to the hotel in the warehouseman's van. Gaetano Scirea was waiting for him. They simply had a bite to eat, accompanied by a glass. 'It seemed silly to us to celebrate in a sensational way,' the Azzurri captain said later, 'it was not like we could go dancing, it would be like dirtying the moment.' They went back to their rooms and lay down on their beds, exhausted, dazed and intoxicated by too much happiness. And they enjoyed their triumph in this way. 'To the last drop. Because nothing like sport can give such joy. But they only last a moment, and you have to make them last in your heart.'

The evening at the Santiago Bernabéu was an unforgettable celebration for Italy. President Pertini and coach Bearzot embraced each other in an way that today is the portrait of a world that no longer exists. Pertini presented Bearzot with a Mauro Armellini pipe and took the Azzurri back to Italy on the presidential plane. It was there that the famous scientific scopone between Bearzot–Pertini and Causio–Zoff was played. Pertini never wanted to lift the cup: 'That belongs to the players, they're the ones who won it!'

To celebrate the victory, however, the day after the final, the president invited the entire Italian delegation to the Quirinale. When he was informed of the arrangement of the diners ('On his right is Minister Signorello, on his left the president of CONI Carraro'), Pertini shouted: 'Signorello and Carraro again? This is the lunch in honour of the world champions: I want Bearzot on my right and Zoff, the captain, on my left.' At the table, they asked him what Chancellor Schmidt looked like. 'Like a beaten dog, but Kissinger was another one who was barking. The game made him suffer, because you have to know, guys, that Kissinger is German.'

Gentile, Tardelli, Scirea and Causio left football on the same day, 1 November 1988, with a match between the 1982 Italy and the world's best. Gentile still has Zico's jersey. Regarding the famous rip, he who, among other activities, worked with textiles in Como, later explained: 'The weave was not the best.' A light honeycomb net, with a wide pattern, in which a fingernail was caught. He was always considered a killer defender (in the list of the most ruthless players compiled by the English newspaper *The Times* he is in eighth place, followed by Bergomi and Tardelli), but unfairly: 'I never hurt anyone, the attackers I marked all played the next game.' In fact, in his entire career he was only sent off once, for a handball in midfield. In the match against Brazil he was cautioned at full stretch. Zico has always admitted that his marking was harsh, but not unfair: 'Gentile did his duty.' The two are still friends today. On 25 March 2017, they performed together during the television programme *Ballando con le stelle*, Italy's version of *Strictly Come Dancing*, scoring top marks.

The Black Jackets

As he himself had predicted, Italy vs Brazil was the last match refereed by Abraham Klein. Arnaldo César Coelho was chosen for the final, a nomination advocated by FIFA president João Havelange, a Brazilian, as compensation for the premature elimination of the green-and-yellow national team. However, Artemio Franchi wanted to pay tribute to the Israeli referee by including him as a linesman, so that he could experience the excitement of a World Cup Final. It was a sort of compensation for the final match in 1978, which he was due but was robbed of. When Cabrini missed the penalty, he rejoiced. In the event of a draw and therefore a replay, he would referee the final himself.

In any case, he could not end his career as a referee any other way. He had refereed Italy and Brazil all his life: Italy in their first international match, in Rome against Poland in 1965; the Seleção, after refereeing them in 1968 against Spain, he had taken charge in Mexico in 1970 against England. This was followed by Brazil vs Scotland and Brazil vs Portugal in 1972, Italy vs England and the Soviet Union vs Brazil in 1976, Italy vs Argentina and Brazil vs Italy in 1978 and Italy vs Yugoslavia in 1980. Not counting the 1979 Argentina vs Rest of the World Cup match, with a line-up coached by Bearzot that included four Italians (Cabrini, Tardelli, Rossi and Causio) and three Brazilians (Leão, Toninho and Zico).

David Miller in *The Times*, during the 1990 Italian World Cup, called him 'the best referee of the last twenty years'. So, the absolute best of his generation. The Brazilians, including Zico, still complain today about the penalty not being awarded for the shirt torn by Claudio Gentile in the first half. When Klein went to Brazil a few years after the match, the Globo television network chased him everywhere for four days, asking him about the episode. He finally replied: 'You forget that there was an offside, the linesman had raised his flag and the game was therefore stopped.' Klein, by the way, received a score of 9.2 for that match, the highest ever for a referee in a World Cup game.

In 2009, *08397B*, the documentary dedicated to FC Bayern Hof's tour of Israel in 1969, told the story of his refereeing in the first post-war match between a Jewish and a German team. In 2016, on the occasion of his 82nd birthday, he was interviewed by *Haaretz* reporter Uzi Dann. The journalist found himself in Haifa, in a small flat overlooking the sea, among photos and memorabilia: flags, magazines, emblems, ties, badges, cups, whistles and various trophies. There was the England vs Brazil ball, the same one that Pelé and Moore, Tostão and Charlton had kicked in 1970 and that, when it was headed by Pelé, was stopped by Banks with 'the save of the century'. There was the one from the 1982 final. And inside a plastic bag from the supermarket was the historic Italy vs Brazil ball. Uzi Dann asked to touch it. His hands were shaking. Touching the ball with which Paolo Rossi had scored a hat-trick, he felt one of the strongest emotions of his life: 'If football is a religion, I have touched the holy ark.'

In 2014 Klein had tried to donate his incredible collection, without encountering interest. But he – as he told Dann – did not want his memorabilia locked away in a private individual's flat. He wanted to see his collection in a museum, so that anyone could admire it, including generations born after the matches of his life. The educational intent remained intact. Finding no one, he auctioned off his memorabilia, including that from Italy vs Brazil, on eBay in

November 2016. The black kit (Adidas, made in France, 100 per cent polyester), the whistle (Balilla/2 G. Baldi, Florence), the cloth badge with the FIFA logo, the yellow card for cautions, the match report, the Tango ball and the digital watch (Seiko Sports 100 branded FIFA, serial number 120303). A few months later, FIFA, via the newspaper *Haaretz*, became aware of the auction and finally realised the rarity of Klein's memorabilia. Moritz Ansorge, curator of the FIFA Football Museum, asked Klein to close the eBay auction to acquire the entire collection.

At the beginning of July 2017, 35 years after the Italy vs Brazil match, referee Klein and his wife Bracha travelled to Zürich to bring back the kit he wore that day and the match ball. He touched it for the last time and handed it over to an emotional Ansorge: 'It is an incredible treasure that I have found in my hands.' In honour of this legacy, on 25 October 2017 at 7.30pm the FIFA World Football Museum paid tribute to Klein in front of Israeli Football Federation president Ofer Eini, referee president Uzi Itzhaki and Haifa mayor Yona Yahav. The dream of seeing his collection in a museum came true.

His son Amit, who returned safely from the war in Lebanon, followed in his footsteps and became a professional referee.

Bulgarian referee Bogdan Dochev was the linesman for Argentina vs England four years after Italy vs Brazil at the Azteca Stadium in Mexico City. From his line he saw 'the goal of the century' and validated the goal remembered as *'La mano de Dios'*, or 'Hand of God'. Both goals were scored by Diego Armando Maradona. In 2014 the Bulgarian admitted that he saw the player's irregularity but could not report it because at the time FIFA regulations allowed the linesman to give his opinion only if he was involved by the referee: 'On that occasion the referee Ali Bin Nasser validated the goal without even looking at me.' It is a reconstruction denied by the Tunisian black jacket: 'It was not my fault. In that World Cup the assistants were not considered as they are now, the referee had to decide on everything. At the time FIFA gave us a piece of advice: only listen to the linesman if he is better placed than you. I had doubts, but I saw Dochev running towards midfield and I had to adjust. Did Dochev blame me? He too was fooled by Shilton's hand.'

For that hand, Dochev died (on 29 May 2017) tormented by remorse. His wife Emily a year later revealed to *The Sun* that the failure to report it had ruined her husband's life. After the mistake, in fact, he had written on the back of a photo of the Argentine champion 'Maradona is my gravedigger'. 'That World Cup,' she said, 'ruined our lives, because Bogdan isolated himself from everyone and our friends didn't even say hello to us anymore.' The widow Dochev laid the blame on Bin Nasser, who was guilty of ordering her husband: 'You do nothing, the calls will be mine alone.' Thus the world knew '*La mano de Dios*' and thus Dochev became the linesman who had not seen it.

For the other assistant, Thomson Chan Tam-Sun, Mundial 82 remained the highest peak of his career. Despite holding the title of the only Hong Kong referee ever to have participated in the final stage of a World Cup, the championships in Spain turned out to be a bad deal for him. He had been thinking of turning down the invitation since the call-up, having received a very good job offer. When he returned home after Italy vs Brazil, the job had already been given to someone else. But if he is still remembered today, it is only because of that World Cup.

The Scopone Plane

The plane that brought home the 1982 world champion national team found itself at the centre of much debate between 2013 and 2016. The historic aircraft used for the scientific scopone between Pertini, Bearzot, Zoff and Causio was the McDonnell Douglas DC9-30 of the air force, purchased in 1974 with funds from the Council Presidency and used by the 31st Wing for medical and VIP transport.

Its story hides a lie. It began at the end of 1973 when, in order to meet the need to provide the Italian General Staff with a more modern

THE MATCH

fleet, the Italian government decided to purchase two brand-new DC9-30 aircraft. They were practically identical to those intended for the civilian market, but with the passenger cabin modified for VIP transport. The capacity was reduced to 45 passengers to allow the two aircraft to offer considerably more comfort. In fact, the empty space at the front of the fuselage was fitted out with two reserved lounges.

For the purchase order, presented to McDonnell Douglas not by the Ministry of Defence but directly by the Presidency of the Council of Ministers, 6.9 billion lire was allocated from the 1973 budget. However, management was entrusted entirely to the air force through the Reparto Volo Stato Maggiore in Rome-Ciampino. In their history they have flown three presidents (Pertini, Cossiga and Scalfaro), a pontiff (John Paul II) and a World Cup. One of the two aircraft was decommissioned by the air force in 2001 and sold first to Boeing as part of the purchase of KC-767 tankers, then to Alitalia in 2007, when it was transported by urban route from Ciampino to Fiumicino. It was no longer able to fly and was therefore assigned to the company's maintenance school for the training of its technicians.

In 2010, the fleet was renewed and Alitalia decided to equip the school with a more modern and therefore more suitable aircraft. The DC9 was thus replaced and Alitalia, not wanting to dismantle it, kept it at Fiumicino, parking it in the square in front of the Avio 5 hangar at Leonardo da Vinci airport, where it occupied a full maintenance bay.

Alitalia was the first to realise that it could not get rid of this piece of history and, over the years, the company tried to donate the aircraft to entities interested in preserving and enhancing it. Between 2013 and 2015, three different entities (a museum, a company and a training institute) showed interest, but in the end, frightened by the complexity of the transport operations, they gave up the project. Since it was impossible to donate the aircraft, Alitalia was forced to consider scrapping it. 'For years we have been trying to save what has become a symbol of our country,' said the company's president, Luca Cordero di Montezemolo, who was present at the Sarriá in Barcelona on 5

THE SCOPONE PLANE

July 1982. 'We are ready to donate it, but so far we have not found anyone willing. We've been trying to save it since 2010, looking for buyers, but those who initially expressed an interest have since taken a step back.'

However, the Alitalia managers were confident: 'We will not be left alone in this endeavour.' They then made contact with the FIGC. The idea was to save at least one piece of that historical page of Italian football: the lounge that hosted the card players, four seats and a wooden table, so as to recreate the iconic scene in the Museum of Football in Florence. It was still an embryonic hypothesis, but it began to appear in the top management of Via Allegri. Luca Di Bartolomei, responsible for sport in the Democratic Party, made an appeal to the two parties involved: 'It would be nice if Alitalia dismantled that piece of sports history and the FIGC found a place to recreate that scene in the Florence Football Museum.' However, the hypothesis fell through.

Thus began a race against time. Italy mobilised. The web became the primary forum for controversy. There were those who considered it shameful to abandon a piece of history, and those who considered it equally shameful to preserve it while the country was experiencing one of the worst economic crises in its history. On 17 March 2016, Alitalia finally reached an agreement with the Fondazione Museo dell'Aeronautica Volandia, and four months later the aircraft came to occupy the space adjacent to Milan-Malpensa Airport, the only one able to preserve it in its integrity. The piece of history, it was promised, would soon be on display for all to see. 'We are very happy that this affair has ended in the best possible way,' Montezemolo commented. 'Alitalia has always tried to prevent a symbol of national memory from being lost. In that shot,' he said, referring to the famous photo, 'are represented some of the figures most loved and dearest to all Italians.' The Italian airline then thanked those who had generously offered to protect a piece of the country's history.

In reality, the epic misrepresented the story. The first of the two military DC9-30s registered MM62012 arrived at Ciampino in the first half of 1974, followed a few weeks later by the second one registered MM62013. On 8 February 1999, the latter was parked at Moscow's Vnukovo airport waiting to pick up Prime Minister Massimo D'Alema to take him back to Rome after a visit to the Russian capital. President Boris Yeltsin had just landed at the same airport on his return from Amman. The wing of his Ilyushin II-96 military aircraft seriously damaged the tail of the Italian aircraft during taxiing in the parking phase. Following the incident, Russian Prime Minister Primakov played down the situation: 'Our two countries are so close that even our aircraft felt the need to meet.' He then presented D'Alema with a model of a plane. But the DC9 remained on the ground, injured, never to rise again. Its repair was economically valued much higher than the residual value of the airframe. So it was 'forcibly' decommissioned, and then dismantled on site. It was the 'Mundial aircraft', the one with the designation MM62013. The spirits of all parties involved have for years revolved around an aircraft that was not what it was thought to be.

The aircraft that had instead taken the Azzurri to Spain (the Alitalia Boeing 727-243/Adv I-DIRS cn 22168/1770 City of Sulmona, delivered to Alitalia on 3 September 1981 and then decommissioned in favour of People Express, in 1985, Continental Airlines, 1987, and Hinduja Cargo Services, 1997) crashed into a hill on 7 July 1999, after taking off from Kathmandu-Tribhuvan airport, in Nepal, causing the death of five crew members. Curiously, the outbound and inbound aircraft stopped in the same year, within five months.

Jumping on the Bandwagon

The day after the Sarriá match, the circulation of the *Gazzetta dello Sport* and *Corriere dello Sport* exceeded one million copies, while *Tuttosport* broke the 400,000 mark. On 6 July 1982, part of the Italian newspapers used the title '*Il Brasile siamo noi*' (Brazil is us). The *Corriere dello Sport-Stadio*, which the day before had headlined '*Avanti Brasil!*' (Come forward Brazil!), came out with '*Perdonaci, Brasil!*'

(Forgive us, Brazil!) The *Gazzetta* had *'Fantastico!' La Repubblica*, for the first time, gave a huge space to football on its front page with the headline *'L'Italia nel pallone'* (Italy on the ball). Guglielmo Zucconi compared the Italian victory to Gino Bartali's feat in the 1948 Tour de France. 'Italian skill crushes Brazilian art', *The Times* headlined. *El Periodico* proposed: 'Let's turn the Sarriá into a museum. One of the best matches in the history of the World Cup. We haven't seen football like this for years. Bearzot is a prestigious coach.' The future Nobel Prize winner Mario Vargas Llosa also joined the chorus, praising the Azzurri in the *Corriere della Sera*: 'It would be a resounding injustice to say that Enzo Bearzot's team won the match because Telê Santana's team played badly.' The Spanish journalist Quique Peinado, years later, referring to Brazil, wrote: 'The 1982 World Cup welcomed what for many was the best national team of any country of any era in the history of football, and certainly the strongest team that participated in a World Cup without winning it.'

A few days after the match, it came out that the reporter of *Avvenire*, Bruno Amatucci, had convinced Bearzot, during the long night before the match, to put Gentile, instead of Tardelli, against Zico. The director of *Unità*, Emanuele Macaluso, congratulated him. The public praise of a communist to a Catholic was yet another miracle of the World Cup.

With the Mundial victory, sales increased further. The *Gazzetta dello Sport* exceeded 1.4 million copies; the *Corriere dello Sport* sold 1.6 million, an unbeaten record among all Italian newspapers. In order to save time, Giorgio Tosatti had written his piece cold the day before. The record circulation was also made possible by the fact that *La Repubblica*, with which the sports daily shared its printing house, did not come out on the newsstands on Mondays. The *Guerin Sportivo* exceeded 300,000 copies. Oreste del Buono's editorial remained famous: 'Bearzot has not missed a name, a mark or a move. I realise I'm writing rubbish. I stop, it is the night of a true national triumph. In Italy, I'm told, something is happening that resembles all the national holidays put together, 24th May, 28th October, 25th

THE MATCH

July, 25th April and so on, then tomorrow we'll wake up from this true dream to a reality, or rather a shitty unreality. We don't have a penny. Patience, let's make this night last. It should never pass.' These numbers marked the start of the great publishing boom of the 1980s. The sports dailies doubled their usual circulation and reached their highest audience ever. But in order to satisfy the ever-growing demand for news, they began to raise the tone and lower the quality.

If the publishers were gloating, the Italian journalists were the real losers of that World Cup. The day after the match, some rushed to give explanations or justifications ('A clarification with the readers is appropriate ...' wrote Carlo Grandini in the *Corriere della Sera*). Most, however, began to jump on the Bearzot bandwagon with the utmost indifference and the typical Italian art of making do. Only a few apologised: Claudio Carabba in the *Nazione* wrote: 'I regret having doubted to the end the intelligence of Enzo Bearzot, whom I believed to be a poor man, and who instead was an indestructible leader ... I regret having humiliated and offended Paolo Rossi ... Finally, I regret having repeatedly mocked the 40 years of Zoff, magnificent captain of the future, who ... avoided tragedy by flying to block, right on the fatal goal line, the ball hit by the head of a Brazilian whose name I don't even want to know.'

It was not the only *mea culpa*. 'Let's acknowledge it openly,' wrote Candido Cannavò in the *Gazzetta dello Sport*, 'the greatness of what happened also lies in this stupendous remorse of ours.' 'After having criticised him so harshly,' wrote Bearzot's most bitter critic, Giorgio Tosatti, in the *Corriere dello Sport*, 'let's take our hat off to him and apologise. He will lose friendlies, he will make mistakes, but at the moment that counts, his team flourishes, his stubbornness proves to be wise, his choices exact, his tactics apt. It would be cowardly not to tell him he was right.'

Bearzot, for his part, in the press conference after the match, did not want to take revenge against anyone. Giampiero Masieri wrote in the *Nazione*, 'And this, too, is a way of winning.' Roberto Renga, a rookie reporter at the 82 Mundial, admitted in 2008: 'As a

JUMPING ON THE BANDWAGON

category we were completely wrong in our evaluation of the Italian national team.'

Italy, by winning the title, managed to prove everyone wrong, and the journalists made a world-class fool of themselves. Before 1982, the pen hurt more than the sword, the reporters used cutting judgements, rejecting everything. Since then, however, caution had become the watchword. The press was careful not to make predictions and, at least in the newspapers, Italy were often one of the favourites.

Brera remembered the bet. He wrote in *La Repubblica* after the match: 'I will put on the flagellants' habit and follow the procession of St Bartholomew in August in my village.' A promise that, of course, he did not keep. On questioning the Lombardy lunarian, he realised that, fortunately for him, the procession had been abolished years ago. He had once again managed to gamble, lose and not pay the price.

At the Sarriá, Michele Plastino managed to capture exclusive footage of the first statements made by Falcão, Sócrates and Zico, as well as Sordillo and Matarrese, as they left the stadium. He also stole the unexpected joy of the RAI reporters, a now voiceless Gianfranco De Laurentiis and a sweaty Beppe Viola: 'I feel like I'm going crazy. I've finally lost ten kilos.'

'Even ten years,' replied Plastino.

'I've gained ten years.'

Unfortunately, this was not the case. Once the Mundial summer was over, a sudden illness put an end to his short, dazzling life. He joked that he had only one dream: to meet at least one Albanian. 'How will it be done? We've never seen one in Italy.' If only he had lived a little longer: nine years later, on board merchant ships and boats of all kinds, thousands of refugees began to arrive in the port of Brindisi, fleeing dictatorship and the crisis, in search of a better future.

Six months after the match, on 3 January 1983, the heart also proved fatal for photojournalist João Batista Scalco, the 'Van Gogh of the Pampas', who had immortalised Falcão's exultation and turned it into an iconic image. At only 32 years of age, he left behind two children, Mariano and Juliana. A street in Rio de Janeiro is dedicated

THE MATCH

to him. After the Mundial, Jurema, the woman who, according to the Brazilian press, had had a mystical influence on her husband Roberto Dinamite's two World Cup convocations, also left us.

In the space of a few years, the asphalt took away the diplomatic Franchi, the timid Scirea, the arch-rival Brera and the likeable Dirceu. Five years after the Spanish championships, the director of *Tuttosport*, Pier Cesare Baretti, died in a plane crash.

The 17-year-old Fabio Fazio, hidden in the hedge of Alassio, once an adult conquered full popularity with a programme dedicated to Sunday football. In giving it a name, he wanted to pay homage to the reporter Beppe Viola, the man who had 'covered' him in 1982, calling it *Quelli che … il calcio* (Those who … football), paraphrasing the title of a famous song, 'Quelli che …' (sung by Enzo Jannacci, who never, however, credited it to his journalist friend).

Since the 1970 World Cup Final, Nando Martellini had been waiting for the moment to shout his joy. He waited for three World Cups. At the final whistle, with his voice broken by emotion, he shouted three times: 'World champions, world champions, world champions.'

Shortly after the Mundial, Paolo Samarelli knocked on the door of *La Repubblica*. The same day, Mario Sconcerti, the head of the sports pages, asked him to stay on. After almost a decade, he joined Scalfari's court as a professional journalist, later becoming head of the graphics department, a role from which he resigned in 2013, after 32 years working for the newspaper. His 'moviole' from the days of the *Guerino* are a cult object among collectors. He has not kept a single original sketch.

Finland's Juha Tamminen continued to follow Italy until the final. The year after the Mundial he became a professional photographer. He took part in four more World Cups (1986, 1990, 1994 and 1998), interviewed Pelé and shot over 100,000 pictures. He no longer follows football. His biggest regret is related to Maradona's '*Mano de Dios*': he lowered his camera at the moment the ball was in the air: 'It was the mistake of my life.'

464

Four years after the Mundial, one of the four reporters of *La Repubblica*, Oliviero Beha, together with Stefano Chiodi, claimed that the draw between Italy and Cameroon was the result of an agreement. The hypothesis, supported by testimonies deemed unreliable, above all that of a cook who acted as an intermediary between the reporters and some Cameroonian players, was never proven but gave the journalist enormous celebrity. When he died in 2017, he was remembered mainly for his investigation into the so-called Mundialgate.

The Fate of the 'Powers'

Spadolini's government ended in the same summer of 1982 (on 22 August), due to what he himself called the 'quarrel of the housewives' (between the two finance ministers of his government, the Christian Democrat Nino Andreatta, Treasury, and the Socialist Rino Formica, Finance). The following day he reconstituted a government perfectly identical to the previous one but in November he had to resign because of the disengagement of Bettino Craxi's Italian Socialist Party. He became defence minister in both the first and second governments headed by Bettino Craxi. Crushed by the coalition government (the Pentapartito or CAF), he no longer took part in other such governments. He became president of the Senate of the Republic and was appointed senator for life. In 1994, a few months after another Italy vs Brazil match, he was put forward again for the presidency of the Senate in the legislature that marked the beginning of the Second Republic. He lost by a single (disputed) vote. It was the end of an era, his era. He died two weeks after the Pasadena World Cup Final. He was one of the few politicians who was never touched by the Tangentopoli investigations. Considered one of the best Italian statesmen, he was far-sighted in hypothesising a blue 1982 in the collective memory.

After winning the World Cup in Spain, Bearzot became director of all the FIGC national teams, while Allodi was exiled from

THE MATCH

the Coverciano Technical Centre. Their 15 years of silence were interrupted six years later, in Coverciano, with an emotional embrace. Involved and then acquitted in the second lacerating episode of the betting scandal, Allodi spent his final years in endless bitterness, living his melancholic twilight in oblivion. He died in a clinic in Florence, struck down by a heart attack on 3 June 1999 at the age of 71, taking with him forever the glory of monumental successes (from the Inter of Angelo Moratti and Helenio Herrera to the construction of Maradona's Naples, passing through the Juventus cycle of the early 1970s) and the shadow of unfathomable mysteries.

The physical and emotional wear and tear that came with being president of the Royal Mundial Organisation Committee cost Raimundo Saporta his health, depression and finally his life. Bernabéu's prophecy ('The highest chair will only cause you pain') had come true. Saporta had avoided any kind of prominence all his life, making an exception only for the World Cup, but he was never the same again. A few months after the Mundial he asked the Banco Exterior de España for retirement. Later, the imminence of the end led him to make a statement: 'I was a bad athlete when I was young. But after that I was neither a player, nor a referee, nor a coach, nor even a spectator. From the stands I never watched a game: I had to make sure that everything was going well. Only at the end did I check the result. I was only the manager of two teams: the poorest one, in high school, where I had to buy balls and paint the lines on the field, and the richest one.'

A few weeks before his death, during a Spanish tournament (the 32nd Christmas Tournament), the people in the stadium paid him a warm tribute. Moved, he replied: 'I thank you with all my heart, I know that this will be the last tournament I will see in my life.' And so it was. A little over a month later, on a cold February Sunday, the huge heart of one of the best sports directors of all time stopped beating. Shortly before his departure, with the death of Doña Simona, he had paid off the debt of gratitude that bound him to his mother and, at almost 70 years of age, had married Arlette Politi Treves, his

THE FATE OF THE 'POWERS'

discreet lifelong companion (officially another Frenchwoman living in Madrid, like him, but in reality also a Sephardic). The figure of Saporta, in Italy, has been completely forgotten.

Manager Carlo De Gaudio followed the final against Germany from the stands, alongside Cabrini's wife, who he had to console after her husband's missed penalty. Then the enthusiasm dragged him on to the pitch, crouching behind a billboard, to enjoy the Italian triumph. He was also head of the Italian national football team at the 1984 Los Angeles Olympics and the 1986 World Cup in Mexico. At the World Cup in Italy four years later, he was the president of the organising committee in Naples. Five matches were played at the San Paolo, including the semi-final that Italy lost on penalties to Maradona's Argentina. Pressed by the requests of personalities, he enlarged the VIP stand to find seats for Kissinger, Agnelli, Spadolini, Andreotti, Carraro, the mayor Lezzi, Gardini, Pescante, Matarrese, Boniperti and Neapolitan politicians.

Four years after the Spanish Mundial, there was a new betting scandal (Totonero bis), then Italy, the defending champions, were eliminated in the round of 16 of the 1986 World Cup by France. These events led the president of the FIGC, Federico Sordillo, to resign on 4 July. Matarrese, on the other hand, continued his collection of chairs (after being president of Bari, of the league and Christian Democracy deputy for five legislatures, he sat on the FIGC, UEFA and UNIRE), managing to float at the highest levels for 30 years. He represented Italy during the 1994 World Cup in the United States, that of Roberto Baggio, but always remained an instinctive and authoritarian blunderer. Sitting in his chauffeur-driven blue car, on his way to the national team's retreat, he stuck his hand out of the window and handed a pair of horns to another car he had just overtaken, which was guilty of going too slowly. On board was the Bishop of Frascati, Monsignor Giuseppe Matarrese, his brother.

João Havelange remained president until 1998. During his 24 years as president, he doubled the number of participating teams from the traditional 16 to 24 in 1982 in Spain and then to 32 in 1998 in

THE MATCH

France, his last World Cup. With these changes, continents such as Africa, North America and Asia were able to have more teams in the finals of the World Cup. On 8 June 1998, two days before the start of the French World Cup, Joseph Blatter of Switzerland, who had been secretary since 1981, beat the UEFA president, Lennart Johansson of Sweden, to be elected Havelange's successor, and officially took office the following month, after the event. The Estádio Parque do Sabiá (Estádio Municipal João Havelange) in 1982 and the Estádio Olímpico de Rio (Estádio Olímpico João Havelange) in 2007 were named after the Brazilian president. He remained honorary president of FIFA until 18 April 2013, when, at the age of 97, he was forced to resign following his involvement in the ISL corruption case. After 8,760 days in office, 7,200 of which were spent away from home, 800 hours a year in the air (a total of 288 flights between Rio and Zürich), he died at 100 years old in 2016, overwhelmed by the deluge of scandals into which FIFA was sinking. Mocked by fate, he passed away just four days before the football final of the Rio Games that he himself had so strongly wanted, without being able to witness Brazil's first epic Olympic victory.

The Adidas Tango was the last leather ball in a World Cup. Its creator, Horst Dassler, died on 9 April 1987 at the age of 51. Emanuela Audisio paid tribute to him in *La Repubblica* as follows:

> Dassler was a great mediator between worlds that were too different to talk to each other. Thanks to Dassler, professionalism has made and is still making an appearance in worlds that had previously rejected it (see the USSR, see the Olympic world). Not only is the great representative of an economic empire leaving (the sisters will be there to run a factory with a turnover of three thousand billion lire), but also a period of fluidity and sports-political stability. Dassler was many things: the most important needle in the scales, the public relations man, the dispenser of votes. Dassler built up a dangerous monopoly, but it is also thanks

to his diabolical talent that the sport was able to grow and multiply. As of today he leaves many orphans and much anarchy.

Three years later he was followed by his cousin Armin, son of Rudolf (the father of the Puma). The Dassler war ended with them. Distracted by this, the two factions underestimated the rise of running and athletics in general in the 80s, encouraging Reebok and Nike to enter the market. The last member of the founding family to take up the reins was Frank Dassler, Rudolf's grandson, who until 2018 headed the group's legal department, but within Adidas. An unthinkable situation just a few years earlier. In 2010, the Tango ball was described as 'the best football of all time' by Goal.com.

Tycoon Rolf Deyhle, the only private citizen in possession of a FIFA World Cup, took his own life with a firearm on 2 May 2014 in a nursing home in Badenweiler. Devastated by depression, which he did not want to consider and therefore treat, he died just a few weeks before the World Cup in Brazil. In addition to collecting paintings, sports marketing and staging musicals, he had produced successful films such as *Sommersby, One Day of Ordinary Madness* and *JFK*. In 2006 he commissioned Germany's oldest auction house to sell the cup. 'I've had it for almost 30 years,' he told the Associated Press in Stuttgart. 'I'll be 70 in two years. I have six children and I want to put my house in order, as they say here. I can't divide this trophy into six and that's why I've decided to sell it while I still can.' Auctioneer Lars Axendorf declared, 'The starting price is one million euros; we hope to get 10, 15 or 20.' The winner of the world's most coveted sports trophy was to be announced on 28 June (on the day between the round of 16 and the quarter-finals of the German World Cup). FIFA, fearing that the winner might start trading it, put pressure on Deyhle to curb his intention, who replied: 'I received this cup as a gift for my contribution to FIFA and I can manage it as I see fit. I have to provide for my children, the proceeds will be part of their inheritance.' FIFA, through a spokesman, let it be known that it would have recourse to its lawyers to prevent the sale of a trophy, according to it, protected by copyright. In the end Deyhle, in agreement with FIFA, decided to stop the auction. Seven years later, Bernd Weissbrod was the last person to photograph him with his trophies. In the picture taken on 30 September 2013, Deyhle posed in his Stuttgart studio, caressing the FIFA Fair Play Trophy he had invented with one hand and the cup given to him by Helmut Käser with the other. But his eyes were already lost in the void.

The editor of the *Corriere della Sera*, Angelo Rizzoli, was arrested in 1983 on charges of having made disappear the funds intended for the 1981 capital increase of the RCS group, and was then sentenced to three years and four months in prison. He suffered 407 days of detention (first in San Vittore, then in Como, then in Lodi, and finally in Bergamo), the worsening in his cell of the multiple sclerosis from which he had been suffering since 1963, the robbery of the most important Italian publishing company founded by his grandfather Angelo, the death of his father Andrea by heartbreak, the suicide of his sister Isabella at the age of 23, and the unjustified arrest of his brother Alberto. Shortly before he died, his father said: 'After working for 48 years, I lost everything. The company, the name, the children in prison. The house in Via del Gesù is mortgaged, I gave away the land and the plane. I'm burdened with debts, more than a hundred billion in debts incurred by my son. Today I have nothing of my own. Only debts. If you add up my father's labours and mine, we have worked exactly one hundred years to build the Rizzoli empire. Angelo destroyed it in two years.'

All of Angelone's assets, including the 50.2 per cent of the publishing house that remained in his possession, were seized and entrusted to judicial custodians. After six definitive acquittals in the Court of Cassation, Rizzoli could not dispose of them even after his return to freedom. In a subsequent trial, in 1992, the Court of Cassation ruled that the entrepreneur had not retained part of the funds paid by Roberto Calvi's *La Centrale*. Those funds had disappeared at the hands of Tassan Din, Gelli and Ortolani. In 2006 the crime for which

THE FATE OF THE 'POWERS'

he was arrested in 1983 was decriminalised. He lived the last years of his life in Rome, in the Parioli neighbourhood, in via Pietro Paolo Rubens, a few steps from where Juan Carlos lived. On 14 February 2013 he was arrested on charges of fraudulent bankruptcy. Suffering from sclerosis, diabetes mellitus, chronic renal failure, hypertension, pancreatitis and a cervical myopathy, he was admitted to the detention ward of the Sandro Pertini hospital. After being placed under house arrest and released, on 30 November he was admitted to the Policlinico Gemelli, where he died during the evening of 11 December 2013, at the age of 70. His final destiny linked him to Bruno Tassan Din, his managing director at Rizzoli-Corriere della Sera. Caught up in the P2 affair and sentenced to eight years for the bankruptcy of the old Banco Ambrosiano, he too fell ill with multiple sclerosis and died in 2000 at the age of 65 from a cerebral haemorrhage.

Franco D'Attoma, the president of the 'Perugia of miracles', undefeated for an entire championship (1978/79), the man who bought Paolo Rossi and introduced sponsorship to the Italian league, returned to manage the Umbrian team until an incurable illness ended his life in 1991. The foundation he had conceived (in order to circumvent federal rules) of a knitwear factory with the name of a pasta factory changed the history of football forever, triggering an unstoppable process. As a result of his attempts, in the pre-Mundial season, the FIGC and the leagues raised the white flag and opened the doors to commercial sponsors, allowing them to be displayed on shirts. The real surrender was signed when D'Attoma himself was entrusted with the direction of Promocalcio, the league structure created to manage sponsorship.

Rino Gaetano and Antonello Venditti dedicated a verse to the flight of Felice Riva, president of Milan between Rizzoli and Carraro. In the 'Switzerland of the East', former president Riva had returned to live like a young lord. But in 1982 the wind changed and his hotel became a battleground, the one fought by Amit Klein. He returned to Italy with a Lebanese passport on 15 June, his birthday. The World Cup in Spain had just started, and a few hours earlier Italy had met Poland and Brazil played the Soviet Union. Fate came to his rescue once again. Pardons, amnesties and foreign citizenship saved him: he was not punishable because he was a foreign citizen. After the Mundial no one looked for him anymore: forgotten, but free for the rest of his life, which ended in 2017.

The Man Who Did Not Want America

Artemio Franchi was under all kinds of pressure from former Secretary of State Henry Kissinger, a great football lover, to allow the United States to host a World Cup. Already during the Mundial he had publicly expressed his desire. The day after the Sarriá match, Kissinger flew to Spain to watch the final stages. On that occasion, after praising the organisation – 'It was a perfect World Cup' – and congratulating Raimundo Saporta, he told the press: 'If for some reason Colombia is unable to organise the 1986 World Cup in their country, the United States would be willing to do it.' Then, after regretting the elimination of the Brazilians and welcoming the Italian victory, he hoped to find Italy and Germany in the final. And that is what happened. When Colombia withdrew on 5 November 1982, his other wish did not come true.

Four months later, in the spring of 1983, FIFA was to decide in Stockholm on the venue for the 1986 World Cup (for which the United States was also in the running) and lay the groundwork for the 1990 tournament. The Americans had sniffed out the business. The organising committee estimated a revenue of $400 million, a quarter of which would come from television rights alone. Among the main sponsors, Pepsi could have supplanted its competitor Coca-Cola and was represented by Pelé. Alongside him was Franz Beckenbauer, captain of the 1974 World Cup champions Germany and Horst Dassler's ally. The day before the award, Kissinger invited Franchi to breakfast on the French veranda of the Grand Hotel in the heart of the old city, overlooking the Royal Palace. With him were Havelange and Elliot S. Berry, manager of an agency that managed television rights. The team offered 20 per cent more than the sum guaranteed by the Mexicans. Franchi listened in obvious embarrassment, then explained his reasons: 'You cannot turn a football championship into an advertising business for its own sake.' The following day the votes went as he had planned (Mexico was unanimously awarded the 1986 edition; Italy was given the option for 1990).

The next day Franchi confided to Franco Mentana: 'I will never agree to a World Cup for multinationals. The Americans wanted to put football in the hands of the multinationals, to have it played on tartan and in artificial light, even during the day, in covered stadiums. It would completely distort the game, transform it into something that would no longer be football. A world championship cannot be distorted, not even for a billion dollars. They will have to go over my dead body to get there.'

Having lost the opportunity of the 1986 and 1990 editions, the United States, two months later, started again with a request for the 1994 finals. The usual exchange between Kissinger and Franchi had the same epilogue. The following month Franchi found two Americans waiting for him in the Rome hotel where he was staying. The UEFA president explained to them that, to be optimistic, it would not be possible before 1998: 'FIFA's effort is to bring football to African nations, so one of them will host the World Cup. It won't be big business, but football cannot live only on business.' The following day Franchi had lunch with Dassler in Rome. 'European shoe exports are starting to annoy the Americans,' explained the German, 'and their insistence comes precisely from the desire to relaunch an entire US sportswear sector at world level.' It was their last meeting, exactly one year after Italy vs Brazil: 5 July 1983.

If his friend's words worried him, the family news was bringing him much joy. Earlier in the year, Giovanna's daughter had given birth to her first granddaughter, Maria (named after her mother), to whom her son Francesco would soon add a second grandchild.

Thirty-eight days after his meeting with Dassler, a Fiat Argenta was waiting for him in front of the Bruzzi building, the oil company he had founded. A little earlier he had telephoned the jockey Silvano

THE MATCH

Vigni, known as 'Bastiano': 'I'm in the piazza, I'm leaving soon and I'll come to you.' Franchi took state road 438 that would have taken him first to Vescona, to pick up Vigni, then to Siena for the traditional dinner of the contrada della Torre, on the eve of the Palio dell'Assunta. The car he was driving crashed into a lorry travelling in the opposite direction. By a melancholy coincidence, the owner of the vehicle was Danilo Boschi, captain of the Bruco, a dear friend and adversary of Franchi. Intervention was immediate and the rescuers soon realised that the driver of the Argenta was UEFA president Franchi. They did everything they could to revive him, but to no avail. Artemio died in the ambulance that was transporting him at breakneck speed to the Le Scotte polyclinic in Siena. This was the demise of the greatest Italian sports manager of the post-war period, the man that everyone designated as Havelange's successor.

The autopsy report spoke of a crushed chest and ruptured aorta. Shortly after 7.30pm, the Ansa news agency issued its first, brief announcement of Artemio Franchi's death. In those minutes, the telephone also rang in the Franchi family's beach house in Vittoria Apuana. During the night, the contrada della Torre transferred the body of their captain to the chapel of Salicotto dedicated to the patron saints Anne and James. From dawn, a continuous flow of relatives, friends, acquaintances, authorities and sports personalities began, all gathered around his wife Alda and children Francesco and Giovanna. Outside the church, bouquets and wreaths of flowers from the Torre and the other contrade, from Sienese personalities and from the world of football, from friends and authorities, piled up along the road. From Siena, his body was taken to Coverciano, the technical centre that he had wanted and made important. At the funeral there were, among others, the president of FIFA João Havelange, who had arrived from Rio de Janeiro, Jacques Georges, who would replace Franchi as president of UEFA, the representatives of the European federations, the presidents of CONI, Carraro, of the FIGC, Sordillo, of the football league, Matarrese, Fino Fini, doctor of the national team, the Fiorentina team and the Azzurri coach Bearzot.

474

MADE IN ITALY

Artemio's last tribute to Italian football came indirectly on the day of his funeral, when Havelange said: 'Many nations, including Italy, have asked to organise the 1990 World Cup. In order to honour Artemio Franchi's memory, FIFA will award the organisation to his country next year.' In front of the coffin he added: 'We must commit ourselves to fulfilling Artemio's wish.' And that is what happened. The stadiums in Florence and Siena were named after Franchi. In 1995, referee Klein dedicated his autobiography to him.

The accidental death of Franchi never convinced the journalist Alberto Ballarin, who dedicated a series of journalistic investigations to the episode, at the end of which his doubts were reinforced: 'One wonders whether it was really fate or not a murderous hand that drove that car.'

Ballarin, who had grown up in the circle of Gianni Brera and worked for *Gazzetta* and *Guerino*, noticed that the Carabinieri had found no sign of braking on Franchi's car (whose braking system was intact) and that no autopsy had been performed. As the investigation continued, it became apparent that the fire brigade's intervention to extract his body was untrue and that the window to the right of the driver was down. Nor did the times add up: more than 30 minutes to cover 12 kilometres of a road with which he was more than familiar. His investigation focused on the hypothesis of two foreign motorcyclists who allegedly stopped him with an excuse, rendered him unconscious (if not lifeless) and left him for a collision without being able to offer any resistance (as shown by the fractures on his arms). Whether this hypothesis is true or not, once and Dassler died, by the United States won the right to host the 1994 World Cup, beating Morocco by three votes.

Made in Italy

Winning the World Cup contributed decisively to generating a newfound national pride. For the first time since the end of the war, the tricolour was hoisted on balconies all over the country and adopted by marketing and advertising. Identifying with 'Made in Italy', it became synonymous with success. Abroad, it became a business card capable of attracting interest in all fields, from fashion (with Armani, Valentino and Versace) to the food industry. Many companies rushed to enjoy the reflected light of that triumph, and Sordillo was frightened by an unexpected revolution that he did not want to handle: 'Not only do I not want to eat this cake, I don't even want to touch it.' But the cake was there, within reach, it could be translated into the sponsorship of the national football team, world champions in 1982, and it was too tempting.

Artemio Franchi brought home Dassler, the owner of Adidas, to convince him to close a deal with the newly formed marketing company ISL, whose offers were less than a billion lire a year, including stadium posters that made a billion a season. Sordillo was not convinced. But it was necessary to strike while the iron was hot to take advantage of the enthusiasm of world success. On 25 May 1983, in Athens, on the day of the European Cup Final between Juventus and Hamburg, Dassler, together with an Italian partner, MKT, with Fiat capital, raised the stakes to 1.1 billion a year. But this time, too, his offer was not considered adequate and Sordillo did not even want to attend the meeting. A commission of sponsors was set up, consisting of Gianni De Felice, the new head of the press office, the lawyer Pesce and Dario Borgogno, secretary of the federation. But it was Riccardo Corato, owner of Network, a Roman public relations agency, who resolved the situation by turning up at Sordillo's office.

In the summer of 1984 the contract was signed and in the autumn the agreement was announced. A shower of billions was pouring into Italian football. The FIGC was totally unprepared. The methods of sponsoring the national team up to that point had been obviously and inevitably sloppy. Sordillo declared publicly, 'I don't know about these advertising things, they can get complicated, there's money here, money there.' And money did come in. Dassler had set an example. Corato created a package of eight companies (Coca-Cola, Kodak, Assitalia, G.F.T. Armani, Pop '84, Alivar-Pavesi, Grana

Padano and Cinzano), to which Diadora was added, with a total annual turnover of more than 6,000 billion lire, which in the first 27 months (September 1984–December 1986) paid about 6 billion lire into the federal coffers, to which was added the value of technical supplies and advertising induced. A record figure, one of the highest in the world for sports sponsorship of national teams.

The Evolution of Football in Italy

With the allowance of a second foreign player, within a few months all the other stars of the Mundial (besides the Brazilians: Maradona, Rummenigge, Boniek and Platini, to name but a few) came to play in Italy. In those years, the Italian championship experienced its most shining phase and began to be considered 'the most beautiful in the world'. But soon everything changed. Everything became standardised, stiffened, predictable, expected. Football lost its spontaneity, if not its innocence, which it may not have had for a long time. Even the celebrations of the players began to be decided at the table. The shouts of Tardelli and Falcão, or the arms raised to the sky by Rossi and Sócrates were the last acts of spontaneous joy celebrated on the pitch. Even the fans organised themselves with pre-packaged uniforms and choruses, so the chaotic and naive shouts of the Sarriá fans became a distant memory. No one wrote on a sign any more 'Italia facci sognare', 'Forza Azzurri' or 'W Italia'. Even 'Volare' disappeared from the stadiums.

First the sponsors and then the television rights changed habits. Football was transformed into spectacle, business and fashion. Championship matches, which were only ever played on Sundays, were extended throughout the week, as were cup matches, which used to be played only on Wednesdays. Shirt numbers also exploded. Players, who once had normal physiques, conscious of being on stage in front of millions of people, swelled their muscles, started to comb or shave their hair in fancy ways and covered themselves with tattoos. A more cunning and less 'sporty' way of playing began to take hold among them, using techniques that were also tried out in training sessions, where they tried to hone their guile. Players learned to fall, to simulate, to show pain and to challenge the referee's decisions. Sportsmanship was no longer a part of football, which was reduced to a mere activity. Rather than hand the ball to an opponent, it was left on the spot, or kicked or thrown away. Anything to annoy the opponent. Éder delivering the ball into Zoff's hands remains a shining example of sportsmanship. Obvious then, but unthinkable now, in times when fair play has been reduced to a financial category.

After Count Rognoni's recommendation, Allodi sent the young Sacchi to cut his teeth with relegated Parma in Serie C1. He immediately brought him back to Serie B and in 1986/87 he made headlines by eliminating AC Milan from the Coppa Italia at the San Siro. Rossoneri president Silvio Berlusconi was impressed by his game – based on zonal defence and pressing – and wanted him on his staff at all costs. His arrival marked a watershed in the history of modern Italian football.

Tardelli and Sconcerti, the two Tuscans involved in the quarrel on the eve of the Sarriá match, later found themselves alongside each other as commentators on *Domenica Sportiva*. During this, at the end of January 2018, the two, 36 years after the Mundial, found themselves again involved in a quarrel: 'Marco,' said the journalist on live television, 'you can't have won with Juventus and be eternally in the right. Be happy to win.'

Bearzot

Bearzot, preserving the heroes of Spain for the Mexican Mundial, chose to die with his soldiers. Having resigned, he walked away from a football he no longer recognised. He remained for everyone the symbol of an era to be regretted, of a football that has disappeared forever. In the land of opportunists, he took no advantage of the Spanish venture that made him and his pipe the icon of at least three generations of Italians. After his adventure with the Azzurri, he did not look for clubs to coach, he did not go on talk shows, he did not accept advertising deals, nor did he sign consultancy contracts. He simply set himself aside (spending his days cycling alone in Milan, between Via Washington and Piazza Piemonte, or frequenting the café in Via Oriani, where he used to talk about football and politics, always in a whisper, as was his nature), with an impeccable sense of exit, without clinging to the nostalgia of glory. It was more than enough for him to cherish the memory. He still remembered the afternoon of 19 June 1938: 'When we were all in the square in Gradisca listening to Carosio's voice over the loudspeakers.' And of the 1982 final: 'The boys throwing me in the air.' But the most vivid image of the World Cup in Spain, for him, was the kiss from Zoff after the match against Brazil.

He returned to Barcelona ten years later, on the occasion of the 1992 Olympics. He presented himself as an ambassador for the Olympic dreams of a 'Milan 2000' that would never come true. That evening, it was 24 July, the Italy team led by Maldini and Tardelli, would play its first match against the United States: 'I am here because of an invitation from Massimo Moratti, the FIFA host, not because the federation thought of me. Those in the national team are my boys even if I have nothing to do with them anymore. And my boys are above all Cesare Maldini and Marco Tardelli: I'll phone them. I won't go to the village: it's federal territory, I don't want to be reported for trespassing.'

In 2005 he confessed to Gianni Mura that as a boy he was terrified of the idea of death. 'Now I'm not afraid of anything, really.' Five years later he dpassed away. By a twist of fate, he died on 21 December, like the other world champion coach Vittorio Pozzo (who departed this world in 1968, in the year of the European Championship won by Italy). Exactly as he had done on the night of the Bernabéu, on leaving the parish of Santa Maria al Paradiso, in Milan, he was lifted up by his boys who accompanied him on his last journey: on one side Conti, Rossi, Maldini, Collovati and Marini, on the other Zoff, Cabrini, Tardelli and Altobelli. But also Antognoni and Bergomi. All

THE MATCH

there to greet the Old Man. Gianni Mura, describing him as a serious, honest, loyal, sincere and cultured man, wrote in *La Repubblica*: 'Since yesterday, there has been one less gentleman in Italy, Enzo Bearzot.' Three years earlier, on his birthday, the last question he had asked him, 'How would you like to be remembered in a few years' time?' had been answered by: 'As a man who has been remembered in the past.' He had received the answer: 'As a decent person.'

A year after Bearzot's death, Sepp Blatter, FIFA secretary at the time of the World Cup in Spain and now president, sent a letter with Christmas and New Year greetings, addressed personally to Enzo Bearzot, in his Milan home where he had lived until his last day. On the inside of the card was his signature and that of general secretary Jérôme Valcke. It was a sensational gaffe on the occasion of the first anniversary of the coach's death. On the same day, his wife Luisa accompanied one of the Mundial '82 correspondents, Alberto Cerruti, to a meadow in the Paderno d'Adda cemetery. 'He liked to come and visit my parents, because there is so much green and it looks like a garden instead of a cemetery.' And the Old Man wanted to be buried there. Behind the grave in which he lay, children played football: 'Many of them, before going home, stop in front of my husband's gravestone to say a prayer.' One day, Mrs Luisa found a flower with a card signed 'One of your boys in '82'.

Simple and reserved, the coach's family never allowed themselves public appearances, not even at the stadium. Even on the unforgettable night in Madrid, Mrs Bearzot was not in the stands. 'We were all at home, with the children and the children's friends. In the end we were happy, even if we didn't have any special parties. I know it will seem strange, but what do you want, that's how we are.' When Franco Mentana of the *Gazzetta* called her from Madrid to ask her what she thought of that triumph, she could not believe her ears: 'My husband only did his duty and at most I can make him an extra cake, Enzo loves sweets very much.'

In addition to the solid values in which he believed, the coach managed to pass on to his family his love of classical studies. His daughter Cinzia became a full professor of Greek history and epigraphy and coordinator of the doctoral school in humanities at the Faculty of Arts of the Università Cattolica del Sacro Cuore in Milan; his granddaughter Giulia graduated in history, while Livia graduated in ancient literature with first-class honours on the very morning of her grandfather's death.

By winning the Spanish Mundial 'on the counter-attack', Bearzot was to become one of the most important masters in the history of football, and one of the most beloved figures of the Italian 20th century.

What he did for Rossi was unique. It has never happened again that a coach would gamble on a debilitated and out-of-shape player just in the name of deep trust. Exactly 20 years later, Roberto Baggio, the only Azzurri player who was loved like Pablito, was not called up by Giovanni Trapattoni for the World Cup in South Korea and Japan, despite an incredible recovery from injury, the mobilisation of football, the invocation of the fans and a clamorous sit-in in front of the FIGC headquarters.

Ermido Santi, the socialist member of parliament who was the author of the question on the awards for Bearzot's national team (in which he asked the government if it was right that public money should be spent on a football match at a time when the country was suffering from difficult economic problems), was, three years after the Mundial, hit by an arrest warrant from the Milan judges, for having received bribes as president of the Istituto Autonomo Case Popolari in Genoa. The Court of Cassation, ten years after the Mundial, then sentenced him to three years and six months. The other signatory of a question, Publio Fiori (who had asked President Spadolini whether he considered the awarding of prizes to the Azzurri to be just and morally acceptable), made headlines when his 2004 income tax return put him in second place in the ranking of the richest MPs in the Chamber, with €1,441,865 and a life annuity of €9,950 per month.

Leonardo Vecchiet was arrested in Naples on 7 April 1994. He ended up in Poggioreale. Those were the most tumultuous years of

THE MATCH

Mani Pulite. Duilio Poggiolini, the king of healthcare, confessed to the shenanigans of a sector in ruins, referring to the miracle doctor. According to the Naples Public Prosecutor's Office, he received 'undue remuneration in order to speed up the processing and positive evaluation of files relating to certain pharmaceutical products at the Single Commission for Pharmaceuticals'. The case was transferred to Rome, where the Public Prosecutor's Office immediately changed its approach, recognising that Vecchiet was not at fault. He was only released from prison on 27 June. He was placed under house arrest. Ten years later the tenth criminal section of the Court of Rome acquitted him in the first instance because the fact did not exist, at the request of the public prosecutor. 'This affair destroyed me and caused me so much suffering,' he declared, 'both morally and physically, it was a terrible decade. Now, finally, everything has passed with the complete recognition of the correctness of my behaviour.' The professor accepted money, duly invoiced, to fund the university struggling with chronic underfunding.

The Sigma Tau money went to fellows who would otherwise have had to leave research. In any case, the funding stopped in 1990, so Vecchiet did not receive any money while he was at the Single Drug Commission. He also phoned Gianni Mura: 'I am Professor Vecchiet, do you remember me? I wanted to tell you that I was fully acquitted in the first instance because the fact does not exist, and the request came from the public prosecution.' Mura sensed that Vecchiet was asking him to speak, even in a few lines, of his proven innocence. The journalist, in *La Repubblica*, on 1 February 2004, dedicated a space to him 'not as compensation for the alleged dishonesty slammed on the front pages, but because it is right that it should be so. No one will compensate him for the two surgeries and five by-passes.' Vecchiet died three years later.

The press did not tell the story of the Villa Pamphili slap. After that occurrence, Bearzot took Anna Ceci aside and explained to her the reasons that had led him to exclude Beccalossi, the player she had asked for, from his team. The girl, mortified, declared herself in agreement with his choices and apologised amid sobs, until the two embraced and exchanged their respective addresses. Afterwards Anna Ceci invited Bearzot to her wedding.

After Bearzot

After Bearzot, his most trusted men sat on the Azzurri bench. They all missed out on glory by a whisker. His two deputies, Azeglio Vicini and Cesare Maldini, were both foiled by penalties (in the 1990 and 1998 World Cups). The captain of his Azzurri, Dino Zoff, was denied the satisfaction of winning the European Championship in 2000 by a golden goal. In the same year, Marco Tardelli and Claudio Gentile won the European Under-21 Championship as coaches. Both triumphed in the wake of Maldini's previous successes, as he was three times European champion in 1992, 1994 and 1996, in years when the under-21 team was sometimes more exciting than the national team and made headlines. Maldini died in 2016. The credit for creating the myth of the under-21s, however, goes to Vicini, who was only beaten by penalties in the 1986 final. The coach did not collect any trophies but brought home great records: no other Italian coach has taken part in six World Cups, either as assistant or head coach, leading all the representative teams, from junior to senior. He was also responsible for the record of 27 million television viewers for Italy vs Argentina in 1990, the match that ended on penalties, and which, in the end, decreed his end, despite the fact that the national team had played the best football of the Italian 'magic nights'. He risked not participating: during the summer of 1987, while he was in Brazil to study South American football, he was carried away by a sudden wave and risked drowning. He was saved by Fabio Capello. He died in his bed, in 2018, remembered by all as the coach of a smile and common sense.

Zoff's place was taken by Trapattoni, the man who had provided the Juventus block (including Zoff) for Bearzot's national team. That Italy failed in three consecutive World Cups (at home in 1990, in the United States in 1994, in France in 1998) and by a golden goal (2002), then won its fourth World Cup under Lippi in 2006, on penalties, against France in a context apparently similar to that of 1982 (the betting scandal before the World Cup, the team alone against everyone, a newly arrived federal president, etc.) but in a world now completely transformed, without flags, examples and romanticism.

'The fourth Italian World Cup,' noted *Il Post* on the occasion of the 30th anniversary of the 1982 victory, 'was won by very different players, in a very different Italy and a very different world. It was different.' A year earlier, the editor of the same newspaper, Luca Sofri, had summed up the same concept in his book *Un grande paese* (A Great Country): 'Twenty-four years later, the Italian national team won the World Cup again and the images of celebration were very different, both on the field and at the Circus Maximus: with the players – "the gladiators" – unleashed in the exhibition of themselves, their bodies, their pride, their conquest. A generation had passed.'

For the Italians who had lived through the Spanish nights, the thought was unanimous: 'In 1982 it was something else.' When Bearzot died, a reader named Hendrie wrote in *Latin Lions*: 'The 1982 World Cup is worth a hundred times that of 2006. The difference can only be understood by comparing Bearzot's humanity with the arrogance of … I don't even remember the name …'

Lippi's title came thanks to a mistake from the penalty spot by a French player, Trezeguet (thus giving something back to the Azzurri, as he had taken the European title away from Zoff's Italy in 2000), after Italy had met, with the exception of the hosts Germany, teams considered mediocre (Ghana, United States, Czech Republic, Australia, Ukraine). The Azzurri counted on an impeccable goalkeeper (Buffon), a defender in a state of grace (captain Cannavaro, later Golden Ball winner) and a brilliant director (Pirlo) but, apart from them, the rest of the team, despite their excellent form, would not be remembered by history. On the contrary, a place in the annals would be occupied by the ebullient Materazzi who, having only come on after Nesta's injury, after scoring a goal and being sent off in the first phase, would unexpectedly become 'the man of the final'. He did it all: he caused the penalty for the French lead, scored the equaliser with his header, insulted Zidane, suffered the legendary headbutt that marked the 'Bleu' captain's farewell to football and scored one of the final five shots from the penalty spot.

Few people remember him, but Ivano Bordon, Zoff's backup goalkeeper, one of the five Azzurri to sit on the bench at the Sarriá that 5 July, also won the 2006 World Cup as goalkeeper coach. He is therefore the only living Italian footballer to have won the World Cup twice, as a player and as a coach.

Santana

Defended by the entire team, the Brazilian coach resigned, taking full responsibility for the defeat, and went into voluntary exile in Saudi Arabia. Without him the Brazilian team was in serious danger of not qualifying for the 1986 World Cup in Mexico until, on 23 March 1985, the Brazilian federation recalled him to replace the disastrous Evaristo de Macedo. The Brazilian journalists did not deny their schizophrenia this time either. Quickly forgetting the nickname 'Pé frio' (literally 'cold foot', used to indicate a loser), they renamed him 'O Mestre' (The Master). And the saviour of the country succeeded: the national team qualified for the World Cup in Mexico.

In Brazil, which had just freed itself from the grip of the military dictatorship, Telê began the purges. First the left-winger, Éder, was expelled after a monstrous retaliation foul during a match against Peru. Then it was the turn of striker Renato Gaucho, for being caught by the paparazzi while returning drunk late at night during a training camp. He was followed by full-back Leandro, who was accused of sticking up for him. Finally, forward Sidney was also sent home for indiscipline. Instead, the coach wanted to give another chance to some of the players who had lived the shattered dream with him in the summer of 1982: Zico, Falcão, Júnior and

THE MATCH

Sócrates. But not even in Mexico did his Brazil find better luck. Like Italy, they lost to France. Once again, they stopped just short of the semi-finals.

A year later, Santana returned to the benches of Atlético Mineiro, Flamengo and São Paulo, with whom he won ten titles, two Copas Libertadores and as many Intercontinental Cups. Triumphs that brought journalists to reconcile with him. In 1997 the magazine *Placar* crowned him the best Brazilian coach in the history of football. He did not have time to enjoy that title. In the same year he began the long agony that would lead to his death in 2006.

Gilberto Tim, who had always dreamed of becoming a football coach, got his chance six years after the match against Italy, in 1988 at Coritiba, but the experience turned out to be a disappointment, so he returned to the role of physical training. Ten years later he died in Porto Alegre, at the age of 54, a victim of Alzheimer's disease.

The Brazilian coach who was dismissed in 1970, João Saldanha, followed the match against Italy at the Sarriá. He left Brazil optimistic but was soon convinced that Telê Santana was 'a loser', and when Brazil were defeated on the pitch he showed no mercy. 'Moral champions? Champions of stupidity, if anything. With the quality of our splendid players, we could have won this cup hands down. Unfortunately, however, we lacked modesty and had no idea how to position ourselves on a football pitch. We lost, whatever.' In 1990 his doctors gave him three months to live. He left for Italy to attend the last World Cup of his life. He found himself following them in Rome from a hotel bed, where he was confined by illness. Italy vs Argentina was his last commentary. He died in Italy, in a room of the Sant'Eugenio Hospital, in the heart of the Eur district, and was buried in Rio, at the São João Batista cemetery, with the flag of the PCB, Botafogo and the Portela school. Holding his coffin was Zagallo himself, the man who had taken his place on the bench. A couple of streets are named after him, as well as the press room at the Maracanã and the bicycle path that connects Ipanema to Copacabana.

The Defeated Generation

The 1982 Seleção was considered the best Brazilian national team ever, along with Pelé's 1970 team, and compared to Puskás's 1954 Hungary and Cruyff's 1974 Netherlands, the other two legendary teams that failed to win the World Cup. But that group of demigods never played together again: Italy vs Brazil on 5 July 1982 was the last match that Telê Santana's dream team played. After the Mundial, Brazil's best players found opportunity in Italy: Cerezo, Zico, Sócrates, Júnior, Dirceu, Edinho and Batista, not to mention Falcão. The legendary Magic Square became Italian. After the Italian experience, Zico and Sócrates met again in 1986 in the ranks of Flamengo but only played one match together. That year they played their last World Cup, their third. Sócrates missed in the penalty shootout against France. The elimination definitely consecrated them as the 'defeated generation'.

Toninho Cerezo was not forgiven for the glaring error that allowed Rossi to score his second goal. Thanks to his excellent physical condition he continued to play at a high level for another decade, but never played in a World Cup again. According to his team-mates, Cerezo felt under pressure for the rest of the match because of his mistake. Three decades later, Júnior would deny threatening Cerezo following the mistake that facilitated Rossi's second goal. 'I called Cerezo's attention but I just said to him: oh, man, there's the whole game ahead!' The Júnior–Cerezo confrontation after the latter cried has filled the pages of the press, especially the Brazilian press, for decades. Cerezo has always denied being upset after the Italian double, stating that he remained lucid throughout the match: 'I confess that I cried, but it was after Falcão's goal. It was the second equaliser and I felt something strange at that moment, such a great joy that I couldn't avoid tears when we were returning to midfield. It was a spontaneous emotion that came out of the depths of my heart. It felt like I was the one who scored that goal.' Cerezo, for better or worse, had been an accomplice in the last two goals, the one that

THE MATCH

made it 2-1 to Italy and the one that gave Brazil their equaliser (if he had not faked the overlap the Azzurri defence would not have opened up). 'That's why I cried. But I was in full control of my actions,' he guaranteed. Zico confirmed at the time that Cerezo was shocked after the mistake in the first half: 'That goal by Rossi influenced him a lot. Cerezo made a mistake as if he had missed a penalty.' The No. 10 also recalls a possible second collapse of the midfielder: 'When we equalised, he cried a lot and we tried to calm him down.' And it was at that moment that, according to Cerezo, Falcão himself, along with Júnior, approached him and said, 'Come on boy, let's go and win this game.'

On the occasion of the 30th anniversary of the match, Cerezo declined all invitations received to avoid having to repeat his version of that episode. He only responded to *Placar* when asked to name the 11 best players of all time. He unexpectedly confirmed the 1982 Brazil defence en bloc (Waldir Peres, Leandro, Oscar, Luizinho and Júnior), but did not mention any of the men from the Magic Square (instead of which he put Cruyff, Rivelino, Gerson and Vialli). In front of everyone, along with Reinaldo, he put Bruno Conti. Cerezo, who had received from Leandro what became an assist for Paolo Rossi's goal for 2-1, the worst ball ever played by his feet, named one of his sons after the defender. When he grew up, Leandro Medeiros Cerezo changed sex, becoming, under the name Lea T, the first transwoman to walk the catwalk and one of the highest-paid models in the world. She was also a finalist in the 2013 edition of the TV show *Dancing with the Stars*, the Italian adaptation of the BBC talent show *Strictly Come Dancing*, doing better than Paolo Rossi who, in the 2011 edition had gone out halfway through.

The other great suspect, Waldir Peres, returned to defend the São Paulo goal. Abandoned by his defenders, he ended up taking all the blame for the team. His responsibilities were no greater than those of his team-mates, yet, just as happened to Moacir Barbosa in 1950 (again when Brazil only needed a draw), he became the scapegoat for a tragedy that had many causes. A few years later, at Guarani,

THE DEFEATED GENERATION

he saved three penalties in one match, including one from the great Bebeto, who played for Flamengo. But still he continued to suffer the merciless judgement of the people, and for the people he always remained *O Frangueiro*, the chicken. He often dreamed of the Sarriá match and he always managed to catch that ball that he handled too casually when giving away the corner kick, the only one for Italy, which resulted in the third goal for the Azzurri. 'If it had gone like that, everything would have changed. My life and the lives of my team-mates would have been different.' He remained convinced that the flap of a butterfly's wings in that case had changed the history of his country. The match against Italy, few remember, was the only one the Seleção lost with him in goal.

On 23 July 2017, Waldir Peres was in Mogi Mirim for a birthday party. He had just finished eating when he was struck down by a heart attack. He died at the age of 66 as an 'idolo do São Paulo', having defended his goal for 617 matches (played between 3 November 1973 and 26 May 1984). Bola de Ouro in 1975, three-time Paulista champion (1975, 1980 and 1981) and hero of the 1977 Brasileirão ended on penalties against Atlético-MG. In Italy the news of his death was reported, in brief, with four lines appearing in *La Repubblica* and five in the *Corriere dello Sport*, while it was neglected by the rest of the main newspapers.

Serginho never wore the Brazil jersey again; Italy was his last match. He was considered one of the scapegoats of the Sarriá tragedy. In reality, it was not his fault that Brazil only managed to avoid conceding goals against New Zealand: Cerezo, with his horizontal pass, created Rossi's second goal and, with his clumsy header, caused the corner that led to the third goal, on which Júnior, nailed to the goal line, was not blameless. Nor was it his fault that Brazil failed to equalise in the final minutes because, after Falcão's goal, he was no longer on the pitch. After that World Cup he began a downward spiral that would lead him to abandon football over the years. Thirty-seven years later (on 20 February 2015), he confessed to Globo's *Sport News* that he had kicked linesman Vandevaldo Rangel in the 1977

THE MATCH

Brasileirão final (played in 1978), an episode that cost him 11 months banned and subsequent exclusion from the World Cup in Argentina: 'If I had known I would have had a year's suspension I would have ripped his head off.' He remains to this day the man who has scored the most goals, 242, in the history of São Paulo.

Luizinho stopped playing for Vila Nova, where he had started, in 1995 and tried to start a coaching career with Atlético's youth team, won some titles and was called by Marcelo to help him in the first team. It was a horrible experience for him: 'I saw players who had won nothing and thought they were phenomenal.' He understood that football had reached a point of no return. The players knew nothing about the history of their teams, there was no more respect for the coach and no more willingness to learn from their elders: 'Nowadays young people think they are great, and they don't want to listen.' It was very difficult for him and he felt that the best choice was to call it quits on his coaching career. From that Brazil of 1982, he has remained very close to Serginho, Júnior, Cerezo, Éder and Zico: 'Today it is very difficult to meet, but when we have the opportunity it is a wonderful opportunity to recall our stories.'

Oscar became captain of the Seleção and remained a key player until a week before the World Cup in Mexico when, surprisingly, he ended up in the reserves. He was on the bench for all the matches and never set foot on the pitch. Twenty years later he admitted that the ball he headed towards Italy's goal in the last minute was stopped on the line: 'It wasn't a goal. Five centimetres further, just five, and we would have had a draw and our generation would have had a different life. Instead, we were defeated: not only that day, but forever. In Brazil, even today, we are the ones who lost. Zoff said that it was the save of his life. On the other hand, it would have been the goal of my life. Five centimetres and everything would have changed.' He has always been critical of his team: 'Even Leandro and Júnior were attacking, leaving Luizinho and I alone against Conti, Rossi and Graziani. The defeat was fair. They say: if we played a hundred times, Brazil would always win. False, Italy would win

THE DEFEATED GENERATION

again because we, even though we were dancing, hadn't understood anything.'

Two weeks before the elections, on 31 October 1982, the black-and-white team of Corinthians entered the pitch against Palmeiras with an epoch-making inscription on their shirts: 'Dia 15 vote' (on the 15th day go and vote), signed by Washington Olivetto. In 1982 Corinthians won the national championship in São Paulo with the word 'Democracy' printed on their shirts. For Sócrates it was the best moment of his life. He and his team-mates won the championship the following year, the club managed to keep its accounts in the black and the self-management of Corinthian democracy triggered a virtuous process that led Brazil to regain democracy two years later with the return to direct election of the President of the Republic.

Contrary to what he had planned, O Doutor also participated in the 1986 World Cup. In the first match, Brazil won against Spain thanks to his goal after the Australian referee Christopher Bambridge had disallowed a fair goal for Spain. After the match, Sócrates told the press: 'Everyone knows that for obvious political and economic reasons it is preferable for Mexico, the host, and Brazil, the national team with the most fans, to go as far ahead as possible in this World Cup.' In other words, the two teams that sell the most tickets and ensure that the stands are always full. Havelange was shocked and opened an investigation. The president of the Brazilian Football Federation, Nabi Adi Chedid, immediately rebuffed the captain of the Seleção. Sócrates appeared before journalists again to confirm this. A few days later he kicked the first of the penalties against France without a run-up. He missed . His mistake and that of a team-mate sent Brazil and its generation of talent home without a win.

At the end of the derby with São Paulo, which was worth the Paulista championship, on Wednesday, 14 December 1983, Radio Jovem Pan asked him how he wanted to die: *'Quero morrer em um Domingo e com o Corinthians Campeão'* (I want to die on a Sunday and with Corinthians as champions). His wish was, incredibly, respected: he left on the Sunday of the fifth Campeão do Brasil title in the club's history, 4 December 2011, at the age of 57, destroyed by alcohol and smoking.

In 1986 Dirceu was supposed to play his fourth World Cup, equalling Pelé, but due to an injury one month before the start of the championship, Telê Santana took no chances and chose to take young Edivaldo to Mexico. On the night of 15 September 1995, the former midfielder was returning from a football match. While crossing Avenida das Américas in Rio de Janeiro's Barra da Tijuca district, his car was hit by another vehicle. Dirceu died a few metres from the house where his wife Vania was waiting for him. Not only was she waiting for him, she was also carrying his fourth child. Having participated in three Olympics and three World Cups in ten years, between 1972 and 1982, although he did not win any of these tournaments, he became Brazil's most successful player, surpassing even Pelé.

João Batista da Silva landed at Lazio and had a relationship with journalist Francesca Guidato Berger, from whom Elizabeth Salomè da Silva was born, later raised in Rome by her stepfather Helmut Berger. On 18 January 2017, the girl found her 15 minutes of fame when she wrote a tweet that sparked panic on social media: 'A building collapsed in the Flaminio area behind the Teatro Olimpico.' The news was unfounded.

His role as a mentor to a new young generation of creatives continued to increase Washington Olivetto's fame. In 2001, he was kidnapped on the streets of São Paulo and held for 53 days. After he managed to free himself, he returned to his job as head of W/Brasil, the well-known Brazilian advertising agency. That same year, more than 300 entrepreneurs were kidnapped in Brazil.

The Search for Explanations

The match is considered the watershed between two phases of football but it has also conventionally gone down in history as an allegory, the paradigm of the confrontation between two opposing currents: spectacle football and organised football.

THE SEARCH FOR EXPLANATIONS

As for almost all the players of the Seleção, the meeting with Italy was the match of a lifetime for Zico. He once said that if he could have scored just one more goal in his career he would have wanted to score it in that match. And, he claimed, he would have scored it if Serginho had not stolen the ball from him in the first half. Thirty years later, on 28 November 2012, Zico declared that Italy vs Brazil 1982 was the match that changed football history forever. 'If we had won it, football would probably have been different,' he vented. 'After that, however, we began to lay the foundations for a football in which the result must be achieved at any cost, a football based on the destruction of the opponent's game and systematic fouls. That defeat was not good for the world of football.' But he also admitted: 'If we had scored five goals that day, Italy would have scored six, because they always found a way to capitalise on our mistakes.'

As on that day at the Sarriá, Pablito had the last word: 'That 3-2 was a lesson for which Brazil should thank us and give us a prize. A defeat from which they learned a lot. Above all, to play more defensively. So much so that they went on to win two more editions of the World Cup. Since then their approach has changed, they have become more cautious and Europeanised. Also because many Brazilians have become acquainted with the championships of our continent. Still, watching them play is always a spectacle. Although they have evolved, their football has remained the mirror of a country where the spectacle remains important.'

Italy vs Brazil was not the day when football died but the day when a certain naivety disappeared. The time tactics, the reasoned manoeuvre, won. From that moment on it was no longer possible to simply pick the best players, put them on the pitch and send them into attack. There would still be room for talent but it had to be incorporated into a game plan that also thought about how to protect the defence.

The search for explanations for that defeat will remain a constant in Brazil. Hundreds of articles, television programmes and books, some written by the protagonists of that World Cup, have continued for decades to try, in vain, to give an answer. For all Brazilians, Italy vs Brazil 1982 is considered '*O jogo que nunca acabou*' (The game that never ended).

Marcelo Idiarte, a fan, has watched this match 20 times since then. Now that football no longer matters to him, he has learned that there is always something imponderable and unpredictable about a match. 'But the Sarriá game is particularly difficult to accept and forget. Every time I watch it again on an old VHS tape, I get the impression that Brazil is going to score at any moment. Every triangulation move, every dribble, every ball that whizzes into the Italian area gives the feeling that it will pierce Zoff. But time passed and the ball did not go, even many years later. After that World Cup, the Brazilian national team has become synonymous with tragedy for me. I prefer to watch Flamengo de Varginha against Asa de Arapiraca. Or take the VCR out of the wardrobe and put in the old VHS tape of Brazil–Italy. Because I don't know, sometimes I have the impression that you can still score.'

After the Sarriá tragedy, Daniel Souza, the young fan who first heard Gentile's screams, has not wanted to shed a single tear for any other team. He does not remember how he got back to his hotel after that match. Distraught, lost and terribly angry, he spent two sleepless nights in the hotel located in Gran Vía 2, just 15 minutes from the Sarriá. Even today, however, he proudly boasts of his presence in Barcelona on the day that 'our football died'. He is convinced that the cry 'It's over!' will carry him to his grave.

The Sad Destinies of the Champions

Italy and Brazil also crossed Mané Garrincha's life. It was during the days of the Mundial in Spain that the two-time world champion experienced the most tragic phase of his life: totally cut off from society, unable to relate to his children and mistreated by his companions. And he was the model that Santana's Seleção players indirectly used as a pretext for the issue of awards, so as not to end up like him.

THE SAD DESTINIES OF THE CHAMPIONS

His life was indeed marred by tragedies of all kinds. Devastated by alcohol and destitution, he was responsible for a tragic car accident in which his mother-in-law lost her life. Guilt led him to depression and a suicide attempt by inhaling gas. His wife Elza Soares, a singer who supported the reformist president João Goulart, convinced him to leave Brazil and move to Rome. Later the two lived in Torvajanica, where Garrincha played football with amateur teams, also competing in the Canottieri Cup of the Circolo Canottieri Lazio. In 1970 Sacrofano, a small team from the province of Rome that had just been promoted to the First Category and was coached by Dino da Costa, a former Italian-Brazilian striker for Roma and Juventus and Garrincha's former team-mate at Botafogo, called him up for a quadrangular match in Mignano Monte Lungo. Garrincha, by then penniless, prey to alcoholism and depression, agreed to play for 100,000 lire per match and dragged Sacrofano to victory with a double straight from the penalty spot. Returning to Brazil and abandoned by his wife because of the constant aggression she suffered, he began a long, slow agony that would lead to his premature death, five months after the Spanish Mundial, at the age of 49, in destitute conditions, due to the consequences of cirrhosis of the liver and pulmonary oedema. Death spared him one last sorrow: his son Manuel Garrincha dos Santos Júnio, known as Garrinchinha, would die three years later, at the age of nine, in a car accident.

Moacir Barbosa, considered the scapegoat of the 1950 Maracanã defeat, slipped into oblivion until 1993. It was a Brazilian TV station that rescued him: they offered him a job as a TV commentator ahead of the United States World Cup. He was sent to Brazil's training camp on the eve of a qualifying match against Uruguay but he did not even have time to settle into the hotel: the Brazilian federation demanded that he be removed from his post. His presence near the team was a cause for concern. 'Bad luck,' wrote the federation. Moacir left in tears. He said, 'If there is no memory, at least let there be respect.' He returned home. Many years later, when old ladies met him in the street, they would point him out to their grandchildren:

495

'See that man? A long time ago he made the whole of Brazil cry.' Before he died, he had the strength to say, 'The maximum sentence under Brazilian law is 30 years, but the sentence I'm serving is 50 years.' All he had to do was wait for it to be carried out. His extreme poverty moved many football fans and his story reminded the world of the cruelty of modern sport.

The End of the Sarriá and the Match of the Century

As in an inexorable mantra, 12 years after the Spanish Mundial and 24 after the Mexican final that awarded the Jules Rimet Trophy to the Brazilians, Italy and Brazil found themselves once again facing each other in the most precious World Cup Final in history, that of 1994 in the United States, to which they came with three titles each. It was the first final to end on penalties. Roberto Baggio, who had been unbeatable in that World Cup, missed the decisive shot and gave an impenetrable Brazil their fourth title. That Italy team was coached by Arrigo Sacchi, the man who in 1982, a few days before Bearzot triumphed in Spain, had led Cesena to win the Primavera championship. In the years that followed, a singular phenomenon occurred: the Brazilian people expressed more and more esteem for the 1982 national team than for the 1994 one. Even today, the Brazil of Telê Santana, together with that of Pelé, continues to remain in the collective memory as the most beautiful ever.

The 74-year-old Sarriá Stadium was sold to pay off the debts of the Catalan club Espanyol and 15 years after the match, on 21 September 1997, again at 5pm, it was demolished to make way for a shopping centre. It disappeared forever. Together with 50 journalists, dozens of cameras and followed by live television coverage on Tv3, the Catalan state channel, 5,000 people wanted to witness the last breath of the historic facility, braving the police cordons to deposit flowers and tear up a last tuft of grass as a relic. Seventy kilos of explosives did not immediately bend the old grandstand. 'The stadium is standing,

THE END OF THE SARRIÁ AND THE MATCH OF THE CENTURY

not dying,' the crowd shouted. Sixty seconds later, the thud. The old bastion, where the feet of Zamora, Di Stéfano, Maradona, Zico and Paolo Rossi had performed, folded in on itself, exhausted. The Sarriá was no more.

Interviewed by half the world, the man who owes his immortality to that stadium and who in the year of the World Cup was called 'Mr Sarriá' did not blink an eye. 'I'm not going to lose sleep,' said Pablito. 'After all, I only played two games there. They had asked me to go and attend the demolition. But it was not right for me to do so. They are demolishing it, that's all, because time is passing, because interests are more important than other things, because it is an old stadium, which nobody needs anymore. The collapse won't take away anything from my life. The games, on the other hand, remain.'

On the day of the match between Italy and Brazil in 1982, two footballers were born, one Italian and the other Brazilian: Alberto Gilardino and Fabrício de Souza. The Azzurro would become a world champion in 2006.

Three years after the Sarriá challenge, Zé Tadeu, a Brazilian trying to invent himself as a footballer, determined to pass on the myth of his two idols – Marco Tardelli and Diego Maradona – named his son Diego Tardelli, linking the two stars of the Group of Death in one name. The boy went on to become a Seleção footballer. When in 2014 in a Superclásico de las Américas played in Beijing, Brazil defeated Messi's Argentina 2-0, Diego Tardelli won the match single-handedly, scoring both goals, his first ones for the national team, thus stealing the show from Messi and Neymar.

On 28 March 2015, coach Antonio Conte brought a Brazilian footballer naturalised as an Italian (his great-grandfather Battista Righetto was from Nove, in the province of Vicenza) to the Azzurri national team, named Éder Citadin Martins, known simply as Éder. Named by his father as a tribute to Éder Aleixo de Assis, the 1982 Seleção forward.

In 1983, in the wake of the huge success of the Spanish World Cup, the Japanese cartoon *Captain Tsubasa* was created (released in

Italy in 1986 under the title *Holly and Benji, due fuoriclasse*). In it, the Brazilian Roberto Sedinho wore the shirt of broken dreams, the 1982 Seleção. In the same cartoon, during the final of the national primary school championship between Oliver Hutton's New Team and Mark Lenders' Muppet Team, Hutton and Tom Becker's combined shot (Twin Shot), later repeated in the World Youth final against Brazil, was evidently inspired by Rossi and Graziani's shot that resulted in Italy's third goal against Peres.

In 2017, to coincide with the 35th anniversary of the World Cup, the Azzurri created a group on WhatsApp, immediately dubbed 'the chat of the champions' by the press. The *Corriere della Sera* wrote: 'They still exchange good morning every morning, like 35 years ago, like when they were in training camp in Vigo, World Cup of Spain 1982. Today as then.' Demonstrating that those boys, now in their 60s 'were and are a team'.

At the end of the same year, 'Il Canto degli Italiani', adopted on 12 October 1946 as the provisional anthem of the Italian Republic (and still unofficial during the 1982 World Cup), thanks to Law No. 181 of 4 December 2017, after more than 70 years, finally achieved the status of *de jure* national anthem.

In 2019, Azzurri captain Dino Zoff proudly declared, 'The 1982 victory will be unrepeatable. There will never be another World Cup like it. With a team capable of scoring so much [12 goals], scoring in open play, against the best teams. It almost never happens. I think it's something you won't see again.'

He was not the only one who thought so. In 2010, *Time* declared 1982's Italy vs Brazil 'not only the best World Cup match, but the greatest match ever played'. Defining that match as the most beautiful of the century, it undermined another of the Azzurri, Italy vs Germany (4-3) in 1970, which until then, in the collective memory, held the record. Since then, the Sarriá battle has become 'the match'.

Author's Notes

The Air of the Mundial

Perhaps I have always breathed the air of the Spanish Mundial. If I look at my life backwards I have the impression that everything refers to the Sarriá match.

I came into the world at the same time as Angelo Rizzoli, a few weeks after the 1970 final between Italy and Brazil, on the same day as Pertini, one before Bearzot, one after Tardelli, two before Gentile, two after Rossi. All under the sign of Libra. My grandmother lived in the palace where Juan Carlos grew up, in Viale dei Parioli in Rome. I saw Italy vs Brazil in 1982 with my family, a stone's throw away, in the same street where Juan Alberto Schiaffino, the hero of the *Maracanazo*, had lived. The first newspapers I kept in my life were those bought by my father the morning after the match. Six days later I bought my first newspaper, *La Gazzetta dello Sport* with the title 'Campioni del Mondo' (both the first and this one are still with me).

From that moment on, I searched, collected and collated everything that had to do with those days: they were mostly newspaper cuttings, stickers, photographs from inserts, and illustrations of the goals; materials that I shortly afterwards collected in a large album. I then started looking for documents, memorabilia, trophies, tickets, seats, glasses, medals, stamps, cups, stickers, coins, scarves, cushions, shirts, books and all sorts of relics. Among them, the pennant of the Madrid final signed by the players, the agency slides of Italy vs Brazil, hundreds of photos (including the one, taken by Daniele Massaro, of Tardelli's famous scream), match tickets, players' suits, negatives and films.

Even then the story had reached a fair level of obsession in me. This intensified as I began to locate the houses of the protagonists, walk their own routes, smoke combinations of tobacco mixed by

Bearzot and Pertini, and look for bottles of the '82 vintage. I then began to track down the original Mundial organisation papers, the Mundiespaña airline package brochures, the forms to be filled out for journalists' accreditation, the plans for the Sarriá stadium. And of course I found myself immersed in watching films, examining stills or reading documentation, technical sheets, leaflets, tickets, letters, cards, postcards, communiqués and articles directly or indirectly related to the events in question, up to analysing the most insignificant details in order to try to reconstruct the invisible plots of *those men*, within *that* match, contained in *that* World Cup, played in *that* year.

The 'Mundial' winds continued to cross my existence, influencing my steps. I went to live halfway between Mario Sconcerti's house and Lino Cascioli's studio (the two correspondents of *La Repubblica* and *Il Messaggero* who quarrelled with the Azzurri on the eve of the match), almost opposite the house of Paolo Samarelli, the sketcher for the *Guerin Sportivo* match reports, a stone's throw from the FIGC headquarters. It was within those walls that I stood in front of Dino Zoff on the morning he resigned as coach of the national team, using the same words he had spoken in Spain. For me it was like stepping back in time. And a little later, outside of there, in the days when Sky was being born, I managed to work with Darwin Pastorin, the correspondent of *Tuttosport*, who in 1982 was at his first World Cup, crossing my path with the world champion José Altafini and the 'white Pelé' Angelo Benedicto Sormani, the most famous Brazilians in Italy.

Continuing my research, I came across the photographer Giuseppe Calzuola, who later gave me a 'magic box', unexpectedly found in a cupboard after 35 years, containing hundreds of unpublished negatives of the 1982 World Cup. It was on that occasion that I had the opportunity to put my mortal hands inside the 'World Cup' gloves that Zoff gave to 'Peppe' at the end of the match. The circle was then closed with the referee Abraham Klein, from whom I had the honour of receiving three incredible relics of the Sarriá match (just

THE AIR OF THE MUNDIAL

before he handed over his treasures to the FIFA Museum): the match report, compiled in his own hand, the yellow card for cautions (with the names of Gentile and Oriali) and the Balilla whistle with which he had refereed the match. With these I could finally see and even touch what I had only imagined for decades. They were my holy grail. The journey was over for me. Perhaps the time had come to tell it.

That match was always talked about. It was consumed by its own legend. From the words that were repeated and the images that were replayed on each occasion. I had noticed that those 90 minutes frequently led to fixed points, with no particular variations on the theme. The same statements from the protagonists were repeated from year to year. In fact, the battle of the Sarriá was already a perfect story and changing it would have made no sense. On the other hand, I had no intention of changing it. I simply wanted to tell it in my own way, going along with what I had seen but had not had the chance to read. The epicentre was always the tale, of course. A coach from another era who, against all odds, gambles until the very end on a player considered finished and is repaid by him when destiny seemed already written. It was impossible not to start from there. The myth was also involved. The biblical one of David versus Goliath. Then history. And the stories. There were so many, some splendid, others extraordinarily unusual. Like, for example, the often recalled story of a handful of players and journalists from the same country who, instead of participating in building a success, found themselves at war with each other in Galicia. Finally, there was the match itself, which seemed to be written on a scoreboard.

Already among the most obvious elements of this, related to his actions and his men, there were many things that appeared fascinating to my eyes, but seemed to me to have been overlooked from the beginning. Sometimes they were simple moments, apparently insignificant. But each of them could have had a story. And I had the desire to stop them, dilate them, study them, as if under a lens.

What I wanted most of all, however, was to reconstruct the events hidden behind each aspect, even inanimate ones – searching not so

THE MATCH

much for the causes but for the origins – in order to see the match in a new light. Because an event, whatever it is, is also a point of arrival. The fateful tip of an iceberg. So I started to follow the threads to trace the 'whys' hidden at the beginning. To be able to do this lucidly, I set two parameters: space and time. The first helped me to understand what the elements were (the what and the where), the second where they came from (the how, the when and the why). So I accumulated facts, stories and people, then organised them into levels (human, political, sporting, journalistic, technical, philosophical, scientific, sociological, etc.), then created maps and started cross-referencing the data (also finding fascinating combinations, albeit on the verge of absurdity, such as the one linked to the 2-1, when a subtle and mocking marketing thread tied the ball's path by spinning it from one boot, Cerezo's, to the other, Rossi's, in the name of Lancer, the sportswear company that had a contract with both).

The density of the story opened up infinite possibilities for me and I beat many paths and edited the individual stories several times until I chose the most linear approach, one that forms an orderly progression according to a basically chronological logic, within which the single narrative strands are broken up and alternated.

Every aspect of reality today requires us to simplify it, so I have tried to translate a potential complexity into an evident simplicity, without the latter distorting the former: by assembling a work composed of a large number of individual self-contained and self-sufficient units, which, when added together (and almost without, I hope, perceiving their heaviness), are capable of conveying a certain idea of complexity. In order to do this, however, I first had to organise the thousands of oral and written sources, in all possible languages, that I had come across. Then I had to verify every single episode back to the mother source. To be on the safe side, I always tried to obtain certain data, which I then translated into numbers, because this helped me to give accuracy to the past. And I found a lot of them, of the most diverse types, although I almost never reported them.

THE AIR OF THE MUNDIAL

I mention some of them, here, dissimilàr and unusual (for me it is a way to do justice to their representation and in any case, their whole can tell a story). *10,358*: the decree by which Brazil declared war on Italy on 31 August 1942. *80*: the minute in which, on 15 January 1950 in Florence, during Fiorentina vs Juventus, Carlo Parola's prowess was caught by photographer Corrado Bianchi crouching in a hole behind the goal; it would become the emblem of the Panini stickers. *112*: the house number of a building without heating in Viale dei Parioli where Juan Carlos of Bourbon, born in exile in Rome, lived on the first floor. *500*: the lire that in 1974 President Pertini handed over to the waiter who had placed an orange juice and a cup of coffee (for the guest) on his table in front of an astonished journalist, Nantas Salvalaggio, who then wrote: 'It's the first time I've seen a high-ranking politician make such a blatant gesture. Normally they don't stoop to such a level, they let the state pay.' *2354/2346*: the other decree of 29 September 1978 signed by Juan Carlos, on the proposal of the Minister of Culture Pio Cabanillas Gallas, by which Saporta was appointed president of the Real Comité Organizador de la Copa Mundial de Fútbol on 9 October 1978. *10 per cent, 25 per cent, 65 per cent*: the division of the Mundial's revenues between FIFA, the Spanish federation and the 24 participating teams, as announced by Saporta already a year before the uproar raised by Italian politicians in an interview given to the newspaper *Le Monde* (also reported in *Olympic Review* no. 162, April 1981). *11 June 1981*: date of the first article signed by Enzo Biagi in *La Repubblica* after he left *Corriere*. *26*: the episodes of the series created by Sport Billy Productions, owner of the Sport Billy franchise, and licensed to Filmation Associates, broadcast in Europe and Latin America. *288*: the number of Rio–Zürich trips made by Havelange during his 8,760 days in office. *502*: the resolution adopted by the United Nations Security Council on 3 April 1982 calling for an immediate cessation of hostilities between Argentina and the United Kingdom and a complete withdrawal of Argentina's forces. *500,000*: the lire to be deposited as a payment for the reporters' access to the Mundial (a request developed in three stages: filling in the form at the FIGC, issuing the bank deposit and, finally, in Spain, collecting the pass together with the deposit. On that occasion, while standing in line, Sconcerti, Brera and Calzuola were one behind the other). *Top 10*: the song of the year in 1982 is *Felicità* by Romina and Al Bano. Followed by the worldwide hit 'Paradise' by Phoebe Cates, 'Il ballo del qua qua', by Romina Power, and the theme song from *Lady Oscar*. Culturally, Italy is naive, and in the cinema Italians console themselves with Paolo Villaggio (*Fracchia la belva umana*), Lino Banfi (*Vieni avanti cretino*), Diego Abatantuono (*Eccezzziunale veramente*), Renato Pozzetto (*La casa stregata*), Alvaro Vitali (*Pierino contro tutti*), Jerry Calà (*Vado a vivere da solo*) and Adriano Celentano (*Innamorato pazzo*). The great season of Italian comedy, which began with *I soliti ignoti* and *La Grande Guerra* (The Great War), which Bearzot showed his boys on the first day, has now come to an end with the genre's melancholy swan song: *Amici miei*, again by Monicelli, the film discussed at the dinner at Mondadori's house when *La Repubblica* was born. *61.7*: the kilometres travelled by coach by the Azzurri from Santiago de Compostela, where they landed, to the training camp in Pontevedra. *M7242R4*: the number plate of the Pegaso 6100S coach used by the Italian national team in Spain. *3*: the street number of Calle del Marqués de Valladares, the address in Vigo where the barber Manuel Blanco Varela, called Manolo works, where Soldati went to be shaved for 14 mornings. *19*: the lines entitled *Le mogli in premio (se passano)* written by Claudio Pea on page 3 of the insert dedicated to the World Cup in the newspaper *Il Giorno* of 7 June 1982. *8pm*: the time on 18 June 1982, when, in Madrid, Klein reads his son's telegram and, in Seville, Santana made his Magic Square official. *2*: the suitcases lost by Mario Soldati in Spain. The first on the flight from Milan to Santiago de Compostela (the luggage contained, among other things, the text of a lecture that the writer was to give in Paris on 25 June during the break between the first round and the quarter-finals); the second the day after the lecture, returning from Orly to Barcelona (in that case it was his glasses that were lost). *19 out of 22*:

THE AIR OF THE MUNDIAL

the Azzurri sitting in the stands at the Sarriá on 2 July 1982 to watch Brazil vs Argentina (only Graziani, Causio and Antognoni were missing). *105 x 69.5*: the dimensions in metres of the Sarriá pitch. *4,496,000*: the cost in pesetas of the Sarriá pitch (the rest: dressing rooms 21,098,000, lighting 43,853,000, press box 21,344,000, car park 6,683,000, general improvements 159,349,000). The restoration was carried out by the architects Francisco Cavaller Soteras, José Soteras Mauri, Antonio Bergnes de las Casas Soteras and Juan Pablo Mitjans Perello and the construction company Agromán S.A. *Between 8 and 12 centimetres*: the thickness of the Sarriá lines lime-washed by Tonino Fernández. *147*: the square metres of the changing room used by the Azzurri in the Sarriá (which had a massage table, sauna, bathtub and bathrooms). The guest dressing room was for the Brazilians: 105 square metres, equally austere, without the sauna and bath (which would not have been used in any case). The referees' changing room was 29 square metres, while the two rooms in the Sarriá subway leading from the changing rooms to the pitch occupied 84 and 42 square metres. *35*: Falcão's heartbeats per minute in the hours leading up to the match; the only member of his team not to record an increase in frequency, a sign of perfect self-control and an incredible ability to control any state of anxiety. *13.45*: the time set at the start of the match on one of Klein's two Seiko Sports 100 watches (the quartz one) to better follow the 45 minutes. *120303*: the serial number of Klein's second watch. *47/441*: the number of the bib worn by photographer Calzuola at Sarriá. *71 per cent*: the percentage of the 571 people intercepted at the Fluminense stadium who had blind faith in Brazil's victory (66 per cent of the 624 people interviewed at the Paulista stadium believed in it). *C2*: the league in which Pavia Calcio played, including Mauro Aguzzoni, the local favourite to whom the frequenters of Mirabello's Bar Oratorio had dedicated a banner ('Mauro facci sognare') later corrected to 'Italia facci sognare' (Italy let us dream) and taken to Spain to support the national team. Photographed in Vigo, that shy cry on a small rectangular sheet became a mediatic catchphrase, as well as the lucky picture on the

THE MATCH

front page of the *Gazzetta dello Sport*, which also published it on 5 July 1982. *5.3*: the folders written by Gianni Brera to the Sarriá after the match. *1,034,049*: the circulation in copies of the *Gazzetta dello Sport* the day after the Sarriá match. That of the *Corriere dello Sport* was 1,067,000 (1,063,503 according to other sources).

In the myriad of data, the same number could lead to many paths. Thirteen, for example, were the kilos accumulated by Zico after the care of the fitness trainer José Francalacci; the goals scored by Italy and Brazil in previous direct clashes; the teams from which Santana took his 22 players; the minutes, each, of ball possession by Italy and Brazil in the first half (but also those played by Careca on 10 June before he was injured); the hours spent between Trinca and Cruciani's appointment with the *Corriere dello Sport* and the one with the FIGC; the months needed to build the Torrespaña antenna for RTVE in Madrid; the years spent together by Sconcerti and Bearzot touring stadiums (and those that will pass before Sydney Samuelson, one of the cameramen of the Sarriá, received a knighthood from Prince Charles).

Numbers aside, I would never have managed to get that much information on my own. To mention a few not included in the text, I learned that in 1970, during a party in Guadalajara, someone had put poison in Klein's glass to prevent him from refereeing the Italy vs Mexico quarter-final for which he had been chosen; that on the table of the Chalet delle Rose, in Sasso Marconi, where in 1975 the publisher Luciano Conti and Italo Cucci met to relaunch the *Guerino*, there were a bottle of water, a glass and a gun; that the pinball machine model used by Edinho was 'Space Invaders Pinball Machine' (with which he scored 2,000 points); that Santana's three grandchildren were named Diogo, Mariana and Camila; that Havelange met Soldati when he went to the Sanctuary of Santiago de Compostela to have the Mundial cup blessed in the cathedral; that, with regard to Gentile's moustache, so much criticised by his wife, the cyclist Giuseppe Saronni had only been able to see his daughter, born a few days before the departure for the Mundial, thanks to a photo

THE AIR OF THE MUNDIAL

published by the *Corriere dello Sport* (because at that time families, in one way or another, only had news of the absentees through the *Corriere dello Sport*), or that the footballer Roberto Dinamite was on the field during the Operário vs Vasco da Gama match on the evening of 6 March 1982, when a flying saucer (an unidentified luminous object in the shape of a cigar) flew through the stadium at the Morenão, sending spectators fleeing.

I therefore owe a debt of gratitude to everyone who has directly or indirectly helped me in this endeavour: people and things, stories and texts, films and images, historians and spectators, journalists and photographers. Starting with those who most wanted to convey those weeks in 1982 – Mario Sconcerti, Italo Cucci and Darwin Pastorin – along with those who contributed impeccably to the portraits of Enzo Bearzot: Gigi Garanzini, Franco Mentana and Gianni Mura.

Precious were all the memories of the Azzurri: Paolo Rossi, Dino Zoff, Marco Tardelli, Antonio Cabrini, Claudio Gentile, Bruno Conti, Giuseppe Bergomi, Fulvio Collovati, Francesco Graziani and Franco Causio.

Then, of course, Gianni Brera, Giovanni Arpino, Mario Soldati and Oreste del Buono. With them, the main newspapers of the time. Mainly *Guerin Sportivo, Placar, La Repubblica, Corriere della Sera, La Stampa, Il Giornale, Il Messaggero, Il Tempo, Paese Sera, l'Unità, Il Giorno, La Nazione, Il Mattino, Avvenire, La Gazzetta dello Sport, Corriere dello Sport, Tuttosport, Panorama, L'Espresso, Epoca, L'Europeo, El País, ABC, La Vanguardia, Jornal do Brasil, Jornal da Tarde, Veja, Folha de S. Paulo, El Mundo, Paulo, El Mundo Deportivo, The Times, New York Times, The Guardian, Die Welt* and many others. But also *The Post, The Last Man, Football Stories* and *UOL.*

Debts continue to be owed to the Adi & Käthe Dassler Memorial Foundation, the Gianni Brera Archive of the Arnoldo and Alberto Mondadori Foundation, the Historical Archive of the Presidency of the Republic, Fernando Arrechea, Alberto Ballarin, Alex Bellos, José Oscar Bernardi, Marco Bernardini, Enzo Biagi, Gianni Bondini, Nicola Carraro, Alfio Caruso, Solange Cavalcante, the Centro de

THE MATCH

Investigaciones de Historia y Estadística del Fútbol Espanyol, the Centro de Pesquisa e Documentação de História Contemporânea do Brasil, the Cuadernos de Fútbol del Cihefe, Giulia Maria Crespi, Franco Di Bella, Beppe Di Corrado/Giuseppe De Bellis, Elio Domeniconi, Paulo Roberto Falcão, the Fédération Internationale de Football Association, the Federazione Italiana Giuoco Calcio, Massimo Ferrari, Luiz Carlos Ferreira, Fabrizio Ferron, Raffaele Fiengo, the FIFA/Coca-Cola World Football Development Programme, the Artemio Franchi Foundation, the Forward Association, Dan Friedman, Fundação Getúlio Vargas, Luigi Garlando, Mario Gherarducci, Antonio Ghirelli, Carlo Grandini, Alberto Helena Jr, Marcelo Idiarte, Lorenzo Iervolino, Andrew Jennings, Antonella Leoncini, Pablo Llonto, Riccardo Lorenzetti, Carlos Maranhão, Víctor Martínez Patón, Francesco Luti Mazzolani, Indro Montanelli, Marcello Mora, Carlo Nesti, Gianluca Oddenino, Giampaolo Pansa, Quique Peinado, Mario Pennacchia, Waldir Peres de Arruda, Angelo Maria Perrino, Carlo Petrini, Michele Plastino, the Presidium of Sports Fabulation Em Bycicleta (Stefano Corsi and Gino Cervi), RAI, the Real Comité Organizador de la Copa Mundial de Fútbol de 1982, Franco Recanatesi, Roberto Renga, Gianfranco Ricci, Rivista di Studi Breriani, Alberto Rizzoli, Gustavo Roman, João Saldanha, Nantas Salvalaggio, Eugenio Scalfari, Vittorio Sermonti, Juan Antonio Simón, Rob Smyth, Luca Sofri, Daniel Souza, Juha Tamminen, Giorgio Tosatti, Giovanni Valentini, Mario Vargas Llosa, Marina Viola, Adriano Wilkson, Jonathan Wilson, David Yallop, Renato Zanata, Furio Zara, West Nally Group and any other person who participated in the reconstruction of that day, even if only through a comment on a blog, a forum or a social network.

Thanks again to Cinzia Bearzot for her kindness, Abraham Klein for his answers, Giuseppe 'Peppe' Calzuola for his memories, Paolo Samarelli for his affection. And to Mary Elizabeth Pickford, for the enlightening walks. Not to mention the support of my sister Valeria Trellini added to the (unjustified) enthusiasm of Giulia D'Anna Lupo and Pietro 'Petricca' Macaluso, the first to have read these pages in

THE AIR OF THE MUNDIAL

instalments when they were just flying PDF files (later composed and printed thanks to the incessant availability of Antonio Fagioli).

I would also like to thank Matteo Codignola and Giovanni Nucci for their words. And above all Beatrice Masini: for letting him go without letting me go.

I also have old material debts to friends: Gianluca Marziani, for the stickers of España 82 (spring 1982); Andrea Brunelli, for the World Cup Epoca insert (summer 1982) (spring 1982); the unnamed Daniele Zannoni for the issues of *Guerin Sportivo* of May and June 1982 (autumn 1984); Vincenzo 'Vicius' Daniele for the *Corriere dello Sport* of 5 July 1982 (winter 1995); Francesco 'Cecchino' De Facendis, for the album España 82 (spring 2010).

I apologise to those who, in these pages, find themselves undeservedly playing a marginal role or to those who have felt ill-described: in reconstructing the events related to the match I have always relied on oral or written sources, as verified as possible, with the sole intent of trying to tell a story that could at least come close to the authenticity of the facts. This may not have been achieved, but the intention was authentic.

However, this story, originally twice as long and sadistically padded with notes, would never have crossed the bridge that separates a wish from its fulfilment without the love-work of my agents Fiammetta Biancatelli, Ombretta Borgia and Paolo Valentini, the audacious passion of Giovanni Francesio and the meticulous care of Mario de Laurentiis. But before that it would never have been written without the desire for knowledge instilled in me by my parents and the continuous support of my Dabò, who is solely responsible for all the good things that have happened in our lives. At the top of these are Arturo and Olivia.

A special dedication goes to Enzo Bearzot, wherever he is. Without his morals and his example I would never have had the desire to breathe the air of the Mundial.